LOVE, HOPE AND HATRED

The story of English League
Football Derbies

for dan
best wishes

Mike Mosley

Dec. 2012

Written and published in Norwich, UNESCO City of Literature
November 2012

A catalogue copy of this publication is available at The British Library

ISBN 978-0-9575019-0-4

Love, Hope and Hatred 288pp typeset in Georgia 10/12pt with Gill Sans 10/12pt
Design and typesetting by Marion de Mello Catlin, Design Shift
Printed and bound by TJ International, Padstow
Cover design by Marion de Mello Catlin, Design Shift
from an idea by John Mosley

Shift Publishing
Bracondale Millgate
Norwich NR1 2EQ
www.shiftpublishing.co.uk

Norwich is England's 1st UNESCO City of Literature
and a member of the UNESCO Creative Cities Network

Dedication

For Jacky and John and in memory of Stevie Foster

Acknowledgements

My special thanks go to

Marion Catlin
(for publishing, design and encouragement)

John Mosley (cover design)

Gill Vance (proof reading)

Jason Mills (information about the Southern League)

and my wife Jacky (for putting up with me through hours
and hours of research).

Thanks also to hundreds of football fans, far too numerous
to mention by name, for their stories of love, hope and
hatred about the beautiful game.

Contents

The warm-up

'Love' plays 'Hope' in a thrilling, tense football derby. The stadium is packed. Fans are frenzied and the tackling is grim. Love scores. Half the stadium erupts; the other half is plunged into despair. Red flares rain down, thrown by what look like demons in red and white horns. They chant *"love, love, love"*, but in a menacing way which is anything but loving. In a scene reminiscent of visions of hell, hundreds of creatures dance, wail and scream in fires engulfing part of the stadium. Poor souls you think, until it dawns on you that those in the flames are in fact deliriously happy supporters of Love. Supporters of Hope can only look on and.... hope.

This is not a bizarre dream. This is not fantasy football. This is Casablanca and the city's two biggest and best supported clubs are Wydad, meaning *'Love'* in Arabic and Raja, which means *'Hope'*. The very name Casablanca conjures up images of beauty, romance and intrigue for anyone who has seen the film of the same name. Humphrey Bogart and Ingrid Bergman; *"here's looking at you kid"*; *"play it again Sam"*, which is one of the most often quoted lines in cinematic history, even though Bogart's character didn't actually say it. The final scene is one of the finest ever made and the film has been ranked amongst the best-loved of all time. But the Casablanca in the film is Hollywood's fantasy. In reality, Casablanca is Morocco's main port and its biggest city; a bustling industrial metropolis of more than three million people and it is neither romantic nor beautiful. The ground, Stade Mohammed V, is not pretty either.

In the stadium, Wydad score again. Raja players protest in vain. More flares rain down from the terraces, thrown by Wydad fans. They are supposed to be the more genteel of the two sets of supporters. If so, you shudder to think what will happen if the green 'oiks' of Raja have anything to celebrate. As you survey a scene of mayhem, fires are now burning by the side of the pitch itself and you realise, if you haven't done so already, that 'Love' and 'Hope' absolutely *hate* each other. Their mutual venom is so toxic that they happily create this vision of hell in a corner of an ordinary city and indeed in the stadium they share with each other.

And so to the title of this book – *'Love, Hope and Hatred'*. Fittingly, the book is presented in two halves. The first half explores the history and development of football and the background to English League derbies (not forgetting that England's League contains Welsh clubs). We will also take a peek at a few of the world's best and most divisive derbies. The second half concentrates solely upon the main purpose of the book, which is to find and describe in more detail the best and most competitive English League derbies.

Hopefully readers will be happy to stay for the whole 'game' but, as a general guide to the book, you may wish to consider three points. Firstly, there are meanderings, for example to find the origins of the term 'derby' and a trip to derbies in ancient Rome. Treat these as being equivalent to buying a half-time meat pie or a match programme. They are there for your enjoyment, but they are not essential, so save them for later if you like.

Secondly, if you are already an aficionado and/or anorak of football history and its associated facts, you may find the first half entertaining, but probably you will already know the vast majority of what it contains. The second half is more detailed and contains statistical information about English League derbies which, *if* it has been produced in an easily accessible format previously, I haven't been able to find it. Feel free therefore to attend only for the second half. You can be like a visiting international manager who doesn't need to see the whole thing, but who pops in for half a game to check out technical details.

Thirdly, if you have only a limited interest in football, the first part of the book should be of general social and historical interest. It should also give you sufficient insight into football derbies to answer the odd pub quiz question and to understand what on earth the aficionados/anoraks are going on about. However, some of the stats at the end of the first half and explanations at the beginning of the second half may get a little turgid for you. If you feel the need to skip them or to leave early to catch your bus, no-one will blame you.

Two explanations are required about terminology in the book. Grammar checkers and editors issue constant reminders that a football club is a singular noun, an 'it'. Maybe, but football supporters think of their clubs as collectives. Really 'it' should be 'us' and when it comes to derbies it is definitely Us against Them, so the plural is used throughout the book when referring to clubs.

Historical records in the English League can be confusing because the names (and constitutional entities) of its divisions have been altered over time. Hence, for most of football's history 'Division One' referred to the top tier of the English League, but when the Premier League was established in 1992 'Division One' became the second tier. In 2004 the Championship was formed and 'League One' became the third tier. The proper names of the divisions are used in the book where there can be no doubt as to their meaning (e.g. Premier League, Division Three South etc) but, in order to avoid confusion, the terms 'first tier', 'third tier' etc are used extensively.

***

"Some people believe football is a matter of life and death. I'm very disappointed with that attitude. I can assure you it is much, much more important than that'.

This is probably Bill Shankly's most famous quote. As manager of Liverpool, Shankly was instrumental in transforming a mediocre club, then languishing in the second tier of the league, into a football dynasty that largely ruled English football during the 1970s and 80s. Bill Shankly died in September 1981 and so his quote was made a few years before the Heysel, Bradford and Hillsborough disasters. Had Shankly witnessed those tragedies, it is unlikely he would have made the comment, given that Bill was always sensitive to the feelings of fans. Clearly, football is *not* a matter of life and death and it is *not* more important than many other things in life. Nevertheless, for millions of people in virtually every country, football is far more than a game. It is an overwhelming passion. Apart from family, close friends and maybe the odd pet, the love of their lives for millions of people is their football club. Many clubs have banned the scattering of ashes in goal mouths and centre spots. Pragmatically, had they not done so, goalkeepers would have to perform on a pile of ashes large enough to be a baseball pitcher's mound, such is the demand from thousands of fans to make one last public gesture of devotion to their beloved clubs.

Anyone who doubts the importance of football should consider one fact. It is estimated that nearly half the world's population watches the World Cup final. This audience dwarfs those for any other occasion, be it sporting, religious, political or artistic, in the history of the planet. If Martians were to pay us a visit, they would struggle to generate more interest. If football in general is a passion, there is one ongoing clash in football that supercedes all others in its ability to generate emotions and angst – that is the 'derby' match.

The famous Shankly quote may be an exaggeration, but it is probably true to say that, apart from the loss of a family member, friend, job, or home, the worst thing that can happen to a true football fan is defeat at the hands of the local enemy. Logically, this doesn't make a great deal of sense. The people of Bristol, Birmingham or Sheffield, for example, are fiercely proud of their cities. Yet the blue halves of these cities would probably rather gouge out their own eyes than see their red or claret neighbours bring the FA Cup back to the cities they love. This is true, even though Birmingham hasn't seen the FA Cup come home since 1957; Sheffield since 1935 and Bristol since, for ever, as neither Bristol club has ever won it. Of course, the feeling is reciprocated by reds and clarets. If the blues of their respective cities were drawn against Beelzebub Wanderers, there is little doubt as to where red or claret loyalties would lie, difficult as it would be to find an appropriate chant.

This animosity is not confined to rivalries within cities. The same resentments occur between neighbouring communities. The residents of Burnley and Blackburn, for instance, think all things Lancastrian are wonderful. People from Newcastle and Sunderland believe that God's own country was created in the region north of the Tees and south of Scotland. But, when it comes to football derbies; friends and neighbours from the same city, county or region are often seen as loathsome sub-humans, to be despised, abused or, on occasions, even assaulted. In football, especially in football derbies, sense and logic rarely get a look in and, as we shall see later in the book, tribalism within local derbies has tended to escalate significantly over the years.

Returning to Casablanca – the city's derby is more fervent than most but, as we are about to see, similar scenes of love, hope and hatred are replicated every year in towns and cities across England and Wales and almost everywhere else on the globe.

FIRST HALF

1

Origins of football

Before studying the early days of derbies, it is worthwhile charting the origins and development of football itself. Football has been played for millennia. FIFA officially recognises China as the birthplace of the game, although many would argue that in awarding the accolade to China, world football's governing body made a politically expedient decision, rather than one based upon clear historical accuracy. The Chinese certainly played a game called 'tsu-chu' and the Japanese 'kemari'. The Greeks played 'pheninda', which the Romans adapted as 'harpastum'. All were recognisable forms of football, as were various games played in Central and South America, long before the Spanish conquest.

The earliest recorded date for football in England is disputed. However, it was definitely being played before the 14th century and it was specifically banned in 1314 by Edward II. In fairness to Edward, he had more important things on his mind at the time, as England lost quite an important 'derby' in 1314 – they were routed by the Scots at the Battle of Bannockburn. Even Scotland's 3-2 victory over England's world champions at Wembley in 1967 wasn't as famous as Bannockburn.

Edward's was the first of many attempts by authorities and churches to put an end to the game. Football was deemed sinful and a distraction from more worthy pursuits, such as killing Scottish people. At a much later date, football would be seen as a laudable distraction from even greater evils, but the prevailing view in the 14th century and throughout the next half millennium was that football should be stamped out. Indeed, anti-football legislation passed by Henry VIII in 1541 was not repealed until 1845. It should be understood that the authorities were not concerned about football as such, but they did worry a great deal about large groups of impassioned ordinary people. Fear of the 'mob' and potential insurrection was a regular feature of English life until well into the 19th century.

Modern football began to emerge in the 19th century, although people may be forgiven for thinking it is a much more recent phenomenon, as those in the higher echelons of the English Premier League (and many media pundits) seemingly want us to believe that football started only in 1992, when their own greedy baby was born. Incidentally, records in this book refer to the whole of football's history and do not distinguish between top tier successes pre- and post- the coming of the Premiership.

Birth of the modern game.

Conventional football history emphasises the role of English public schools in the development of the game and suggests that public schools invented organised football; formulated their own distinct rules and then passed on the game to the rest of the population by means of rule books and/or the missionary zeal of former pupils. In part this is a fair reflection of the role of public schools. But, as is so often the case with conventionally accepted English history, this explanation more accurately reflects developments in the south of the country, rather than in the north and midlands. Furthermore, even in the south the game existed long before it was adopted by schools.

It is certainly true that it was in public schools where people first began to *write down* formal playing codes. Differing written codes in individual schools prompted the first attempt to pull together a single set of rules. Representatives from public schools sought a compromise between many codes in existence at the time and created the Cambridge University Rules between 1846 and 1848. The influence of public schools and other institutions, for instance the military, continued to dominate the growth of football in southern England for many years, as is demonstrated by the names of clubs like Old Etonians, Old Carthusians and Royal Engineers. However, public schools provided only one element in the development of the game and, in the north, public schools had much less impact than in the south. 'Mass' or 'mob' football had been played in many parts of the country for centuries and, as we have already seen, had frequently been the bane of the authorities. Mob football is usually portrayed as sheer anarchy and, in part, it was and is. But anyone who witnesses the few examples of mass football still in existence will soon recognise that there are rules and conventions and there are also tactics, coaches and specific playing roles.

More importantly, mob football had already been partly codified and standardised by the early 19th century, at least at local level, in *unwritten* 'rules' or traditions. Part of the reason for this local standardisation was that many games involved wagers and so a level playing field, so to speak, became a necessity. People continued to play in bigger mob football games, usually at festival times, but a more organised form of the sport became increasingly popular at other times. Typically in the north teams were based upon localities, rather than institutions and the influence of public schools was minimal or non-existent. As early as 1831, an old Etonian opined in his *'Reminiscences of Eton'* – *"I cannot consider the game of football as being gentlemanly; after all the Yorkshire common people play it"*.

Changing times and changing values.

Football reflects the society in which it is played. For example, the basis upon which clubs were formed often reflected social divisions present in their countries of birth; dominance by certain clubs in totalitarian states is frequently linked to the whims of dictators or regimes; the basis upon which leagues are run often reflects a country's general stance with regard to laissez-faire economics, and so on. The development of football in England and Wales reflected early-19th century and (a little later) Victorian values and it provided one of the answers to the needs of a changing society. For the upper and middle classes, in particular, 'muscular Christianity' became very much in vogue, with its belief in a healthy body and a healthy mind; its codes of honour and codes of behaviour – essentially, Victorians had codes for everything.

Early football had largely been a 'people's' game, played in towns and villages by ordinary folk. Its adoption by public schools was not accidental. Public schools in the 18th Century were unruly dens of vice for the aristocracy. Gambling and bullying were rife. Education was at best a secondary pastime. Eton, for example, had a full scale rebellion in 1788; Harrow, one which lasted for three weeks in 1771. The army crushed a pupils' revolt at Rugby in 1797 and numerous riots in Westminster School at around the same period were suppressed by troops. Changing values in the 19th century coincided with the growth of the nouveau riche, made wealthy as the Industrial Revolution gained pace. They were not willing to pay to send their sons to nurseries of vice. Hence a new breed of headmaster emerged, typified by Thomas Arnold at Rugby School and Edward Thring, celebrated head of Uppingham School. They were determined to take control of their schools and to produce fine, upstanding young men for the expansion and upkeep of the British Empire. Thring condemned the *"depravity of self-abuse"* and *"the worm-life of foul earthly desires"*. He whole-heartedly encouraged 'muscular Christianity' as a counter-weight to these 'vices'.

Darwinian theories, whilst presenting a challenge to many tenets of religion, bolstered the concept of a healthy body and a healthy mind as crucial to the survival of the fittest. Football, once a sinful distraction from more worthy pastimes, was now deemed a healthy, 'manly' pursuit for the winter months, cricket already being well-established as the game for summer.

For Britain's working classes, leisure time was changing. From the beginning of the Industrial Revolution their leisure time had been squeezed and their traditional holidays taken away. Their working time had become longer and more regulated, to a point whereby they didn't really have any free time. However, Factory Acts, passed in the middle part of the century, introduced half-day working on Saturdays and opened up opportunities for organised activities. Many older leisure activities were frowned upon because they were associated with cruelty to animals and, much worse in the eyes of the powers that be, gambling and drunkenness. The working classes therefore came under the same encouragement to adopt new, healthy pursuits to develop team spirit and codes of behaviour that would be transferable into the workplace.

The battle for football's identity.

In order to fulfil its destiny as the game for all classes in winter, football had to overcome two substantial obstacles. First, although already popular in many parts of the country, football was by no means the only winter game vying for the attention of sports enthusiasts. Sport generally was blossoming. Hockey in particular and also games such as lacrosse and rowing were seen as potential alternatives to football. Anyone who questions the drawing power of rowing at the time need consider only two points. First, timing of the 1873 F A Cup final was switched, as it clashed with the Oxford v Cambridge boat race. The timing was changed, not only because the boat race was a massively bigger attraction, but also because participants in the Cup final wanted to see it. Secondly, several football clubs, including Flamengo, the most popular club in the whole of South America, and Brentford, the most popular club in the whole of, well, Brentford, started life as rowing clubs, before adding minor sports such as football to their activities.

A second and even more difficult obstacle to football's expansion arose from the question – *what exactly was football*? Cricket had a national governing body, the MCC, founded in 1787 and it had clearly codified its laws by 1835. In contrast, by 1850, football had no governing body and lacked standardised rules at national level, despite the efforts of the Cambridge students. People watching 'football' at the time in different parts of the country would have seen a wide variety of games. All would have similarities, but there would also be significant differences based upon the amount of handling allowed, interpretations of offside and the use of 'hacking' (hacking basically meant the legitimate kicking of opponents' shins). In many instances these games were not so much akin to either modern football or rugby, but were like a cross between a rugby maul and Australian Rules football.

Teams inevitably had to adjust to playing to different rules. Many clubs played a more rugby oriented game one week and a game a little closer to football the next. Sometimes it would be agreed to play to the rules of one club in the first half of a game and the rules of the other club for the second half, which explains one of the origins of the half-time break – it wasn't just for a cup of tea and half an orange. More usually the practice was for teams to play the entire game according to the rules of the home side, giving a whole new dimension to the concept of home advantage.

As an aside, people question why home teams tend to win more often than away teams. The reasons usually given are that home players respond to the support of their home crowd and/or they are more familiar with the pitch and/or they are more rested, not having had to travel. None of these explanations seem very plausible in modern times. Away fans frequently now provide at least as great, if not greater, vocal support than home fans. Pitches are pretty standard – they hardly contain devilish nooks and crannies only known to home players. Players travel in luxury to games or stay overnight and therefore should be equally rested. Perhaps a psychologist should explore the possibility that footballers have a weird form of collective memory, passed down over decades from times when being the away team meant really being at a disadvantage. In those days, the away team might have little or no support; have to play on pitches that actually did have unknown nooks and crannies and arrive, exhausted after a long journey, just in time to play the game. Even worse, they might also have had to play to a set of rules that were, at best, unusual or, at worst, virtually unknown to them.

Football's simplicity, affordability and accessibility fairly quickly overcame the first obstacle and saw off alternative sports in the race to be the preferred winter pastime, but the second obstacle, the battle for the definition of football itself, was altogether much more difficult.

Coming of the Football Association.

In October 1863, Ebenezer Cobb Morley, a solicitor from Hull living in Barnes, prompted a small number of London based clubs to meet to consider the formation of an Association *"for the purpose of settling a code of rules for the regulation of the game of football"*. Although the clubs present were all from London, they were influenced by letters received from clubs in Sheffield and Lincoln. They also had a copy of the latest version of the Cambridge University Rules. Their debate centred upon a choice between the Cambridge Rules or adapted rules of Rugby School. In particular, the issues of carrying the ball and hacking were contentious.

In their letter to the Football Association (FA), Sheffield described hacking as more suitable for wrestling than football (modern wrestlers presumably wouldn't agree that the deliberate kicking of shins with specially re-enforced boots would be suitable, even for them). Blackheath, on the other hand, believed the new Cambridge Rules would destroy the game and that hacking was a fundamental aspect of it. Blackheath's representative made a passionate speech or, more accurately, a wild rant to the effect that football without hacking was not manly and would quickly be taken over by wine quaffing, effeminate foreigners – so much for 'soft southerners'. Morley responded with characteristic pragmatism by saying *"if we have hacking, no-one who has arrived at the age of discretion will play at football and it will be entirely left to schoolboys"*.

Ultimately, the newly founded Football Association opted for the Cambridge Rules. Blackheath left in acrimonious circumstances and the seeds of the great schism between what became association football ('soccer') and rugby football ('rugger') were sown. Even at this point, when football was beginning to get its act together, many remained unconvinced about its long term prospects. The Sporting Gazette in October 1863 pronounced that *"football can never attain the proud position among the national sports of England which its admirers so fondly look forward to – the cricket of the winter months"*. Nevertheless, in spite of doom-mongers, association football had stolen a crucial march on rugby football in the struggle to become the nation's number one winter sport. It had an embryonic national body and it had made an attempt to codify a common set of rules. That having been said, it should be pointed out that, even as late as 1885, there were still roughly twice as many rugby clubs in England and Wales as football clubs.

It should also be said that 'association football', as agreed by the FA in 1863, would not have been recognisable as similar to the modern game and was still as much like rugby and Australian Rules. Running with the ball in hand was not allowed, but handling to control the ball was legitimate. Therefore, the ball would not be kicked or headed if in the air, but would be brought to ground by handling. The game was very much slower than it is today. Passing was unusual because of the offside rule and was used largely as a last resort. It was frowned upon as failure on the part of the individual player who passed the ball away. Goalkeepers didn't exist as such, but most teams played a defensive full-back similar to the modern full-back in rugby. Usually, eight of the eleven players were forwards (as in today's rugby union scrum), who would attack the opponents' goal together in a V-shaped 'scrimmage'. They would usually score goals from close range, often bundling opponents over the line along with the ball. In this manoeuvre, the mass 'grassing' of 'goalkeepers' was a fine art. Incidentally, Norwich City's '*On the ball, City*', allegedly the oldest football song still in existence, contains the line '*have a little scrimmage*'. There were no corner kicks etc so, if the ball went out of play, the first person to 'touch it down' would be given the ball to resume play, thereby explaining the otherwise meaningless use of the term 'touch' in the modern game, where touching the ball is specifically forbidden. Given the nature of football at the time, it is not so surprising to find that Clapham Rovers, FA Cup winners in 1880, were primarily a top rugby club rather than an association football club.

The events of 1863 were crucial from a historical perspective but, at the time, things did not fall neatly into place for a number of reasons. First, the formation of the Football Association was a great idea but, for many football clubs, it was seen as a London body, not a national body. Its decisions and rules were of no consequence to many in the provinces. Indeed, for the next few years, the FA found it very difficult to make progress; the south generally remained a rugby stronghold and at one point the only club outside London in membership of the Football Association was Sheffield FC.

Second, the rugby tradition was strong not only in the south, but also in large parts of the north and midlands. If people are asked today to name the biggest strongholds of English football, most would probably suggest Manchester, Liverpool and the North East. However, in the early days of football, these places were predominantly rugby fortresses. Football was expanding rapidly around them, firstly in and near South Yorkshire and the East Midlands and, shortly afterwards, in the Lancashire cotton towns north of Manchester and the West Midlands, but rugby still held sway in many major northern towns and cities.

Third, there developed the real possibility of a schism within association football itself. Sheffield FC had remained loyal to the Football Association and had been the main ambassador for the FA in northern England. However, with the approval of the FA, Sheffield had continued to use its own rules which, first published in 1858, pre-dated the FA's version. There were a number of differences and, in fact, Sheffield's rules were closer to those of the modern game. Football was progressing much more quickly in the north and midlands than in the south. Even more worryingly for the FA, many new clubs in the north and midlands were choosing to adopt Sheffield Rules, to such an extent that, by 1870, Sheffield Rules were predominant.

Association football unites.

Two events in the 1870s avoided a split and eventually consolidated football's ascendancy over rugby. First, in 1871, in the same year that rugby finally formed a national body, the struggling FA introduced the FA Cup. In the sense of its immediate impact, the new cup competition was neither novel nor momentous. There had been earlier examples of cup competitions; the number of entrants for the FA Cup was disappointing and, as almost all entrants were from the London area, it was seen by many as the London Cup and therefore no different to other local competitions. However, within a few years, the FA Cup had captured the imagination of the public and it provided a national focus for the sport, which rugby could not or, more accurately, chose not to match. The decision by rugby's elite to disparage organised competition as 'pot hunting' ultimately helped consign rugby to secondary status but, in truth, most of them didn't want rugby to be a mass participation sport anyway.

Second, in 1877, from a position of strength, the Sheffield FA accepted the primacy of FA Rules, without engaging in what could have been a very damaging fight. The FA altered its rules to incorporate a few of those from Sheffield and the FA's authority became unchallenged. In March 1877 The Wednesday (as Sheffield Wednesday were known at the time) beat Heeley 4-3 in the Sheffield Challenge Cup final at Bramall Lane. It was to be the last major game played under Sheffield Rules. A schism had been avoided and the game was united around one ruling body and one set of rules.

The clarity of the rules gave further impetus to the growth of football and clubs were now forming even more rapidly. Significantly, many were being established in areas which had previously been solid rugby country – Everton, Manchester United, Manchester City, Sunderland and Newcastle were all formed in the years between 1878 and 1882. The power base of English club football was shifting, but it wasn't yet moving to big cities. Instead, the cotton towns of north Lancashire, in particular Blackburn, Preston and to a lesser extent Darwen, Accrington and Bolton, came into ascendency and for one very good reason – professionalism.

Professionalism.

Professionalism was not new in sport. English cricket had long before openly accepted professionalism, albeit with a clear distinction between gentlemen and players. Baseball in the States had a fully professional league as early as 1871. Australian Rules had a professional league in Melbourne in the early 1880s. Professionals also existed in Britain in a variety of other sports, especially in various forms of athletics, most notably pedestrianism. Therein lay a problem. Pedestrianism was extremely popular, but it had long been tainted with betting and its associated scourge of cheating. The football authorities were afraid that professionalism would take their game down the same slippery slope. They were also concerned that, in a professional era, big city clubs would inevitably overtake clubs from smaller towns because of their ability to attract bigger crowds and therefore accumulate greater finances to pay the best professionals.

A question for readers to ponder would be – *in hindsight, were the authorities right to be worried on either or both counts?*

The fact remained that football was expanding rapidly. Crowds and revenues were increasing and demands upon the time of the best footballers were becoming ever greater as a result. However, it was changes in society that again had more impact upon the growth of professionalism, rather than changes in football itself. Victorian values encouraged a perceived need to make your mark for posterity in an increasingly competitive world. A number of wealthy businessmen in the cotton towns of Lancashire saw football clubs as their own way of making their mark and enhancing their civic status. They did so in competition with each other. Local talent was limited and so, increasingly, the route to success lay in buying-in the best talent from elsewhere, especially by using 'professors' from Scotland. In addition, by the mid-1880s, the country was in a prolonged economic slump. The momentum of the Industrial Revolution was petering out and unemployment was rising fast. The amateur spirit might be applauded, but it didn't pay the bills. Something had to give.

The fall-out from the debate about professionalism threatened to destroy the relatively newly-found and fragile unity of football. In the early 1880s a number of clubs, mainly from Lancashire, were thrown out of the FA Cup, following accusations of illegal use of professional players. The situation was best typified by a game between Preston North End and Upton Park in January 1884. The match ended in a 1-1 draw. Before the replay, Upton Park complained about Preston's professionals, of which there were indeed seven Scottish 'professors'. Preston, a significant and growing force in the game, remained unrepentant and were thrown out. However, it was also well known that Upton Park had specifically recruited players from Oxbridge Universities and elsewhere for their cup side. This was not professionalism as such, but it was dubious practice. Double standards appeared to be applied. That having been said, it is perhaps too easy to judge the authorities of the time by our own standards. Professionalism is now clearly part and parcel of the game but, at the time, the use of professionals was seen as cheating, pure and simple.

A crunch was inevitable and it came in October 1884, when a large number of clubs, primarily from Lancashire, met to consider forming the British Football Association, as a breakaway from the FA. The FA had to act and it chose not to swim against the growing tide, described by William Sudell, Preston's chairman, as "*like trying to stop Niagara with a three-legged stool*". Professionalism was accepted in 1885, albeit initially in a limited form.

A few years later, rugby's authorities faced a similar crisis and decision. This time the professional rebellion was led primarily by clubs from across the Pennines in Yorkshire, where the rugby clubs of West Yorkshire were equally as strong and valuable to their game as the football clubs of North Lancashire were to the FA. Rugby's authorities chose conflict and schism and the Northern Rugby Union clubs went their own way, eventually creating the substantially different game of Rugby League. Meanwhile Rugby Union remained amateur, at least officially, for many decades afterwards.

It may seem safe to assume that the battle for and against professionalism in football was a straightforward conflict between the wealthy gentleman players of the south against the horny-handed sons of toil from the north and their accomplices and providers of talent, from across the border in Scotland. Rarely is anything so simple in the politics of football. Most southern representatives at crucial meetings of the FA were indeed wealthy gentlemen who were opposed to professionalism. However, first, they had decided to remain amateur themselves and so felt that they would not be directly affected by any decision to allow professionalism 'up north'. They were wrong. The big northern clubs were soon to turn their attention southwards for talent, as well as continuing to import from Scotland. Second, the majority had come to the conclusion that William Sudell's three-legged stool analogy was correct and they would have to bow to the inevitable sooner or later. Most southern votes therefore were cast in favour of change.

The most implacable opponents of professionalism were not from the south, but from traditional heartlands of the game in Sheffield, Nottinghamshire and Birmingham. The Sheffield FA tried to soldier on in opposition to professionalism, believing its clubs were strong enough to resist. They were not. Individual Sheffield clubs and Sheffield FA's representative side began to take hammerings. By 1887, this last bastion of amateurism outside the south conceded defeat when, under threat of the formation of a professional outfit called Sheffield Rovers, made up principally of their own players, The Wednesday turned pro.

Although Scottish 'professors' were often at the centre of the professionalism debate, it would be wrong to believe that the Scottish FA were complicit in the encroachment of professionalism – quite the opposite. The Scottish FA and the other home countries opposed professionalism. The Scots made it clear that they would refuse to play England if the English team contained professional players. The Scottish FA also wrote to all Scots playing professionally south of the border, basically telling them not to darken Scottish doors again without specific clearance. When England did field the first-ever professional in an international match against Scotland in 1885, the Scots insisted that teenager James Forrest had to wear a different coloured shirt from the rest of the English team, to distinguish him as a professional. One dreads to think what would have happened to young Forrest had hacking still been allowed.

There were a few oddities in the argument about professionalism that demonstrate not so much duplicity on the part of the people concerned, but more that strong feelings on either side of the debate existed even within individual clubs, as well as within associations. The first example takes us back to The Wednesday's victory in the final of the 1877 Sheffield Challenge Cup. Playing in Wednesday's side that day was one James Lang, a Scottish international, who was employed by a cutlery firm, owned by a member of Wednesday's Committee. Whether Lang's later claim to be the very first professional footballer is correct or not (it is a title claimed by or on behalf of others), it seems clear that Lang's duties at the cutlery firm consisted of reading the paper. The self-styled first professional was therefore plying his trade for the biggest, 'strictly amateur' club, in the very association which was most vehemently opposed to professionalism.

Perhaps even stranger is the example of Dr Edward Morley, who represented Blackburn Rovers at many crucial meetings in this period. Rovers were the best team in England. They had been favourites to win the FA Cup in 1882 and 1883, but failed to do so. They then did win it for the next three years in a row. Basically then, Rovers were big news and everyone knew they did not achieve their feats without resorting to professionalism. Indeed, their transfer from Darwen of Fergie Suter, another Scottish 'professor', had been so controversial that it led not only to adverse press comment, but to fighting between the two teams and supporters when they met shortly after the transfer. Yet Dr Morley opposed the proposed professional breakaway from the FA and described professional footballers as *"money-grabbing-get-rich loafers"*. It is a quote to ring down the ages of football and many will agree with the sentiment today. But it is inconceivable that Dr Morley was unaware of the professionals in his own club. As he was neither mad nor bad, it seems that he personally opposed professionalism but, despite his position as a representative of Rovers, his views made little difference to the actions of his club.

Scotland's professors

This book is not about the development of football in Scotland, but it would be remiss if the section on professionalism in England and Wales ended without a special mention of the people who became the meat in the sandwich during the controversy – the Scottish 'professors'. Why Scots became so overwhelming good at football in the 19th century (and for most of the 20th century) has been debated elsewhere. It is the subject of as much conjecture as there is about the reasons for the decline of Scottish football in more recent years. An example of Scottish dominance in the early years is the fact that they won eleven and lost only three of the first nineteen internationals against the 'old enemy' England. Scots were good – very good – and they were much in demand. They were the first masters of the passing or 'combination' game that began to flourish as a result of a crucial change in the offside law. The introduction of the rule whereby a player was deemed not to be offside, as long as there were at least three opponents (later reduced to two) between the attacker and the opponents' goal, was the single most important rule change in creating modern football. It opened up the game, made it much faster and replaced mass dribbling and scrimmaging amongst the forwards with passing between players.

Over time controversies in football tend to re-appear again and again, in slightly different forms, and there are many similarities between the 19th century debate about the employment of Scottish professionals and the current debate about the number of foreign players in the Premier League. Scots were derided as money-grabbing mercenaries who had no underlying loyalty to clubs or to the towns and cities in which they played. The employment of Scots was attacked for depriving local talent of the opportunity to play and be nurtured. Local newspapers generally approved the importation of talent if it genuinely improved the quality of football on show, but frequently complained that too many 'journeymen' Scots were flooding into clubs without any discernable increase in the quality of local teams. A quote from the era sums up the animosity and frequent class prejudice to which Scottish professionals were subjected – *"the employment of the scum of Scottish villages has tended, in no small degree, to brutalise the game"*. And finally, of course, club owners blamed increases in the costs of employing Scottish professionals for increases in ticket prices – *"do you want the club to be successful? – then you have to pay the price"* is another familiar refrain to echo down the ages to football fans of today.

Just how reliant the new powerhouses of English football were upon their Scottish imports is illustrated by two examples. The fabulous Preston North End side of 1888/9 won the first ever Football League title, without losing a game, and completed the 'double' by winning the FA Cup, without conceding a goal. Of the twelve players who played at least ten games for the 'Invincibles' during that season, seven were Scottish, the goalkeeper was Welsh and, of the four Englishmen, one was John Goodall. Goodall was born to Scottish parents and grew up in Kilmarnock. There is of course no doubt that, had Goodall been born more recently, he would have qualified as a Scottish player and Preston's great team would have had eight Scots. However, the rules regarding nationality were very different in Victorian times and so, as Goodall had been born in London, he was deemed to be English (incidentally, his brother Archie was born in Belfast and so was supposedly Irish and the Goodall brothers became the first brothers to play internationally for different countries).

The second example shows both that the use of Scottish professionals was not confined to the north and that it was not just a short-lived, passing phase in the very earliest days of professional football. When Tottenham Hotspur won the FA Cup in 1901, to become the only club from outside the Football League to win the cup after the League's foundation, their feat was understandably hailed as a great victory for the south. However, the Spurs' team was reminiscent of the 'no English players' Arsenal sides of the early 21st century. Not a single southern English player appeared for Spurs in the final. Tottenham's team consisted of five Scottish, two Welsh and one Irish player, together with three Englishmen who were from Cheshire, Lincolnshire and, what is now, Cumbria.

As a final footnote to Scotland's wonderful players – it is often assumed that Scottish players were very successful, but that Scottish club teams were poor, having been drained of talent by English League clubs. This is not the case. The example of Queen's Park, avowedly amateur and the outstanding team in early Scottish football is well documented. Suffice it to say here that they appeared in two FA Cup finals (1884 and 1885) and would almost certainly have won it had they persevered. Not so well known is that, in 1888, a match was played between the winners of the FA Cup and the winners of the Scottish Cup for the 'Championship of the World'. England's cup holders were West Bromwich Albion. Scotland was represented by Renton. Renton won 4-1.

Coming of the Football League.

The advent of professional football triggered an inevitable train of events, as football continued to become more and more popular. There was money to be made and prestige to be gained, but it was risky and competitive and there were pesky, if valuable, professional players to be paid. Cup competitions at national or local level drew big crowds but, obviously, half the clubs involved were knocked out in each round. Fearing the consequences of early exits, clubs would enter more than one competition, but success could lead to the alternative problem of fixture congestion and cancellations. Bigger friendly or challenge games still drew sizeable crowds too, but they didn't provide excitement to compare with competitive fixtures. The unpredictability of fixtures and revenues, especially from competitive games, became increasingly unacceptable.

Again an *external* factor provided lubrication for the next stage in football's development. The growth of railways changed Britain fundamentally, to a degree hard to appreciate in our world of instant mass communication. Before railways, people rarely travelled outside their localities and, if they did so, they moved at a speed of about ten miles an hour maximum. So slow was movement that there wasn't even the need for standard time in different places (Greenwich Mean Time was not adopted in Britain as a whole until 1880, although 'railway time' had been introduced a few decades earlier). In order to pay their bills, big football clubs needed *regular*, competitive football and a greater, *regular* stream of income. They now had a means of transport to facilitate *regular* trips to relatively faraway places. But how should *regular* competition be organised? William McGregor of Aston Villa is credited with proposing an answer – the Football League.

Although there had been earlier cup competitions in the north, the FA Cup had been a thoroughly southern invention, contested largely by London based clubs in its early years and won by southern clubs in the first eleven years of its existence. The Football League, by contrast, was thoroughly not southern. The original members, all of them professional, consisted of six clubs from Lancashire and six from the midlands (with apologies to those people in Stoke who consider Staffordshire to be in the north). It was a success from the start and it quickly spawned imitations. In part, alternative leagues were formed because, initially, the Football League was seen as a closed shop. The original rules of the new league were radical, as it was agreed that the bottom four clubs at the end of the first season (ie one third of its members) would have to seek re-election for year two. However, a self-interested old boys' mentality, which was to dog football for decades to come, quickly reared its head, as all four clubs at the bottom were re-elected at the end of the first year.

It was already apparent that the twelve founders were not the best twelve clubs and so other leagues formed in the north and midlands and they threatened to become parallel rivals to the Football League. The sham didn't last for long. Reasonably quickly, leaders of the Football League understood that, if it was to retain its primacy as the top English league, it had to open up entry to the very best clubs, even if this created risks for founder members. It was a wise decision, as may be illustrated by two outcomes. The first was that, although not all imitations disappeared altogether, the primacy of the Football League became unchallenged virtually immediately, at least in the north and midlands. Secondly, within only eight years of the entry of new clubs into the League, the championship had been won four times by clubs who had earlier been denied membership (Sunderland in 1891/2, 1892/3 and 1894/5 and Sheffield United in 1897/8).

For all its success, the early Football League encountered similar problems to those of the modern day. Two original members, Stoke and Accrington, went bust. Stoke returned, but Accrington disappeared altogether (the current club in the town, Accrington Stanley, is not linked to the founder member of the League). Other clubs, who had been big players in the early days of professionalism, also bit the dust in the new dog-eats-dog world of league football. A notable example was Blackburn Olympic who, in 1883, had been the first northern club to win the FA Cup. Effectively their fate was sealed by the decision of the Football League to allow only one club from a city or town to be in the original twelve founder members. Professional and with all the financial commitments that entailed; unable to compete with Rovers for the big prize of representing Blackburn and therefore with no way of progressing, the Light Blues folded in 1889, shortly after completion of the League's first season.

What of the FA during this period? Again there are parallels with the modern day. The Football League flexed its muscles in much the same way as the Premier League does today. In many senses the threat to the FA in the late 19th Century was even greater than the problems it faces today, because the Football League's northern/midland, professional base, as opposed to the FA's primarily southern, amateur set up, was even more starkly confrontational than the current relationship between the FA and Premier League. The FA survived and the Football League prospered for two main reasons. First, whatever travails faced individual clubs (and it was an incomparable time of sink or swim and changing fortunes), the majority of clubs were doing very well. In any event, there was a queue of new clubs more than willing and able to take the place of those falling by the wayside. Second, for all the power of the Football League and tensions between its leaders and the hierarchy of the FA, people running the FA had the wherewithal to go with the flow at crucial times and to stand up to the expansionist ambitions of the Football League when required.

A special mention has to be made at this juncture of Charles W. Alcock, who is credited with being '*the father of modern sport*' by Keith Booth in his '*Life and times of Charles W. Alcock*'. Born in Sunderland and educated at Harrow, Alcock was secretary of the FA throughout the tumultuous years 1870 to 1895. He, more than anyone, steered football through the choppy waters of the introduction of the FA Cup; the threat of a breakaway professional British Football Association; legalisation of professionalism and the advent of the Football League. It remains to be seen whether or not the current crop of big wigs running English football in the early 21st century have comparable abilities.

Football in the South.

The Football League was an entirely northern and midlands based institution, but it would be wrong to think that it had no impact on the south of England. As new leagues were springing up in the north and midlands, as potential alternative options for clubs denied access to the Football League, similar initiatives were being considered in the south. Football was changing in southern counties. This is perhaps best demonstrated by the fact that of all the London based attendees at the historic meeting to create the FA back in October 1863, only one survives and the lone survivor, ironically, is Blackheath, the club which chose rugby. As had always been the case further north, clubs in the south increasingly became based upon localities, rather than schools or other institutions, and more and more became fully or partially professional. There was therefore a desire and a financial need for regular, competitive, league football. London's first club to turn professional, Woolwich Arsenal (in 1891), led the push for a new league. However, powerful amateur vested interests in the London and other Southern County associations succeeded in delaying the introduction of a Southern League for a few crucial years.

When the Southern League finally made its debut in 1894/5, largely at the instigation of Millwall, it contained a mixture of professional and amateur clubs, but the amateur clubs were not old ones of FA Cup glories past. No school clubs were present and the only institutional club in the new league was Royal Ordnance Factories, a club formed by workers at the same factories from which Woolwich Arsenal had emerged. By the time the Southern League was formed, Woolwich Arsenal themselves had flown, joining the Football League in 1893/4 as its first southern member. It was something of a coup for the Football League and one they were to repeat in the coming years.

It has been suggested that the Southern League was on a par with the Football League at this time. The evidence strongly suggests otherwise. As an example, clubs from both leagues continued to meet in the FA Cup for twenty-two seasons in the period when the leagues supposedly ran in parallel. In that period, Southern League clubs won the cup only once (Tottenham in 1901); reached the final on only two other occasions (Southampton in 1900 and again in 1902) and had a total of nine semi-final appearances. In the same twenty-two years of would-be parallel running, the Football League's *Division Two* was more successful than the Southern League, having two FA Cup winners (Wolves in 1908 and Barnsley in 1912); three beaten finalists (Bolton in 1904, Barnsley in 1910 and Huddersfield in 1920) and eleven semi-finalists.

As the new century progressed, the Southern League was further weakened by the switch of allegiance of some of its bigger clubs. These included Bristol City in 1901, Fulham in 1907, Tottenham in 1908 and West Ham in 1919 and, as further evidence that the Southern League was not on a par with the Football League, its big clubs were not especially successful after they made the switch to the national league. Perhaps the most telling way to compare the relative strength of leagues is to look at attendance figures. The paying public is remarkably adept at adjusting its appearances at games in direct correlation with the quality on show. The Southern League never competed with the Football League's top tier in terms of its crowds. In early years, the Southern League's crowds were only half as big on average as those in the top tier of the Football League, but they were at least marginally bigger than average crowds in the Football League's second tier. By 1911/12, however, the Football League's top division was attracting average crowds of over 16,000 and its second division over 9,500, whilst the Southern League could attract an average of less than 7,000 per game.

The relatively poor crowds in the Southern League were certainly not due to a lack of interest in football amongst southerners. Southern clubs who joined the Football League were generally very well supported. In fact Chelsea, formed only in 1905, were the best supported club in the whole country in three out of five seasons immediately preceding the First World War. Tottenham's support was not far behind. They had been struggling financially and were finding it hard to attract enough fans before leaving the Southern League. By contrast, in 1908/9, although in Division Two, they had the fourth largest crowds in the entire Football League.

Incidentally, Woolwich Arsenal were not faring as well in the battle to attract support. In the five years prior to their move north of the river in 1913/14, Arsenal were the top London club in terms of league performance three times, but their attendances were way behind those of Chelsea and Tottenham. The final straw came in the Gunners' relegation year of 1912/3 when their average crowds of just over 9,000 failed to beat those of Second Division Fulham or Clapton Orient. Arsenal therefore had the poorest Football League attendances in London. Chelsea and Tottenham, by comparison, although both fighting relegation for most of the season, enjoyed crowds of over 32,000 and 24,000 respectively, the best and third best figures in the entire League. Something drastic had to be done and something very drastic was done, as Woolwich Arsenal upped sticks and moved north.

In the second season after the resumption of football, following the First World War, the Southern League was, in effect, incorporated into the Football League, but only as its Third Division. By that stage, third tier probably accurately reflected its standing. The Southern League continued on from 1920/1, but with a completely different set up of teams, many of which were reserve sides of the new Football League Division Three clubs.

The paragraphs charting progress of the Southern League may give an impression that football in the south of England was significantly weaker than elsewhere in the country. This does not paint an entirely accurate picture. *Professional and league* football in the south were weaker, but amateur football remained stronger in the south and incomparably stronger than it is today. In particular, the south had Corinthian 'Club'. Corinthian were an odd lot really. They were formed in 1882, primarily to help England counteract the power of Scottish football. They boasted many England internationals in the following years and provided the entire English side on occasions in the 1890s. They were strictly amateur, although they were not averse to claiming substantial expenses, commensurate with their elite social standing. Corinthian did not deign to compete in leagues or the FA Cup. It is, however, a moot point as to whether or not they could have entered the FA Cup anyway, because Corinthian members were usually also members of other clubs and many participated in cup competitions on behalf of their other clubs.

Corinthian were, therefore, not so much a club in the normal sense of the term, but more an amalgam of the best amateur talent in England. For the purpose of evaluating the strength of football in the south, it need only be said that Corinthian were brilliant. For example, in 1889, they played the double-winning 'Invincibles' of Preston North End and won 5-0. In 1903, they met the Bury side which had created a, still existing, FA Cup final record by beating Derby 6-0. Corinthian won 10-3. Corinthian, made up of toffs, might be expected to have played a refined form of the game. They didn't, although they helped develop the passing game in England. Blackburn Rovers, the best professional team in the mid-1880s, were said to play in 'Corinthian style'. It was not a compliment. It meant that they were, shall we say, 'robust' and Corinthian can perhaps be likened to a (much better) 19th century version of Dave Bassett's Wimbledon – again, so much for 'soft southerners'.

Birth of the fan and the derby.

Modern football emerged at a time of enormous cultural and social change. The biggest change of all was urbanisation created as a result of the Industrial Revolution. In the late 17th century, the biggest places in England outside London were Norwich, York and Bristol. Liverpool, Manchester and Birmingham, the big three by 1861, were not even in the top forty in the 17th century. In essence, although London was the largest city in the world by the beginning of the 19th century, in the rest of England big cities simply didn't exist. In 1801, only 20% of the population lived in towns/urban areas. By 1881, nearly 70% did so. In addition, as we have seen, before the Industrial Revolution and the advent of railways, people didn't move around very much. People generally lived in relatively small places, having little contact with the outside world. Even if they lived in an urban area their loyalty would be to their immediate communities rather than to a wider town or city.

The early 19th century was a turbulent period. It began with the Napoleonic Wars and a threat of revolution and it continued with regular bouts of rioting and repression. Crime, violence and alcohol abuse were rife amongst all classes and were at significantly greater levels than later in the century. People were forced by economic circumstances to move from much smaller communities into ever expanding, disease and crime ridden cities. Their living conditions in shoddy, back-to-back housing were poor and their working conditions harsh. Leisure time for the vast majority of people was restricted. Mass gatherings were frowned upon and suppressed by authorities who feared insurrection. The Highways Act of 1835 was used to put an end to most examples of traditional street football. Therefore, ironically, traditional football was in serious decline at precisely the time when 'organised' football was about to take off.

The authorities had to find solutions to these dilemmas and to control potential tinder-boxes in their burgeoning cities. The concept of 'muscular Christianity' has already been explored as one of the pillars upon which a 'better' society was to be built. Another was 'civic pride'. This was not just about wealthy entrepreneurs erecting grand buildings and statues of themselves. Nor was it just about attempts to improve the lot of ordinary people by, for example, providing parks and open spaces. Civic pride also meant trying to generate a sense of belonging and pride in their cities amongst the general public, many of who were newcomers, with no sense of being a Mancunian or Loiner (someone from Leeds by the way). It was important, not least because those with a sense of pride in their city might think twice before burning it down. Football provided a vehicle. It is no coincidence that many of our current football clubs trace their roots back to churches, schools or works' teams, or that employers enthusiastically supported embryonic clubs. The authorities and employers were anxious not only to find healthy alternatives to drunkenness, by encouraging the 'muscular Christian' *playing* of football; they were also keen to encourage *support* for local clubs as an expression of 'civic pride'.

Of course, not everyone was so keen to see working people congregating at football matches. There was still a fear of the 'mob' and the upper classes began to drift away from football as the game became increasingly dominated by working class players and supporters. The Temperance Movement remained suspicious of mass gatherings and condemned the propensity of fans to drink before and after games. The scouting movement didn't like the idea of people spending their time passively watching football matches, rather than participating in activities. Working class political organisations were lukewarm, or positively hostile towards football, viewing sport as a distraction from more important issues.

Nevertheless, many civic leaders were happy to encourage and ride the ever-growing enthusiasm of working class supporters for their clubs and their towns. The opening of a new football ground was a major civic event. It put the city/town on the map and provided an opportunity for club owners to bask in the salutations of their fellow citizens. Nowhere was this new-found sense of civic pride better illustrated than in the welcome afforded to victorious FA Cup teams, returning north from the capital, a place which most northerners had never visited. Blackburn was the first town to experience the joy. Olympic, a team drawn from the working and middle classes and benefitting from training in Blackpool, paid for by collections in the town's mills and foundries, beat Old Etonians 2-1 in March 1883. It was a defeat for the elite; a victory for north over south; professional over amateur; modern tactics over the relics of a 1-2-1-7 formation. In the longer term, it heralded the start of a new order in football. At the time, however, above any of these broader implications, it was a victory for the *town of Blackburn* and marching bands and a horse drawn parade milked the sense of civic pride for all it was worth. Rovers fans joined in the celebrations, as did Olympic fans when Rovers kept the cup in Blackburn for the next three years (it is still the only place to have won the cup for four years in a row).

Football supporters and local derbies existed long before the birth of the Football League. However, the introduction of league football, with its season long, planned, competitive matches against teams from faraway places, made the game much more interesting for the general public, let alone for existing football lovers. Throughout the year, people could track the fortunes of their clubs, the representatives of their communities on the national stage, in league tables published regularly in the press.

There were no derbies within individual towns or cities at the start of the Football League because of the rule forbidding more than one team from one city or town. This was to change shortly afterwards, in 1892/3, when Nottingham, Birmingham, Stoke, Sheffield and Liverpool were granted two Football League clubs each (Liverpool's second club, after Everton, was Bootle, not Liverpool AFC). However, from the start of the Football League, derby rivalry quickly grew between Lancashire's clubs, especially between Preston and Blackburn Rovers – more so at that time than Blackburn and Burnley – and Midlands' clubs, especially between Aston Villa and West Brom – more so at that time than West Brom and Wolves.

As we shall examine later, relationships between local rivals were a good deal less hostile than they are now – but the big derby days had been born.

2

Why are they 'derbies'?

The origin of the term 'derby' is disputed. The most appealing explanation is that the name derives from a surviving example of 'mob' football, played on each Shrove Tuesday and Ash Wednesday, in Ashbourne, Derbyshire. This annual bout of wonderful madness involves dozens of people pushing and pulling each other for up to eight hours a day for two days, whilst trying to score into goals which are *three miles* apart. The teams are the Up'ards from north of the River Henmore and the Down'ards from south of the river. The playing area is as much of Ashbourne as they choose to use and much of the activity takes place in the river itself.There are rules to protect private property, but boarding up of windows and removal of vehicles from the area is still highly recommended.People born in Ashbourne are clearly designated to one half of this 'derby' from birth although, in 1972, a born Down'ard 'goaled' for the Up'ards. Apparently, the justification for this brazen act of treachery was that his mum, an Up'ard, had asked him to do it. The scorer therefore was the victim of age-old tensions falling upon those who are products of football's mixed marriages. The traitor was never forgiven by Down'ards, including other members of his predominantly Down'ard family, but no doubt his mum loved him.

The game may look like complete mayhem but in fact there are strict conventions which govern, for example, how goals are scored and who is allowed to score them. There are tactics too, with individual runners strategically placed and trained to be American football style wide-receivers, should the ball ever emerge from the 'hug' (scrum) of the assembled masses. Although scoring is not exactly prolific, nor is it as uncommon as might be expected, given the size of the playing area. A full list of scorers from 1891 onwards has been lovingly recorded in the town.

The Shrovetide event in 2010 took a special place in folklore. After fifteen years without a victory, the Down'ards entered day two in good heart, having goaled on Shrove Tuesday. On Wednesday, after a long spell in the river, proceedings livened up when Lenny Lyon, a stalwart Up'ard, took a seemingly risky decision to lob the huge ball over his head into a seriously muddy ploughed field. As the snow of the 2010 winter fell relentlessly, a scene reminiscent of Napoleon's retreat from Moscow unfolded, as the Down'ards gradually drove the Up'ards backwards. The battle continued in gardens, on top of a farmer's truck, in a Homebase car park and on a major roundabout, holding up traffic for well over an hour. With only fifteen minutes to go to the cut off point of 10pm, Down'ards were still in control and within sight of their goal. The Up'ards were down and out surely, but no – this is a derby after all. In a classic counter-attack, the Up'ards broke out and headed up river where, over two and a half miles later, they 'goaled'.

Up'ard celebrations were short-lived, however, because Down'ards objected that the goal had been scored after the deadline. Their challenge was upheld by 'the Committee' and Up'ards were left to rue the fact that, after eight hours of largely defensive toil, they had been within a couple of minutes of retaining their undefeated record. It is difficult to imagine what Alex Ferguson or Arsene Wenger would have made of the timekeeper – a large meat pie in all probability. In comparison, Lenny Lyon seemed to take it all very phlegmatically, but then maybe eight hours in the cold, much of it in a river, is enough to dampen anyone's fighting spirit.

The 2011 event was less contentious, but produced a feast of attacking 'football'. For the first time in seventy-five years the contest ended in a 2-2 draw, the maximum possible score. 2012 saw a return to normality and a 1-1 draw.

The Ashbourne game is probably the biggest and most famous surviving example of mass street football, but it isn't unique even now, there being the Ba' game in Kirkwall and Uppies versus Downies in Workington, to name but two. As we saw earlier, in the past similar games were common in many towns and cities. One was held in Derby itself, where St.Peter's tackled All Saints every Shrove Tuesday until the mid-19th Century. Unfortunately, in 1847, things got a little out of hand; the Mayor felt the need to read the Riot Act; two companies of dragoons charged the crowd and this particular derby in Derby itself was no more. Many commentators say that the origin of the term 'derby' comes from the St.Peter's/All Saints clash and not from Ashbourne, as they are after all called 'derbies', not 'ashbournes' or 'derbyshires'. This may be so but, at the time, there was nothing particularly special or unusual about the event in Derby to warrant its inclusion in the language.

After observing an example of 'mob' football, a French visitor commented that *"if Englishmen call this playing it would be impossible to say what they call fighting"*. However, this is not an example of pure British eccentricity, as these types of games were played in other parts of the world and still are played in places such as the cultured city of Florence. It being Florence the whole event is much more colourful than its counterpart in Ashbourne and is generally a good excuse for dressing up. Pageantry, medieval costumes and a street procession are all part of the build up to the main event. It is also a bit more ordered, in the sense that there are a set number of players in each of the four teams representing the quarters of the city. However, any thoughts that this may be more a fashion show than an Ashbourne style scrummage are quickly dispatched once the action starts. This is, after all, the city of the cunning and violent Medici family and the *calcio storico* has been described as being *"as fun filled as a full blown riot in a maximum security prison"*.

There are more prosaic explanations of the origins of the name 'derby'. One is that it derives from an old slang term, 'derbies', meaning handcuffs, the idea presumably being that two opponents are unbreakably cuffed together in a struggle. Another is that the term came into common use as a way of describing big games, following the 1886 FA Cup final replay, played at Derby. It was the first time the final had been held outside London and the game attracted huge interest and a relatively big crowd (about 15,000), greater than for any previous final. Yet another possible explanation, popular in Liverpool, is that the term refers to the battle across Stanley Park between Everton and Liverpool, as Stanley is the family name of the Earls of Derby. The latter two explanations can be discounted, however, because the term 'derby' was in use before 1886 and before either Liverpool club came into existence.

By far the most likely explanation of the origin of the term 'derby' is that it is taken from the famous horse race, established in 1780 by the Earl of Derby. So big were crowds at the Epsom race that, so the story goes, any important sporting event attended by a large crowd became known as a 'derby'. In the early days of football, travelling to away games in other towns and cities was difficult. In fact, other than at major FA Cup ties, the presence of away fans from other places was quite rare until after World War 1. Therefore, the biggest football crowds by far were those at games between local rivals. Hence they became known as 'derbies'.

The latter explanation of the name may be more likely to be correct, but romantics and those with an eye and ear for a good story will still go with the Ashbourne connection – long may their madcap football of the streets continue and flourish.

3

Derbies of old – a detour to Ancient Rome

Whatever the origins of the term, the concept of passionately supported team contests between local rivals is very old indeed. The best examples of 'derbies' in ancient times are those associated with chariot-racing in Rome. It was very much a team sport, with each 'faction' or 'colour' fielding up to three chariots in races. The parallels between Roman chariot-racing and modern football are striking. The factions attracted fervent, partisan fans, many of who would arrive in the evening before races to ensure getting a good view. Mass hysteria generated at the events even had its own name, *furor circensis*.

Charioteers were sporting superstars who earned fortunes and the adoration of young women and men in Rome. Records suggest that top charioteers were by far the best paid sportspeople *in history*, their comparative rewards far outstripping those of gladiators, modern American baseball and basketball stars and making David Beckham look like a journeyman pauper. Most charioteers came from humble backgrounds. Unlike today's footballers, who have been known to describe themselves as wage-slaves, charioteers often really were slaves.

Stars could be transferred from one team to another. There were old pros who survived long enough to race over one hundred and fifty times a year for twenty odd years – and our footballers talk about burn out. There were sports' stattos too who would lovingly record every race, transfer and career record. Superstars were adored to extremes. In 77 BC, a distraught supporter threw himself on the funeral pyre of a Red favourite. At first this may seem a little over the top in comparison to modern fans' behaviour. However, a number of countries, especially in South America, report increased illnesses and even suicides following defeats in major football games. When River Plate, darlings of about one-third of Argentinians, were relegated in 2011 for the first time in their history, emergency services, hospitals and support groups were put on red alert.

As in football, where the proliferation outside grounds of busts of favourite players is a modern fashion, charioteer fans erected statues of the greats. One was erected to a Green hero, Scorpus. Unfortunately, his was a shooting star career. He died in a 'shipwreck', the name given to chariot crashes. He had earned a fortune, but he died young. Of course, individual superstars in gladiatorial contests were also adored and venerated. What made chariot-racing different and more akin to modern football is that the real allegiance of the crowd was to the team and the 'colours', not to individuals. Pliny the Younger observed disapprovingly:-

"I am the more astonished that so many thousands of grown men should be possessed again and again with the childish passion to look at galloping horses and men standing upright in their chariots. If, indeed, they were attracted by the swiftness of the horses or the skill of the men, one could account for this enthusiasm. But in fact it is a bit of cloth they favour, a bit of cloth that captivates them. And if, during the running, the racers were to exchange colours, their partizans would change sides, and instantly forsake the very drivers whom they were just before clamorously saluting by name".
There are many modern footballers who will wince and recognise the truth of Pliny's observation.

At least 150,000 people attended chariot-racing in Rome's *Circus Maximus*, making it far more popular than gladiatorial contests. The impression created by the records is that Romans viewed gladiatorial combats in the Colosseum in the same way we might think about a cross between a boxing match and a circus (professional wrestling springs to mind!). Certainly, it was enjoyable and popular. Sure, people had their favourites amongst gladiators. However, it didn't really matter how many crocodiles or Christians were dispatched by Gluteus Maximus at the weekend. It wouldn't lead to sleepless nights or sheepish looks on Monday morning. What did matter; what determined bragging rights in Rome, was the outcome of chariot-racing.

The fortunes of factions varied over time, as they do in football. Originally there were only two, Red and White. These were joined later by Green and Blue and gradually the newcomers became the dominant colours, with Red and White effectively disappearing. Fans of the Red and White factions therefore became the first to experience the cruel pain of seeing their rivals overtake them and eventually disappear over the horizon – a pain felt on many occasions by fans of modern football clubs. During his reign Domitian introduced two more colours, Purple and Gold, but these were short-lived, disappearing after Domitian died. There are similarities here, for example, with the rise and fall of Gretna in the Scottish League.

When the Roman Empire split, chariot-racing not only continued, it became even more fervent. People in Byzantium wore their green or blue colours as a norm, in much the same way that football fans wear replica kits. Fortunately there is no record of either Blue or Green having a day-glo orange away kit, to be worn on package holidays across the Bosphorus. Fans had to be segregated at races and there appears to have been a class divide between them, with Green fans usually coming from poorer areas of the city.

Associations developed around chariot-racing factions and became involved in politics. Trouble broke out at races and factions became the focal point of dissent. Things came to a head in 532 AD, during the reign of Justinian. Following the arrest of supporters at an earlier racing event, Blue and Green fans came together in the Nika Riots to challenge Justinian and replace him as Emperor. After five days, Justinian made an approach to Blue leaders. In addition to bribing them, Justinian reminded them that he had always supported the Blue, whereas his rival was a Green. The Blues withdrew, leaving Greens to face Imperial troops, who stormed the Hippodrome and killed thousands.

Again all of this may seem a little extreme in comparison to modern day football. Politics does not feature as a dividing force in English football. However, this is not the case in a number of other countries, where politics, as well as religion, class and national identities frequently define club allegiance from birth. Nor is it unusual for modern continental 'ultras' to use football affinities as a base for political activities.

Furthermore, violence associated with modern football is not, alas, always confined to relatively minor skirmishing between rival 'firms'. In 1969, in the build up to the 1970 Mexico World Cup finals, El Salvador and Honduras were drawn against each other in the qualifying stages. The games coincided with a dispute between the two countries about land and immigration. Emotions were fanned in the build up to the qualification play-off game in June 1969 and, following El Salvador's 3-2 victory, press reports in both countries exaggerated what were in any event violent clashes between fans. The outcome triggered what became known as the 'Football War' when El Salvador invaded Honduras in July 1969.

As an example of club football spilling over into politics, it should be remembered that the first serious violence of the Balkan Wars in the 1990's began at a derby between the former Yugoslavian rivals, Dynamo Zagreb (now Croatian) and Red Star Belgrade (now Serbian). More recently, Al-Ahly fans in Cairo were at the forefront of demonstrations that helped bring down Mubarrek's regime in Egypt. In a chilling echo of Justinian's attack on the Greens, it was alleged that government forces were responsible for organised retribution in the subsequent attack in Port Said which resulted in the killing of dozens of Al-Ahly fans.

Before moving on from chariot-racing, here is a final tribute to its devoted fans in the Roman Empire. A Roman custom was to write curses on stone or lead tablets to encourage gods to support them and bring calamity to their enemies. If the gods couldn't be relied on to do the job, fans might take things into their own hands by striking nails through lead tablets and lobbing them at rival charioteers as they passed by. One fan took the time to write this tablet to curse his rivals before a crucial derby and all 21st Century fans will empathise with the sentiments expressed.

"Help me in the Circus on 8th November. Bind every limb, every sinew, the shoulders, the ankles and the elbows of Olympus, Olympianus, Scortious and Juvencus, the charioteers of the Red. Torment their minds, their intelligence and their senses, so that they may not know what they are doing, and knock out their eyes so that they may not see where they are going – neither they nor the horses they are going to drive".

'*Red scum*' scrawled on a modern wall may be more succinct, but somehow it doesn't quite compare does it ?

4

The first 'modern' derby

The first derby in a properly organised, association football match unsurprisingly involved a clash between the two oldest football clubs in the world. It was the first Sheffield derby, not be confused with the current 'Steel City' derby between the professional clubs of Sheffield United and Sheffield Wednesday. The historic first derby was between two clubs who are still playing today, at a similar level to each other, in the amateur ranks of English football – Sheffield and Hallam. Sheffield FC, founded in 1857, is indisputably the oldest football club in the world and is officially recognised as such by FIFA. Incidentally, only two clubs in the world have been awarded FIFA's greatest honour, its order of merit. One is Real Madrid – the other is Sheffield FC.

It should be said that Hallam's claim to be the second oldest club is disputed by Cray Wanderers who are from Kent, many miles from Sheffield. The 'Countrymen' (Hallam) and the 'Wands' (Cray) were both formed in 1860. In keeping with the competitive nature of the great game, neither club acknowledges the claim of the other in the historical sections of their respective websites. Both clubs state categorically and without question that they are the number two club in history. This is an example of a difficulty that football researchers will encounter regularly when examining club histories. It sometimes suits clubs to make claims about their origins that are not entirely accurate or, at least, which are open to debate.

Whether Hallam is the second or third oldest club in the history of the game, their meeting on Boxing Day 1860 with their neighbours Sheffield was a momentous occasion. It heralded the great football derbies of the world. It was the first meeting of Red, Sheffield, against Blue, Hallam; the quintessential clash of colours which has been played out millions of times on bar-football tables and with standard Subbuteo sets for over one hundred and fifty years.

Football in the early days was much more robust than it is now. Barging and hacking were not only allowed, they were skills to be admired and positively honed. A Sheffield player recalled "*often seeing the ball lying quietly on the ground whilst, yards away, opposing players were blocking, ramming and butting each other*". Despite the rough play, the first derby was "*conducted with good temper and in a friendly spirit*". Sheffield won 2-0 and their small band of supporters thereby had the pleasure of being the very first football fans on the planet to experience the happy glow of a derby victory and the bragging rights which go with it.

Two years later, the clubs met again on Boxing Day, this time at Bramall Lane. The result, 0-0, easily slipped from the memories of those present, but *'the manner of play'* was not so easily forgotten by anyone who was there to witness it.The game set the scene for the sheer animosity between neighbours that has been replicated time and time again, in virtually every large city on almost every continent. To say that it was not a friendly affair would be a considerable understatement, especially bearing in mind that the game was played at Christmas and in aid of charity. There occurred what was described as a *"waistcoats off and fighting"* incident. It involved, amongst others, John Charles Shaw. Shaw was a prominent Conservative politician who, although playing for Hallam, was a member of both clubs. Recriminations and accusatory letters from players and supporters continued in the press for days afterwards and relations between the clubs became so frosty that a planned return fixture was cancelled. In fact, the first elevens of the two clubs didn't play each other again until 1905, forty-three years later!

5

An introduction to English League derbies

What is a derby anyway?

A pause is needed at this point to think about what precisely constitutes a football derby. The answer is not as obvious as it may seem. What should be clear is that a derby is not the same as a rivalry. Arsenal v Manchester United or Liverpool v Chelsea are clashes between deadly rivals, but these clashes are not derbies, because London and Lancashire are too far apart geographically. Derbies are games between *local* rivals. However, the definition of what is meant by 'local' is not always straightforward. It does not necessarily mean that places and their football clubs are close neighbours. Norwich and Ipswich are nearly fifty miles from each other. Crystal Palace is about forty miles from Brighton. Yet, in both cases, matches between the clubs are considered to be derbies.

Nor does 'local' mean that clubs always see their closest geographical neighbours as their primary derby foes. In the examples above, Norwich and Ipswich are a long way from each other, but Ipswich are still the nearest club for Norwich and therefore are the Canaries' logical geographical rivals. However, Norwich are not the closest club for Ipswich. A trip to Colchester United is much shorter. Crystal Palace present a more extreme example because a number of clubs, especially their fellow South Londoners, Charlton and Millwall, are closer to Palace than Brighton. Palace and Millwall too, choose clubs from further away to be their main derby rivals. Palace choose Brighton on the south coast. Millwall choose East London, as their biggest rivals are West Ham. These geographical distortions continue, even though the Palace v Millwall derby has usually been a more closely fought affair than either of the derbies involving Palace v Brighton and Millwall v West Ham. In fact there are numerous examples where, for various reasons, clubs have chosen close, but not *the closest* clubs geographically, to be the main focus of their hatred. As a result, the difference between a supposedly local derby and a rivalry is not entirely clear cut.

'General' and 'Primary' derbies.

To add further blurring to the mix, a distinction has to be made between what might be termed *general* derbies and much more important *primary* derbies. Every year there are dozens of *general* derbies. Whenever two sides from London meet, there is a London derby. We have Midlands' derbies, South West derbies, Lancashire v Yorkshire derbies and so on. Using this definition of *general* derbies, in 2011/2 in the Premier League alone, there were twenty derby matches in London and an amazing forty-two in Lancashire.

However, by no means all general derbies are passionate affairs. Barnet v Leyton Orient or Burnley v Oldham both qualify for the category, but it is unlikely that fans see these clashes as being significantly spicier than Barnet v Oldham or Orient v Burnley. To illustrate the point, the lowest attendance at *any* third tier game in 2010/11 saw Dagenham and Redbridge play Brentford in a *general* London derby.

In the midst of their frequent general derbies, most clubs have just a few fixtures against local opponents that really matter. To use Dagenham and Redbridge as an example; they may not be overly excited about fellow London opponents like Brentford, but contests against Orient or, if they had the opportunity, West Ham, would matter a great deal.

A smaller number of clubs are more focussed still and each has one special 'primary' derby that is all-, or virtually all-consuming. True focussed derbies are less numerous than most people think. A few years ago the Football Fans' Census (www.footballfanscensus.com), in their '*Rivalries Uncovered*' report, concluded that there were only twenty-three clashes involving English League clubs where the supporters of both clubs mutually identified each other as their number one derby opponents. Moreover, that number exaggerates the existence of real and regular primary league derbies. Firstly, as the report was looking at rivalries rather than derbies, the list included, for example, Colchester United v Wycombe Wanderers. For historical reasons these are rivals, but Essex v Buckinghamshire is certainly not local. Secondly, a small number of the listed derbies involved a Football League club against a non-league club. Therefore, overall, the number of League clubs who were identified as having a *primary* derby against another League club was less than half the total.

Even where clubs have clear cut, virtually all-consuming *primary* derbies, many still save just a bit of bile for other local rivals. Newcastle and Sunderland have an extremely focussed hatred for each other, but both save a glass or two of poison for Middlesbrough. Cardiff and Swansea devote most of their energies to their own Welsh derby, but keep just enough powder dry for trips across the border to Bristol. Arsenal and Tottenham have been traditional top dogs in London and have little time for anyone else, but both treat clashes with West Ham and Chelsea as a good deal more than just another London derby. There are therefore very few primary derbies where the clubs concerned are 100% focussed upon each other. The purist examples of derby feuds are probably to be found on the south coast between Southampton and Portsmouth and in the 'old farm' derby in East Anglia between Norwich City and Ipswich Town. Nothing and no-one else really gets into the frame to distract participants in these derbies.

Given that primary derbies are relatively few in number, it may seem logical to conclude that no club can have more than one primary derby. However, how could that rule be applied in Liverpool, Manchester and Nottingham? Forest fans would undoubtedly argue that, at present at least, their primary derby is with Derby County, and Derby fans agree. Does this mean that Forest's clashes with their city neighbours Notts. County are not primary derbies? Similarly, does Manchester United's reciprocated fascination with Liverpool relegate the Manchester and Liverpool city derbies to the also-ran category of general derbies? If it did so before 2011/12, it certainly does not do so now.

To summarise, defining precisely what is a derby, rather than a rivalry, and what is a primary derby, as opposed to a general derby, is not as easy as at first it seems. It is easy to recognise a clear cut primary derby when you see one and to identify what is an obvious rivalry or a minor general derby, but there are significant grey areas in between.

Earliest competitive derbies involving current League clubs.

The first big *competitive* derbies between current *primary* or *general* derby rivals were played before the establishment of the Football League. All occurred in the FA Cup, as it was the only national competition at the time. There had been earlier clashes in 'friendlies' or in minor, local cup competitions. Nottingham's clubs first met in a friendly in 1866. At that point only two other current League clubs existed (Stoke and Chesterfield). The Nottingham derby was also the earliest competitive encounter in a national contest. Given their age, County being the oldest current League club and Forest the third oldest, it is perhaps not surprising to find Nottingham at the top of the list. However, the longevity of other derbies may be less predictable.

1. Nov 1878. Notts County 1 Nottingham Forest 3. Forest went on to become the first of the new breed of midland and northern clubs to reach an FA Cup semi-final, where they lost 2-1 to eventual winners, Old Etonians.

2. Nov 1881. Blackburn Rovers 6 Bolton Wanderers 2. This is not a primary derby and it never has been for either club, but it has always been an important Lancastrian derby. In the 1881/2 season Rovers went on to become the first current League club to reach an FA Cup final, where they lost 1-0 to Old Etonians.

3=. Jan 1885. Grimsby Town 1 Lincoln City 0. The teams met again in the following season's Cup competition. Grimsby won again. Grimsby were already well established, whereas Lincoln had been founded only in 1884. Having to meet their Lincolnshire rivals twice in two years was therefore something of a baptism of fire for the Red Imps.

3=. Jan 1885. Aston Villa 0 West Bromwich Albion 0. Although it may not be a primary derby now, this was the big West Midlands' derby at the time. West Brom won the replay 3-0.

5. Jan 1886. West Bromwich Albion 3 Wolverhampton Wanderers 1. West Brom went on to reach the FA Cup final, where they lost to Blackburn Rovers. On the way, they put out another West Midlands' foe, Small Heath Alliance (now Birmingham City), in the semi-final.

6. Oct. 1887. Stoke 1 Port Vale 0.

7. 5th Nov. 1887. Aston Villa 4 Birmingham City 0. The Blues were still known as Small Heath Alliance at the time.

8. 26th Nov. 1887. Middlesbrough 2 Sunderland 2. Newcastle v Sunderland is clearly the big North East derby now but, arguably, the Wear/Tees derby was at least as big in 1887, because both clubs were longer established than Newcastle. Sunderland won the replay 4-2.

These eight derbies were the only ones to begin competitively at national level before the start of the Football League.

Earliest Football League derbies.

The first local derbies in the Football League took place on Saturday 8th September 1888, the first day of the campaign in the League's inaugural year. In Lancashire, Preston won 5-2 at home to Burnley and in the West Midlands, Wolves and Villa played out a 1-1 draw. However, at the time, as now, these were not primary derbies.

The big primary derbies in 1888 were Preston v Blackburn in Lancashire and Villa v West Brom in the Midlands. Preston first met Blackburn in the League in December 1888 and won 1-0 at home. Villa first met West Brom in January 1889 and won 2-0 at home.

The first of the current, primary derbies to be played in the League was Burnley at home to Blackburn in November 1888, but Burnley fans should look away now – Rovers won 7-1. In the West Midlands, the first League clash was Wolves' 2-0 home win against West Brom in January 1889.

The nature of early derbies.

When properly organised association football began, arguably derbies were even more important than they are now, due to the difficulties of travelling to games. It was often impractical and/or too costly for fans to travel to away games and therefore for many people local derbies offered the only opportunities for them to experience the thrill of entering an enemy's den. Derbies were always eagerly contested and crowd trouble was more common than is often assumed. Those who believe that problems at football matches began in the 1960s are mistaken. In the very first Sheffield derby, described earlier, the behaviour of Hallam fans was heavily criticised in the local press. In the second Grimsby v Lincoln FA Cup tie in 1885, Grimsby players were chased from the pitch and into a shed by irate Lincoln fans. However, most football related trouble in the early years involved encroachment onto the pitch and/or boisterous complaints about the decisions of officials, rather than violence directed towards opposing fans. There were a number of well-documented violent occurrences, but they were relatively uncommon. It should be pointed out that this lack of violence was not specific to football. Society in general was less violent in the latter part of the 19th century and the first half of the 20th century than it had been before or than it has been since around the mid-1950s. Again, football crowds reflect the society in which they exist.

Important as derbies were, most were not as vitriolic as they are now. Partisanship in English derbies has tended to increase significantly over time. For example, when fixtures were first organised to avoid clashes of home games for teams from the same city, most people assume that it must have been for policing, crowd control and transportation reasons. In modern times these are indeed the reasons for organising fixtures in this way. But, originally, a primary reason for keeping home games apart was to enable fans to watch both clubs in the city on a regular basis. While the vast majority of fans would have a favourite team for derby day, it was much more common than it is now for people to support both clubs.

Similar arrangements and sentiments were not confined to single-city derbies. It was quite common for neighbouring communities to organise transport for people to travel to support local rivals when their own team was playing further afield. Well into the 1960s, these 'double' support arrangements were far more numerous than they are today. Now the idea of, say, Burnley fans travelling to support Blackburn when the Clarets are away may not be completely unthinkable, but it would certainly be very unusual.

A major change in attitudes over the years has been in the loyalty of supporters to their areas. Most fans these days look for two results before any others. First is their own team's score, but that is quickly followed by looking for the result of their primary local rivals. A perfect weekend is usually deemed to be a clear-cut victory for the favourites and a whopping defeat for local enemies. Even if local rivals are playing an unpopular club from the other side of the country, the vast majority of fans want their neighbours to get a thorough stuffing. The same principle often applies in European games, in which English League clubs cannot necessarily rely upon the support of English/Welsh fans as a whole, let alone from fans of their closest derby rivals.

It wasn't always so. Unless the result would have a direct negative impact upon their own side, the majority of fans used to support local teams against opposition from another area. In the early days of the Football League, for example, a strong rivalry developed between Lancashire and the West Midlands because a large majority of the initial twelve clubs came from those two areas. In spite of their local derby rivalries, supporters of all West Midlands' clubs would tend to support any of their neighbours against Lancastrian opponents and vice versa. Today it is somewhat unlikely that, for example, West Brom fans would wish Wolves every success on a trip to Bolton Wanderers.

A particularly good example of the change in loyalties to an area comes from the south coast. When Portsmouth won the FA Cup in 1939, the Pompey team were invited to parade the cup around the Dell (Southampton's old ground). There they were greeted with cheers by Saints' fans delighted to see the cup arriving in Hampshire for the first time. If someone had suggested a similar parade, following Pompey's victory in the 2008 final, a hardened police chief wouldn't have known whether to laugh or cry – times and attitudes have changed.

In summary then, derbies historically were competitive, but not always full of bile. Neighbouring clubs were frequently the second favourites of supporters.

On the whole, northern clubs would enjoy the support of other northern fans when playing southern clubs and vice-versa. Clubs themselves were in competition with other clubs in their area for success and for fans, but usually had no particular axe to grind with their neighbours.

Bitter early derbies.

However, in the midst of this general picture of local co-operation, or at least of mutual respect between local clubs, there are examples of derby rivalries that were acrimonious from the very start.

Arsenal v Tottenham. Arsenal's relationship with southern clubs as a whole was not good. In hindsight, their decisions to become the first London club to turn professional and the first to join the Football League may seem inspired, but both decisions were derided at the time as sheer treachery in the south. To add to the general southern disdain for Arsenal, Tottenham would quickly have two much more specific reasons to dislike their North London neighbours. The first reason is that originally Arsenal were not North London neighbours anyway. They moved onto Tottenham's patch chasing better crowds than they could attract south of the river, and thereby posed very unwelcome competition for Spurs. The move was opposed by other London clubs and led to a campaign by the local press to *'keep the interlopers out'*.

The second reason centred upon decisions of the Football League in the first season after the First World War. It had been agreed that both divisions of the league should be extended, from twenty to twenty-two teams. This meant that decisions had to be made about who should be promoted and who should be relegated, in the light of the pre-war table. Derby and Preston, champions and runners-up in Division Two, clearly would be promoted as usual. The choice for the remaining two places in the top division appeared to be between four clubs – Chelsea and Tottenham (next to bottom and bottom in Division One in 1914/5) and Barnsley and Wolves (third and fourth in Division Two). Another possibility was to open up a further place, by relegating Manchester United, who had finished third from bottom in 1914/5, but whose players had subsequently been found guilty of match-fixing.

The most logical choice seemed to be to save Chelsea from relegation and promote Barnsley. However, there had been a precedent for saving both bottom clubs when the top division had been extended previously in 1905/6. Added to factors to be taken into account in making the decision was the Football League's desire to root itself more firmly in the south. With the exception of 1914/5 which, for obvious reasons, was an odd year for crowds, Spurs had been one of the best supported clubs in the country. Tottenham had attracted crowds in excess of 25,000 on average since joining the League. Barnsley, on the other hand, had struggled to maintain crowds a quarter of that size. In the circumstances, the League surely had to choose Tottenham, despite Barnsley's valiant efforts.

To the sheer amazement of everyone, except those who have seen football politics in action before, the League chose Arsenal rather than any of the four more deserving candidates. Arsenal had finished fifth in Division Two in 1914/5 and therefore did not appear to be an option for promotion. The need to encourage the south may have been an understandable, if hardly fair, reason for considering Arsenal over Barnsley or fourth placed Wolves, but was clearly not a reason for dismissing Tottenham's claim. Arsenal's crowds had improved, following their move north of the Thames, but there was no evidence to suggest that they could consistently match those of Tottenham. The 'official' explanation for the decision was that Arsenal were rewarded for long service to the Football League, seemingly ignoring the fact that fourth placed Wolves were original members of the League. Dark stories emerged of corruption. Arsenal's chairman, Sir Henry Norris, allegedly made a deal with the League's President, who was also chairman of Liverpool. 'Honest' John McKenna allegedly received a cut-price house in London via Norris's property company. Nothing was ever proven. Whatever may have been the reason for the League's decision, it further fanned the flames of ill-feeling in North London.

Chelsea v Fulham. Staying in London, the derby between Chelsea and Fulham is not, and has never been, as fervent as its North London equivalent, but there was an early twist in its story. Stamford Bridge was an important ground and it needed a football club. Fulham are the oldest club in the capital and had been nomadic, having had ten previous grounds, before settling at Craven Cottage in 1896. The Mears family, owners of the Bridge, were confident of attracting nearby Fulham to their magnificent stadium, a stadium good enough to become the venue for FA Cup finals prior to the opening of Wembley. Surprisingly, the Cottagers turned down the offer; chose to stay at Craven Cottage and decided to remain in the Southern League, rather than join the Football League. Bemused but undaunted, the Mears decided to create their own club and so, in 1905, Chelsea became one of the few clubs to be formed specifically to fill an existing stadium. They also joined Bradford City as a club admitted to the Football League without ever having played a competitive game. By the time Fulham joined the Football League only two years later, Chelsea had become the best supported club in England. Since that momentous decision, gates at Craven Cottage have never in any season exceeded those at Stamford Bridge. Chelsea, one of the youngest clubs in London, have fifteen pieces of domestic silverware and a European Cup in their trophy cabinet. Fulham, oldest of them all, have none.

As an aside, a few years later the Cottagers almost had another chance to join the big time. Henry Norris was originally a director of Fulham. Whilst still a director at Craven Cottage, he became struggling Arsenal's chairman. His first big football idea was to create a major new force, by merging Woolwich Arsenal with Fulham, playing at the Cottage. For the FA, the thought of moving a club from South East London right across to the other side of the capital was a bridge too far. With his proposal rejected, Norris turned his attention to Arsenal's move to Highbury.

Everton v Liverpool. Liverpool are another club born specifically to play in an existing stadium and their arrival on the Merseyside scene was controversial. The Reds may never have existed, had it not been for a dispute about the behaviour of Anfield's landlord and his proposal to massively increase the rent charged to Everton. In 1892, the majority of the Everton club decided to quit Anfield in protest and move across Stanley Park to Goodison. The landlord, John Houlding, set about forming a new club which, to add heat to the situation, he decided to call Everton. The 'old' Everton were none too pleased and they challenged Houlding's right to take their name. The League found in the existing club's favour and so Liverpool AFC were born (it had to be AFC, because a long-standing agreement with rugby's authorities prevented Liverpool from using the title FC, the name of an established rugby club).

Ill-feeling between the clubs continued into the following season (and well beyond of course). In 1892/3, the League was expanded to twenty-eight clubs from fourteen. The new club, Liverpool, applied for a place but were rejected before voting began. Another new club from the area, Liverpool Caledonians, also applied and were allowed to get further in the process than the club from Anfield, although Caledonians too were eventually denied a place in the League. Yet another Merseyside club, Bootle, were selected instead and Liverpool believed that Everton had a hand in denying them a League place. It should be said that Bootle were a well-established club. They had been strong alternative candidates when Everton were selected as original members of the League. In contrast, neither Liverpool nor Liverpool Caledonians had track records. However, suspicion is stronger than reason in football derbies and Everton stood accused. *If* Everton were involved in denying the Reds, it would not be entirely surprising, given the antics of Mr. Houlding.

Liverpool had to wait only a year before they were elected to the League. Also, Bootle resigned before the start of Liverpool's inaugural season and so the city's top-class, bitter derby had not been delayed for long.

Sheffield United v Sheffield Wednesday. A third 'ground before a team' club are Sheffield United. Their emergence was not greeted with as much heat as in the examples of Arsenal or Liverpool, but it was far from being the uniting experience that their name suggests. The biggest club in the city at the time, The Wednesday, had often played their bigger games at Bramall Lane, now home of United, although Wednesday had never treated it as their home ground as such. The Wednesday had frequently quarrelled with the Lane's authorities and eventually they moved to a new ground outside the city at Owlerton (hence their Owls nickname, though the 'owl' in the name of the district is pronounced as in 'bowl', not as in 'owl'). It was later re-named Hillsborough. Bramall Lane's authorities, including Yorkshire County Cricket Club, decided to form a professional football club to challenge Wednesday after witnessing the huge crowd that attended the Lane for the 1889 FA Cup semi-final between West Brom and Preston.

Having in a sense taken Wednesday's stadium, United initially proceeded to overtake Wednesday to become Sheffield's first League champions in 1897/8 and to cap it all they took Wednesday's nickname, the Blades. In fact, the nickname had been used by Sheffield teams in general, not just by Wednesday, but originally United were called either Junior Blades, to reflect their 'young' status, or the Cutlers. Well into the 20th Century, older Wednesday fans continued to complain about the 'theft' of Sheffield's historic Blades' tag.

.... *and one that got away.* Staying with the theme of clubs formed to fill existing major stadiums, it should be noted that not all similar plans were successful and, as an aside, there is a remarkable story of a potentially bitter derby that didn't take off. If people are asked today to name the biggest club stadium ever built in England, in terms of its regular maximum attendance, most would point to Old Trafford or Villa Park or to the old Maine Road, as it holds the attendance record. The answer, however, is that West Ham Stadium, situated fairly close to where the current City Airport stands in East London, was built to welcome about 120,000 people and was therefore bigger than any other club ground. The stadium was home to the West Ham Hammers and this is where its story gets even stranger. The Hammers were a speedway club, not a football club, and they had nothing to do with the 'Hammers' of West Ham United. The vast stadium was not built primarily as a football venue at all, but its owners decided that commercially it needed a football club and they duly set about creating one. The beast to emerge was Thames Association. By the time their creation appeared on the scene, Millwall had moved away from the East End and into South London and so Thames, in their huge stadium, were potentially new derby rivals for West Ham – United that is for anyone who is completely confused at this point. To add further to the confusion, West Ham United's original name was Thames Ironworks, but this had nothing to do with Thames Association in the West Ham Stadium!

The venture was a complete failure. Entering Division Three South in 1930/1, Thames finished third from bottom in their first season and bottom in their second, at which point they resigned. As for the huge stadium; had it been possible to put together all the crowds to have attended the forty-two home games played by Thames Association over two years, the combined attendance would not have filled their West Ham Stadium. There is one further twist to the story. As Thames were on the verge of folding, Clapton (now Leyton) Orient offered to merge with them. Orient were a struggling side but were firmly established. Who knows what may have happened had Thames taken up the offer?

The section about the bitterest of early derbies ends with a much more recent example. This one is 'early' in the sense that it has been very bitter from the birth of the clubs involved. In fact by the end of the 2011/12 season, the clubs have yet to meet each other in a derby (which is why this derby doesn't appear later in the book). Moreover, the clubs are further apart geographically than Norwich and Ipswich or Palace and Brighton. The clubs concerned are, of course, ***Milton Keynes Dons and AFC Wimbledon.*** Their story is well known and is only briefly outlined here. In essence, Wimbledon FC were moved to Milton Keynes on the grounds that London could not sustain as many football clubs as it had, whereas Milton Keynes, the fastest growing city in England, could sustain an ambitious club and needed league football. Understandably, the move was furiously opposed by Wimbledon's fans and was seen by the wider football community as an abandonment of fans and the beginning of American-style franchising of clubs.

This was not the first major move made by a Football League club. As we have seen, Arsenal moved from their traditional South London home and Millwall from theirs in the East End. Nor was it the first time a proposal had been made to move a club to a new town or city. Robert Maxwell proposed merging Oxford United and Reading and moving both of them to Didcot. The owners of Elland Road tried to persuade Huddersfield Town to move lock, stock and barrel to Leeds after the First World War. South Shields moved to Gateshead chasing a bigger fan base and there are various other examples of proposed mergers and relatively minor re-locations. Wimbledon's move to Milton Keynes, however, was the first time a League club had been re-located to a different place unreasonably far away for its supporters to travel to home games. Wimbledon's fans rallied and formed a new club, AFC Wimbledon, who have gone from strength to strength. At the end of 2010/11, after five promotions, the club gained entry into the Football League. The MK Dons have done reasonably well too but, in 2012/13, are just one tier above their simmering rivals. Therefore, not only could the lottery of a cup draw throw them together, they could also meet in the League itself in the near future. A neutral might prefer to give that particular first derby a miss.

To give fans in Milton Keynes credit, firstly, they were largely innocent parties in the machinations leading to the original Wimbledon's demise. All they wanted was a league club. Secondly, they appear to have a strong sense of self-awareness, as occasionally they adopt Millwall's *'nobody likes us, we don't care'* anthem, which the Lions took on board for very different reasons. MK Dons' fans also refer to themselves as a 'franchise', especially when goading opposing fans.

One piece of the story not so well known is the fate of Wimbledon FC's 1988 FA Cup victory. Which club can place the trophy in its cabinet? The answer is that neither of them is able to do so. Under pressure from supporters groups across the country, MK Dons agreed to relinquish any claims to the achievements of the former Wimbledon, but these were not accorded to the new AFC Wimbledon either. Instead, Wimbledon's achievements, 1988 FA Cup success included, were given to the London Borough of Merton, their former local authority home. South London therefore has its precious second FA Cup victory back where it belongs, but only one of its clubs, Charlton, can officially claim to have won the cup.

Finally, many would argue that, as the clubs are so far apart geographically, this has to be a rivalry not a derby. Given the earlier definition of a derby being local, technically it has to be only a rivalry, but AFC Wimbledon fans deserve a bit of special treatment and they will get it here – after all, who else has had their club stolen and transported?

Three types of English League derby.

There are three main types of derby in England and Wales. All are geographically based.

Inter-City. First, there are reasonably straightforward inter-city (or town) derbies, like those between Southampton and Portsmouth; Newcastle and Sunderland etc. In combat terms these are equivalent to the traditional enmity and mutual suspicion between neighbouring countries, such as England and France – except that there is little possibility of an entente cordiale being signed any time in the near future. If you come from Newcastle, you're a Geordie 'takem' and you are very unlikely to support non-Geordie 'mackems' from down the road in Sunderland. No doubt one of your first culinary lessons, taught to you by your parents, will be not to eat streaky bacon unless it is very well done. It will thereby have a blackish hue, rather than being red and white striped, Sunderland-style. You will never enjoy the real taste of bacon, but that's a price you're willing to pay for your beloved Geordie Magpies.

These geographical rivalries are not necessarily between very close neighbours. As we saw earlier, Norwich and Ipswich are almost fifty miles apart. However, their derby is a modern day embodiment of the ancient division of territory in East Anglia between the north folk and south folk. Therefore, although the places are not very close to each other, their respective counties share a border. It is *'Suffolk 'n' good'* versus *'Norfolk 'n' good'*, as Ipswich fans would have it, but a *'fine city'* versus a mere town according to Canaries.

Many inter-city derbies stay on a roughly even keel decade after decade. However, sometimes the fortunes of clubs shift dramatically. For example, in Hertfordshire and Bedfordshire, Luton Town have always been the biggest club. Unfortunately, in recent years, they have fallen on hard times and have been overtaken in performance terms, if not in overall size, not only by traditional rivals Watford, but also by newcomers Stevenage.

Traditional derbies can be altered, not by changes in the performance of the participating clubs, but by the emergence of clubs from cities and towns not previously on the League map. For example, the arrival of Oxford United significantly altered the dynamics of the traditional Reading v Swindon derby. The arrival of MK Dons is of interest, not only to AFC Wimbledon, but also to a number of older clubs close to Milton Keynes. Who knows what impact the emergence of Crawley Town may have on the Brighton v Crystal Palace derby or Fleetwood Town's meteoric rise on Blackpool v Preston or Morecombe v Accrington? Most English League derbies fall into the inter-city/town category and we shall examine many of them in detail in the second half of the book.

Single-city. Second, there are intra-city derbies in Bristol, Stoke and Nottingham etc. In combat terms, these are more like civil wars. Loyalties split families, work colleagues and school friends in the same city. In four of the eight main city derbies, the older, longer established clubs have been overtaken by younger upstarts. In Bristol, Liverpool, Nottingham and North London; Rovers, Everton, County and Spurs are older than their more successful local rivals. The chart below sets out how things have changed over time in these single-city derbies. It lists the most successful clubs now, taking the whole of their histories into account, and what the position was at the start of World War 1 and World War 2. World Wars are used as convenient dividing lines at various times in the book, partly because they were cataclysmic events and partly because football was suspended during those years:-

---

Clubs with the best historical record in single-city derbies (based upon success in the League, FA Cup, and League Cup)

City	At 1914/5	At 1938/9	Now (2012/13)
Birmingham	Villa	Villa	Villa
Bristol	City	City	City
Liverpool [*1]	Everton	Everton	Liverpool
Manchester [*2]	United	City	United
North London [*3]	Tottenham	Arsenal	Arsenal
Nottingham [*4]	County	County	Forest
Sheffield [*5]	Wednesday	Wednesday	Wednesday
Stoke	City	City	City

*1-It was not until 1977 that Liverpool overtook Everton's overall domestic record, though they took the lead a few years earlier if European success is taken into account.

*2-City led Manchester United until 1909 and regained the lead in 1932. United re-took supremacy only in 1951.

*3-Arsenal overtook Spurs in 1930.

*4-Forest's FA Cup victory in 1959 saw them overtake County

*5-United briefly overtook Wednesday at the turn of the 20th century and again in the mid-1920s, but Wednesday have held the lead ever since their League championships in 1929 and 1930.

Many people may be particularly surprised to read that Notts County were not overtaken by Forest until the late 1950s. Not only were County historically the more successful of the two, admittedly pretty unsuccessful, clubs at that point, they were also usually the better supported club prior to the Second World War. They still had attendances on a par with Forest's well into the fifties. It was only when County slumped into the fourth tier in the late fifties and early sixties, at the same time as Forest were doing reasonably well in the top tier, that the yawning gap in size and support between the clubs began to develop.

There is an odd coincidence to note about England's intra-city derbies. In seven out of eight cases, the club playing in red is the dominant one historically (counting Villa's claret as leaning towards red, at least in comparison to the blue of Birmingham City). Only Sheffield Wednesday successfully fly the flag for clubs in blue or black. Even then, the Sheffield derby is by far the closest run of the eight. The eight reds have fifty-nine League titles and sixty-four domestic cups to their credit, against only eighteen League titles and thirty-two cups achieved by blues/blacks.

Furthermore, it has been getting even better for reds. In eleven seasons of the 21st Century before 2011/12, intra-city derbies were amazingly one-sided and firmly painted red. In six out of eight cases, the red club finished above the blue in the League in all eleven seasons – United above City in Manchester, Stoke above Port Vale, Forest above County in Nottingham, City above Rovers in Bristol, Arsenal above Spurs in North London and United above Wednesday in Sheffield. In the remaining two cases, the score was 10-1 to the reds – Liverpool over Everton (the exceptional year being 2004/5) and Villa over Birmingham (the exceptional year being 2002/3). The overall total of higher League finishes in those eleven seasons was therefore an incredible 86-2 to clubs playing in red.

At last, 2011/12 saw a fight-back, led by the blue moon rising over Manchester. Reds of Forest, Stoke, Bristol City and Aston Villa were still in higher divisions than their blue rivals, but Everton and Sheffield Wednesday added blue victories to the one achieved by Manchester City. Arsenal, on behalf of the reds, pipped Tottenham and so 2011/12 witnessed a closer score of 5-3 to red clubs, making the 21st Century total 91-5.

In seven out of eight cases, recent red dominance has had the effect of significantly widening even further the gaps between historically dominant clubs and historic underdogs. The exception is again in Sheffield where (red) United, whose overall record is still behind (blue) Wednesday's, had been closing the gap throughout the 21st Century, until Wednesday edged their contest in 2011/12. Promotion for Owls and failure in the play-offs for Blades guaranteed that blues would have at least one more higher placing in 2012/13.

Complex relations. The third principal type of derby involves complicated relationships in large conurbations, such as the West Midlands and London, or in places like Humberside/ Lincolnshire and the Thames Valley. Primary derby rivalries are more likely to shift over time in these areas. In a number of instances, the development of clear cut primary derbies, which may well have thrived in less complex areas, has been prevented or, at least, stunted.

London If inter-city derbies are like wars between neighbouring countries and single-city derbies are like civil wars, London is more like the Balkans. Conflict is seemingly ever present. Certain animosities are endless, but others change according to shifts in power over time. And so, Arsenal v Tottenham is the consistent big event in North London. It has existed, largely undisturbed, ever since Spurs furiously opposed Arsenal's move from south of the River Thames in 1913.

Other rivalries are less clear. In West London, Chelsea have usually been the top club but at various times their *primary* derbies have been against Fulham or QPR, or even Brentford for a short time in the 1930s. More recently, Chelsea's elevation to the top echelons of English football has led them increasingly to ignore local West London rivals and to look towards Arsenal or occasionally Tottenham for their primary 'derby'.

West Ham show small-sibling contempt or, at times, brotherly concern for their East End local rivals, Leyton Orient and Dagenham and Redbridge, but there exists a long-standing derby with Millwall. It began in the Southern League when both clubs were based in East London, before Millwall's move south of the river in 1910. At a later date, new London clubs joined the Southern League, including Crystal Palace, who could have provided a genuine South London derby for Millwall. However, Palace, founded in 1905, didn't even exist when the Millwall v West Ham derby began. Furthermore, Palace had their own local derby in the early days with a club called Croydon Common. Incidentally, before folding, Croydon Common beat Palace 5-1 in their final away derby. Significantly, Charlton, also formed in 1905, were not around, as they didn't join the Southern League until 1920/1, by which time all previous members had left to become the new Third Division of the Football League.

People may argue that Millwall should concentrate on their South London neighbours. After all, Charlton's Valley and Millwall's Den are only four miles apart. Moreover, Charlton and Palace have records broadly comparable with Millwall's, whereas West Ham's is far superior. History, however, is a tenacious beast. As we will see in the second half of the book, Lions and Hammers are unlikely to abandon each other any time soon.

It is often said that the number of derbies in London puts added pressure upon the capital's clubs and has led over the years to their relative lack of collective success. There may be an element of truth in this observation, although northerners would no doubt dismiss it as a convenient excuse. In recent years, the capital's clubs have become more powerful and successful, with Arsenal and Chelsea winning six Premier League titles and a number of London clubs achieving Premiership status. Nevertheless, London shares with other capital cities in large Western European countries, the dubious and unusual distinction of limited achievement in both domestic and European competitions. Throughout the world, the biggest and most successful clubs usually hail from capital cities. Although there are a few notable exceptions in Europe, such as Oslo and Warsaw, this dominance by a club or clubs from capitals also applies in small and medium sized European countries. However, until Chelsea's ground-breaking victory in 2011/12, no team from London, Paris, Rome or Berlin had ever won the primary trophy in Europe. i.e. the European Cup or the Champions League, whereas clubs from Manchester, Marseilles, Milan and Munich have seventeen titles between them.

West Midlands. Primary derby relationships in the West Midlands have changed over time. In recent years, things have settled down and the primary derbies are now established as being Villa v Birmingham and Wolves v West Brom, with all four having a healthy dislike for each other.

Coventry long to be in on the act. From 1967 to 2001, they put in a magnificent shift of thirty-four consecutive seasons in the top tier in an attempt to establish their credentials as worthy derby foes. They also won the FA Cup in 1987, something Birmingham City have never achieved and which the other three have not managed since West Brom's victory in 1968. Coventry's efforts were to no avail. History and, to a lesser extent, geography ensure that none of the other four are bothered about Coventry, who are therefore left with Leicester as a primary derby, even though neither of them want it to be. For their part, Leicester are more interested in Forest and Derby in the East Midlands. It is harder still for Walsall, as they don't have any top tier credentials or silverware to their name. Like poor saddlers trying to gain admittance to an exclusive pony club, Walsall like to think of themselves as desirable, but it is not a requited love affair. The big four show no signs of admitting anyone new to the derby club.

The current primary derbies make sense in terms of administrative geography. Villa and City are from Birmingham, whereas Wolves and West Brom are from outside the city boundary in the Black Country. However, this is another example of a club opting for primary derby rivals who are not their closest geographical neighbours. The Baggies' ground, the Hawthorns, is closer to both Villa Park and St.Andrews, homes of Aston Villa and Birmingham City, than it is to Molineux, home of Wolves.

Historically, derby plates have shifted. Shortly before the Football League began, West Brom were rated the top club in the West Midlands, but both Wolves and especially Villa were more successful in the early days of the League. Villa won five of the first twelve titles and very quickly established themselves as by far the most successful and best supported club in the region. Despite disappointments in the League, West Brom retained their place as the main early derby for Villa for three main reasons. First, they already had a slightly stronger reputation than Wolves. Second, and most importantly, they continued to be successful in the FA Cup. Their three meetings with Villa in the finals of 1887, 1892 and 1895 solidified their rivalry. Third, Birmingham City were relatively weak and unable to make any significant headway to attract Villa away from West Brom.

Therefore, the initial relationship between the four was established, with Villa as the dominant club, Birmingham as the weakest link and West Brom and Wolves in the middle, vying for the attention of Villa and trying to knock them off their pedestal. Birmingham didn't really figure greatly on the radar of the other three. They were no threat to Villa, whereas Wolves and Albion probably took pity on them for having to share the same city with the almighty and despised Villans. However, in 1935/6, Birmingham came top of the West Midlands' 'league' and it heralded a shift in the fortunes of the clubs. In the same year, the almost unthinkable happened when, for the first time in their history, Aston Villa were relegated. To put this into perspective, on a 'most successful club in history' list at the time, Villa were Number One.

There followed a period right up to the end of the seventies in which Wolves and West Brom held sway. In the fifties they were two of the most successful clubs in England and it was in this period that Wolves v West Brom and, to a lesser degree, Villa v Birmingham began to be seen as primary derbies. In 1980/1, Villa returned to the top in style. Not only did they re-take the West

Midlands' crown, they were also League champions and they followed it up by becoming champions of Europe in 1981/2. In the next thirty seasons, Villa were top dogs in the West Midlands twenty-four times, Coventry five times and Birmingham once. Neither Wolves nor West Brom registered. The Black Country's 'new' primary derby between Wolves and West Brom may not have been covered in glory in those years, but it became more firmly anchored, though even today many older Baggies still think of Villa as primary, or at least equal, derby rivals.

Lincolnshire and Humberside. The clubs currently involved are Hull, Grimsby, Scunthorpe and Lincoln. In the early days of the League, Gainsborough and Loughborough were included and, more recently, Boston United entered the fray for a few seasons. Gainsborough Trinity were Grimsby's main competitors in Lincolnshire initially, being generally stronger, though less well supported, than Lincoln City.

The area is characterised not so much by its shifting derby rivalries, although they do vary according to changes in strength over time, but more by a relatively lukewarm feeling towards what could be fervent primary derbies. According to research, the three other clubs currently involved named Scunthorpe as their main rivals in the area. Hull and Grimsby didn't place Lincoln even in their top three rivalries and Scunthorpe placed Lincoln only third, behind Hull and Grimsby. Quite why Scunthorpe should be so despised (Doncaster don't like them either) is as big a mystery as why everyone is seemingly unwilling to dislike Lincoln. Of the two sets of fans, the Red Imps of Lincoln definitely have a more devilish reputation. In their book 'Rivals', Geoff Harvey and Vanessa Strowger produced a 'nutter rating' for every club. Lincoln's fans were right up there, or down there depending upon how you look at it, with the likes of Cardiff, Stoke and Millwall. Scunthorpe fans were judged to be positively sane in comparison. In addition, Iron have been in the League only since 1950, whereas the others have had many decades more to build up their mutual animosities.

Lincoln have a long history with Grimsby, which was revived as the two desperately fought to avoid the drop into the Conference in 2009/10. Lincoln survived on that occasion. Grimsby did not. It was, however, a short reprieve, because Lincoln slipped into the Conference in 2010/11. Their derby history in the FA Cup goes way back to 1885, making it the third equal oldest primary derby of them all. Their League derbies started in 1892/3, when both clubs were elected as original members of Division Two. Neither Scunthorpe nor Hull existed when the Red Imps and Mariners first locked horns in the League. When Lincoln lost their League place in 1911/12, they were replaced by Grimsby. In general, Grimsby have been dominant, for example leading Lincoln 80-25 in higher league placings. However, in competitive terms, Lincoln's rivalry with Grimsby is still stronger than any of the derby combinations involving Scunthorpe. It is therefore surprising that this ancient derby is not rated very highly by either of its participants, although their presence together in the doldrums of the Conference is currently injecting heat.

By far the potentially juiciest derby of all in the area is Grimsby v Hull and again it is hard to see why this derby doesn't have a greater prominence. This may seem a crazy suggestion from the standpoint of 2012/13, with Hull having recently basked in the glory of the Premiership while Grimsby have fallen into the depths of the Conference. However, the same crazy tag might have been applied in reverse just fourteen years ago when Hull avoided relegation to the Conference by only five points and Grimsby finished a respectable eleventh in the second tier.

Hull is in Yorkshire, not Lincolnshire. It was briefly thrown together with Grimsby in the local authority area of Humberside, a decision that may well have made sense economically, but was never accepted psychologically on either side of the Humber. The border issue may explain why City tend to look westwards to the likes of Sheffield and especially to Leeds for their primary derby, rather than to nearer neighbours in Lincolnshire. However, it is highly unlikely that any other Yorkshire club will ever see the Tigers as their own primary derby.

South Yorkshire. We travel westwards ourselves to South Yorkshire where the clubs involved are Sheffield's United and Wednesday, Barnsley, Rotherham and Doncaster (and to some extent Chesterfield, over the border in Derbyshire). In reality the Sheffield clubs are reluctant participants in the South Yorkshire melee. The Sheffield derby is fervent and generally Blades and Owls only have eyes for each other. But, in recent times, they have had to be more involved in other South Yorkshire derbies because their 'superiority' has been challenged by all three smaller clubs.

Dislike of the Sheffield clubs creates an unfortunate form of tunnel vision amongst others in the area and it stunts the development of their own derbies. There is a bit of a thing between Doncaster and Rotherham, fuelled by their recently fluctuating fortunes. In 2002/3, Rotherham were safely placed in mid-table in the second tier, ahead not only of Doncaster, but of Sheffield Wednesday and Barnsley. Doncaster, meanwhile, were clawing their way out of the Conference. Fast forward a mere six years and Doncaster were safely placed in the second tier while Rotherham, although not quite in the reverse situation, had survived a very difficult year in tier four, having been deducted seventeen points at the start of the season.

Barnsley vent their spleens firmly southwards towards Sheffield. In a sense this is legitimate. The Sheffield clubs are not the powerhouses of old. Wednesday's League Cup triumph in 1991 is the only piece of silverware to be placed in either Sheffield trophy cabinet since 1935. Barnsley meanwhile finally reached the top tier in 1997/8 for the first time. Although Barnsley's recent record is more comparable than in the past, their desire for a primary derby against either Sheffield club is not built upon solid ground. The Owls and Blades have five League championships, seven FA Cups and 126 years in the top tier between them. Barnsley have their solitary Premiership year and an FA Cup victory (as a second tier side) in 1912 to their credit.

Barnsley do, however, have a respectably placed derby available to them in South Yorkshire, against Rotherham, but both choose largely to ignore it. The

Sheffield derby aside, Tykes v Millers is statistically the most competitive derby in the area. Barnsley dominate it, but not by much. For example, their head-to-head count against Rotherham is equal closest of all derbies, with twenty-one wins each.

M4/M40 Corridor. An alternative description of the area would be the Thames Valley but, as we shall see, in a football context this term has unfortunate connotations. The clubs involved are Reading, Swindon, Oxford United and latterly Wycombe. Also included, at least on the fringes, are Bristol's clubs, especially with regard to their relationships with Swindon, and Aldershot Town for historical reasons.

Logically, the stand-out derby is undoubtedly Reading v Swindon. The Royals of Reading are the oldest Football League club in the south of England and the Robins of Swindon are third oldest, equal with Leyton Orient. Reading and Swindon were both founder members of the Southern League and theirs is the oldest southern derby of current League clubs. Their Football League derbies began in 1920, whereas Oxford didn't enter the League until 1962 and Wycombe not until 1993. The Royals v Robins contest is also more competitive than any other combination of sides in the area, although all are fairly close. An oddity in their derby records is that, in the number of derby victories and also in higher league placings, Swindon lead Oxford and Oxford lead Reading, but Reading lead Swindon. Although Reading v Swindon may seem the obvious primary derby, it isn't necessarily so. In the past, Reading had a rivalry with, the now defunct Aldershot, but this has not yet been revived with the later re-incarnation, Aldershot Town. Reading therefore do see Swindon as their main rivals, though only marginally. But Swindon view meetings with Oxford as their primary derby.

The three places are roughly equidistant and, if anything, Reading should be the ones to dislike Oxford. Enter Robert Maxwell. He had one of those plans that make sense only to megalomaniacs who all too often frequent football's corridors of power. He wanted to create Thames Valley Royals, a combination of Reading and Oxford (United that is, remembering that there is an Oxford City). It didn't happen, but Maxwell sowed seeds which led to the questioning of football's 'givens'. Arguably, he paved the way for later examples, such as the forced removal of Wimbledon from their traditional home.

Hatred of Oxford may stem from the fact that they achieved success all too quickly for their upstart status in the area. They were first to reach the top tier, something they achieved in 1985, after less than twenty-five seasons in the League. Swindon didn't make it to the summit until 1993 and Reading not until 2006. To say the least, it must have been annoying for clubs who had been plugging away for decades to see Oxford progress so quickly. Oxford also lasted longer at the top, although for only three seasons. Oxford's ascent and descent from non-league to top tier and back to the Conference was pretty dramatic and they picked up welcome and not so welcome 'firsts' on the way. They were the first fourth tier club to reach the sixth round of the FA Cup and the first club to have won a major national trophy (the League Cup in 1986) subsequently to drop out of the League.

To add to the oddity of rivalries in this area, Wycombe fans name Colchester as their main rivalry, rather than any local club and the animosity, it seems, is reciprocated in North Essex. The Bristol clubs are not heavily involved and do not wish to be, as they have enough trouble with each other and Cardiff City, but both see Swindon as their next most important derby.

The northern surrounds of Manchester. In north Lancashire, primary derbies have changed over time, but have now solidified. Preston v Blackpool, Blackburn v Burnley and, to a lesser extent, Accrington v Morecambe are all accepted primary derbies. But slightly further south, on the northern outskirts of Manchester, the situation is not so clear cut. The clubs involved are Bolton, Bury, Oldham, Rochdale and Wigan. By far the biggest club in the area historically are Bolton Wanderers. They tend to scoff at the idea that any of the other four are worthy derby opponents. Trotters look south to Manchester or north to Blackburn. However, Mancunians have no great interest in Bolton. Blackburn, although more willing to participate, view Bolton as important, but way behind their first 'loves' in Burnley.

In the early days of football, derby configurations in the area were different. Bolton were founder members of the Football League. Shortly afterwards, in 1894, Bury joined the League and gained promotion in their first year. A healthy and very close derby began and continued into the late 1920s. Bury won the FA Cup in 1900 and 1903, something Bolton didn't achieve until 1923. In 1924/5, the Trotters of Bolton and Shakers of Bury finished third and fifth respectively in the top tier. In the following year, Bury came fourth and Bolton won the cup, beating another local rival, Manchester City in the final. Their derby was at its peak. Indeed, for three out of four seasons in the mid-1920s, Bolton v Bury was the top derby in the whole League.

Into the fray, Oldham joined the League in 1907 and gained promotion to the top tier in 1909/10. In 1914/5, the Latics were runners-up in the League by one point to Everton. Who knows what Oldham might have achieved had war not intervened when they were in their prime. Their second place finish is still higher than either Bury or Bolton ever attained. Oldham fell from the top tier in 1922/3. Bury went down in 1928/9 and never returned. Oldham did return, but not until the nineties and then for only three seasons. Altogether, Bury and Oldham have spent twenty-two and twelve years respectively at the top.

The potted history of past glories helps explain attitudes towards current potential derbies in the area. Bury largely ignore others and still see Bolton as their primary derby, even though Bolton consider themselves long flown on to a different plane. Both Bury and especially Oldham think they are far too good to be messing about with the likes of Rochdale, much as Dale would simply love to mess about with them. The other four all think Wigan to be upstarts from oval-ball land who don't deserve to be where they are and who won't last long enough to be worthy of primary derby status. Oldham have a particular dislike for Wigan, partly because both have the 'Latics' nickname, Oldham's claim to it being much older.

Wigan's preferred primary derby would be with Bolton. However, in many senses, their main derby is not with an association football club at all. It is with

Wigan Warriors, giants of rugby league. Athletic face an ongoing battle to rid Wigan of the tag of being purely a rugby town. Their dream of a Wigan v Bolton primary derby received a significant boost in 2011/12 as they fought with both Bolton and Blackburn to avoid relegation from the Premiership. The 'upstarts' of Wigan survived, as both founder members of the Football League succumbed. What effect the outcome will have on future relationships is hard to say, but the bitter seeds of a new primary derby may have been sown. Currently there are no clear cut primary derbies in the area. Given their histories and general standing, the biggest surprise is that Bury and Oldham are not more interested in each other.

Derbies are not always static. It is often assumed that current hotly contested derbies have been around from time immemorial. Many have been. However, the strength and vehemence of both general and primary derbies can vary periodically and, in a few cases, clubs may switch even their primary derby rivals. Such variations or changes of target are usually caused by differences over time in the relative success of the clubs concerned. As long as derby rivals remain roughly on a par with each other, their derby tends to remain safe but, if one club becomes significantly stronger than the other for a substantial period of time, derby relations may change.

As we saw north of Manchester, in the early days of League football, Bury were primary derby rivals of Bolton. However, in the past seventy-six seasons, they have finished above the Trotters of Bolton on just three occasions. In essence, Bolton have disappeared over the horizon and the primary derby has died as a consequence, even though Bury fans cling to the hope of its revival.

A little more recently, Huddersfield and Leeds were primary derby competitors, with the Terriers of Huddersfield maintaining a significant lead over their big city rivals up to the 1960s. Their geographical rivalry was enhanced by the career of Herbert Chapman. Chapman was the first manager to win League championships with two different clubs and deserves his place alongside the likes of Clough, Shankly, Ramsey, Ferguson and Busby as one of the greatest managers of all time. He is best known for his success at Arsenal in the 1930s and many will also know that, before joining Arsenal, he was the catalyst for Huddersfield's magnificent achievements in the 1920s. Less well known is that he joined Huddersfield after being involved in the scandal of Leeds City, the forerunners of Leeds United. The illegal payments scandal led to the dissolution of City and earned Chapman a temporary ban from football. His arrival at Huddersfield was therefore controversial. To make matters worse, an attempt was made at around the same time to move Huddersfield to Leeds to fill the void left by City. Remarkably, the Terriers not only survived this threat to their very existence but, within five years, had become the most successful club in England.

The derby was therefore well-established but, from the 1960s onwards, Leeds United moved into a completely different gear. They became much more successful than Huddersfield and began to see Manchester United as their primary derby rivals (the geographical justification for their rivalry being classed as a derby relied on antipathy between the neighbouring counties of Yorkshire and Lancashire). Huddersfield, of course, still continued to hate Leeds but, in reality, their primary derby had to become their meetings with Bradford City, especially as Bradford's other club, Park Avenue, had to depart the League in 1970.

In Leeds' case the biter has subsequently been bitten. As Leeds declined in the 21st century and Manchester United continued to win trophy after trophy, their own derby relationship changed. Leeds fans still think of it as their primary derby but Reds fans, although still hating Leeds, have moved the Yorkshire club well down their own pecking order of derby days. The potential for a revival of a Leeds/Huddersfield derby was given a significant shot in the arm in 2011/12, as the Terriers of Huddersfield won the tier three play-off final to join Leeds in the Championship for 2012/13.

Dominance can distort. The derbies mentioned above could make a return to the primary derby list eventually, but there is a long way to go, given recent history. There are other derbies, currently downgraded because of the dominance of one partner, which could quickly be restored. This is especially the case where one club has forsaken its closest geographical rival in search of a more competitive derby. Fortunes change; geography doesn't.

The most famous example of dominance distorting geography in English derbies is in the case of the footballing relationships of Manchester and Liverpool. For the vast majority of fans of the underdogs in these cities, City and Everton, their biggest derbies undoubtedly have always been against their neighbours in their respective cities. However, for the majority of fans of the dominant clubs, United and Liverpool, the primary derby has been when these two meet. In a poll conducted in the late 2000s, less than one in twenty Liverpool fans named Everton as their biggest derby rivals.

Many people believe that Manchester United and Liverpool have always been at each others' throats. It is, we are told, the natural consequence of cold relations between the two cities, which began as a result of disputes about the building of the Manchester Ship Canal. There is an element of truth in this explanation. Most neighbouring cities compete in fields other than football and, at points in time, most have commercial or political disputes with their neighbours. Some of these disputes have been more serious than others. The Ship Canal saga was certainly unlikely to be conducive to friendly relations between the two cities but, if hatred between the cities is so ingrained, why is it not a significant factor when Manchester City meet Everton? The two are hardly bosom pals, but vehement hatred of each other, created as a result of the history of their cities, is not obvious.

In fact, Manchester United's rivalry with Liverpool has *not* always been an all-consuming passion. As big clubs in neighbouring big cities they always had a weather eye upon each other. However, until after the Second World War, Manchester United were not that big a club anyway (United were 18th on the all time success list in 1939 - see appendices on pages 272-274 for the full lists). Manchester City (13th) could reasonably have argued that they were bigger at the time. Furthermore, despite their successes in the fifties and sixties, it was not until the Premiership era that United moved on to a different level from City.

The story in Liverpool is similar. On the same 'up to 1939' success list, Liverpool were 12th and therefore were not so great. Everton were ahead of them, in 2nd place. Only in the 1970s did Liverpool begin to disappear over the horizon, winning eleven titles in eighteen years between 1972/3 and 1989/90 (Everton won a further two), as well as the small matter of four European Cups in the same period.

For many decades, therefore, the main derbies for both Liverpool and Manchester United were with their respective city rivals, not with each other. The pre-eminence of their duals in the past few decades is a consequence of Red success, not historic inter-city rivalry. In recent seasons, traditional divisions have quickly been enhanced as the strength of the clubs has changed. City have taken on the mantle of 'richest club on earth'. Liverpool have failed to mount a challenge to United. United v Liverpool is still vitriolic and ultra-competitive historically, but it is under threat.

Everton v Liverpool is still not as vehement as its Manchester equivalent. Nevertheless, it has been given a substantial boost by the Toffees' higher league placing in 2011/12, as well as Liverpool's relatively low ebb. The biggest change, understandably, is in the standing of Manchester's derby. City's first title in forty-four years and their access to a bulging war chest to defend that title completely altered the *current* dominance scene although, as Sir Alex Ferguson was quick to point out, changing *historic* dominance will take a good deal longer.

There are a number of other instances where the dominance of one club in a city or an area distorts close geographical rivalries. Plymouth, for example, should probably view clashes with their fellow Devonians, Exeter and Torquay, as their primary derbies. However, Argyle have been top team in Devon so frequently that they have been dismissive of their local rivals. In eighty-five seasons to 2011/12, since Argyle joined the Football League in 1920/21, they finished highest of the three seventy-five times. Exeter have been top Devonians only six times and Torquay four. This lack of Devonian competition led the Pilgrims on a constant search for their big derby. Portsmouth, in the 'dockyards derby', has been one possible adversary, but Portsmouth have other closer neighbours in mind and are about as dismissive of Plymouth, as Plymouth have been of Torquay. Other South Western clubs are in the frame. Historically, focus has occasionally been on Bristol's clubs, who themselves not only have each other to contend with, but also have clashes with Cardiff City and associated Welsh/English antipathies. More recently, Yeovil entered the list of possible contenders for Plymouth's loathing, especially as they are from over the county border in Somerset.

The best cure for a derby-starved Green Army is to enjoy a revival on their doorstep and here perhaps comfort can be found in adversity. Plymouth's stay in the second tier sadly came to an end in 2009/10 and was followed by a further relegation and threats to the club's very existence in 2010/11. Their demise coincided with the coming of relatively good times for the Grecians of Exeter, back from dark days in the Conference. 2011/12 saw Exeter in tier three, with Plymouth and Torquay together in the tier below. Furthermore, for the first time ever, Argyle ended the season below *both* fellow Devonian clubs. Meetings with Torquay hopefully gave Plymouth fans chance to dust off one of the best football chants of all when Argyle's faithful, from the most southerly club in England, shout "*you dirty northern bastards*" at Torquay players and fans, from the second most southerly club.

Events which changed derbies.

Occasionally, major changes in derby relationships are triggered, not so much by differences in power, but by specific things or events occurring over short periods of time. The following examples of current primary derbies were not created entirely by the events outlined, but were certainly significantly enhanced by them.

Brighton v Crystal Palace was a general derby between two southern clubs with a history of competition stretching back to their days together in the Southern League, but it wasn't a vehement derby, let alone a primary derby. Neither had particularly strong local derbies, but Palace looked more to South London neighbours, Charlton and Millwall, while Brighton tended to look along the coast, rather than to London.

Over a short period of time in the 1970s things changed. The clubs locked horns for a few seasons, culminating in promotions together to tier two in 1976/7 and to the top tier in 1978/9. Both had high profile managers, who were not exactly best of friends. At the same time, both clubs became increasingly fashionable. To top it all, one of the managers, Alan Mullery, having stirred the pot by being highly critical of Palace management, duly jumped ship, left Brighton and within a year returned as manager of... Palace! Later, he re-joined Brighton. Allegedly, Brighton even created their new nickname, the Seagulls, in response to Palace fans chanting their own new nickname, the Eagles, before a derby in the 1970s. Their derby has never since reached the heights of the seventies, but it endures to this day, as we saw as they clashed again in the Championship in 2011/2.

Derby v Forest was a general derby in the past and one likely to grow in importance naturally, given Forest's recent dominance over their city rivals Notts. County. However, it became a primary derby in the 1970s, mainly thanks to Brian Clough. The story of Clough's reign and success at both clubs is told in more detail in the second half of the book and its effect upon Notts County is related shortly. At this point, it need only be said that Clough's impact upon the Rams and Forest is cemented into history, literally, as part of the road connecting Nottingham with Derby is called Brian Clough Way.

A little further north, a simmering derby exists between **Chesterfield and Mansfield Town.** They have been derby rivals for many years, as the towns are fairly close to each other and there is competition between their counties, Derbyshire (Chesterfield) and Nottinghamshire (Mansfield). Both are seen as fringe participants in the rivalries of South Yorkshire, and Mansfield are also rivals with Nottingham's clubs. A derby between the clubs therefore already existed, but at a relatively low level – until 1984 that is. The miners' strike of 1984/5 ripped the area apart. North Derbyshire, with Chesterfield as its main town, remained loyal to the strike. Most of Nottinghamshire did not. Ever since the strike, fans of all Nottinghamshire sides have heard calls of 'scabs' on their visits to the coalfields of South Yorkshire and Derbyshire. But, in reality, Nottingham itself had little to do with mining, whereas Mansfield is at the heart of the former Nottinghamshire coalfield. The outcome is that Spireites versus Stags is one of the bitterest derbies of them all.

The saddest derbies. A remarkably consistent trait exists amongst football fans. Most of us forget successes or those little pieces of luck which combine in our teams' favour to change the outcome of games, gain promotion or stave off relegation. Almost all fans think we are hard done by; that the gods or, in particular, 'tin pot gods' who officiate at games, have it in for us. Our own club suffers more than any other in the entire Universe, there is absolutely no doubt about it. A look at the history of clubs does indicate that certain clubs seem to have more bad luck than others. It isn't true that luck evens out over time. Many fans suspect that bigger and/or more fashionable clubs get more favourable treatment and there appears to be statistical evidence to support their suspicions. However, on the whole, hard luck stories are much exaggerated and even, supposedly 'lucky', Arsenal don't always have it all their own way.

The saddest stories of all in football involve the removal of your club to another area (e.g. Wimbledon) or financial collapse (e.g. Chester City or Darlington), but the next worst thing is probably having to stand by helplessly as your bitterest rivals go from success to success. We have already seen a number of examples which could be nominated for the title of 'saddest derby' story and it can happen to big boys as well as to minnows. Manchester City and Everton have seen their neighbours race ahead of them, after decades of close rivalry in which blues of both cities held the upper hand, if only just.

There was Fulham, not taking an opportunity to be kings of West London, by foregoing the offer of a move to Stamford Bridge. Thereby they failed to kill off Chelsea at birth and had to suffer as Chelsea outstripped them and almost always beat them in derby encounters. Reading and Swindon both had to watch the emergence of Oxford United, who were first to reach the top tier, even though the Royals and Robins had been trying for decades before United had even entered the League. More recently Luton Town, traditionally the dominant partner in the Bedfordshire and Hertfordshire derby with Watford, have not only had to endure the humiliation of losing their Football League status, while Watford sat comfortably in the second tier, but have also seen Hertfordshire club Stevenage leap over them into the Football League. There are many more examples of bad luck stories; temporary and not so temporary reversals of fortune and tales of 'what might have been'. However, for the saddest story of all in the League itself, we probably have to return to Nottingham and to the toughest chapter in the history of the League's oldest club, Notts. County.

Nottingham's clubs are the closest football neighbours in England. Their grounds are separated by only a few yards, which include the River Trent, and in Britain only Dundee's clubs are closer to each other. However, whilst County fans may consider games against Forest to be their main derbies, the feeling is not reciprocated by Forest fans, who see Derby as their derby. Forest's dominance in recent times has led them to seek more challenging and regular derby encounters than those offered by their neighbours across the river. Historically, though, Forest's dominance over Notts. County has not been so pronounced. Although Forest have finished above County every year since 1976, overall Forest have had more league encounters with the County from their own city than with the one from Derby, meaning that they have been in the same division as Notts County more often than with Derby County. Furthermore, Notts. County were the top Nottingham club up to World War Two, albeit marginally – County were 19th in the all-time success list in 1939 whereas Forest were 22nd. It is said that Notts. County, enjoying credit for being the League's oldest club and not even being disliked that much by their near neighbours, are the least hated club in England and that their fans' greatest ambition is to be truly loathed by someone, anyone. This lovable image is reinforced by their original nickname, the 'Lambs', although it should be pointed out that the 'Lambs' from which the name derives, far from being cuddly, were a pretty unpleasant street gang in the nineteenth century.

Given this background; relating what happened to County in the late 1970s is a horror story so awful that every modern football fan would probably immediately wish it upon his or her local rivals. Although broadly on a par with Forest in the decades before the Second World War, County fell on hard times in the 1950s. Prior to County's promotion from tier three in 1972/3, they had not been in the same division as Forest since 1956/7 and had not finished above them since 1950/1. In 1970/1 Forest were in the top tier, whereas County were in the fourth. Things then changed very quickly. Following two promotions for County and relegation for Forest, both clubs ended up in tier two. For two glorious seasons, in 1974/5 and 1975/6, County were again top dogs in Nottingham.

County fans must have thought that all the years of heartache were at an end; that normal service had been resumed and that Nottingham's derby, oldest of all professional derbies, would be revived and last forever as a genuinely competitive fixture. It must have felt like a marathon runner gradually hunting down and overtaking her greatest rival. Alas for County, they were about to find out that fairly dramatic 'ups' can be followed by even more dramatic 'downs'. Forest had recruited from Derby, via brief stays at Brighton and Leeds, the equivalent in marathon terms of someone even better than Paula Radcliffe, a certain Mr Brian Clough.

In 1976/7, after trailing County for two seasons, Forest were promoted to the top tier, although they finished only third in tier two. Amazingly, in the following year, Forest were League champions and, for good measure, they won the League Cup as well. In winning the title, they lost only three of forty-two games (they had lost eleven a year earlier in the lower tier). In the following year, Forest failed to defend their title, but still finished second, again losing only three of forty-two games. They won the League Cup again and capped another outstanding season by adding a small trinket to their newly extended trophy cabinet – the European Cup. They successfully defended their European crown in 1980, thereby winning two European Cups on the back of only one League championship, the only club in Europe to do so.

A Forest fan who had dreamt of these things happening would have been sectioned as a deluded maniac. In just *four* years, Forest had gone from being not even the best team in their home city, incidentally the smallest city ever to win the European Cup, to being undisputed champions of the continent – not once, but twice! A County fan who had imagined this happening would probably have thrown himself in the Trent and most of his fellow Magpies would have thought this the wisest course of action in the circumstances.

Meanwhile, County muddled along in an understandable state of shock. Briefly they joined Forest in the top tier in the early eighties and they did so again in the early nineties but, to date (2012/3), County have never again been the top team in Nottingham. They are now miles behind Forest in the all-time success league and no-one has the courtesy to treat them as primary derby rivals. Even fellow Nottinghamshire club, Mansfield, are more interested in Chesterfield. About the only miniscule consolation for them is that the last time they met Forest in a league clash in February 1994, County won 2-1. There must be a positive chant in that fact somewhere, somehow.

In order to find an even more heartbreaking story of derby fortunes, we have to leave the Football League and visit another city to have played a crucial role in creating modern football. The city of Cambridge has never been blessed with the best of luck in football terms and has not always received the recognition it deserves for its early contribution to the game. As we saw at the beginning of the book, the role of universities and public schools in the evolution of modern football is sometimes exaggerated, but there is no doubt that we owe a debt of gratitude to Cambridge University, for having the foresight to try to standardise rules in the mid 19th Century. A small plaque to acknowledge this role was placed in Parker's Piece, a green space in the centre of Cambridge, where many early games were played.

Unfortunately, Cambridge didn't reap many rewards for its efforts. It was Oxford University who became the only university side to reach FA Cup finals, losing to Wanderers in 1873, winning the cup in 1874, in a shock victory over Royal Engineers, before again losing finals in 1877 and 1880. Cambridge University managed just one semi-final appearance, in 1877. Currently (2012/3), Cambridge doesn't have a Football League team and it hasn't had one for most of the time since the League was created. The city first hosted a League club in 1970 and it is here where the saddest derby story of all begins.

Cambridge City, the 'Lilywhites', founded in 1908, are older than local rivals Cambridge United and, historically, they were always the city's biggest club. In fact, United, as Abbey United, did not become a senior side until the 1940's. In the 1930s City, then Cambridge Town, had a serious non-league derby with Ipswich Town but, when both clubs were offered a chance to join the Football League, the Lilywhites chose to stay amateur in the Southern League. Ipswich turned professional, joined the Football League and found new 'friends' in Norwich. By the time Cambridge City began a serious quest to join the Football League Ipswich had been guided all the way to a League title by Alf Ramsey.

In the 1960s, the Cambridge clubs were together in the Southern League and were equally successful, but the Lilywhites, along with Chelmsford City and Bath City, were the best supported clubs in non-league football and regularly attracted crowds roughly twice the size of United's. At the time there was no automatic promotion from non-league football into the Football League and the Conference didn't exist. Instead, clubs finishing bottom of the Football League had to go through an annual process of applying for re-election, in which they competed for votes with top non-league clubs. Unsurprisingly, as the voting electorate consisted of League clubs themselves, an 'old pals' act' existed which led to few League outfits losing their places and endless frustration for bigger non-league clubs. To put the situation into perspective, when Peterborough United replaced Gateshead in 1960, it was the first victory for a non-league club since 1951. Throughout the sixties, both Cambridge City and United joined a queue of clubs applying to be admitted to the League. In 1962/3, City were Southern League champions, with United as runners-up. City confirmed the title by doing the double over their neighbours in the season's derbies and their home game at Milton Road attracted a record crowd of over 11,500 fans. But the clubs received virtually no votes in the election process. No more League clubs were replaced in the sixties and the situation for both Cambridge clubs seemed hopeless. However, things quickly changed.

In 1969/70, Bradford Park Avenue finished bottom of the League for a third year in succession. Even the old pals' act couldn't save them this time. By chance, Avenue's plight coincided with the emergence of a good Cambridge United side who won the Southern League in 1968/9 and 1969/70, whereas Cambridge City had been relegated from its Premier Division. This short window of opportunity set the scene for United to beat Park Avenue in the voting; to join the Football League and to leave City behind. City achieved promotion back into the Southern League Premier Division in 1969/70 and finished as runners-up in 1970/1. They applied again for election to the Football League, but the chances of another team from Cambridge being elected were non-existent. City received only two votes and their 'junior' rivals had flown. Had the opportunity occurred at virtually any other time, City rather than United would have become Cambridge's first League club.

United fared well, albeit that their record was somewhat topsy-turvy. Twice they were promoted between fourth and second tiers in successive years and once they made the reverse journey to the League's basement in successive years. In 1991/2, they finished fifth in the old Division Two. Only defeat in end of season play-offs prevented them from being the first club to be promoted from fourth tier to first in successive seasons. However, they fell into decline and in 2004/5 United finished bottom of the League and were relegated to the Conference. At the time, Cambridge City were well placed in the tier immediately below the Conference and only defeat in play-offs prevented City from achieving their dream of reviving derby matches against United for the first time since the 1960s.

Were the Gods finally smiling upon City? Alas not.

In 2006, City were subjected to a scandalous and fraudulent attempt to deprive them of their ground. It led to a High Court case. Furthermore, City's Board made plans to scrap the first team and reduce City to a youth feeder club for United. All of this undermined the team and the club, but it didn't deter their fans. A Supporters' Trust was formed and the High Court case won. Even then, things didn't go City's way.

Having been saved only by the efforts and determination of their fans, their 'reward' was to be relegated from the tier below the Conference into the next lower tier (the seventh tier of English football), not because of results on the pitch but because their ground, for many years the biggest in non-league football, was deemed unfit for tier six.

By now most fans would have considered abandoning football altogether and taking up something as awful as the comical British version of American football. But even worse was to follow for City fans. They had to watch in disbelief as yet another 'junior' club, from just outside Cambridge, made an astonishing rise through the ranks. Histon FC trace their history back to before the formation of either Cambridge City or United, having been formed in 1904 as Histon Institute. The 'Stutes', however, were a junior side until very recently and were nowhere in the frame when City v United rivalry was at its height in the sixties. Four promotions in seven years saw Histon, rather than City join United in the Conference, passing City on the way. When Histon beat United 5-0, in a FA Trophy tie, Lilywhites' fans must have had mixed feelings of joy and envy. When the Stutes were drawn against and then beat Leeds United in the FA Cup in 2008, in front of an adoring TV audience, City fans must simply have cried. To rub salt into the wounds of City faithful, once part of the biggest crowds outside the League; Histon, the highest placed team in Cambridge at the time, created a first in September 2010 when they visited Wrexham in the Conference without a single away supporter.

Many fans have experienced the pain of seeing local rivals emerge and overtake their own clubs, but Cambridge City fans have seen lightning strike twice, as well as being defrauded and threatened with oblivion by their own Board. If there is an unluckier club in England it will be difficult to find and their fans must be in need of permanent counselling.

6

Derby records

Before derby records can be compiled, two issues have to be clarified – they are, a) which derbies should be considered? and b) which competitions count for the purpose of collating records?

Which derbies should be considered? For the purposes of this book, sixty English League derbies have been researched, a top thirty of which are studied in more detail in the second half. Many of the sixty are clearly primary derbies, for example Arsenal v Tottenham; others are more general derbies, such as Arsenal v Chelsea. Overall they probably constitute the premier derby clashes in the English League. There are, of course, lots of excellent and passionate derbies to be found elsewhere in the football pyramid but, to make the task manageable, a line has to be drawn somewhere. Most derbies in the list are between two clubs in the Premier League, Championship or Football League, but the criteria for consideration allow a few others to be included. *The basic rule adopted is that, to be considered for inclusion, **both** clubs must have been in the League **together** at some time within the past ten years and **both** clubs must at least be as high as the Conference National (ie fifth tier) in the 2012/13 season.*

On that basis, Chesterfield v Mansfield and Luton v Watford, for example, qualify for consideration, although Mansfield and Luton are currently in the Conference. So does Lincoln v Grimsby, even though both have dropped into the Conference. On the other hand, Macclesfield's derby with Altrincham, or Cheltenham's with Gloucester City, do not qualify, because Altrincham and Gloucester have not been in the League in the past ten years.

Unfortunately, two fervent derbies have fallen by the wayside in recent times. Chester City v Wrexham no longer qualifies, as both clubs were relegated from the League and poor Chester City folded altogether. Shrewsbury v Wrexham is included, although it is fair to say that Wrexham viewed Chester City as their greater derby partners and may do so again, as the new Chester club, hopefully, rises like a phoenix from the ashes of the past few years. Another even more competitive derby bit the dust in 2011/12. Darlington, alas, were relegated from the Conference National at the end of 2011/12 in disastrous financial circumstances. The club had to be re-formed and the new club has been placed in the ninth tier of English football and so their highly rated clash with Hartlepool does not meet the criteria for consideration in 2012/13.

The sixty derbies (in alphabetical order).

Accrington v Morecambe	Charlton v Crystal Palace	Leeds v Man Utd
Arsenal v Tottenham	Charlton v Millwall	Leyton Orient v Southend
Arsenal v Chelsea	Chelsea v Fulham	Liverpool v Man Utd
Aston Villa v Birmingham	Chelsea v QPR	Luton v Watford
Aston Villa v West Brom	Chesterfield v Mansfield	Macclesfield v Stockport
Barnsley v Rotherham	Colchester v Southend	Man City v Man Utd
Blackburn v Bolton	Coventry v Leicester	Millwall v West Ham
Blackburn v Burnley	Crewe v Port Vale	Middlesbrough v Newcastle
Blackburn v Preston	Crystal Palace v Millwall	Middlesbrough v Sunderland
Blackpool v Preston	Derby v Nott'm Forest	Newcastle v Sunderland
Bolton v Wigan	Doncaster v Rotherham	Northampton v Peterboro
Bolton v Bury	Everton v Liverpool	Notts. County v Nott'm Forest
Bradford City v Huddersfield	Exeter v Plymouth	Oxford Utd v Reading
Brentford v QPR	Exeter v Torquay	Oxford Utd v Swindon
Brighton v Crystal Palace	Fulham v QPR	Portsmouth v Southampton
Bristol City v Bristol Rovers	Grimsby v Lincoln	Port Vale v Stoke
Bristol City v Cardiff	Grimsby v Scunthorpe	Reading v Swindon
Bury v Rochdale	Hull v Grimsby	Sheffield Utd v Sheffield Wed
Cambridge Utd v Peterboro'	Hull v Scunthorpe	Shrewsbury v Wrexham
Cardiff v Swansea	Ipswich v Norwich	West Brom v Wolves

Undoubtedly, disgusted supporters of clubs such as Gillingham, Walsall and Bournemouth will already have put the book in the toilet (and not for the purpose of reading at leisure), having realised that their clubs are not mentioned in the list of sixty derbies, whereas the likes of Manchester United and even Grimsby get three bites of the cherry. It does seem unfair and their absence from the list doesn't mean that clubs who are missed out do not have derbies themselves. In the Football Fans Census report mentioned earlier, Walsall fans named Wolves, West Brom and Stoke as derby rivals. Gillingham wanted to have a dig at Millwall, Swindon and Fulham. Bournemouth went for Reading, Southampton and Brighton. The problem, however, is that none of the clubs named as potential derby rivals showed much interest in having a dig back.

Which competitions count?

We also have to be clear about which games in which competitions are to be taken into account when club records are compiled. Anyone wishing to know their club's record in derby matches may assume the task is easy and that information will be consistent. In fact, he or she will find an array of interpretations of records in different publications.

(Readers who are not that interested in the fine details of football records may wish to give the next few paragraphs a miss and jump straight to the first derby record on page 64. Readers with an interest in football statistics, however, will wish to know how the book's conclusions are reached and it is only fair to provide a guide, nerdy as it may seem to non-stattos).

Variations in recorded derby stats exist because different authors or organisations take different matches into account when creating their databases. At one extreme, people include every fixture played between two clubs, no matter what the status of the game. They may even take friendly games into the reckoning. At the other extreme, only league fixtures are considered by a few statisticians. The problems created by different interpretations of which games count is perhaps best illustrated by looking at an example. In the case below the record of the Portsmouth versus Southampton derby is outlined.

If all their clashes are taken into account, the south coast derby has been played 139 times and Pompey lead 62-56 in wins. However, this total aggregates all sorts of games, including those in minor competitions and in wartime games involving guest players. These matches are not classed officially as senior games. In other words, use of the 139 figure equates non-senior matches as being on a par with competitive clashes in the Football League or the FA Cup.

Most commentators reject this all-inclusive approach. The most common basis upon which derby totals are calculated is to include the FA Cup and League Cup competitions, alongside Football League and Premier League results. Using this calculation, Portsmouth and Southampton have met only 38 times, with Saints leading 19-9. This latter approach may seem reasonable. However, it works to the disadvantage of a number of southern derbies when a pecking order of derbies is being compiled. Specifically, it underestimates the derby record of those clubs who played in the Southern League before its First Division was incorporated into the Football League after World War One.

The debate about the comparative standard of the Southern League during its formative years has been covered earlier. Suffice it to say here that those who believe it was on a par with the Football League's top tier are (in a borrowed cockney accent) ''avin' a laugh'. However, it is fair to say that, in its earliest years, the Southern League was on a par with the second tier of the Football League and it wasn't that far behind the second tier by the time the Southern League effectively became the Football League's new third tier in 1920. Given the relative strength of the Southern League in those years, it would be unfair to ignore derby matches between clubs in the south, while at the same time including games of equivalent standard played mainly between northern and midlands' clubs in the second tier of the Football League. The inclusion of Southern League games up to 1919/20 makes a huge difference to the record in our south coast example. Pompey and Saints had a long-standing, healthy rivalry in the Southern League and so the total number of derbies jumps from 38 to 70 games, with Southampton leading 34-21.

Northern readers may argue that there were other leagues in the early days which deserve similar recognition. What about the Central League or the Northern League, especially as the latter pre-dates the Southern League and the former provided many member clubs for the new Division Three North in 1921/22? However, during this period the top northern and midlands' clubs were already playing in the Football League, and not in these alternative leagues, because the Football League was very northern/midlands dominated.

By contrast, although a small number of top southern clubs joined the Football League, many others stayed in the Southern League and so the Southern League was at a higher standard. To illustrate the point; of the twenty-two southern clubs who switched to the Football League in 1920, eighteen are still in the top four tiers of English football and five of those clubs have subsequently won national titles. Of the twenty clubs who created Division Three North in 1921, only seven are still in the top four tiers and none of them have ever won a national title.

With one exception, no other league in the North or Midlands could compare with the Southern League, let alone with the Football League. The exception was the Football Alliance, but the Alliance lasted for only three seasons before many of its clubs joined the Football League. Importantly, only one current derby was played in the Alliance, Grimsby versus Lincoln, and that for only one season in 1891/2. For completeness, that year in the history of the Lincolnshire derby has been included.

In summary – all records are based upon derby results up to the end of season 2011/2012 in:-

- **The Football League/Premier League/ Championship**
  (including results in end-of-season play-off matches).
- **The FA Cup**
- **The League Cup**
- **The Southern League up to 1919/20**
- **The Football Alliance in 1891/2**

Results of derby matches in 'friendly' games, minor cup competitions, minor leagues, charity shield games, wartime competitions etc are NOT included.

Having decided which derbies to study and which competitions and results to include in the research, we can set out a number of derby records.

Which derbies have been played most often?

Twenty-one of the sixty derbies have been played at least one hundred times up to the end of the 2011/12 season.

1.	213	Everton v Liverpool
2.	180	Liverpool v Manchester Utd
3.	174	Arsenal v Chelsea
4.	167	Arsenal v Tottenham
= 5.	160	Manchester City v Manchester Utd
= 5.	160	Blackburn v Bolton
7.	159	West Brom v Wolves
8.	158	Aston Villa v West Brom
9.	146	Newcastle v Sunderland

= 10. 141   Reading v Swindon

= 10. 141   Middlesbrough v Sunderland

12.   126   Sheffield Utd v Sheffield Wed

13.   125   Middlesbrough v Newcastle

= 14. 120   Aston Villa v Birmingham

= 14. 120   Luton v Watford

16.   114   Crystal Palace v Millwall

17.   112   Exeter v Torquay

18.   111   Grimsby v Lincoln

19.   110   Brighton v Crystal Palace

= 20. 107   Bristol City v Bristol Rovers

= 20. 107   Leeds v Manchester Utd

Note that Blackburn v Bolton is very high in the list, whereas Blackburn v Burnley, the primary derby for both clubs, has been played only ninety-three times. The 'Cotton Towns' derby sits just outside the top twenty-one in 24th equal place, coincidentally alongside two other important derbies – Blackpool v Preston and East Anglia's 'Old Farm' clash – and just one derby and one place behind Nottingham's city clash. Other notable derbies that do not appear in the 'most played' list include Derby v Forest (89) and Cardiff v Swansea (66). Two southern derbies, Southampton v Portsmouth (70) and Millwall v West Ham (60) do not get anywhere near the centurions list, even though the total of their Football League and cup derbies is roughly doubled by the inclusion of their early meetings in the Southern League.

Primary derbies in FA Cup finals

1887	Aston Villa v West Brom	2-0	
1892	West Brom v Aston Villa	3-0	
1895	Aston Villa v West Brom	1-0	
1898	Nott'm Forest v Derby	3-1	
1977	Manchester Utd v Liverpool	2-1	
1986	Liverpool v Everton	3-1	
1989	Liverpool v Everton	3-2	(aet)
1996	Manchester Utd v Liverpool	1-0	

Villa v West Brom is included here as a primary derby because it was one at the time. There have been very few primary derby clashes in FA Cup finals and there was a huge gap between 1898 and 1977 during which period there were none.

General derbies in FA Cup finals

There have been a number of *general* derbies in FA Cup finals, as follows:-

1904	Manchester City v Bolton	1-0
1926	Bolton v Manchester City	1-0
1931	West Brom v Birmingham	2-1
1933	Everton v Manchester City	3-0
1967	Tottenham v Chelsea	2-1
1975	West Ham v Fulham	2-0
1980	West Ham v Arsenal	1-0
1982	Tottenham v QPR	1-0
1985	Manchester Utd v Everton	1-0
1995	Everton v Manchester Utd	1-0
2002	Arsenal v Chelsea	2-0

Setting aside very early finals, many of which were all-London affairs because most clubs entering the competition were from London, an unusual feature of FA Cup finals is the absence of single-city clashes until 1967, when Tottenham beat Chelsea. There have been seven single-city derbies since. In the capital, derbies in finals have been like proverbial London buses. There were no all-London finals for well over eighty years, but then along came four in sixteen seasons between 1967 and 1982. We then had to wait another twenty years for the next one.

Primary derbies in League Cup finals

1963	Birmingham v Aston Villa	3-1 and 0-0 (over two legs)
1983	Liverpool v Manchester Utd	3-1 (aet)
1984	Liverpool v Everton	1-0 (after 0-0 draw)
2003	Liverpool v Manchester Utd	2-0

General derbies in League Cup finals-

2006	Manchester Utd v Wigan Ath.	4-0
2007	Chelsea v Arsenal	2-1
2008	Tottenham v Chelsea	2-1

An abiding memory of the 1980s was Merseyside's finals, two in the FA Cup and one in the League Cup in six seasons. Liverpool's buses must be even more bunched together than those in the capital, as the Merseyside derby has not been played out in a final before or since that six year period. Memories may not be sweet in the blue half of the city, as Liverpool beat Everton on all three occasions.

Derby Doubles and Trebles – Listed below are seasons in which derby partners have shared two or three of England's major domestic honours (i.e. the list does not include instances where one club has achieved a double).

1889/90   Preston (League) and Blackburn (FA Cup).

1905/06   Liverpool (League) and Everton (FA Cup).

1913/14   Blackburn (League) and Burnley (FA Cup).

1919/20   West Brom (League) and Aston Villa (FA Cup).

1953/54   Wolves (League) and West Brom (FA Cup).

1955/56   Man Utd (League) and Man City (FA Cup).

1961/62   Ipswich (League) and Norwich (League Cup).

1964/65   Man Utd (League) and Liverpool (FA Cup).

1965/66   Liverpool (League) and Everton (FA Cup).

1970/71   Arsenal (League+FA Cup) and Tottenham (League Cup).

1976/77   Liverpool (League) and Man Utd (FA Cup).

1982/83   Liverpool (League+League Cup) and Man Utd (FA Cup).

1983/84   Liverpool (League+League Cup) and Everton (FA Cup).

1989/90   Liverpool (League) and Man Utd (FA Cup).

1990/91   Arsenal (League) and Tottenham (FA Cup).

1991/92   Leeds (League) and Man Utd (League Cup).

1994/95   Everton (FA Cup) and Liverpool (League Cup).

1997/98   Arsenal (League+FA Cup) and Chelsea (League Cup).

2000/01   Man Utd (League) and Liverpool (FA Cup+League Cup).

2002/03   Man Utd (League) and Liverpool (League Cup).

2004/05   Chelsea (League+League Cup) and Arsenal (FA Cup).

2005/06   Liverpool (FA Cup) and Man Utd (League Cup).

2010/11   Man Utd (League) and Man City (FA Cup).

Top English League Derbies – year by year (the list sets out which of the sixty derbies was the top derby in each season, based upon combined League positions of the clubs involved, except where stated in the notes)

1888/89   Preston (1st) + Blackburn (4th)

1889/90   Preston (1st) + Blackburn (3rd)

1890/91   Preston (2nd) + Blackburn (6th)

1891/92   Preston (2nd) + Blackburn (9th)-note*1

1892/93   Preston (2nd) + Blackburn (9th)

1893/94	Blackburn (4th) + Burnley (5th)
1894/95	Preston (4th) + Blackburn (5th)-note*2
1895/96	Bolton (4th) + Blackburn (8th)
1896/97	Sheff Utd (2nd) + Sheff Wed (6th)
1897/98	Sheff Utd (1st) + Sheff Wed (5th)-note*3
1898/99	Liverpool (2nd) + Everton (4th)
1899/00	Sunderland (3rd) + Newcastle (5th)
1900/01	Notts Co (3rd) + Nottm Forest (4th)
1901/02	Sunderland (1st) + Newcastle (3rd)
1902/03	Sheff Wed (1st) + Sheff Utd (4th)
1903/04	Sheff Wed (1st) + Sheff Utd (7th)
1904/05	Newcastle (1st) + Sunderland (5th)
1905/06	Liverpool (1st) + Everton (11th)-note*4
1906/07	Newcastle (1st) + Sunderland (10th)
1907/08	Man Utd (1st) + Man City (3rd)
1908/09	Newcastle (1st) + Sunderland (3rd)
1909/10	Newcastle (4th) + Sunderland (8th)-note*5
1910/11	Sunderland (3rd) + Newcastle (8th)
1911/12	Blackburn (1st) + Bolton (4th)
1912/13	Man Utd (4th) + Man City (6th)
1913/14	Blackburn (1st) + Bolton (6th)-note*6
1914/15	Blackburn (3rd) + Burnley (4th)
1919/20	West Brom (1st) + Aston Villa (9th)
1920/21	Liverpool (4th) + Everton (7th)
1921/22	Newcastle (7th) + Middlesbrough (8th)
1922/23	Liverpool (1st) + Everton (5th)-note*7
1923/24	Sunderland (3rd) + Newcastle (9th)-note*8
1924/25	Bolton (3rd) + Bury (5th)
1925/26	Bury (4th) + Bolton (8th)
1926/27	Newcastle (1st) + Sunderland (3rd)
1927/28	Bury (5th) + Bolton (7th)
1928/29	Sheff Wed (1st) + Sheff Utd (11th)
1929/30	Aston Villa (4th) + Birmingham (11th)

1930/31	Arsenal (1st) + Chelsea (12th)
1931/32	Sheff Wed (3rd) + Sheff Utd (7th)
1932/33	Aston Villa (2nd) + West Brom (4th)
1933/34	Arsenal (1st) + Tottenham (3rd)
1934/35	Arsenal (1st) + Chelsea (12th)
1935/36	Arsenal (6th) + Chelsea (8th)-note *9
1936/37	Middlesbrough (7th) + Sunderland (8th)
1937/38	Arsenal (1st) + Chelsea (10th)
1938/39	Everton (1st) + Liverpool (11th)
1946/47	Liverpool (1st) + Man Utd (2nd)
1947/48	Man Utd (2nd) + Man City (10th)
1948/49	Man Utd (2nd) + Man City (7th)
1949/50	Sunderland (3rd) + Newcastle (5th)
1950/51	Tottenham (1st) + Arsenal (5th)
1951/52	Tottenham (2nd) + Arsenal (3rd)
1952/53	Wolves (3rd) + West Brom (4th)-note *10
1953/54	Wolves (1st) + West Brom (2nd)
1954/55	Chelsea (1st) + Arsenal (9th)
1955/56	Man Utd (1st) + Man City (4th)
1956/57	Preston (3rd) + Blackpool (4th)
1957/58	Wolves (1st) + West Brom (4th)
1958/59	Wolves (1st) + West Brom (5th)
1959/60	Wolves (2nd) + West Brom (4th)
1960/61	Tottenham (1st) + Arsenal (11th)
1961/62	Sheff Utd (5th) + Sheff Wed (6th)-note*11
1962/63	Everton (1st) + Liverpool (8th)-note*12
1963/64	Liverpool (1st) + Man Utd (2nd)
1964/65	Man Utd (1st) + Leeds (2nd)
1965/66	Liverpool (1st) + Everton (11th)-note*13
1966/67	Man Utd (1st) + Leeds (4th)
1967/68	Man City (1st) + Man Utd (2nd)
1968/69	Liverpool (2nd) + Everton (3rd)
1969/70	Everton (1st) + Liverpool (5th)

1970/71	Arsenal (1st) + Tottenham (3rd)
1971/72	Leeds (2nd) + Man Utd (8th)
1972/73	Arsenal (2nd) + Tottenham (8th)
1973/74	Liverpool (2nd) + Everton (7th)
1974/75	Liverpool (2nd) + Everton (4th)
1975/76	Liverpool (1st) + Man Utd (3rd)
1976/77	Liverpool (1st) + Man Utd (6th)
1977/78	Liverpool (2nd) + Everton (3rd)
1978/79	Liverpool (1st) + Everton (4th)
1979/80	Liverpool (1st) + Man Utd (2nd)
1980/81	Aston Villa (1st) + West Brom (4th)
1981/82	Liverpool (1st) + Man Utd (3rd)
1982/83	Liverpool (1st) + Man Utd (3rd)
1983/84	Liverpool (1st) + Everton (7th)-note *14
1984/85	Everton (1st) + Liverpool (2nd)
1985/86	Liverpool (1st) + Everton (2nd)
1986/87	Everton (1st) + Liverpool (2nd)
1987/88	Liverpool (1st) + Man Utd (2nd)
1988/89	Arsenal (1st) + Tottenham (6th)
1989/90	Liverpool (1st) + Man Utd (13th)-note*15
1990/91	Arsenal (1st) + Tottenham (10th)-note*16
1991/92	Leeds (1st) + Man Utd (2nd)
1992/93	Man Utd (1st) + Liverpool (6th)
1993/94	Man Utd (1st) + Leeds (5th)
1994/95	Man Utd (2nd) + Liverpool (4th)
1995/96	Man Utd (1st) + Liverpool (3rd)
1996/97	Man Utd (1st) + Liverpool (4th)
1997/98	Arsenal (1st) + Chelsea (4th)
1998/99	Man Utd (1st) + Leeds (4th)-note*17
1999/00	Man Utd (1st) + Leeds (3rd)
2000/01	Man Utd (1st) + Liverpool (3rd)
2001/02	Arsenal (1st) + Chelsea (6th)-note*18
2002/03	Man Utd (1st) + Liverpool (5th)-note*19
2003/04	Arsenal (1st) + Chelsea (2nd)

2004/05   Chelsea (1st) + Arsenal (2nd)

2005/06   Man Utd (2nd) + Liverpool (3rd)-note*20

2006/07   Man Utd (1st) + Liverpool (3rd)

2007/08   Chelsea (2nd) + Arsenal (3rd)-note*21

2008/09   Man Utd (1st) + Liverpool (2nd)

2009/10   Chelsea (1st) + Arsenal (3rd)

2010/11   Man Utd (1st) + Man City (3rd)

2011/12   Man City (1st) + Man Utd (2nd)

Top Derbies Summary

1.	Liverpool v Man. Utd (18 times)
2.	Everton v Liverpool (17)
3.	Arsenal v Chelsea (11)
4.	Newcastle v Sunderland (10)
5=	Arsenal v Tottenham (8)
5=	Man.City v Man.Utd (8)
7=	Sheff.Utd v Sheff. Wed (7)
7=	Leeds v Man Utd (7)
9.	Blackburn v Preston (6)
10.	West Brom v Wolves (5)
11=	West Brom v Aston Villa (3)
11=	Blackburn v Bolton (3)
11=	Bolton v Bury (3)
14.	Blackburn v Burnley (2)
15=	Notts. Co v Nottm.Forest (1)
15=	Middlesbrough v Sunderland (1)
15=	Middlesbrough v Newcastle (1)
15=	Birmingham v Aston Villa (1)
15=	Blackpool v Preston (1)

Notes

*1 – arguably, 1891/92 belonged to West Brom and Aston Villa. They were only 12th and 4th in the League, but West Brom beat Villa in the FA Cup final.

*2 – similarly, in 1894/5, Villa (3rd) and West Brom (13th) contested the final. Villa won.

*3 – Forest (8th) beat Derby (10th) in the FA Cup final.

*4 – Strictly according to League positions, Preston (2nd) and Blackburn (9th) were marginally better. However, Everton also won the FA Cup, so Merseyside did the double.

*5 – Liverpool (2nd) and Everton (10th) were level with the North East on League positions, but Newcastle also won the Cup.

*6 – Villa (2nd) and West Brom (5th) were equal, but Blackburn/Bolton edged it with more points.

*7 – Sunderland (2nd) and Newcastle (4th) were equal, but Liverpool/Everton had more points.

*8 – Bolton (4th) and Blackburn (8th) were level on League positions, but Newcastle also won the Cup.

*9 – An alternative contender from outside the sixty derbies would be Brentford v Chelsea, because Brentford finished 5th, one place ahead of Arsenal. However, Arsenal also won the FA Cup.

*10 – Preston (2nd) and Blackpool (7th), though marginally behind on League positions, could make a claim, as Blackpool won the Cup.

*11 – Tottenham (3rd) and Arsenal (10th), though marginally behind on League positions, could make a claim, as Spurs won the Cup.

*12 – Tottenham (2nd) and Arsenal (7th) were equal on League positions, but Everton/Liverpool had more points.

*13 – Leeds (2nd) and Man Utd (4th) had a better overall record in League positions, but Everton won the FA Cup, which meant that Merseyside completed the double.

*14 – Liverpool's derby with Man Utd (4th) was higher in League positions, but Everton won the Cup. As Liverpool also won the League Cup, beating Everton in the final, Merseyside swept the honours board.

*15 – Liverpool's derby with Everton (6th) was higher in League positions, but Man Utd won the FA Cup and so the Liverpool/Man Utd derby completed a double.

*16 – Leeds (4th) and Man Utd (6th) were marginally higher in League positions, but Tottenham won the FA Cup and so North London completed a double.

*17 – Arsenal and Chelsea were equal on League positions and had more points, but Man. Utd also won the FA Cup.

*18 – Liverpool and Man. Utd had slightly better League positions overall, but Arsenal completed a League and FA Cup double and met 6th place Chelsea in the FA Cup final.

*19 – Arsenal and Chelsea were level on League places, but Man.Utd/Liverpool had more points.

*20 – Chelsea and Arsenal were equal on League positions, but Man. Utd/Liverpool had more points and won both cups.

*21 – Man. Utd and Liverpool were equal on League positions, but Arsenal/Chelsea had more points.

Derbies in 2011/12

2011/12 was truly a vintage season for English League derbies, especially in the Premier League. Usually fairly predictable big-city derbies were anything but predictable in 2011/12. In the Premier League alone, three went to the wire on the last day of the season. The highlight was, of course, Manchester's epic battle for the title, as City emerged from years of hurt to snatch the championship from United. On the way the men in light blue recorded the equal biggest victory in Manchester's derby history, winning 6-1 at Old Trafford and turning United's '*Theatre of Dreams*' into a nightmare for the day. United exacted minor revenge by despatching City from the FA Cup, but it provided scant consolation for a club so used to putting their 'noisy neighbours' in their place. The shoot-out on the final day was pure drama. City's two injury time goals against obstinate ten-man QPR which transformed typical City heartache into blue heaven couldn't have been scripted in fiction, except in far-fetched comic book style.

Manchester provided icing on the cake but throughout the league structure there were more closely fought derby struggles than usual. North London giants Arsenal and Tottenham battled for Champions' League places. Both saw off Chelsea's challenge in the League, but looked across London in envy as the Blues out-smarted both Barcelona and Bayern on their way to becoming the capital's first ever European champions. Arsenal fans in particular will treasure memories of the season's major London derbies, as the Gunners beat Chelsea 5-3 at Stamford Bridge in October and came from two down to hammer Spurs 5-2 at the Emirates in February. For good measure, Chelsea beat Spurs 5-1 in the semi-finals of the FA Cup. Much worse was to come for Tottenham. Chelsea's success in the Champions' League denied Spurs a place in the 2012/13 tournament. They were left to rue the fact that part way through the final afternoon of the season they, rather than bitter rivals Arsenal, were sitting in the automatic qualification spot.

Liverpool's clubs had a relatively low key year, but their parochial joust was tighter than usual. Ascendancy in the League was decided on the last day, with Everton victorious. Had Liverpool not won both league encounters, Everton would have been out of sight long before the season's conclusion. In the FA Cup, the clubs revived memories of the marvellous eighties, as they clashed in the semi-finals. Alas for Evertonians, they were reminded of their defeats in that decade, as Liverpool triumphed again.

Lower down the Premiership table, West Brom fans enjoyed the rare satisfaction of sitting comfortably in mid-table watching primary foes, Wolves, crash into the Championship. Secondary rivals and 'betters', Villa, almost suffered the same fate, amidst internal turmoil and anger directed at their (former Birmingham) manager. As if that wasn't enough, the Baggies were undefeated in the four West Midlands' derbies. They won three, including victories at Villa Park and 5-1 at Molyneux. The contented sounds of Throstles crowing could be heard across the West Midlands, as West Brom topped the regional pile for the first time in thirty-three years.

Queen's Park Rangers made a dramatic return to West London's derby battleground and they, Chelsea and Fulham played together in the top tier for the first time ever. Hopes were high and Rangers savoured victory over Chelsea at Loftus Road. But they crashed to earth, losing 6-0 and 6-1 at Craven Cottage and Stamford Bridge respectively, both of which were record defeats against their local rivals. At least Rangers won their battle against relegation – just – and their part in the final day drama in Manchester will ensure them a place in history.

The North East's year was not as dramatic, but it was as heated as always. Newcastle finished above Sunderland for the first time in four years and surprised even themselves by mixing it with the big boys in an, ultimately fruitless, chase for Champions' League places. They also rubbed Black Cat noses in it by winning one and drawing the other derby clash, meaning that Sunderland have won only once in the last fourteen encounters.

In the Championship three rarely played derbies made a welcome return. West Ham and Millwall met in the same division of the League for only the twelfth time in eighty-four seasons. West Ham's promotion meant that season thirteen will have to wait. Portsmouth and Southampton came together for only the sixteenth season and, as both departed the Championship in opposite directions, Saints into the higher echelons of the Premier League and Pompey into tier three, they may not be adding to that total in the near future. Meanwhile, Brighton renewed acquaintances with Crystal Palace for only the third time in twenty-four seasons, reviving memories of their glory days in the seventies. Elsewhere in the second tier, Coventry could thank derby rivals Leicester for helping them on their way to relegation, as the Foxes won both derby matches. Derby tried to do the same to Nottingham Forest but, despite losing both fixtures to the Rams, Forest survived.

In the third tier Sheffield's United and Wednesday fought out a titanic struggle every bit as bitter as the top of the Premier League clash over the Pennines in Manchester. It went to the final day and ultimately Wednesday's 1-0 victory in the derby at Hillsborough towards the end of the season proved decisive in snatching the second automatic promotion slot from the Blades. A second case of blue heaven and red woe was compounded when United lost on penalties in the play-off final, thereby becoming only the second League team ever (the other being Sunderland) to reach ninety points and yet not achieve promotion.

In tier four, something strange happened in Devon. Perennial bosses in this part of the world, Plymouth Argyle, suffered the indignity of finishing the season below both county rivals, Exeter and Torquay, for the first time in their league career and they also lost both derbies to Torquay (Exeter were in tier three). Exeter's relegation, combined with Torquay's failure in the play-offs and Plymouth's survival in their own relegation battle, means that all three meet in tier four in 2012/13. Oxford United tried hard to rain on Swindon's parade by beating the Robins in both derby encounters, but it was Swindon who had the last laugh. The Robins ended the season as fourth tier champions while United failed to make it to the play-offs.

There was derby excitement aplenty, even where clubs didn't play each other. Burnley fans may have been in a division lower, but they took great delight in the off-field internal wrangling and on-field defeats of deadly enemies, Blackburn Rovers. Like hungry wolves, the Clarets waited for the trap door to open and for Rovers to drop through to meet them in the Championship in 2012/13. In tier three, Notts. County fans lived in hope of a similar fate befalling city rivals Forest. Better still, for much of the season County had realistic hopes of reaching the play-offs and potentially replacing Forest in tier two. In the end neither part of the dream materialised, but it was at least the nearest County have come for many a year – the last time they finished above their neighbours was in 1976.

New kids on the block Stevenage took giant steps towards elevating their Hertfordshire derby with Watford. They almost became the first club to achieve three promotions in successive seasons in the higher reaches of the league structure, but fell short in the tier three play-offs. For a time, fellow newcomers AFC Wimbledon harboured hopes of promotion to meet their hated 'half-brothers' MK Dons, but their challenge faded away. MK Dons in turn did their best to keep running from the chasing original Dons, by reaching the play-offs in tier three, but they lost. The hunt goes on.

For all that it was an excellent year for derbies, some old favourites failed to join in the party. There was no sign of Bristol Rovers closing the gap on Bristol City and even less so of struggling Port Vale catching up with rampant Stoke City. Mansfield hoped to take advantage of Chesterfield's relegation to tier four, but their attempt to renew old acquaintances failed in the semi-finals of the Conference play-offs. Luton did better in the Conference play-offs, but lost in the final and their journey to catch Watford still looks long and arduous. And for one old favourite, the thrill of the derby is at an all-time low. Having been locked together like co-joined twins for most of their existence, Hartlepool and Darlington have gone their separate ways. While Pool earned the right to enjoy another season at the giddy heights of the third tier, desperate Darlington plunged out of the Conference. Worse was to come as Darlo lost their ground; were demoted even further and seemed to be going out of existence altogether. Finally, Morecambe still could not manage a Football League derby victory against Accrington.

7

Around the world in (about) eighty derby days

Britain's gift. Before returning to the detail of English League derbies, this section offers an optional detour around derbies of the world. Space doesn't allow detailed examination of many, but a few examples of world derbies are described in order to make comparisons with our own. Our love of sports such as cricket and rugby, as well as our passion for football, sometimes leads Britons to believe that we gave to the world all its great games. Britain was indeed the premier cradle of new sports, but we forget that many of 'our' sports, cricket and rugby included, are not that popular in world terms. We forget that more important world sports were invented elsewhere, for example basketball and volleyball (born in the USA) or handball (Danish). Organised football, however, is by a long, long distance the most important and popular sport on the planet and it is arguably the most appreciated of Britain's gifts to the world. The way in which Britons (and at a later date other Europeans, notably the Swiss) spread football around the globe had a profound effect upon the nature of derbies in other countries, as we will examine shortly.

But first we need to consider a conundrum. At the same time that football was emerging as Britain's favourite sport, the British Empire covered a quarter of the globe. Yet most countries in the Empire either rejected or were slow to take up the sport. No former British colony is a top football country (though Nigeria and Egypt, for example, are very good) and *only* England itself has won football's World Cup.

A potential explanation for this relative absence of football in British colonies might be that subjects of hated empires reject the trappings of their masters. However, of course, countries of the former British Empire avidly embrace rugby and, in particular, the quintessential English game of cricket. Indeed *only* former British colonies have won the World Cups of rugby and cricket. Explanations for the puzzling difference in the spread of Britain's sporting inventions are too complex for detailed consideration here. (People interested in learning more are advised to read two excellent books – '*Parish to Planet*' by Eric Midwinter and '*The Ball is Round*' by David Goldblatt). In essence, however, three factors came into play:-

First, cricket was a more established game than football. It was already fully codified and being played to consistent rules throughout the Empire before football had become a properly organised sport. Cricket was also England's summer game and most of the Empire was hot. Colonial rulers and administrators were therefore far more interested in cricket, especially as football in England gradually became associated with the working classes, whilst cricket and rugby were generally games for the middle and upper classes.

Second, Britain's football authorities made very little effort to spread the game abroad, within the Empire or elsewhere. At best ambivalent to the concept of international football outside Britain, the Home Nations' Football Associations were positively hostile to the founding of FIFA – in 1904 several European FAs went ahead anyway, without the British.

Third, it was left to entrepreneurs and workers, rather than colonialists or football administrators, to take football to the world. Crucially, they did so more in countries *outside* the British Empire than within it. By this time, the Empire was at least as interested in commercial expansion and influence as it was in direct conquest and colonialism. Britain had financial clout for investment, a huge merchant navy and, in case things got difficult, control of the seas via the Royal Navy. A number of independent countries, especially in South America, became part of Britain's 'informal Empire'. British and other Europeans flooded into places such as Argentina and Uruguay. They were influential and, at the time, British customs were admired. Britain was seen as powerful, rich and at the forefront of modernity. The playing of sport became an integral part of being 'modern' and football was the most modern and accessible sport of them all.

In a sense, football was to the turn of the 20th century what iconic American commercial brands such as KFC, Coca Cola and McDonalds are at the turn of the 21st century. Today, people in China and elsewhere flock to those brands, not because they particularly like or wish to ape Americans, but because elements of American culture are seen as modern and fashionable. Similarly, people flocked to football at the turn of the 20th century, not because the British were particularly popular, but because they and their game were seen as the future. Therefore, football became not only a 'home from home' diversion for home-sick Europeans, but a novel and fashionable attraction for populations in Britain's 'informal Empire'.

Different types of derby. English League football really only has geographical derbies, although the presence of Welsh clubs adds a national dimension. Most people simply support their home town club or the nearest club to where they live. Social dividing factors in England and Wales were either never relevant as reasons for supporting a football club or, where they did exist, they have faded over time.

In many countries, football was introduced into societies that had significant social dividing lines. Clubs were founded by specific social groups and those original allegiances are often still relevant in the choices made by supporters today. Geography is by no means the only factor to divide clubs and their fans. There are derbies based upon class, religion, politics, language, ethnic communities and national/regional identities. It isn't always easy to compartmentalise these derbies as being based upon single issues as, in many instances, fans choose their clubs because of a combination of two or more social factors. Many dividing lines are more intense and personal for people than where they happen to live and so, frequently, the club a fan will support is already determined at birth.

It should be said that, as with geographical factors, nothing is set in concrete. Even in the starkest religiously based derbies, there will be exceptions, for example, where a Catholic supports Glasgow Rangers – rare, but not unique. Furthermore, the importance of class and ethnicity can vary over time. In general, such divisions have tended to reduce over the years, as is the case in many South American derbies. However, whenever there are tensions in a region, societal ruptures are reflected in football, the most obvious recent example being in the Balkans.

We begin our trip by looking at ***class-based*** derbies.

It may be argued that the English League has derbies based upon class, as there is evidence to show that average wealth amongst supporters differs considerably from club to club. However, class divides in modern English League football are secondary consequences of geography. Wycombe Wanderers and Cheltenham Town, for example, have a higher proportion of middle class supporters than average, but it is not because the middle classes are specifically attracted to them. It is because there are more middle class people than average in and around High Wycombe and Cheltenham. Bristol City draw most of their support from the south of the city which, on the whole, is leafier than the north. Therefore, City have more middle class fans than Bristol Rovers. Portsmouth is a more working class place than its rival neighbouring city of Southampton. But working class people in south Bristol or in Southampton wouldn't choose to support Rovers or Pompey, specifically *because* they are more working class. Similarly, West London clubs have proportionately more wealthy fans than clubs in the rest of London because, in general, West London is wealthier. Relatively wealthy people, therefore, are simply doing what most fans do – they usually support the closest clubs to their homes or to where they grew up.

To find the nearest thing to a class based derby that existed in English football, we probably have to return yet again to Nottingham. In the early years there is evidence that Notts. Forest, as they were often referred to at the time, had greater working class support than Nottingham FC, later to become County. However, even this historic example pales into insignificance in comparison with examples elsewhere in the world.

In a number of countries, class *itself* is something that distinctly affects club allegiance. There are many examples where clubs play in the same stadium and/or originate from the same district of a city, and yet the class base of their support differs significantly. In the title of the book, we have already seen one example of a class divide, although it is by no means the most extreme example. In Casablanca, 'Love' (Wydad) draw support largely from relatively well to do people. 'Hope' (Raja) draw their supporters from relatively poor people in the suburbs, but the clubs share the same stadium.

One of the strongest class-based derbies is in Teheran, Iran, between Persepolis and Esteghlal who, again, share a stadium, the 90,000 capacity Azadi. Persepolis are the working peoples' club and boast support from more than sixty percent of Iranians, making them arguably Asia's best loved club. They have had a difficult history, to say the least. They suffered the dissolution of a forerunner club, during the Shah's reign; massive decline and sequestration of property, following the Iranian Revolution, and enforced name changes. Technically, their current name is Pirouzi. But the 'Reds' or 'Lions' have remained strong against all odds and should be seen as a model of persistence for clubs facing adversity – you can't keep a good club down for long, at least not a big one, even in the harshest of environments. Persepolis's opponents, Esteghlal were the Shah's club in past times, when they were known as Taj (meaning 'Crown'). They too have survived obstacles in recent years, but they were and they remain a club for the elite.

In South America, it is common to find class as a determining factor in support for clubs and class often combines with ethnicity to compartmentalise supporters. Probably the most famous class-based football derby of all is in Buenos Aires, although its specific class dimension has diluted in recent years. Boca Juniors are a classic club from the other side of the tracks. Their Bombonera Stadium (the 'Chocolate Box') is situated in La Boca, the run-down dockland part of the city. Their great rivals, River Plate, originated in the same area, but subsequently moved out to a much more upmarket suburb. Even before their move, River were seen as representing the middle classes. River's nickname, 'Los Millonarios', stems from a period when they were splashing out in the transfer market, rather than being a reference to the wealth of their supporters, but it all adds to the image.

Similarly, Boca's nickname, 'Los Bosteros', which roughly translated means 'the Shit Handlers' or simply 'Shits', was initially an insult thrown at them by other fans, but has now been enthusiastically adopted by Boca fans as their own. Again, all part of a lower class image. When River fans attend the Bombonera, they frequently wear surgical masks to protect them from the supposed smell of the place. Another divisive element is added to the derby because of Boca's early links to the Italian immigrant community which, being less well-established, tended to be poorer at the time.

If all this creates a picture of being welcomed to River's ground by fans in boaters, sipping Pimms, rather than Bovril, at half-time, think again. Everything is relative. Anyone who has been to River's ground, 'El Monumental' (image again), and seen their 'Drunks from the Board' ultras would probably wonder how on earth Boca fans could possibly be harder. Both stadia are said to physically tremble on match days and a reporter for the Observer said that *"derby day in Buenos Aires makes the Old Firm game between Rangers and Celtic look like a primary school kick about."* The comment may be a bit of an exaggeration, and there are after all some pretty tough primary schools in Glasgow, but it is true to say that *El Superclasico* ranks as one of the greatest derbies of all, probably matched only by Barcelona v Real Madrid and Galatasaray v Fenerbahce in its ability to terrify. It is by no means a parochial affair for citizens of Buenos Aires alone. A survey in 2006 estimated that almost three-quarters of Argentina's population supports one of these two clubs. Maradona is a committed Boca fan. He also played for them and vowed never to play for their middle class rivals. An incident in 1994 gives an indication of just how intense and how low El Superclasico can become. Following a 2-0 derby victory for their side, a bus full of River fans was ambushed and two fans were shot dead. Shortly afterwards, graffiti appeared in the city. It read '*River 2 Boca 2*'.

About 160 miles north-west of Buenos Aires, the biggest and oldest Argentine derby outside the capital is played in Rosario and it too is class-based. Both Newell's Old Boys and Rosario Central were formed by Englishmen, the former by a teacher and the latter by railway workers. Newell's have generally been adopted by better off people, while Central have a tradition of left-wing political connections and greater working class support. It therefore comes as no surprise to learn that Che Guevara, famous for his revolutionary activities in Cuba, but Argentine by birth, opted to support the Blue and Golds of Central. The nicknames of Rosario's clubs bear testament to the fact that a single incident can create everlasting mythology in football. Newell's are the 'Lepers' and Central the 'Scoundrels'. Many years ago, the two teams were invited to play a match in aid of a leprosy charity. Newell's agreed, but the 'Scoundrels' of Central refused and the names have stuck ever since. Arguably the world's greatest current player, Lionel Messi, is a committed Newell's 'Leper'.

Over the borders of Argentina, in Uruguay, Brazil and Chile, similar class-based derbies are common. The sheer brilliance of early Uruguayan football is often forgotten. If Scotland would have vied with Austria and Hungary, in the formative years of football, for the European title of 'greatest number of excellent footballers per head of population', there is no doubt that the world champions would have been Uruguay. With a population of only around three million, Uruguay were the first World Cup winners. Many commentators dismiss their achievement in 1930, because the number and strength of teams competing, especially those from Europe, was limited and the Uruguayans had the advantage of playing on home soil. However, the reason why Uruguay was chosen to host football's first World Cup was because they had already won the 'unofficial' World Championship at the Olympic Games of both 1924 and 1928. Those victories were achieved in Paris and Amsterdam respectively, in very difficult circumstances, far away from home. Uruguay didn't defend their title in 1934 or enter in 1938. They tried again in 1950, in Brazil, and won again. Therefore, this tiny nation won every world football competition they entered for over a quarter of a century and their accomplishments arguably transcend even those of the 21st century's brilliant Spaniards.

There were three principal reasons for the early pre-eminence of Uruguayan football. First, the country was booming. It was one of the richest countries in the world in the early part of the 20th century and it attracted thousands of European immigrants, keen to play football in their spare time. Second, the immigrants shared styles and experiences and developed a brand of fluid, attacking football that was a revelation to other nations. Third and most importantly, football more quickly passed from being a game for elites to being the game for all Uruguayans. In a relatively new country desperate to establish its credentials as a nation, football soon became an obsession, a symbol of nationhood.

In Montevideo, the oldest derby in the world, outside Britain, began between Penarol and Nacional. It was a fairly complex class-based affair. Penarol were formed by the English, originally as the Central Uruguayan Railways Cricket Club. They still play in the old railway's yellow and black colours. Nacional were formed later by Hispanic students and, as their name suggests, they opposed foreign domination which characterised Penarol. It might therefore be expected that Nacional would be the club of the masses, but they were, and still are, not. Fairly early in their existence, Penarol were adopted by the Italian immigrant community which, as we saw in Buenos Aires, was less established and often poorer than the Spanish community. Gradually, therefore, it was Penarol who became the favourites of poor people and Nacional the representatives of the elite. In keeping with what seems to be a South American fascination with excrement, Penarol became known as the 'Manya Mierdas' which roughly translates as 'Shit Eaters'. It is estimated that 80% of Uruguayans support one or other of these clubs.

It may be surprising to learn that Brazil was relatively slow to embrace football and even slower to percolate the game to all classes of people. Therefore, the great early national clash in South America was Argentina v Uruguay, not Argentina v Brazil as it is today. Furthermore, when football did take a hold in Brazil, it was restricted to being a Rio based phenomenon. The class and community bases of Rio's big derbies are even more complicated than those in Montevideo. Traditionally, the biggest of all is the 'Fla/Flu' derby between Flamengo and Fluminense and they still hold the official world record for the largest attendance ever at a match between club sides. In 1963, 177,000 people crammed into the Maracana to see them. Flamengo is one of the best supported clubs on the planet and is said to be the favourite of a third of all Brazilian fans. 'Fla' grew out of 'Flu', when most of Fluminense's players defected to Flamengo, with a view to establishing a new football section. There is therefore an additional Liverpool/Everton style breakaway dimension to their rivalry. Fluminense, the oldest football club in Rio, was originally a very exclusive sports and social club, based in a relatively prosperous neighbourhood. Flu have therefore long been associated with the affluent middle classes. The club has an unfortunate nickname, 'Po de Arroz'. It means 'White Powder'. It refers to a time when black and mixed-race players were not allowed to play for Fluminense and so a player used white face powder to disguise his skin colour in order to play for the club.

All therefore seems quite clear cut – Flamengo, the club of the people; Fluminense, the club of the elite, with a history of racism. However, things are not as straightforward as they might seem. Racism in Brazil has to be seen in the context of the country's history. Slavery was not abolished in Brazil until

1888 and racial segregation continued for decades afterwards. Therefore, for many years, Flamengo, along with Fluminense and the other big Rio club at the time, Botafogo, all adopted racist policies. Furthermore, in the early days, Flamengo club was so exclusive that it derided the idea of playing such a common game as football.

Enter Vasco da Gama, a club founded by Portuguese immigrants. These days Vasco have a greater fan base than Fluminense, though nowhere near that of Flamengo. Vasco's more recent history is similar to that of Flamengo. They also are a club of the masses. The big difference is that, from very early days, Vasco accepted black, mixed-race and poor (in a financial sense!) white players, all of who were frowned upon by other clubs. Vasco had to fight against discrimination and exclusion to change attitudes in Brazilian football. Frequently, clubs refused to play against them and at one point the other big Rio clubs left to establish a rival league, rather than play Vasco. However, with the advent of professional football in the 1930s, Flamengo saw the light, signed many of the best black players and became South America's biggest club, the red and black darlings of the continent.

A final twist to the story of Rio's derbies is the part played by rowing in the development of Rio's clubs. We saw earlier in the book that rowing was very popular in 19th century England and was a rival to football, vying for the participation of 'muscular Christians'. Europeans exported rowing as part of colonial and commercial expansion and so three of Rio's big football clubs began life as rowers. Ironically, the only one of Rio's big four not to have a rowing background is Fluminense, the club of the elite.

The divisions between big clubs in the Chilean capital, Santiago, are class-based, but with severe additional complications created by the country's difficult political history, again demonstrating the fact that football reflects the nature of the country in which it is played. Colo Colo (Wild Cat) is the most successful and best supported club in Chile. They are named after a heroic indigenous leader who fought against Spanish invaders in the 16th century. Their local rivals are primarily Universidad de Chile ('La U') and to a lesser extent Universidad Catolica. Colo Colo are the club of the people. Universidad de Chile draw support from the middle classes and Universidad Catolica have an even more upper class base than 'La U'.

The fortunes of the clubs differed enormously following General Pinochet's right-wing military coup d'etat in 1973. The dictator favoured Colo Colo and was invited to become the club's honorary President, not necessarily with the agreement of the club's working class supporters of course. On the other hand, 'La U' had a long association with left-wing intellectuals and were therefore discriminated against by the regime. The Catholic Church, and hence Universidad Catolica, initially supported Pinochet and found favour, but subsequently became major opponents of the regime and suffered as a consequence.

South America's class-based rivalries are perhaps not that unexpected in a continent with a history of turbulent politics and massive wealth gaps. More surprisingly, class-based football loyalties are fairly common in Europe too and they exist in places where they would probably be least expected, for example in the relatively egalitarian Nordic countries.

In Oslo the city's big clubs are split along class lines. Valerenga and Lyn share the same stadium, but Valerenga traditionally represent the working class east of the city, whilst Lyn are the club of the better off west. In Copenhagen, FC Copenhagen are traditionally the club of the city's elite. They were formed by a merger which included the oldest football club on mainland Europe, KB Copenhagen (established in 1876 and playing football by 1879). Image conscious Copenhagen are said to have 'cooligans', rather than hooligans. Frem are traditionally the workers' club. They were formed in 1886, ostensibly as a cricket club, but were in fact a front for support of the 'Venstre' ('Left') political party (incidentally, it is now a centre-right party but is still called 'left' – long story!). More recently, Frem have fallen on hard times and Bromby IF have taken over as the main local adversaries of FC Copenhagen. Bromby draw their support from poorer western suburbs and are nicknamed 'Drengene fra Vestegnen', meaning 'the lads from the western suburbs' – very imaginative. In case FC's elite reputation implies that they are exclusive, it has to be said that they are Denmark's most popular club – there are a lot of middle class people in Denmark.

Over the border in Sweden, IFK Gothenburg are arguably the country's biggest club and are decidedly working class. GAIS, also working class, and Orgryte IS, the club of Gothenburg's elite, are older than IFK and were formed at a time when class conflict in Sweden was constantly brewing. Up until the late-1930s, fan violence was something of a 'Swedish disease'. Clashes involving IFK or GAIS versus Orgryte were a considerable embarrassment to the nation, not least because they were not simply fights between rival fans, but battles between opposing classes. Things are relatively calm now, but IFK's 'Anglarna' ('Angels') fans are no, well, angels and Orgryte, IFK and GAIS still have substantially different fan bases.

Beautiful Vienna is one of the world's most sophisticated cities. It regularly appears in lists of the 'top ten places to live'. Where better then to find order and calm, rather than chaos? – not at the city's football derby, that's for certain. Vienna, together with Prague and Budapest, formed the epicentre of football development in Central Europe, and Central Europe, along with parts of South America, lit the torch for football more than anywhere else in the world outside Britain. The world's first international club competition, the Mitropa Cup, was born in Central Europe.

'Red Vienna' was arguably the most important city of all. It is where the first professional football league outside Britain was established. From it emerged some of the finest players in the world immediately before and, for a short time, after World War Two. At the time, Vienna was not the sophisticated place it has become and its 'Red' tag indicates the tensions that existed between different social groups in the city. Rapid Vienna grew out of First Vienna Workers' Club and were forced to change their name because of its explicit class connotations. Austria Vienna emerged from Vienna Cricket and Football Club. There are no prizes for guessing which became which in the capital's class divide. It is a divide that has never been entirely extinguished. When the two met towards the end of the 2010/11 season, the game lasted less than half an hour. With Austria leading 2-0, masked Rapid fans rioted, the game was abandoned and Austria were awarded a 3-0 victory. Bizarrely, behind a few masks, Viennese police found supporters of Greek club, Panathinaikos, members of their notorious 'Gate 13' ultras. If on trips to Greece you have been puzzled as to why you often see simply '13' scrawled on walls, usually in green and occasionally accompanied by a shamrock, this is the reference point. Panathinaikos play in green, their emblem is a shamrock and their 'Gate 13' ultras are trouble.

Athens itself has a more complicated, three way, class divide. The big two clubs are Panathinaikos from Athens and Olympiakos from just down the road in the port of Piraeus. Both are general sports clubs. Their sheer loathing for each other is perhaps best demonstrated by the fact that people died in fighting between fans at a men's basketball game in 1995 and at a women's volleyball game in 2006. Olympiakos are traditionally a working class club and Panathinaikos a club of the middle classes.

The third, smaller, club in the capital is AEK Athens who, proportionately, have a more working class base than Olympiakos, let alone Panathinaikos. An additional divide is hinted at in AEK's name which does not contain any reference to Athens and means Athletic Union of Constantinople. Following war between the countries in the early 20th century, Greece and Turkey agreed a traumatic population exchange. Many displaced Greeks migrated to Athens. AEK grew out of this community and are still associated with migrants, rather than traditional Athenians. AEK's black and yellow colours and club crest are reminders of a lost homeland. As if this wasn't enough, yet another dividing line is added because, politically, AEK fans are traditionally left-wing. They have a mutual pact with fellow leftists, Livorno in Italy and Marseilles in France.

Prague's class divide has an added mix of ex-Soviet bloc politics. Slavia Prague were originally linked to Czech nationalism and to a Czech language society, from which they drew the support of intellectuals, especially university students and teachers. Sparta Prague were solidly working class. Before the Second World War, the two dominated the league in a fairly equal contest. However, after the war, the incoming Communist Government had a clear view of those who could not be trusted, Slavia. Slavia were discriminated against, had their name changed to Dynamo and declined. The Government had a less clear view of who could be trusted. Therefore, Sparta, though not suffering the same ignominies as Slavia, did not receive the regime's wholehearted support either. Instead the army took over a minor club, changed its name to Dukla Prague, and proceeded to dominate Czech football, as a 'safe' representative of the state. Following the fall of the Communist regime, Sparta and Slavia have resumed their competitive derby and the nuances of their class support bases still exist. Meanwhile, relatively unloved Dukla have fallen upon hard times.

Bruges or Brugge, beautiful 'Venice of the North', has a traditional class/ethnic divide. Club Brugge draw most of their support from working class Flemish people and Cercle Brugge are associated with the middle classes, as well as with Dutch and English immigrants. However, many argue that Cercle are the true club of the city itself, whereas Club represent Flanders as a whole, a distinction to which we will return later.

As in Brazil, football in Germany was slow to develop. The sport was viewed with suspicion as an 'English disease' and instead a national form of gymnastics was promoted as the preferred form of healthy pastime. When football did begin to take root, it was kept strictly amateur and Germany's top sides were more akin to early elite clubs in England. Football was strictly divided along class lines, to such an extent that promotion and relegation was suspended for a time in the 1920s to prevent Schalke, a working class club from industrial Gelsenkirchen, gaining promotion to the top tier.

Before moving on from class-based derbies we should pause to address another puzzling aspect of football's development in England and Wales. The U.K. is one of the most class-ridden countries in Europe. Therefore, is it not strange to find an absence of class-based derbies in the English League, when class divides in football are so common in relatively egalitarian countries?

The answer to the puzzle revolves around the availability of alternative sports in other countries. When football was in its infancy in England, there were in fact many association football clubs which were class exclusive, not only in terms of players and members, but also in terms of supporters. Old Etonians and other public school-based clubs are obvious examples. Royal Engineers, favourites, but beaten in the first ever FA Cup final, were a club specifically for officers, not for lower ranks. The two thousand or so people who watched that final in 1872, against another socially elitist club, the Wanderers, were drawn almost entirely from the middle and upper classes. Football was not unusual in this respect. Most sporting clubs and organised leisure associations were class exclusive at the time.

However, two things happened in most of England (less so in Wales). First, the middle and upper classes began to desert football and to side with the rugby union code or hockey. This trend was most marked in public schools. Having done so much to establish organised football, public schools increasingly rejected the 'association' form of the game. It became, at best, a poor second to rugby or, at worst, was abandoned altogether by schools. Second, partly as a result of this change in sporting affections, the original class-based football clubs either disappeared altogether (eg the Wanderers), or became minor amateur clubs (eg Old Etonians, who still play in the Arthurian League, a competition exclusively for alumni of leading public schools). The new professional clubs replacing elitist clubs in England were based upon broader geographical communities, rather than class or institutions.

This is not to say that England's middle classes opted entirely for rugby union or hockey. Early 20th century football crowds are often depicted as row upon row of flat-hatted working class men. But football stands were not erected for people in flat hats. Many middle class people continued to support their football clubs. However, as a general rule, proportionately fewer middle and upper class people remained faithful to football. Distinctions between a rugby union crowd and one supporting football became stark and, to a lesser degree, they still are.

In contrast to England's experience, in most other countries rugby and hockey didn't take off as alternative sports, especially not in South America or Europe. Argentina developed a largely Welsh inspired liking for the oval ball, but it was never a serious contender for the affections of the vast majority of people in Argentina, or elsewhere on the continent. Under American influence, places such as Venezuela took to baseball, rather than European imports. In Europe, rugby gained strongholds in parts of France, which counteracted the growth of football there. On the whole, however, football reigned supreme and unchallenged as the *only* mass outdoor sport for *all* classes in *most* countries of South America and Europe.

In conclusion, the answer to the puzzle is that England and Wales (again, more so England) *did* and *do still* have class-based clubs, but they are not association football clubs competing with each other. We don't have class-based football derbies, simply because England's class-based clubs play different sports altogether. By contrast, in most other countries, football was and is the only major outdoor mass sport. The game was introduced into societies often divided on class lines. Usually, it was taken up initially by elites, because they were more likely to come into contact with English and other European football players. Those elites created exclusive clubs similar to the original elite clubs in England. Subsequently, at different speeds in different countries, new clubs were formed by those who were denied access to the original clubs for a variety of reasons, one of which was their class. When the new 'peoples' clubs emerged, the elites had no alternative sports to turn to and so class-based derbies, playing the *same* sport, were born. Frequently, those early class divisions are still reflected in the support bases of today's clubs.

We turn next to **religion** and look at examples of religious splits, or supposed religious splits that impact upon football derbies in the English League and elsewhere. Religion clearly plays a part in Scotland, most notably in the well-documented schism between Rangers (Protestant) and Celtic (Catholic) in Glasgow. It is one of the most passionate partitions in the world and creates one of the most vehement derbies of them all. The religious divide in Edinburgh between Hearts (Protestant) and Hibernian (Catholic) will also be familiar to most football fans. Less well known is that Dundee's clubs had a religious divide too. Originally, Dundee United were Dundee Hibernian, having been created by the city's Irish Catholic community in 1909. To emphasise their roots, they played in green and white, as do Celtic and Hibernian today but, unlike their Glasgow and Edinburgh counterparts, Dundee Hibernian replaced the green colours and changed their name to United to broaden the appeal of the club. Religion is not a significant basis for support in the city now. Indeed,

Dundee has the unusual distinction of having a *joint* Dundee/Dundee United hooligan firm. The concept of Rangers and Celtic hooligans joining forces in mutual support is one that only a saint could envisage and the rest of us fear.

Religious loyalties have been ascribed to clubs in England too. The silliest example is probably Tottenham's supposed association with the Jewish faith which, on occasions, leads Spurs fans to sing ironic songs about being 'Yids' and for their hooligan firm to be dubbed the 'Yid Army'. In reality, there is no formal or informal connection between Jews and Spurs, other than that certain areas of North London, where proportionately more Jewish people than usual happen to live, are close to Spurs' home at White Hart Lane.

All of this may be taken as relatively innocent, light-hearted banter, albeit in bad taste. However, two examples from elsewhere in Europe may make people think again. The first involves Ajax from Amsterdam. In many senses their experience is similar to that of Tottenham. They have no real association with the Jewish faith, except that they originate from east Amsterdam where proportionately more Jews lived. Like their counterparts at Tottenham, Ajax fans have adopted the trappings of being Jewish, in an act of defiance against opponents who use the term 'Jew' as an insult. Like Tottenham with their 'Yids' nickname, Ajax fans often call themselves 'Joden'. Ajax fans, however, have taken the issue a good deal further, for example by unfurling huge Israeli flags at games. Unfortunately, the Ajax experience has gone well beyond 'banter'. It should also be said that the histories of North London and East Amsterdam differ in one crucial respect. The important point in the earlier sentence is that East Amsterdam was where more Jews *lived* (past tense). But in the Second World War the Jewish population of the Netherlands were systematically rounded up and exterminated. With that background, the fact that Ajax are routinely subjected to chants of 'death to the Jews' and hissing (in imitation of gas chambers) is an unacceptable face of Dutch football which the authorities are desperately trying to eradicate.

If the experience of Ajax is not enough to convince Spurs' fans, and those who taunt them, that playing with religious divisions is unwise, the second example might do so. It involves MTK Budapest. When World War Two broke out, MTK really were directly associated with the Jewish faith, as well as with intelligentsia in the city. Their working class city rivals Ferencvaros on the other hand had become involved with far right-wing politics. Hungary supported Axis powers in the war and so the fate that befell MTK and their fans in those dark years does not have to be spelt out. Alas, the club still suffers anti-Semitic taunts.

The most commonly quoted example of a religious divide in England is one which allegedly exists in Liverpool with, it is said, Everton being Catholic and Liverpool Protestant. However, Everton and Liverpool come from a common root, arguably a Methodist one, given that the original name of Everton, St. Domingo's, came from a Methodist Church Sunday School. When the club split in 1892, religious division was not a factor in determining those people who chose to leave Anfield with the existing club, Everton, and those people who stayed to form a new club, Liverpool. It is true to say that a number of religious people involved in the club did not like the owner of Anfield's business interests, as they involved the evils of alcohol, but people from different denominations were united in agreement about the issue. The clubs come from the same area of the city, being separated only by Stanley Park, and although religion is sometimes a more divisive issue in Liverpool than in most English cities, there is little evidence of it being a significant element in the choice of football club in recent years.

There are many explanations of Everton's perceived historical connection with Catholicism. One relates to Catholics becoming directors of the club not long after the move to Goodison. Another suggests that it stems partly from their choice of players from the late 40s until the early 1960s. There also appears to have been an earlier connection, with Catholic immigrants from Ireland tending to support Everton and Irish Protestant immigrants tending towards Liverpool. In more recent years, there has been evidence of the supposed divide being turned on its head, with the development of Liverpool/ Celtic connections, all of which reinforces a conclusion that, *if* there is now a religious divide between Liverpool's clubs at all, its existence is greatly exaggerated.

Another religious divide purported to have existed in England is the split between Manchester United (Catholic) and Manchester City (Protestant), but the origins of that alleged divide are even more obscure than the one in Liverpool. It is worth saying however that, when Newton Heath were considering a change of name, following saviour from near bankruptcy in 1902, one name short-listed was Manchester *Celtic*, which would imply a possible Catholic connection at the time.

In a sense, religion *was* an important factor in the early development of football in England and Wales, as a number of English League clubs were formed by churches. In addition to Everton's St.Domingo's, examples include Barnsley (St. Peter's), Bolton (Christ Church), Aston Villa (Villa Cross Wesleyan Chapel), Fulham (St. Andrew's) and Southampton (St. Mary's). In an indirect way, the churches in question no doubt saw a religious benefit from establishing football teams, in that young men would be drawn to 'muscular Christianity' because of the attraction of football. However, in most cases, connections to the original church organisations didn't last long and none of the clubs have religious links now.

Religious attachments or separations are therefore hard to find in the English League, but religious divides are far more common elsewhere in the world. In India, Kolkata, formerly capital of the British Raj, was the main base where football developed and remains a stronghold for the game, as is demonstrated by the fact that its vast Salt Lake Stadium holds 120,000 people. Kolkata has a number of clubs, but the biggest and best established are Mohun Bagan and Mohammedan Sporting Club, both founded in the 19th century, and East Bengal, formed in 1920 as a breakaway from Mohun Bagan. All three have rich histories and all can point to their part in opposing British rule in India, especially Mohun Bagan, who became intrinsically linked with the independence struggle and whose founder became President of the Indian National Congress. But it is Mohammedan SC who had a specific religious link and a role in rallying Muslims, especially poor Muslims. At first their influence was confined to Kolkata itself, but increasingly they were adopted as favourites by Muslims throughout the whole of India.

In South Korea, Hallelujah FC were set up in 1980 by Christian missionaries, with the specific purpose of using the club as a vehicle for spreading the Christian gospel. They were the first professional club in South Korea and won the country's first professional league, the K-League, in 1983. It hasn't been plain sailing since and, in 2003, the club were forced to leave their home in the city of Iksan, following a campaign by radical followers of Won Buddhism, who objected to Hallelujah's up-front missionary objectives.

Religion combines with other issues to divide supporters in less likely places. Eindhoven in the Netherlands is traditionally a Roman Catholic city in a largely Protestant country. It has two clubs, Eindhoven and, the much more successful, PSV. Eindhoven are associated with Catholicism, whereas PSV, if not Protestant as such, are not Catholic either. Added to the religious element, there is a local club (Eindhoven) versus national club (PSV) divide, which we will see repeated elsewhere. Also, PSV are seen as a corporate club, opposed by a traditionally funded club. We are so used to sponsorship in modern football that PSV's association with the Philips' electronics empire may not seem unusual. However, the involvement of Philips is not the standard, fly by night, advertising deal, to be dropped or renewed every few years. PSV is an abbreviation of Philips Sports Vereniging and the club was created as a works team by the company in its home city. Not surprisingly, clashes between Eindhoven's clubs are called 'City of Light' derbies.

Football does not itself create serious divisions in societies, but frequently it reflects those divisions and, at times, football is used as a showcase by political or religious factions. Nowhere is this better demonstrated than in Lebanon, where probably there exist the greatest religious divides of all. There is space here only for a very short potted history of Lebanon's recent past. In essence, a prosperous country with a fine capital city, Beirut, has been ravaged by decades of conflict, to the extent whereby the phrase 'it looked like Beirut' has become synonymous with devastation. The civil war from 1975 to 1990 killed more than 150,000 people. The country has been invaded twice by Israel, most recently in 2006 and, in 2008, the worst fighting since the civil war led to the deaths of dozens of people.

Football has not been immune, far from it. Lebanon's clubs are supported by the country's variety of religious and/or political groups. Leaders of those groups often bankroll clubs. For example, Al-Ansar are the biggest club of the majority Sunni community. Al-Nejmeh ('Star') traditionally have a largely Shi'ite support base but they wear the star symbol of the minority Druze community. Safa are a Druze club. Shabab Al-Sahel are Shi'ite. Al-Ahed are Shia too and have ties with the political group, Hezbollah. Homenetmen and

Homenmen are Armenian Catholics and are wings of wider pan-Armenian organisations, the former being right-wing politically and the latter left-wing. Sagesse are Maronite Christians. Racing Club are Orthodox Christians.

Should anyone need further evidence of the intensity of its religious/political rivalries, there is another unusual and extreme feature of football in Lebanon – until very recently no-one watched football matches in Lebanon, except on TV. This was not because there is no interest in live matches. The country has a number of big stadia which could easily be filled by fervent supporters. However, authorities were too afraid of the potential consequences of allowing rival fans to attend Beirut derbies and so for a number of years players celebrated their goals to the sound of silence. In 2012 tentative steps were taken to re-introduce fans but violence remains a problem and the prospects for domestic football are fragile.

Mixing football with **politics** is generally frowned upon in England and Wales. This does not mean that British political parties have no interest in football. All are anxious to demonstrate their connections with the 'people's game'. We are familiar with Tony Blair's avowed devotion to Newcastle United, David Cameron's to Aston Villa and Gordon Brown's (definitely genuine) love of Raith Rovers. It is also commonplace for political parties, especially those of the far right, to try to use football as a recruitment ground. However, English League clubs are not affiliated to political parties and fans do not make a point of declaring their political allegiances, even if their city is a hotbed of socialism or conservatism. The nearest examples we have to politically based derbies are those to have been influenced by historical events with a political edge, eg Chesterfield v Mansfield (Miners' Strike of 1984/5) or West Ham v Millwall (General Strike of 1926).

In other parts of the world, fans are more than happy to wear their political colours on their sleeves – often literally. In many countries, clubs are directly or indirectly linked with political parties. Before embarking on a short study of politically based derbies, the organisation and role of football 'ultras' has to be taken into account. 'Ultras' are often portrayed as being somehow significantly different to ordinary fans. In essence they are not. Nor are ultras synonymous with hooligans. The origin of ultras is disputed, but most commentators agree that the first examples emerged in South America. Hadjuk Split are generally recognised as being the first European club to have ultras, as long ago as 1950, but it was in Italy where European ultra-culture flourished.

The important difference between 'ultras' and 'traditional', English-style, fans is in the way they are organised, although again it should be stressed that there is not an absolute distinction between the two. In England and Wales, most clubs have one official supporters' club and one hooligan 'firm', although a few bigger clubs have more than one set of hooligans. In general, different gangs put on hold their street differences when they come together to support their football club. In short, English League clubs have one largely united set of fans, a minority of who cause trouble usually as part of a hooligan 'firm'. The hooligan element may be difficult to recognise as, especially in the days of CCTV, they make every effort to be inconspicuous. A glance along football related bookshelves will soon demonstrate that, in their dotage, older hooligans are prone to write their memoirs of the 'good times', when they had hours of fun handing out their calling cards.

By contrast, broadly speaking, ultras are organised along federal rather than unitary lines. There are often many ultra groups within a single club. Street differences between these groups are not always put on hold in support of the club. Competition for members and even fighting between rival ultras from the same club are not unusual. Each ultra group usually has its own territory in the stadium (hence Gate 13 at Panathinaikos). Banners may display the names of the ultra organisation as well as, or in place of, that of the club. Different ultra groups negotiate deals with clubs and are frequently granted favours, such as cheap tickets and/or travel and storage facilities for banners etc. As an aside, have you ever wondered how continental ultras are able to bring hundreds of flares, fireworks, musical instruments and weapons into grounds on match days? The answer is that they don't need to do so, because match day paraphernalia is often already safely tucked away in store rooms within the stadium, provided by the club. Most ultra groups are simply *ultra*-fans (hence the name), but some become particularly identified with hooliganism and therefore become the equivalent of English League 'firms'. A difference is that hooligan ultras are rarely inconspicuous, though they are often masked. More disturbingly, a few ultra groups are involved in organised crime, extortion and extremist politics.

The importance of understanding the organisation of ultras before embarking upon a study of political differences between clubs is that the behaviour and political stance of a *particular* ultra group within a club may be at odds with the club's traditional stance. It is relatively rare, but not unheard of, to find left-wing ultra groups in right-wing clubs. It is more common to find right-wing ultras in traditionally left-wing clubs. Therefore, be very sure of your ground before approaching an ultra from Roma (traditionally a left-wing club) with a hearty *'hello comrade!'* With this proviso about ultras, we can move on to look at examples of politically based derbies.

In Israel most clubs are *formally* affiliated to broad political movements. Many Israeli clubs are 'Hapoels'. Hapoel means 'the worker' and the clubs are linked with left-wing politics and to Histadrut, Israel's equivalent of the Trades' Union Congress. Clubs with a Beitar pre-fix are associated with right-wing politics. Originally, Beitar was the name of a youth movement of a pre-independence Zionist political party, one strand of which grew into today's Likud Party. Maccabi clubs, also generally right-wing, belong to the Maccabi World Union, a world-wide Jewish sports organisation that helped cement Jewish nationhood and now organises what is reputedly the world's third largest sporting gathering, after the Olympics and the Commonwealth Games. Tel Aviv has a Maccabi and a Hapoel, historically the two most successful clubs in Israel, and a less high profile Beitar. They all play at the same stadium, Bloomfield.

Israel's political connections with its football clubs are not simply notional. The most successful 'Beitar' club, Beitar Jerusalem, were saved from relegation in the 1970s by political interference.

Meanwhile, Bnei Sakhnin are the most successful Arab-Israeli club and draw support from a number of Arab countries, as well as from Israeli Arabs. Problems and violence at games are not uncommon, especially at fixtures with Beitar Jerusalem, the most openly anti-Arab club who have never signed an Arab player. Pro-Hamas chants from Bnei fans, countered by 'death to Arabs' chants from Beitar, are regularly heard. When, as Chairman of Beitar, Arkadi Gaydamak (a name familiar to followers of Portsmouth) made a donation to Bnei in a gesture of goodwill, goodwill is not exactly what he received in return from his own fans.

Italy has an especially large number of political derbies and rivalries. In 2007, a report commissioned by Italian police concluded that, of 128 professional clubs studied, 27 had 'deep' connections with fascism and 15 with communism. Rome's derby is probably the most intense in Italy partly because, unlike the big clubs in Milan and Turin, Rome's big two do not have significant support elsewhere in the country and they have been relatively unsuccessful over the years. Their derby is therefore more important and more parochial. The clubs don't have formal connections to political parties, but there is nevertheless a traditional political spilt between left-wing Roma and right-wing Lazio. Lazio's *Irriducibili* ultras are especially associated with fascism. One of their more 'delightful' banners at a Rome derby said '*team of blacks, curva of Jews*', even though Roma have no association with the Jewish faith anyway.

Added to the pot is a geographical separation, though both clubs play in the same stadium. Lazio is the name of the region in which Rome is located and Lazio tend to draw more support from wealthier outlying areas around the city, whereas Roma have more working class supporters in the city itself. Roma fans claim (incorrectly) that Lazio fans are not real Romans. Lazio were supposedly Mussolini's favourite club, although there is little evidence that Mussolini even liked football, let alone Lazio, until he saw the opportunities for a good photo shoot afforded by Italy's World Cup winning sides of 1934 and 1938. In fact, Italian fascists saw football (and rugby) as Anglo-Saxon imports to be stamped out. They invented their own game, Volata, as a potential replacement. Fortunately, football mad Italian fans put an end to that nonsense.

Like Lazio, *both* Verona clubs have right-wing traditions, whereas Arezzo, Pisa and especially Livorno are firmly from the left. A few years ago, there was a widely reported controversial incident in which Paulo Di Canio was seen to raise a fascist salute after scoring a goal for Lazio. Less widely reported was that the incident was not random. Lazio, firmly of the right, were playing Livorno, whose fans regularly drape themselves in Che Guevara flags to demonstrate their far-left credentials.

Milan's clubs share the San Siro, although supporters of AC Milan claim it be solely theirs because the club built the stadium before selling it to the local authority in 1935. Inter have always been tenants. There is a political split between the clubs, but it is a complex affair. AC Milan developed their support base from the working classes and the left. They also garnered the affections of southern Italians migrating to work in Milan although, as we will see shortly, Juventus are substantially more popular amongst southern migrants. Inter traditionally have drawn greater support from native Milanese, especially the middle classes, and they have long been associated with right-wing politics. The class division was reflected in their early nicknames, Milan's 'Spanners' against Inter's 'Braggers'.

Italian politics are never straightforward however and the Milan 'left' and working class versus Inter 'right' and middle class categorisation is a far cry from AC's origins. AC Milan were established as a cricket club by Englishmen from Nottingham (hence the Anglicised form of Milan in their name). The club was very exclusive and decidedly snooty about signing other foreigners. This led to a breakaway and the formation in 1908 of Internationale (ie welcoming all nations, although their core membership was Swiss). Later, incoming Fascists didn't like this 'un-Italian', international outlook on life at all and so Inter were forced to change their name and to adopt patriotic Milanese colours. The political delineation between the clubs is therefore largely a post-war phenomenon. More recently, the traditional divide has been blurred again because media mogul and former Prime Minister Silvio Berlussconi is the owner of AC Milan. Berlussconi may be described as many things, but being of the left is not one of them. Today there is no longer a great deal of difference in the class or political make-up of fans on San Siro's curva sud (Milan) and curva nord (Inter), although Inter are still seen by fans of other clubs as more right-wing. There is also no geographical split and so modern allegiance in Milan is largely determined by family tradition. In comparison with other Italian city derbies, Milan's derby is relatively low key and Inter in particular see Juventus as a major distraction, a la Liverpool/Manchester United.

Turin's split is more complex still. Torino are traditionally the left-wing club but, as in the case of Roma's followers, the tag doesn't prevent elements of Torino's ultras from taking decidedly right-wing stances at times. Juventus do not have right-wing ties as strong as either Lazio or Inter, but are definitely not associated with the left. The added complication comes from Juve's position as the most popular club in Italy. The 'Old Lady', as the club is endearingly nicknamed (except by Torino fans, who prefer the 'Old Bitch'), draw their support from across the country and are said to be the favourites of one-third of all Italians. They are especially popular amongst southern Italians who have migrated north. Juve's national popularity leads Torino to share a claim with Manchester City and others, such as Atletico Madrid, 1860 Munich and Eindhoven, to be the true clubs of their home cities, while their bigger local rivals are national institutions, rather than local clubs.

Although not as common as in Italy, there are numerous examples of political divisions between clubs in other parts of Europe. Frequently, politics combines with class and in such cases, as might be expected, the clubs of the workers tend to be left-wing and clubs supported by the elite tend to be right-wing politically. But it isn't always so. We have already seen that F.C Copenhagen are the middle class team in the city, but it is they who are associated with the left. Seville's derby is probably the bitterest single-city derby in Spain and there are three aspects to the rivalry. Betis were formed by people who defected from Sevilla after a prolonged dispute. Betis are seen as the club of the working classes and Sevilla of the middle classes. However, politically, Sevilla are left-wing and Betis hail from the right.

The history of football in Africa has many political strands. In colonial times, initially the game was played only by foreigners (almost always Europeans) to the exclusion of indigenous populations. Later, football was positively promoted by colonial powers as a means of encouraging 'team spirit' amongst African workers, in much the same way that Victorians encouraged 'muscular Christianity' amongst Britain's workers in the 19th Century. An added dimension in African football was that ethnic divisions were encouraged by colonial overlords, as a means of maintaining splits amongst African workers, in a classic divide and rule manoeuvre. There are many instances where those ethnic divisions continue in African derbies to this day. Later still, football clubs across Africa became rallying points for resistance to colonial rule and for the building of national identities. Following independence from European rulers, football clubs in emerging nations were subjected to political pressures of various sorts by their newly independent governments. Finally, as elsewhere in the world, African football clubs have been heavily influenced by commercial interests and by the buying-power of clubs from other continents (almost always Europeans – returning again).

Three examples will give a flavour of political developments in African football.

The first involves Al-Ahly and Zamalek from Cairo, Egypt, who were respectively the Number 1 and Number 2 ranked clubs in the whole of Africa in the 20th Century, according to the Confederation of African Football. Al-Ahly were one of the first, and certainly the biggest, overtly political football club on the continent. They were formed in 1907 by Egyptian nationalists; their name means 'National' – their colours, red, were designed to be symbolic of patriotic resistance to colonialism and by as early as 1924 they were an all-Egyptian club.

Zamalek were formed by expatriates. Early in their existence they were called Al Mukhatalat ('Mixed'), indicating that they were a mixed Egyptian and European side. Later still they were adopted by King Farouk and increasingly the derby rivalry became a political divide between nationalist Al-Ahly and royalist Zamalek.

Today, the 'Red Devils' of Al-Ahly are the club of Egypt's ordinary people and are said to be supported by fifty million souls in the Arab World. Zamalek are the club of the middle classes and are named after an upmarket area of Cairo, Zamalek Island in the River Nile. Ironically, it is Al-Ahly who are based in the luxury of the island. Zamalek have their headquarters in a decidedly less glamorous part of the city. The history of Cairo's derby is fraught with violence and controversy, so much so that the authorities frequently call upon foreign referees to officiate at games. Top Scottish referee Hugh Dallas said *"I've done many Old Firm matches and even they don't come close to this"*. Maybe – but the fact that Celtic v Rangers is so regularly used as the litmus test for derbies says a great deal about Glasgow's finest.

The second example involves Ghana's Asante Kotoko from Kumasi and Hearts of Oak from the capital, Accra, two of Black Africa's biggest clubs. They rank as third and seventh in the CAF list of Africa's top clubs of the 20th Century. Both have lesser derbies in their home cities, but the really big Ghanaian derby is when the two meet, not surprisingly as between them Asante and Hearts have shared over eighty percent of Ghana's league titles. Unfortunately, their derby holds one record that they would certainly not wish to have. In 2001, at a derby match witnessed by 70,000 fans, trouble started after Asante were denied a goal. Seats were ripped up and the police responded with tear gas in a stadium where most gates were locked. 126 people died in the ensuing panic. It is Africa's worst football disaster.

Kumasi is regional capital of the Ashanti region or, as it is seen by many, the Ashanti nation. Here is where the first big divide between the clubs lies. Hearts are a multi-ethnic, urban club, whereas Kotoko is a name associated with Ashanti nationalism. The club's badge and nickname, the 'Porcupine Warriors', are taken directly from Ashanti heritage, so much so that they had to get permission from the Ashanti King to use the symbols.

The second divide lies in politics. When Ghana gained independence, President Nkrumah sought to use football to transcend divisions in the country and to assert his government's power. Kotoko were seen as an unwelcome, ethnically based, anti-Nkrumah club. Hearts on the other hand were associated with the President's Party.

The situation led to severe problems for Asante, but it did not lead to favouritism for Hearts. Instead, in 1961, the President took what is one of the most directly politically biased steps ever taken in football. He established a new club, Real Republikans, who were expected to do for Ghana what Real Madrid were doing for Spain. 'In the national interest' Real, Republikans that is, were given the right to poach the best two players from each club. By 1962/3, they were champions, but it was to be their only title. Nkrumah was overthrown in 1966, Real were disbanded and Kotoko v Hearts dominance and mutual animosity were restored.

Our quick journey through Africa and its political history ends with a third example from the south of the continent and the modern day. The biggest derby in South Africa is probably the one between Kaiser Chiefs and the club from which the Chiefs emerged, Orlando Pirates. However, the derby that probably best demonstrates today's pressures on South African football does not belong to Soweto's giants. Not far away from Soweto, Pretoria is home to two of the most successful clubs in South Africa's modern Premier Soccer League, Mamelodi Sundowns and Supersport United. Both are products of major investment and are the equivalents of England's Chelsea and

Manchester City. Sundowns, the 'Brazilians' because of their club colours, are owned by a multi-millionaire. United are even more a product of commercialisation. They were pretty ordinary Pretoria City, until along came a company called Multichoice. City were transformed into United with the specific intention of the team being used, in the company's words, "*as a marketing tool for the Supersport TV Channel that broadcasts sport into Africa*". Premiership Champions for three seasons (2007 to 2010), United's nickname – the 'Swanky Boys' – says it all really.

Political divisions in football are not necessarily based upon support for political parties or political philosophies as such. In many countries political divisions have been institutionalised, because certain football clubs represent emanations of the state, for example the country's army or police or government ministries. There are dozens of examples, from Thailand's Royal Thai Navy to Uganda's Revenue Authority; Djibouti's Gendarmerie Nationale to Sri Lanka's Army. Although it is by no means always the case, usually institutionalised clubs attract support from those who are largely supportive of the regime in power. Opponents of the regime or those disaffected in some way tend to choose alternatives, *if* they have a choice.

The best known examples of these institutionalised divisions come from the former Communist bloc where, even though the regimes have fallen, past enmities live on. Many famous names from Eastern Europe were, or still are, army teams. They include Legia Warsaw, Steaua Bucharest, CSKA Moscow, CSKA Sofia and Partizan Belgrade. Perhaps most famous of all amongst the army teams, at least for older people, are Hungary's Honved, who provided many players for the side that slaughtered England twice in the 1950s and paved the way for profound changes in football's tactics. Most of the many 'Dynamos' in Eastern Europe were police clubs, often associated with secret police in the countries concerned.

There are many stories to be told of the impact on its football clubs of changing political fortunes in Eastern Europe. Two examples return us to derbies featured earlier. The first takes us back to Budapest, where we have already seen that the MTK versus Ferencvaros derby took on dark undertones during the Second World War. Fradi's premier derby, however, is with Ujpest, rather than MTK, and it is a derby fraught with political and class divisions. Not surprisingly, given their right-wing connections during the war, Ferencvaros were not looked upon favourably by the incoming Communist government after the war. In fact, for a short time, the club was merged with Honved and effectively disbanded. The club however continued to be the most popular in Hungary and attracted in particular a middle class and an anti-communist support base. It was no coincidence that early fighting in the Hungarian Uprising of 1956 took place near to Fradi's ground.

Ujpest, on the other hand, were more part of the mainstream and drew their support from the working class. They became the police team although, unusually, they were not made to change their name to Dynamo. Today, their derby with Ferencvaros is frequently associated with violence and too often punctuated with racist chanting. Anyone who thinks of Budapest derbies as minor affairs should take a few moments to look at a well known '*YouTube*' clip in which Ujpest's Viola Bulldogs ultras appear to shoot Fradi's goalkeeper.

In comparison with our second example, Budapest's derbies are indeed minor affairs. If ever a list is made of derby games that reflected troubled times, a contender for Number 1 would surely be the game in Zagreb on 13 May 1990 between Dynamo Zagreb and Red Star Belgrade. It took place shortly after the first multi-party elections in half a century, elections in which nationalist parties had been very successful. The crowd was relatively small, because a lot of people stayed away anticipating violence. Other people attended, specifically seeking violence. A certain Zeljko Raznatovic led three thousand of Red Star's 'Delije' ('Heroes') to Zagreb. They clashed with Dynamo's 'Bad Blue Boys' from the start. The police were powerless to stop the violence, hardly surprisingly given that a Dynamo player became a national hero in Croatia for kicking a policeman (who happened to be a Muslim).

Within months, the Yugoslavian state was falling apart, the Balkans War was in full flow and Europe looked on in horror as concentration camps made their unwelcome return to the continent. Mr. Raznatovic had become renowned as 'Arkan', leader of the Serbian paramilitary 'Tigers', who adopted Red Star anthems as their own. In the midst of this tragedy, Red Star had (and still have) another derby in their own city with Partizan. Partizan Belgrade were the club of Yugoslavia's Army, which made their position at the start of the conflict difficult to say the least. They were majority Serbian, but their role was to defend the rapidly disintegrating state.

Since the war, parting of the ways for the two countries, and hence for the Red Star v Dynamo derby, has not led to peace and harmony at home in either country. The Belgrade derby is rated as one of the biggest and most aggressive in the world (for example, rated at Number 10 by '*World Soccer*' in 2008 and at Number 4 by experts for the '*Daily Mail*' in 2009). Red Star fans, who already see themselves as heroes of the Serbian state, have now assumed the mantle of defenders of the faith, by forming an 'Orthodox brotherhood' with Olympiakos of Greece and Spartak Moscow.

As for Dynamo, oddly they were never really the primary nationalist Croatian club in the first place. They now have a fervent and frequently unpleasant derby with the club who have long worn Croatia's checks on their badge, Hajduk Split. Adding to disharmony is the animosity between Dalmatia, supposedly 'real' Croatia, represented by Hajduk, and its capital city represented by Dynamo. Dalmatia feels downtrodden and neglected by centralist politicians. Many feel that the former centralism of Belgrade has simply been replaced by Zagreb. What the Hajduk/Dynamo experience certainly shows is that football fans cannot survive without their derbies. When they had a common enemy in Serbia, the two Croatian clubs got on reasonably well. Now, they are completely at loggerheads.

It is worth emphasising again that football clubs in many parts of the world have been focal points for political causes, political parties or general anti-establishment political dissent. In Germany, there is a particularly good example of a club that always seems to have been in political dissent and who have always had a derby against bigger 'establishment' opponents, no matter what type of regime has been in power. Perennial 'outsiders' 1FC Union Berlin began life in 1906. Predominantly metalworkers, 'Iron Union' were thoroughly working class, at a time when Germany's autocratic elite were suspicious of football per se and were determined to ensure that, if they had to tolerate the unwelcome English import at all, it should be restricted to gentlemen amateur players. Union therefore were not welcomed with open arms when they took to Berlin's football stage alongside middle class clubs such as Viktoria 89 and Tennis Borussia.

After the tribulations of the Second World War, Berlin became a divided city, the embodiment of 'Cold War' politics. The Union club was split in two with a number of its players fleeing to the West to form a minor West German outfit, Sport-Club Union 06 Berlin. However, the greater part of the club stayed in East Berlin under the Communist regime. The regime and in particular the Stasi, East Germany's secret police, set about establishing a super club, Dynamo Berlin. They did so largely by foul means, for example by directing players from champions Dynamo Dresden to transfer to the capital's new club. Unsurprisingly, Stasi sponsorship led to huge success for Dynamo Berlin, who took the East German title ten times in succession from 1979 to 1988. Meanwhile Union, officially sponsored by the State's trade union movement, seethed with increasingly anti-Dynamo and anti-authority contempt.

The fall of Communism and re-unification of Germany saw Dynamo Berlin shrink to a shadow of their former, pampered glories, but they still exist in the fourth tier of German football. Higher up the German pyramid, Union have a 'new' 'establishment' club to despise, although not with the venom vented previously at Dynamo. Hertha Berlin in fact are not new. Far from it, the 'Old Lady' (Juventus do not have copyright on the name) were formed in 1892, but it is only since re-unification that they have become the establishment figure for Union fans.

Hertha have to be one of football's greatest underachievers. They are the only big club in the capital city and have the second biggest stadium in Germany. They are regularly top six in terms of attendances and, in 2010/11, although in the Second Division, their crowds were on a par with those of Manchester City. And yet Hertha have won the German championship only twice, the last time being in 1931 and they spend a yo-yo existence between the country's first and second tiers. Nevertheless, Hertha are everything Union are not. The clubs reflect the continuing enormous economic divide between wealthy former West Berlin, represented by Hertha and the impoverished, largely run-down East, where Union soldier on. After their experiences of different political systems over the past hundred years, perhaps Union Berlin fans should adopt The Who's song *'Won't get fooled again'* as their own. Its final line *"meet the new boss, same as the old boss"* seems to fit the bill perfectly.

Before leaving politically-based derbies, we should consider why politics has had so little influence on English League derbies. There are three principal reasons. First, Britain has not been subjected to colonial rule and there was therefore no need for a football club as a rallying point for nationalist sentiment, although a number of Welsh people may disagree. There was to be no equivalent of Al-Ahly, Mohun Bagan or Slavia Prague in the English League.

Second, in the early days, British political parties showed very little interest in football. Crucially, many political leaders and philosophers on the left positively frowned upon the sport and did not encourage working class people to adopt clubs. There was to be no equivalent of the Israeli TUC's support for Hapoel clubs or Peronist party affiliations with Boca Juniors.

Third, from the start, British sporting authorities in general, including football's leaders, tried desperately to adhere to the concept of keeping politics out of sport. In many senses it was an ideal to be admired but, at times, it has led to Britain's isolation and embarrassment. The problem with the idea that 'politics and sport don't mix' is not the idea itself, but that it often led Britons to fail to appreciate that most other nations see sport and politics as inextricably linked – *they* don't understand why *we* can't see that.

When examining **ethnic** divisions in football, most people would probably think of looking to Africa. African football does indeed have a number of ethnically based derbies. We have already seen Ghana's Asante Kotoko's bond with the Ashanti 'nation'. Algeria's top club, Jeunesse Sportive Kabylie, has long been associated with the minority Berber population, much to the chagrin of the authorities. In Kenya, AFC Leopards are closely allied with Abaluhya people, while Gor Mahia are linked to Luo people.

However, there is a less likely choice for the exploration of ethnic divides. Australia is a surprisingly good place to start. The country's top league is the A-League, which replaced the National Soccer League in 2003. As an example of Australian football's history, we will look at clubs in Melbourne. The city has two representatives in the A-League. Melbourne Victory are older, though formed only in 2003. They are the best supported club in Australia. Melbourne Heart were founded in 2008 and so, what will no doubt become a serious derby, has had little time to embed itself so far. Both are 'modern', geographically based clubs, with little evidence of ethnically based support, but that tells only part of the story.

In its early years, football in Australia was associated with immigration from Europe, so much so that it was considered un-Australian by many. It was frequently referred to as 'wogball' by those who seemingly had quickly forgotten the fact that they were not exactly indigenous themselves. Clubs were formed not simply as outlets for sporting activities, but as focal points for bonding and maintaining ethnic minority communities. Melbourne had an array of ethnically based clubs, some of which have folded, but others are still going strong and are very well supported at the level below the A-League. Examples include(d) South Melbourne (from the Greek community and originally called Hellas), Melbourne Knights (Croatian and the name of their supporters' club, known as MCF, means Melbourne Croatian Fans), Footscray JUST (which stood for

Jugoslav United Soccer Team), Heidelberg United (despite the German name, a Greek supported club), Preston Lions (Macedonian), Springvale White Eagles (Serbian) and Mooroolbark (originally Dutch, but later British).

If these clubs are so ethnically based, readers may wonder why they now have such anodyne names. Why did they not stick with Hellas and Croatia etc.? The answer is that the authorities had always been concerned about the divisive nature of Australian football but, when war in the Balkans inflamed existing animosities still further, their concern began to verge on panic. So, in 1996, Soccer Australia demanded that all clubs neutralise their names and emblems, in an attempt to open up the clubs to broader fan bases. In many senses, Australia's football authorities have been successful, especially at the highest level in the A-League, but neutralisation has been fiercely resisted by a number of clubs which still firmly retain their ethnic affiliations. So determined is this resistance that rivalries have grown based simply upon the fact that clubs are or are not ethnically based. South Melbourne, for example, have added to their existing derbies against Heidelberg (an all Greek affair) and Preston Lions (because of the Macedonian question), a dislike of Perth Glory, merely because Glory were established clearly as a non-ethnic club.

Having seen how Australia's ethnic based football developed, it will now be no surprise to find that Canada has had a similar experience. It has football clubs called Toronto Croatia, Portugal FC and Serbian White Eagles. Canada also has York Region Shooters and St. Catherine's Wolves, both of which sound neutral or English. In fact, both are Italian. Shooters play in the Italian national colours and were previously called Italia Shooters. The Wolf in Wolves refers to Rome and the team play in Roma's colours. The difference between Australia and Canada is that the Canadians have not sought to suppress ethnic divisions. On the contrary, for good or bad, the Canadian Soccer League embraced them by creating an 'International Division' to contain the ethnically based clubs.

In addition to class-based, political, religious and ethnic feuds, the world has a number of derbies that are just ***quirky or positively bizarre***. Three are highlighted here.

The first isn't a foreign derby, but it deserves a mention because it is the most regularly played derby of them all. The Isles of Scilly Football League consists of just two teams, in the yellow corner Garrison Gunners and in the claret Woolpack Wanderers. They play each other every week throughout the league season and, for good measure, meet again in two cup competitions. There is another unique aspect to the league, in that the captains get together at the start of each season to select teams from the available pool of players, thereby ensuring that the league is always competitive – a bit like the old school playground method of selection, in which case hopefully there is counselling available for the last man chosen.

Second is the derby in Hamburg between Hamburg SV and St.Pauli. It is quirky largely because St.Pauli are one of the most unusual, if not the oddest, club in Europe. In part, the split between the two is political, but not because of any political connections involving Hamburg SV. St.Pauli, on the other hand are overtly political and, since the 1980s, have developed a cult following amongst mainstream left-wingers and not so mainstream punks, anarchists and anti-establishment groups. The club itself, as well as its supporters, have regularly taken a stance against racism, sexism, fascism and homophobia. Maybe as a result, the club have more female fans than any in Germany. St. Pauli's skull and crossbones logo has become an alternative fashion item, as have their very unusual brown shirts. The club is based near Hamburg's night spots and the city's famous red-light district which all adds to the offbeat image. It is an image the 'Buccaneers' happily cultivate, for example by organising a football tournament called the FIFI Wild Cup, in which they played as the Republic of St. Pauli against teams from Greenland, Tibet and Zanzibar.

Hamburg SV are positively tame by comparison, although they do for instance have a dedicated graveyard for their fans, which is covered in turf taken from their original pitch. They also have a link with Glasgow Rangers. It is not a meaningful political or religious link, but exists because St. Pauli are linked to Celtic, though St.Pauli do not have a religious connection either.

The third example isn't a derby at all, at least not in any conventional sense. It involves the tragic case of Paris St. Germain. Given its size, it is strange that Paris has only one major football club. As a result, PSG have a huge catchment area and one of the biggest followings in France, second only to Olympique Marseilles. PSG have an intense first city versus second city rivalry with Marseilles, but geography dictates that this cannot be a derby and their rivalry isn't the subject of this tale. The oddity in focus is that PSG, or at least the Parisians' supporters, have a fierce derby of sorts – with themselves. It should be said from the start that PSG's experience is not unique. As we have already seen, across the world there are examples where groups of supporters of the same club occasionally fight each other. However, in recent years, the fans of PSG, unwittingly aided and abetted by the club itself, took internecine hostilities to a whole new plane, where divisions between PSG fans became dangerously institutionalised.

It all started with good intentions. The club is fairly new (established in 1970 from a merger of previous clubs) and in their keenness to build up their fan base, PSG's powers that be encouraged everyone they could. They didn't worry too much when undesirable political elements and others began to take hold in parts of their stadium. Eventually, it became clear that the Boulogne end of the ground had become home to many racist ultras and it was difficult for ethnic minorities to go into the stand. At this point, the authorities made what was perhaps a well-intentioned decision, but one that ultimately proved fatal – literally. Rather than tackle the issue of potential no-go areas in the Boulogne end, PSG took positive action to encourage fans from ethnic minorities to make their home in the other end of the ground, d'Auteuil. Not surprisingly, the authorities found that not everyone is well-intentioned. The practical impact of their decision was to confirm the Kop de Boulogne as a place where, in the words of a Boulogne ultra, "*it remains an unwritten rule that nobody of colour enters, be it supporters or stewards*".

The scene was set for a series of clashes which gradually escalated in their severity. For example, in 2006, on their way to a match in Nantes, the two sets of PSG fans fought each other with the result that, as well as numerous injuries, a motorway service station went up in flames. Ultimately, in 2010, the inevitable happened. Boulogne fought d'Auteuil in advance of the big PSG v Marseilles fixture, ironically a match boycotted by Marseilles fans, and a thirty-eight year old PSG fan died, killed by supporters of his own club.

Recriminations followed of course. Various ultra groups were banned and there was even talk of PSG being disbanded in order to make a new start. However, the ongoing vehemence of the PSG v PSG 'derby' is best illustrated by an incident which occurred only weeks after the fatality. A press conference, arranged in support of the country's bid to host Euro 2016, was interrupted by dozens of protesting PSG fans. Their beef? It was fans from d'Auteuil complaining that sanctions taken against them were harsher than those imposed upon the Boulogne end.

And so we return to **geography**. Some English League clubs in large part represent areas of their cities. If you are from south Bristol, the odds are that you will be a City fan (Bristol City were originally called Bristol South End). Most Port Vale fans are from northern parts of Stoke. People from north Sheffield are usually Wednesday Owls. South Bristolian Rovers' fans, south Stoke Valiants or north Sheffield Blades are not unusual, but they are distinct minorities.

The vast majority of English League clubs are simply the sole representatives of their towns or cities, but there are a few with broader reference points. For example, Norwich and Ipswich represent neighbouring counties. Welsh clubs fly the flag for a nation, although there is no single club that can claim to be *the* Welsh standard bearer.

In other countries, there are many examples where clubs play on behalf of geographical areas much wider than their home cities. In the Netherlands, certain clubs represent regions. A good example is Heerenveen from Friesland, a province in the north of the country. Like Wales, Friesland has its own language, spoken by much of the population, but not by all. Unfortunately, Friesland is viewed as bumpkin-land in other parts of the Netherlands, making Heerenveen more equivalent to the 'Tractor Boys' of Ipswich than, say, Cardiff City. Heerenveen go so far as to wear the Friesian 'national' flag on their shirts and to sing the Friesian 'national' anthem before games. Heerenveen's pose as the 'national' team of Friesland is not accepted by die-hard fans of Cambuur, who hail from Friesland's capital, Leeuwarden. Cambuur historically are the bigger club, although they have never experienced a level of sustained success to compare with Heerenveen's recent triumphs and, in the past few years, Cambuur have fallen upon hard times.

Heerenveen therefore have two types of derby. One is a normal derby within Friesland when they clash with Cambuur, in what is an urban versus rural contest, Leeuwarden being positively metropolitan in comparison with the rest of Friesland. The other is when Heerenveen don the mantle of being Friesland's 'national' side when playing against teams from neighbouring provinces. This applies especially to meetings with fellow northerners Groningen, who similarly see themselves as flag-bearers, not only for the City of Groningen, but also for their Dutch-speaking province. Heerenveen play Groningen in the Netherlands' 'derby of the north' (neither of them is in Holland by the way).

As an aside, in case anyone thinks Heerenveen is just a rural backwater, it is worth looking at their sporting facilities. The town has a population of only just over forty thousand people and yet it has a twenty-seven thousand all-seater football stadium, which is almost always full on match days, and an indoor, twelve thousand capacity, ice hockey and speed skating arena. Add to that a gymnastics stadium and a swimming pool and tiny Heerenveen has sporting facilities to rival most British cities.

Similar, but more intense, provincial divides exist over the border in Belgium. Belgium seems such a sensible country at the very heart of the European Community, but in fact Belgium has divisions so strong that they occasionally threaten the very existence of the state. The country has three provinces. The southern part, Wallonia, is French speaking and on the whole is poorer than Flanders, the Dutch speaking north. The Walloons feel neglected or even downtrodden by the Flemish majority. The third province is the capital Brussels. It is surrounded by Dutch speaking Flanders and is officially bi-lingual, but actually is eighty-five percent French speaking.

All these differences and mutual antipathies are reflected in the country's football derbies. The three biggest clubs are Anderlecht, from a run-down district in the capital; Club Brugge, from Flanders and Standard Liege, from Wallonia. Each has local derby rivals. Anderlecht have FC Brussels and an older rivalry with Union Saint-Gilloise; Club have Cercle Brugge and Standard have FC Liege, but the real derbies occur when the three big clubs clash with each other, as representatives of their different provincial communities.

In comparison to the next case, Heerenveen, Groningen and the big Belgian clubs are relatively tiny examples of clubs representing regions or 'nations' within nations. The daddy of them all is Barcelona. According to footballderbies.com and a 'World Soccer' survey in 2008, Barcelona versus Real Madrid is the biggest derby in world football even though, by any reasonable definition of the term local, this is not a derby at all. Barcelona and Madrid are over three hundred miles apart and their regions don't have a common border. Nevertheless, such is the importance of their history and of games between the clubs that it is difficult not to afford them special 'derby' status.

Barca are Catalunya (or Catalonia). The club is the embodiment of Catalan identity, culture and many would argue nationhood. When he was manager of Barcelona, Sir Bobby Robson said that leading a team out against Real Madrid felt like leading the Catalan army to war. The historical background to this rivalry to top all rivalries has been described many times and is usually portrayed as the 'good' of republican Barcelona against the 'bad' of Franco supported, fascist Real. In part this is a fair representation. Barcelona and

Catalonia suffered very badly under the extreme right-wing regime of Franco, following his victory in the Spanish Civil War. It was a victory achieved largely thanks to massive military support provided by Hitler and Mussolini. Barca's left-wing President was murdered by Franco's supporters at the beginning of the Civil War. After the war, Franco's ruthless regime systematically suppressed regional identities and anything associated with 'non-Spanish' cultures. Flags, regional songs, languages and dialects were banned. The Barcelona club and its colours, an adaptation of the colours of the outlawed Catalan flag, became a rallying point for continued resistance to the regime.

The part of the familiar Barca v Real story that is accurate is therefore the description of the regime's suppression of Catalonia generally and of F.C. Barcelona specifically. The part of the story that is not entirely fair is that which relates to Real Madrid's role in Franco's regime. It was certainly the case that the regime adopted Real as its gleaming white club after the war. The achievements of Real were used as an advert for Spain at a time when Franco was very unpopular in most of the world. On one occasion when Barca, leading 3-0 from the first leg, were due to play Real in the second leg of a cup tie, Barca players received a visit from the regime's 'representatives', who made it more than clear that Franco would like to see a Real victory. Barcelona took the 'hint' and lost 11-1.

However, in general, Franco, like Mussolini and Hitler, was not that interested in football anyway. He was also deeply suspicious of any large gathering of people, unless it had been arranged specifically to honour him or his party. Therefore, while Franco's hatred of Barcelona and everything the club represented was undoubted, his love and support for Real was less clear. In fact, initially, the favoured club was Atletico Madrid, because they had been merged with the regime's air force team. Furthermore, Real's roots lay largely in republicanism. Certainly, a number of Real's big-wigs, especially Santiago Bernabeu, after whom their stadium is named, were fervent fascist supporters. But most people in Madrid, including thousands of ordinary Real supporters, fought to the end on behalf of the Republic and against Franco's troops. In fact, because it was republican held and the capital city, Madrid suffered considerably more at the hands of Franco's fascists than did Barcelona during the Civil War. When Franco's troops finally took the capital, one of their first acts was to murder Real's President, just as they had Barca's President at the beginning of the war. It was only after the war that Franco's regime favoured Real as a centrepiece of his centralist state.

Barcelona have another rival much closer to home who provide a genuine derby by any definition. Espanyol (meaning 'Spanish' in Catalan) are from Barcelona and have provided a local counter-balance to Barca for a long time. Until the 1990's, they were known as Espanol, the Spanish name for 'Spanish', and it was with considerable reluctance that they added the 'y' to transform the name into its Catalan equivalent, in acknowledgement of their home city. Espanyol perform an unusual role in the world of football derbies. In one sense, they are underdogs in Barcelona, and they don't even enjoy the respect of being Barca's biggest rivals. In this regard they are similar to, say, Notts County.

However, in another sense, Espanyol are seen as overlords; symbols in Barcelona itself of the Spanish state, of which Catalonia remains only a part and a reluctant one at that.

It is sometimes assumed that animosity between Barcelona and Espanyol stems in part from Espanyol's 'provocative' name. However, the Parakeets were not called 'Spanish' as an insult to Catalonia. The origin of the name comes from the fact that Espanyol were the first Spanish club to field only Spanish players, whereas other clubs at the time, including Barca, were built around ex-pats. Barca were founded by a Swiss businessman and Espanyol's original constitution dedicated the club to oppose Barca's *foreign* nature, *not* their Catalan identity. Fairly quickly, however, as the country lurched towards its cataclysmic civil war, Espanyol became increasingly fervent Spanish nationalists, as Barcelona became the embodiment of those demanding regional autonomy from the Spanish nation. Violent clashes occurred from the 1920s onwards, long before the development of serious animosity between Barca and Real fans. To this day, Espanyol have remained steadfastly Spanish in every sense. Barca steadfastly have not.

Real Madrid have their local rivals too and there is a strong element of both class and political divisions between Madrid's clubs. Real are seen as upmarket and part of the establishment. Their right-wing tag has developed in Madrid, as well as in Barcelona. Atletico Madrid were founded by Basques and were linked to Athletic Bilbao, with who they shared club colours and, for many years, the Anglicised 'Athletic' name. Today Atletico are more working class and anti-establishment, in opposition to Real. The smaller Rayo Vallecano hail from the Madrid suburb of Vallecas which has strong left-wing traditions and was always a base for resistance to Franco.

Barcelona may be the biggest example of a club representing a 'nation' within a nation, but Catalunya's degree of autonomy within Spain pales into insignificance when compared with our next example. Most people have never heard of the European 'state' of Transnistra, unsurprisingly as it doesn't exist – officially that is. But, following a secessionist civil war in Moldova, for the past twenty years Transnistra has had borders, its own police force, army and parliament and has issued its own passports, even though most other nations don't recognise them. Pro-Russian Transnistra is one of a number of unrecognised 'states' within states which arose as the result of the breakup of the Soviet Union. Generally speaking, Transnistra has as little to do with Moldova as it can, but its football clubs play in the Moldovan League and one of them, Sheriff Tiraspol from Transnistra's 'capital', are outstanding. They have been Moldovan champions eleven times in the past twelve years and represent the country in the Champions' League, even though representing Moldova is the last thing that Sheriff want to do.

Both Barca and Sheriff represent regions/'nations' within recognised states but clubs representing regions are not always confined within the boundaries of one country. Sometimes they represent regions that straddle national boundaries. Silesia, for example, has never been an independent state. It has a harrowing history of invasion, uprisings, forced repatriations and mass murder, all connected with the desire of central European powers to get their hands on Silesia's wealth of natural resources, especially her coal. Today Silesia is largely in Poland, but parts of the region lie in the Czech Republic and Germany. Thousands of people in these countries describe themselves in official censuses as Silesian 'nationals', even though Silesia has never been a nation. History is reflected in Silesian football. Poland's two most successful clubs, Ruch Chorzow and Gornik Zabrze, are from the region. Gornik ('Miner') and Ruch ('Motion') have fourteen Polish League titles each, though they've been stuck together on that total for over twenty years. They share a fierce 'derby of Silesia' against each other, but also have a common bond as representatives of the region. This bond is shared, not only with fellow Polish Silesian clubs, such as Polonia Bytom and GKS Katowice, but also with clubs across the national border, like Banik Ostrava, one of the Czech Republic's leading lights.

At an even grander geographical level, there are examples of clubs that represent long-established countries, or regions which have become countries more recently. For convenience, Monaco, a club from an independent state, play in the French League. In the old Soviet Union, the Supreme League consisted of a handful of Moscow based clubs, together with clubs like Dynamo Kiev and Dynamo Minsk who embodied the spirit of large states within the Union (Ukraine and Belarus respectively). Those states are now independent and have their own leagues.

In terms of representing the largest geographical area of all, there is one club to trump all others – because it plays its football on behalf of an entire *continent*. There are many Asian based clubs in Turkey's League, as well as ones in the European part of the country, but only one of the big three Turkish clubs has its base on the Asian side of the country's biggest city, Istanbul. The beautifully named Fenerbahce (the name means 'Lighthouse Garden') line up for Asia every time they play derbies against the big guns of Galatasaray or Besiktas, both of who hail from the European side of the city. Istanbul's derbies have other connotations too. Both European based clubs are associated with the middle classes and Besiktas have a reputation as left-wingers politically. Fener, or the Yellow Canaries (Norwich City alas are not the biggest 'Canaries' in the world), are the club of the working classes. They were founded in secret, as it was illegal for Turks to play football in the days of the Ottoman Empire. Their original colours and badge were yellow and white and were chosen to replicate an image of daffodils swaying gently in the gardens of the white lighthouse – very sweet. That is, however, probably the only thing that could possibly be considered 'sweet' about Fenerbahce. Their derbies with Besiktas would be considered big, noisy and violent by any normal standards, but their derbies with Galatasaray, the better-supported and more successful of the two clubs from the European side of the Bosphorus, are absolutely mega events. They produce some of the most thrilling and at times terrifying spectacles in world football. Violence on match days is common, not only at the grounds or in the streets of Istanbul, but also in towns and cities across Turkey, such is the nation's passion for the clubs.

Fixtures between Fenerbahce and Galatasary are known as 'Intercontinental Derbies' and our geographical romp around derbies of the world ends with an image of Fenerbahce fans, at the start of a derby, unfurling a huge banner that stretches the entire length of their stand. Against a background of their dark blue and yellow club colours, in which the yellow is transposed over the blue, as in rays of the sun, the banner (in English) reads simply 'THE RISING SUN OVER EUROPE'. Beat that!

Reflections

Having looked at examples of derbies that are either, sad, frightening, plain bonkers or all three combined, it would be tempting to breathe a sigh of relief that such divisions don't exist here in the UK. How lucky we are! However, consider these facts:-

First, ask anyone in the world to name the most divisive religious derby on the planet and a majority would immediately respond, Celtic versus Rangers – it may not be in the English League, but it is an example from our own country.

Second, take a look at videos of ultras in grounds across Europe, Asia and South America. There are three common traits. Firstly, the noise of firecrackers, drums and horns, and the smoke and flames, are way beyond anything you have ever witnessed in an English League ground. Secondly, the violence is at times terrifying and is worse than you've seen in England and Wales for years. However, finally, the banners waved by ultras and the names of ultras themselves are frequently in English. In part this is simply because English is the international language but, in part, it is because many ultras took their lead from England – they learnt from us and they think it is 'hard' to have English names.

Third, for all their terrible feuds, all Lebanese clubs still play in Lebanon; Mohammedan Sporting, India's leading Islamic club, still play in India; Bnei Sakhnin, the country's leading Arab club, still play in Israel. No matter what their class, political, religious or ethnic differences may be, clubs still play together in their own national leagues. In the *whole world*, there is only one club to have found political/religious divides so difficult in their own country that they chose to play their football elsewhere. That example comes from right here in the United Kingdom. Derry City, from Northern Ireland, play their football in the Republic of Ireland, having abandoned the Northern Ireland League years ago, for difficult political and religious reasons and after years of trouble at certain games.

Problems in Northern Ireland have dogged the country's football for decades. Belfast Celtic, a bigger, more successful nationalist/Catholic club than Derry, gave up the ghost and disbanded in 1949. Cliftonville, a more modest club from the same community and the oldest club in Northern Ireland, have remained in the league. However, for many years during the 'Troubles', they were unable to play games against premier Protestant clubs at their home ground, the evocatively named *Solitude*. It was too dangerous. We would do well to remind ourselves that, odd as many foreign football attitudes and practices may be, nowhere else except in our own country have conflicts led to clubs choosing the course of action taken by the Candystripes of Derry City.

HALF-TIME BREAK

In the early days of football, half-time breaks were sometimes used to switch codes from home team rules to those of the away team. These days, the primary purpose of breaks at derby matches is surely medical – it gives supporters a chance to lower their blood pressures for a short period at least. There are options at half-time. Fans can join ludicrously long queues for 'refreshments'. However, heart rates will rise again. Will you join the wrong queue, the slowest one? Will you get back in time for the start of the second half? If you don't get back in time, it will undoubtedly bring bad luck. You dare not risk it.

In any event, the beer is bound to be warm and weak and appear to be coming from pipes suspiciously close to the urinals. Tea is not an alternative, as it's made from the same ingredients famously used by Baldrick in Blackadder. The 'orange juice' is so full of chemicals that, at best, you'll come out in a rash and at worst you will be rendered blind within the hour. Perhaps the referee had been drinking the stuff. What else could explain his failure to see the blatant shove on your centre forward that should clearly have led to a penalty in the first half. As a result, you're trailing 1-0 to the half-wits from down the road – Monday doesn't look like being a good day.

As for food, you pay three quid for a pie which you swear is a tortoise. However you can be confident that it isn't a *real* tortoise, as the genuine creatures cost far more than the mixed animal slurry from which the pies are actually made. You reach for the Mars bar you brought with you. You've lost it. What else have you lost? Where are your house keys? You fidget in your seat. Sir Alex Ferguson famously described the tense nature of the final weeks of a season as "*squeaky bum time*". In derbies, bums squeak *all* the time. If the devil was seeking a Faustian deal with you, now would be the time for him to make an offer – a turnaround 2-1 win, in exchange for your soul.

By now, cheerleaders are on the pitch. It is freezing and they are purple. English League cheerleaders consistently have precise weight to age proportions of one stone per year of age. The only ones old enough to be watched without a furtive sense of unease are the size of the mini-bus you arrived in. You console yourself with the thought that American cheerleaders are older and more beautiful only because, if they were not, no-one would turn up to see what laughingly passes as sport in the States.

In desperation you turn to the match programme. You have no idea why you bought it. It's just tradition, like the hot Bovril you bought earlier, a product you would never dream of drinking at any other time. The programme has been where it always is, under your seat. Amid the usual dross from the chairman and the outpourings of the "*still optimistic*" (despite all) manager, the programme contains an interview with the club's latest signing, a six-foot-seven Latvian. Usefully, he explains that his favourite colour is puce and he keeps a pet tarantula. He loves his baby daughter, who he named Chablis because it has more class than Chardonnay. Quickly turning the page, you come to the "*we've run out of anything better to print, so we'll have a*"....... club quiz.

Question 1. Which player began his career with Forfar Athletic reserves and by an amazing co-incidence likes haggis?

You give in. Thank goodness, half-time is over and players are coming back on the pitch. You touch your lucky socks and promise to get a tattoo of the scorer of the winner if your heroes can turn things round in the second half, even if it is the six-foot-seven Latvian.

If you think the above is going to save you from a quiz in this book's half-time break, it is not...

Welcome to the **DERBY DAZE QUIZ** (all questions relate to the sixty English League derbies up to the end of the 2011/12 season).

Q1. Which was the first derby to be played in a national competition?

Q2. Which derby rivals are furthest apart geographically?

Q3. Which derby has been played most often?

Q4. In which derby has neither club ever completed a 'double' by winning both derby clashes in the League in a single season?

Q5. Which club suffered the biggest home defeat ever in any top-tier English League match and, to make matters worse, did so when playing against their bitterest derby rivals? And why did the defeated side have the last laugh?

Q6. Which derby features a club who were the Magpies *against* a club who play at St. James's Park?

Q7. Who have the worst record of all against their derby rivals, in terms of the gap between total derby games won and lost?

Q8. Which club have the best record of all in cup matches against their derby foes?

Q9. Which club lost its first six encounters with their derby opponents and conceded thirty-one goals in doing so?

Q10. Which derby features the two most itinerant clubs in the League (i.e. the two to have had most home grounds)?

Q11. Which derby is closest run in head-to-head clashes between the clubs?

Q12. Which club responded to the plight of their derby rivals (who had been punished for illegal payments) by buying many of their star players at knock-down prices?

Q13. Which two clubs have erected statues at their grounds of players who never played for them, but who were star players for their greatest derby enemies?

Q14. In most cases, if a club has won more League titles and cups etc, they also lead in head-to-head wins against their derby rivals. But there are exceptions where the underdog leads in derby victories. Which club has the best record in derby games against opponents who have better overall records?

Q15. Which is the closest finish in the League between derby foes and what was particularly important about the outcome?

Q16. Whose fans have been waiting longest for a league or cup win over their bitterest derby rivals?

Q17. Only four footballers have been knighted purely for their football prowess (ie not including people such as Sir Alex Ferguson, who was a decent player but was knighted for his managerial achievements). Two of the four knights played against each other in which derby?

Q18. Which is the oldest derby in the south of England?

Q19. Which English derby originally featured clubs nicknamed the Purdown Poachers versus the Garibaldis?

Q20. Finally, one for connoisseurs. In one season, two fervent derby rivals finished equal on points, but the club with the better goal difference (and better goal average) finished the season one place below their bitter rivals. Why? and who were the derby rivals involved?

Answers may be found in the text of the second half. Alternatively, if you are just far too excited to wait, the answers are on page 262.

SECOND HALF

Welcome back.

The second halves of football matches are sometimes referred to as the 'business end' of games. Sparring is over and the real thing begins. And so it is with this book. Having journeyed through the background to great derbies in the first half, the second half concentrates upon finding and describing the best derbies in the English League.

Searching for the English League's best derbies

There have been several previous attempts to measure passion in football derbies and to determine which are the biggest and most competitive. The most comprehensive study of attitudes in English League derbies is probably contained in the *Football Rivalries Report 2008*, produced by New Football Pools (www.footballpools.com). It canvassed the opinions of six thousand fans and asked questions about the strength of derby affiliations. It is in most senses an excellent piece of work and is well worth reading.

Footballderbies.com runs a poll which constantly updates and measures the heat of derbies across the world, as voted for by fans themselves. It allows anyone to judge any derby and to mark it on a scale of 1 to 10, with 10 being 'one of the best matches in the world' and 1 meaning 'you wouldn't even call it a rivalry'. Each derby is then given an average score of its importance. The democratic, grass roots nature of the exercise is to be welcomed. Unfortunately, fans being who they are, assessments of the importance of other peoples' derbies are not necessarily impartial. For example, 43% of people considering Manchester's derby apparently conclude that it rates as 1 out of 10 in its importance. Perish the thought that this might have anything to do with the mischievous antics of fans from down the motorway in Liverpool, rather than objective judgements by neutral observers. In fairness to footballderbies.com, results from the public vote are added to the views of an expert panel before final average scores are included in a league table. This tends to make overall outcomes more realistic.

The conclusions of these two attempts to assess English League derbies are often similar but sometimes differ significantly. For example, West Brom v Wolves tops the New Football Pools survey, but is rated at only 12th in the footballderbies.com list (in June 2012, remembering that this list is updated). Top scorer in the footballderbies.com table is Sunderland v Newcastle, though the Tyne/Wear derby makes it only to Number 9 in the New Football Pools list.

(People who are not interested in the fine details of how derbies are assessed in this book may wish to take a break here and jump straight to the Derby League Table on page 118).

Come the crunch, any attempt to classify the relative importance and fervour of football derbies is bound to be subjective, at least in part, and conclusions in this book may have no greater merit than earlier studies. The ranking of derbies depends upon what is measured and which measures are considered to be most important. The following Derby League Table starts from the premises that, for a derby to be considered up there with the very best in the English League, it has to be:-

(a) a primary derby for both clubs involved.

(b) very passionate.

(c) played often and regularly over the years.

(d) close and competitive, both historically and in recent times.

All derbies are strong in one, two or three of these characteristics or they wouldn't be worthy of the name 'derby', but only the *very best* are strong in all four characteristics. There will be readers who may not agree with the starting premises. They may argue that things like frequency of derby clashes and the closeness of clubs' respective records are irrelevant. For them, all that matters is focus and passion. It is an understandable point of view. There are, however, a number of problems associated with concentrating solely upon focus and passion.

First, both are difficult to measure objectively. As will be seen shortly, in Factor Ten used in this book, it is possible to find a few measures of focus and passion – arguments between clubs; the number of arrests at derby matches etc. But, if these were the only factors taken into account when deciding upon the best derbies, there would be a danger of overemphasising hooliganism and negativity.

Second, in any event the frequency of derby clashes *is* important. Rarely played derby games are often more passionate, in a one-off sense, than derbies played every year. However, do these one-off, rare opportunities really make up for missing the joy (or despair) of meeting local foes regularly?

Third, if derbies are not occurring regularly, it is because clubs are in different divisions. This in turn means that the top dog for a particular year is known before the season has even started. Surely, one of the beauties of football derbies is the constant competitive jockeying for position with the enemy.

Fourth, the same competitive arguments can be had on a longer term basis, if the historical records of clubs are close – *"we've won the cup more times"*; *"ah, but the cup doesn't count, we've finished higher in the league more often"*... and so on. If derbies are not close-run competitive affairs historically, one set of fans can only ever look on in envy, while the other lot gloatingly wave silverware in their opponents' faces.

Finally, if a derby is not played regularly and is not competitive for a long period of time, eventually the top dog tends to look elsewhere for a more equal contest. The underdog may still be as passionate as ever about their derby, but it takes two to tango. Probably the greatest insult of all is to be deemed unworthy of being the biggest derby rival of your nearest neighbours.

There may be other readers who judge the basic premises above from a completely different standpoint. They may take a modern management view and argue that, if you can't measure it objectively and accurately, a factor should not be included in the calculation. Therefore, as it is difficult to measure passion, ferocity and focus in derbies, those factors shouldn't be taken into account. Only measurable competitiveness should count. Again, this is an understandable point of view, but ranking derbies solely upon objective, competitive measures throws up odd conclusions. There are a number of instances where clear and important primary derbies would be ranked well below relatively minor general derbies, if only objective measures such as frequency of meetings, competitiveness, equality of silverware etc are taken into account.

To summarise, in making judgements to determine the English League's top derbies, the ***frequency and competitiveness of a derby AND its passion and focus*** are taken into account in the list below. The basic starting premises outlined earlier have been translated into ten factors. Most, but not all, can be objectively measured. Certain factors are more important than others and so weightings have been applied where necessary.

The ten factors are:-

No. 1 **'We'll meet again'** – this factor takes into account how often derby rivals have met. The more often, the higher the Derby League Table (DLT) score for their derby.

No. 2 **'Six pointers'** – No. 2 considers the head-to-head record of clubs in derby games against each other. The closer their records, the higher the DLT score.

No. 3 **'Bragging rights'** – this factor takes into account the records of clubs in finishing higher than each other in the League. The closer their records, the higher the DLT score.

No. 4 **'We've got more gongs than you'** – this factor measures the success of each club in league and cup competitions and the amount of silverware each has won. The closer the records of clubs, the higher their DLT score.

No. 5 **'Time at the top'** – No. 5 records the number of years spent in the top tier by each club. Where neither club has spent any significant time in the top tier, the clubs' records in the second tier have been taken into account and so on. The closer their records, the higher the DLT score.

No. 6 **'Modern love'** – this factor measures competitiveness in recent times, on the grounds that, for derbies to be high in the final overall list, they should not live off historic records alone, but should be vibrant contests more *recently*. The closer their records recently, the higher the DLT score.

No. 7 **'How long has this been going on?'** – No. 7 is a relatively lightly weighted factor. It charts when the derby began and therefore how long the bitterness has had to fester. The older the derby, the greater the DLT score.

No. 8 **'Bad Blood'** – by their very nature derbies are full of bad blood, but this relatively small factor takes into account whether or not there are any special reasons from the past to make their rivalry even worse. The greater the evidence of early bad blood, the higher the DLT score.

No. 9 **'Who cares?'** – this factor measures the derby's size and is based upon objective information, such as attendances. It also includes more subjective assessments of how many people care about the result. The higher the numbers who care, the higher the DLT score.

No. 10 **'Ferocious Focus'.** This final, very important and heavily weighted factor is based upon a collection of pointers, such as violence and arrests at derby games, the lack of direct transfers between clubs, disputes and anything else which gives a feel for their mutual antipathy. The factor also measures the strength of focus in a derby – do the clubs focus on each other as their clear primary derby, or does one or both of them have other derby rivals? The clearer the focus and greater the ferocity, the higher the DLT score for their derby.

In addition to scores in the ten factors, the final outcome is modified to take into account two things. First, a derby may be very close in most or all ten factors, but one club may be ahead in all competitive elements whereas, in another derby, dominance may be shared. Shared dominance is scored more highly. Secondly, a derby may be competitive in terms of its overall historical record, but it may not have been competitive regularly throughout history. It may be characterised by one club being dominant for a long period and then the other club gaining ascendancy for a similarly long period. A derby gets a higher score if it has been *consistently competitive* over time.

Before declaring the final outcome – hopefully tension is building – three further notes of explanation are required. First, two contests, Nottingham Forest v Derby and Liverpool v Manchester United may not be accepted as true derbies in some quarters. The option is open to readers to discount them, but most commentators consider these to be genuine and very important English derbies.

Second, a few general derbies that are *clearly not* the current primary derbies for clubs involved score highly but are not included in the Derby League Table. A shortened history of these general derbies is included later. As an example, Blackburn v Bolton is a general Lancashire derby that is more important to fans than an average game. The relative parity of their records also ensures that Blackburn v Bolton scores well in many factors. However, Blackburn's primary derby is very clearly with Burnley, not with Bolton, and Bolton look more towards clubs in or closer to Manchester than they do to Blackburn.

Third, a few derbies *included* in the final DLT list *might* also be challenged as not being main derbies for the clubs concerned. As we saw in the first half, defining what are primary derbies is not as easy as it may seem. As an example, Torquay v Exeter scores well on closeness of records, but it might be argued that Exeter's main rival is Plymouth, even though their derby does not score at all well on competitiveness factors, because Plymouth's historical record is far better than Exeter's. A judgement has to be made about those derbies to include or exclude from the list and a dividing line has to be drawn somewhere. If readers wish to add in or take out what they consider to be general derbies, feel free to do so.

At this juncture, there should perhaps be a fanfare, a drum roll or even an 'X-Factor'-style dramatic pause before results are announced. On second thoughts, let's just get on with it. Here are...

THE ENGLISH LEAGUE'S BEST AND MOST COMPETITIVE DERBIES
(The Derby League Table)

1. Newcastle v Sunderland
2. Derby v Nottingham Forest
3. West Brom v Wolves
4. Liverpool v Manchester United
5. Sheffield. Utd v Sheffield Wed
6. Portsmouth v Southampton
7. Everton v Liverpool
8. Ipswich v Norwich
9. Arsenal v Tottenham
10. Manchester City v Manchester United

11. Luton v Watford
12. Blackburn v Burnley
13. Reading v Swindon
14. Cardiff v Swansea
15. Fulham v QPR
16. Brighton v Crystal Palace
17. Bristol City v Bristol Rovers
18. Hull v Grimsby
19. Blackpool v Preston
20. Aston Villa v Birmingham

21. Chesterfield v Mansfield
22. Exeter v Torquay
23. Millwall v West Ham
24. Shrewsbury v Wrexham

25. Northampton v Peterborough

26. Colchester v Southend

27. Port Vale v Stoke

28. Barnsley v Rotherham

29. Coventry v Leicester

30. Bradford City v Huddersfield

Listed below are the *general* derbies which would have made it into the Derby League Table if they were clear *primary* derbies, complete with the position they would have occupied. A brief statistical history of these derbies begins on page 255.

12 Blackburn v Bolton

14 Arsenal v Chelsea

19 Palace v Millwall

26 Charlton v Palace

28 Cardiff v Bristol City

29 Villa v WBA

There will no doubt be a gnashing of teeth, as readers come to terms with the outrageous idea that other derbies are deemed better than readers' own all-consuming passions. *How could x versus y possibly score more highly than my team against the scum-bags from across town?* It may be worth anticipating a few obvious questions that might arise from conclusions in the Derby League Table.

Big derbies within cities, the *intra*-city derbies, do not fare particularly well in comparison to *inter*-city/town derbies. Four single-city derbies make the top ten, but the highest, the Sheffield derby, is only at number 5. Derbies in Bristol and Birmingham scrape into the top twenty; Stoke's derby is only at number 27 and Nottingham's doesn't make the list at all. Perhaps most surprising is the Manchester derby's position at tenth. It was described, with some justification, as the *"most important derby in the world"* in 2011/12, as the clubs fought to the line for the Premier League title. However, only a few years ago it was described, again with some justification, as only third on Manchester United's own derby list, behind their clashes with Liverpool and Leeds. In anticipation of City's continued wealth and United's health, Manchester's derby will no doubt climb the table in the coming years but, given the clubs' relative histories to date, at present their derby does not warrant a higher standing.

There is no in-built bias in the scoring system against single-city derbies. As Manchester's derby record demonstrates, the reason for their relatively low positions is that, in general, England's single-city derbies are very unequal in terms of the success rates of clubs involved. Therefore, whilst they usually score highly on other factors – passion etc, single-city derbies tend not to score well in competitiveness factors, because one club in each city is generally very dominant. To illustrate this point: Five factors measure competitiveness in each derby (No. 2 – record in derby clashes; No. 3 – record of finishing higher in the League; No. 4 – years spent in the top tier; No. 5 – success and silverware and No. 6 – recent history of success). In almost every single-city derby, one club leads in all five factors and often does so by a huge margin. Only in Liverpool, where Everton lead Liverpool in one factor (the number of years in the top tier) and in Sheffield, where United lead Wednesday in one factor (the number of derby wins) is this 'dominance by one club' sequence broken.

Compare the lack of competitiveness of most single-city derbies with, for example, Nottingham Forest v Derby. Their records are close in all five factors. Furthermore, while Forest lead in their number of derby wins and their accumulation of silverware, the Rams lead in the number of higher league placements and years in the top tier. The two are almost equal in terms of recent success (or lack of it). Had this book been written in the early 1970s, single-city derbies would have fared much better, because the peculiar one-sidedness of these derbies was not so pronounced at that point in time.

A second outcome which may raise eyebrows is the appearance in the top ten of Ipswich v Norwich or Luton v Watford at eleventh. Time and time again these derbies have featured highly in surveys and so their appearance in the upper echelons of English derbies in this book shouldn't really surprise anyone. Indeed, many in East Anglia will be annoyed to find their excellent derby placed as low as Number 8. Luton v Watford may be at low ebb at present but historically it is a fierce and competitive example of the species. Anyone who doubts the standing of these derbies is invited to read their histories below and think again.

The hillsides and valleys of South Wales will not welcome the sight of Cardiff v Swansea lingering as low as Number 14, especially as it is one of the highest scoring clashes in the combined 'ferocity and focus' factor. However, firstly, it is a rarely played derby (only 66 times in league and cup games). Secondly one club, Cardiff, have a much better record overall, although Swansea have more derby victories to their credit and in 2012/13 will be enjoying their spell in the Premiership sun. It may therefore be a derby to challenge any in terms of its passion, but many others are more competitive.

West Ham v Millwall at No. 23 may be thought to be a printing error. It isn't. Their derby also scores well in the 'ferocity and focus' factor. Indeed, it is one of England's most fearsome encounters. However, in overall competitiveness, it is one of the most one-sided derbies of all. Their first meeting in the 2011/12 Championship season was only their 26th derby in league or cup since they joined the Football League, meaning that they have rarely been in the same division. West Ham's dominance is demonstrated by noting that they have finished above Millwall in all but three seasons in the clubs' Football League careers. In fact, were it not for the inclusion of earlier records from their time together in the Southern League, when Millwall were particularly successful, the derby would not make it into the top thirty.

BEST AND MOST COMPETITIVE DERBIES IN DETAIL

The following section lays out the statistical history for each of the top thirty derbies in their ranked positions.

The following tables include statistics and information, as follows:-

1. Older Club – the year the clubs were formed.

2. Head-to-head record – the overall head-to-head record between clubs in derby matches in terms of number of games, the first game and who is ahead in number of wins.

3. Higher finishes in the League – a history of which club has finished higher in the league, broken down *roughly* by decade.
Roughly, because statistics by decade are not neat due to interruptions by World Wars. Therefore, the breakdown used is:-
   * 19th Century (there were twelve seasons in the 19th Century but, of course, most derbies did not start as early as 1888/9);
   * 1900 to World War One (a total of fifteen seasons);
   * 1920s (1919/20 to 1928/29 – ten seasons)
   * 1930s (1929/30 to 1938/39 – ten seasons)
   * 1940s and 50s together (a total of fourteen seasons)
   * ten season decades, beginning with the 00/01 year, for each of the 1960s, 70s, 80s, 90s and 2000s.
   * two seasons, 2010/11 and 2011/12.

4. Silverware – Comparative success in winning the League, FA Cup and League Cup.

5. Years in Top Tier – number of years spent in the top tier.

6. Biggest wins – biggest victories in derby games.

7. Historical notes about each derby's development over time.

Number 1 – Newcastle United v Sunderland

Older club   Sunderland 1879 (Newcastle 1881, sometimes quoted as 1882)

Head-to-head record

Number	146 games	
First one	Sunderland 2 Newcastle 3 *(Dec 1898 in Football League Div 1)*	
Leader (wins)	**Newcastle 53-45**	

Higher finishes in the League

19th C	Sunderland	7-0 (began in 1893/4 when Newcastle joined the League's second tier)
1900-WW1	Newcastle	8-7
1920s	Equal	5-5
1930s	Sunderland	8-2
40s+50s	Newcastle	8-6
1960s	Equal	5-5
1970s	Newcastle	8-2
1980s	Newcastle	6-4
1990s	Newcastle	7-3
2000s	Newcastle	7-3
2010/12	Equal	1-1
TOTAL	**Newcastle**	**57-51**

Silverware (wins)

League	Sunderland	6-4
FA Cup	Newcastle	6-2
League Cup	Equal	*– neither club has won the League Cup. Both have been beaten finalists once.*

Years in Top Tier   Equal   81-81

Biggest Wins

Home	Newcastle 6	Sunderland 1	*(Oct 1920)*	
	Sunderland 5	Newcastle 0	*(Nov 1931)*	
Away	Newcastle 1	Sunderland 9	*(Dec 1908)*	
	Sunderland 1	Newcastle 6	*(Dec 1955)*	

History No. 1 – Newcastle United v Sunderland

The origin of animosity between Newcastle and Sunderland is said to date from the English Civil War, when Geordies supported the king, while the people of Sunderland favoured Parliament. Sunderland already had a beef with King Charles I, as he had granted precious coal trading rights to Newcastle and Tyneside, at the expense of Wearside. More recently, Sunderland has continued to have a bit of a chip on its shoulder, or a legitimate gripe, depending upon whether the Tyne or Wear is nearer home. People from Sunderland believe their city is the region's powerhouse which makes things, the 'mackems', but Geordies, the 'takems' take all the credit. Needless to say, Geordies have a different take on the story behind these names.

Sunderland AFC were founded by teachers and originally played in blue. Newcastle's history is more complex. Two clubs, Newcastle West End and Newcastle East End, both of which were linked to earlier cricket clubs, vied for supremacy in the city in the 1880s. Eventually East End emerged as the more successful club and they effectively took over West End, including West's ground, St James' Park. They became Newcastle United in 1892. Ironically, East End played in red and white stripes.

Most people would think of Newcastle United as the North East's top club and, in recent decades, they have been – just. However, the history of their rivalry is one of Newcastle gradually hunting down Sunderland's lead, a lead established early in the Football League's existence. Sunderland burst onto England's football scene. They were the first new club to be admitted to the League, replacing Stoke in 1890 at the start of the third season. They picked up another, unwelcome, first when they were the first club to be docked points – for fielding an unregistered player. After an average initial season, Sunderland proceeded to take the title in three of the next four years and in the other they came second to Aston Villa. Sunderland had two titles in the bag before Newcastle had entered the League. Sunderland versus Villa was the great national clash in the 1890s, although arguably their most important confrontation came later. In 1912/13, Sunderland won the championship, with Villa as runners-up. They also met in the FA Cup final, in front of what was then the biggest, and is still the second biggest, crowd ever to see an English club game. Villa won 1-0 and therefore the clubs denied each other a 'double'.

By then Newcastle had emerged as a major force. They were England's top side in the first decade of the 20th century, taking the League championship three times in five years and losing three FA Cup finals, before eventually winning the cup in 1910. During those years, Sunderland were in trouble with the authorities again. In 1903, they made a 'loan' to a star player, Andrew McCombie, who had been an essential defensive cog in their title winning side of 1901/2. He said the money was a 'gift' and refused to pay it back. When the dispute was investigated, the FA concluded that Sunderland were guilty of making illegal payments. Directors were banned and McCombie was transferred – to Newcastle. In his first trip back to Roker Park in 1904, McCombie scored in the opening minute. Unfortunately for him and to the great amusement of his former employers, it was an own goal and Sunderland won 3-1. But McCombie had his revenge – Newcastle took the title at the end of the 1904/5 season.

After the early years, and with the exception of the 1930s, on the whole Newcastle have had the edge over Sunderland. However, it was not until the Magpies' appearance in the 1999 FA Cup final that they overtook the Black Cats in their overall record. United now lie eighth in the all-time success list with Sunderland one place behind in ninth. Neither club has ever been far adrift of the other. Except for one year (1987/8), when Sunderland slipped down into tier three, neither club has been outside the top two tiers. In terms of League positions, the longest period of dominance by either club was Newcastle's relatively short run of eleven seasons from 1967/8 to 1977/8. Even then, during that period as underdogs, Sunderland achieved their wonderful FA Cup victory against mighty Leeds in 1973.

The North East is one of England's true football hotbeds. On a number of occasions, especially immediately after World War Two, Newcastle have been the best supported club in the country and Sunderland's support has been nearly as strong. But the North East's record of success in recent times is not great. In fact, it has been argued with some justification that, in the past fifty years, on a ratio of success delivered to the size of their support, Newcastle and Sunderland are among the least successful clubs in the world, let alone England.

The high point for the region's big derby was a long time ago in those years around the turn of the 20th Century. In fifteen seasons from the start of the 20th Century to the outbreak of World War One, North East's giants collected five championships to add to three already gained by Sunderland in the previous decade. They also had fifteen top-four finishes between them. The pinnacle for the derby in the League has been attained on three occasions where one of the clubs took the title, with the other in third place (Sunderland as champions in 1901/2 and Newcastle as champions in 1908/9 and again in 1926/7).

It was during the 1908/9 season that the most remarkable half of a football match ever was played at Newcastle's home, St. James' Park. Newcastle were chasing another league title. In December, they met Sunderland. The first half was uneventful. Sunderland scored first, but Newcastle converted a penalty shortly before half-time. The home fans settled down to watch their heroes overcome the red and white foe in the second half. Sunderland didn't go along with the plot – in a big, big way. They proceeded to score *eight* second half goals in less than half an hour. Their 9-1 victory is still the biggest away win by any team in an English top tier game. To put the scoreline into greater perspective, Newcastle conceded almost 20% of the goals they conceded all season in less than one-third of one of their thirty-eight games (ie in less than 1% of their playing time). The 9-1 victory still sits proudly on Sunderland's record books as their greatest ever league win, home or away. Fortunately for Newcastle, they had already been beaten 0-9 away by Burton Wanderers in 1895 and so the ignominy of their derby defeat does not have to be prominently displayed. Most remarkable of all are the facts that Newcastle had the best defensive record in the division and finished that season *as league champions* – which poses a quandary question for football fans. Who would you rather have been in 1908/9? Would you have preferred to have been a fan of the ultimate champions, despite the humiliation of a record derby defeat, or a fan of third placed Sunderland who witnessed half an hour of pure historic heaven?

There are two postscripts to this incredible game. Firstly, how could it have happened? Supposedly there had been an argument between Newcastle's directors and senior players. Therefore, United's team on the day did not include all their stars. There were no substitutes allowed in those days and so it wasn't possible to roll-out the big guns when the going got tough. Therefore, United's team was not at full strength and included a few relatively inexperienced players. Nevertheless, this was not a reserve side by any means. The absence of a few top players should merely have given Sunderland a better chance, as Newcastle's squad was brim full of internationals. It should not have encouraged anything like the rout of the second half. Secondly, record books do not so prominently report the fact that the clubs met three more times that season. Sunderland completed a league double but, in between the two league clashes, after a draw at St. James', Newcastle took partial revenge by knocking Sunderland out of the cup 3-0 at Roker Park.

Alas, since the heady days of the early 20th century, there have been only two more League titles to celebrate in the North East, for Newcastle in 1926/7 and for Sunderland in 1935/6. Newcastle had a purple patch in the early 1950s, when they won three FA Cups in five years. Their performances in the league derbies of 1955/6 and 1956/7 were probably equally as wonderful for Magpies. They won all four, starting with their record 6-1 away win on Boxing Day 1955. On the very next day they beat Sunderland again, 3-1. Just before Christmas 1956, United won 6-2, their second biggest derby home win. A four-game aggregate of 5-17 must have left Rokerites as festive as Scrooge with piles and toothache. In between their defeats in the League, however, Sunderland despatched holders Newcastle from the FA Cup. United have never graced the competition as holders again. Sunderland's own FA Cup final victory in 1973 is the stuff of legend. Most people, except Sunderland and Manchester United fans, would have 'loved it' had Kevin Keegan's Magpies held on to the twelve point lead they held in January 1996 and gone on to win the title – but they blew it. Therefore, since World War Two, the most competitive derby in England has generally been fought out against a background of frustration and under-achievement.

Incidentally, the North East giants know more than anyone the 'curse of the stripe'. In the first forty-four seasons of the Football League, clubs playing in stripes won nineteen titles, ten of which went to the North East. A relatively small minority of teams played in striped shirts and so, at the time, stripes were considered lucky. However, in sixty-nine seasons since Sunderland's championship victory in 1935/6, no club playing in stripes has won a league title.

Over the years there have been many close finishes between Magpies and Black Cats. Sunderland held the record of being the last club to be relegated from the top tier. When finally facing relegation for the first time in 1957/8, they went down on goal average, just below Portsmouth and the dreaded Newcastle. At that stage they easily led the Magpies by 57-42 in number of years spent in the top tier.

In 1989/90, Newcastle finished third in the second tier, six points ahead of sixth placed Sunderland. Only two years earlier, Newcastle had been eighth in the top division and, as Sunderland were spending their one and only year in tier three, the gap between the clubs had been at its widest ever. As is the norm in play-offs, third were drawn against sixth. The first leg ended in a 0-0 draw and so off they went to St. James' Park with Newcastle as clear favourites. But it was Sunderland who won 2-0. Newcastle fans invaded the pitch and held up play for over half an hour in a vain attempt to get the match abandoned. Sunderland went on to lose the play-off final. However it was to be their lucky year because victors Swindon Town were immediately relegated again for financial irregularities and so Sunderland took their spot in the sun despite the play-off defeat.

The Black Cats were not so lucky a few years later though. In 1997/8 they finished the season in third place in tier two, one point behind automatically-promoted local rivals Middlesbrough. They progressed to compete in one of the best-ever play-off finals. It ended in a thrilling 4-4 draw, with boyhood Sunderland fan Clive Mendonca scoring a hat-trick for their opponents Charlton. Charlton won the subsequent penalty shoot-out 7-6, leaving Sunderland as the first club to gain ninety points in the regular season and yet fail to achieve promotion.

Historically, every aspect of this derby is close but, in recent times, there has been one element that has been one-sided. United have established a 52-45 lead in head-to-head encounters. The gap has grown because Newcastle won eight of the last fourteen derbies up to the end of 2011/12. Sunderland won just one. Even odder is the fact that Sunderland have won only twice in their last twenty-one home derbies (though fourteen games have been draws).

In 2012/13, the North East's premier derby is in good health, as both clubs are in the Premier League. Spice is added by the fact that Sunderland, who had been losing ground until recently, finished above Newcastle for three seasons from 2008 to 2011. Newcastle hit back in 2011/12, by not only overhauling Sunderland, but making a credible, though eventually unsuccessful, bid for a Champions' League place. After all this time, Geordies and Mackems are still locked together like a pair of marathon dancers. Overall, the North East derby fully deserves its position on top of the pile. It scores highly in every factor. It is ferocious, focussed and competitive and it beats other excellent derbies because it has been so *consistently* competitive over the decades. It is truly world class.

Number 2 – Derby County v Nottingham Forest

Older club	**Forest 1865** – *the third oldest football league club.* (Derby 1884)	

Head-to-head record

Number	89 games	
First one	Derby 2 Forest 3 *(Oct 1892 in Football League Div 1)*	
Leader (wins)	**Forest 36-32**	

Higher finishes in the League

19th C	Derby	5-3	*(began in 1892/3 when Forest were elected to the new Division One, following the League's expansion into two divisions)*
1900-WWI	Derby	8-7	
1920s	Derby	6-4	
1930s	Derby	10-0	
40s+50s	Equal	7-7	
1960s	Forest	9-1	
1970s	Derby	7-3	
1980s	Forest	10-0	
1990s	Forest	6-4	
2000s	Derby	7-3	
2010/12	Equal	1-1	
TOTAL	Derby	56-53	

Silverware (wins)	League	Derby	2-1
	FA Cup	Forest	2-1
	League Cup	Forest	4-0

Years in Top Tier	Derby	65-56

Biggest Wins

Home	Derby	5	Forest	0	*(April 1898)*
	Forest	5	Derby	1	*(Mar 1904)*
Away	Derby	2	Forest	6	*(Nov 1903)*
	Forest	2	Derby	5	*(Oct 1895)*

History No. 2 – Derby County v Nottingham Forest

The biggest wins of the clubs are worth exploring. In an otherwise unremarkable season in 1903/4, when Forest finished only three points ahead of Derby, Forest achieved both their biggest home and away wins ever against their dreaded foes, with an aggregate score of 11-3. Oddly, Derby did virtually the same thing in 1895/6. They recorded their biggest ever away win against Forest in October 1895 and their second biggest home win, by 4-0, in December, the aggregate score being 9-2.

Derby were formed in 1884 and that makes them positively youthful in comparison with Nottingham's clubs, the oldest and third oldest of all League clubs. Both Derby and Forest grew out of organisations dedicated to other sports, Derby as an offshoot of Derbyshire County Cricket Club and Forest from a former shinty club. Along with Notts County, the Rams of Derby were founder members of the Football League and shortly afterwards, in 1892/3, they were joined by Forest. For many decades the three, with to a lesser extent Leicester, fought out East Midlands' derbies, but until well after the Second World War the area's primary derby was Forest versus their own city's County, not the one from Derby.

Derby were the dominant side in the East Midlands up to World War Two. In forty-seven seasons, Derby finished highest in the League twenty-three times, Notts County on eleven occasions, Forest on nine and Leicester four times. None of them were tremendously successful. By 1939 Derby lay 16th in the overall all-time success list, Notts County 19th, ahead of Forest 22nd and Leicester 29th.

Things began to change as the gap between Nottingham's clubs widened from the late fifties onwards, but the real shift in derby affections occurred when Brian Clough and his deputy Peter Taylor came onto the scene. Clough's story has been told many times and its impact on Notts County was described in more detail in the first half of the book. In short, Clough joined Derby in 1967. They had been second tier for some time and had not been the top side even in the East Midlands since 1953. Both Forest and Leicester had been happily ensconced in the top tier ever since they were promoted together in 1956/7 and so the growth of a Foxes/Forest primary derby became a possibility.

Within five years of Clough's arrival, Derby were League champions for the first time in their history and, to cap it all, Forest were relegated in the same season. But, after well publicised spats with his board, Clough left Derby and, via Brighton and his disastrous forty-four days with Leeds United, he arrived at Forest in 1975. He was joined again by Taylor in 1976. The circumstances were almost a mirror image of 1967. Derby were champions for the second time in 1974/5 and Leicester were safely in the top tier. Forest, meanwhile, finished sixteenth in the second tier, two places behind Notts County. So Clough and Taylor were taking over the poorest side in the East Midlands. Fast forward a mere three years and Forest were champions of England. Leicester were relegated in the same season. Clough had become the first manager since Herbert Chapman to guide two clubs to the League championship (Kenny Dalglish later became the third to do so). One year on and Forest were champions of Europe and in the following season, while Forest were successfully defending their European crown, Derby went down to the second tier.

Forest's successes in Europe were particularly hard for Derby to swallow and not just because they were local rivals managed by a former manager of theirs. Derby's own venture into Europe under Clough and Taylor in 1972/3 had ended in the semi-final against the Old Lady of Turin, Juventus. The nature of Juve's home win was, to put it mildly, dubious or, as Mr.Clough said in his inimitable direct style, Juventus were *"cheating bastards"*.

Given that the clubs have been in the League together for 109 seasons and between them have been outside the top two tiers for only nine years in total, it is strange to find that they have been in the same division together for only forty seasons. The East Midlands derby has therefore been played on fewer occasions than any top ten derby except Portsmouth v Southampton. It is perhaps even more surprising to find that Forest have been in the same league tier as Notts County more often than with the Rams.

There have been three lengthy periods of dominance, the longest being the twenty-one seasons from 1925/6 to 1952/3 when Derby finished above Forest every year. Forest, however, have had two long runs of superiority, from 1953/4 to 1968/9 (sixteen seasons) and from 1977/8 to 1995/6 (nineteen seasons)

The clubs contested the 1898 FA Cup final. Notts. Forest, as they were known, were considered lucky to have reached the final and Derby were clear favourites, even though they finished marginally behind Forest in the League. The Rams had more experience, having reached semi-finals in 1896 and 1897 and they enjoyed support from a majority of the crowd. Even more significantly, just five days before the final, Derby completed a league double over Forest, winning 5-0, which remains their biggest victory over their rivals. However, allegedly Derby were *"labouring under the handicap of a gypsy's curse, provoked by moving on gypsies camped on the area that was developed as County's ground"*. Almost inevitably, the underdogs of Forest won 3-1.

Derby returned to the final in 1899 and lost 4-1 to Sheffield United. They lost again in the semi-finals of 1902 and 1904 and, in between, were hammered by a record score, 6-0, by Bury in the 1903 final. The 'Daily Chronicle' described that game as a *"fiasco"* and said Derby, who were slight favourites, were so poor that *"it might have been twenty"*, even though Bury didn't play particularly well.

Derby had to wait until 1946 to win the cup. Even then, the curse still seemed almost strong enough to deny them. Playing Charlton, Derby were clearly the better side. Late goals left the score at 1-1. With time running out, Derby had a chance to score but, of all things, the ball burst, denying them a goal-scoring opportunity. The game went into extra time and fortunately, at last they made it, winning 4-1.

One of the oddest goals in derbies between Forest and Derby was scored more recently, in March 2004. Forest's keeper was looking to make a straightforward clearance from a back-pass when the ball struck a coffee cup causing the keeper to loop the ball into the air for a grateful Derby forward to tap it into the net. The 'coffee cup goal' helped the Rams to a 4-2 victory and the win ultimately saved them from relegation.

As comparatively small clubs, their feats in the 1970s seemed improbable at the time and appear to border on being impossible inventions in hindsight. The best days for the derby may well be long gone, but it is still a great example of the beast. Forest and Derby are 17th and 18th respectively in the all-time success list, irrevocably tied together. Every aspect of their derby is close run, except that Forest have a significantly better record in the League Cup. They were two divisions apart in 2007/8, but have been together in the Championship since. Notts County are trying hard to re-establish the primacy of the all-Nottingham derby but Forest v Derby is likely to continue as a top class derby for the foreseeable future.

Derby quote: "Anybody who can do anything in Leicester but make a jumper, has got to be a genius".
Brian Clough about Leicester manager Martin O'Neill (Brian being careful not to have a go at former club, Derby County).

Number 3 – West Bromwich Albion v Wolverhampton Wanderers

Older club	**Wolves 1877** (WBA 1878)	

Head-to-head record

Number	159 games	
First one	WBA 3 Wolves 1 *(Jan 1886 in the FA Cup)*	
Leader (wins)	**WBA 64-53**	

Higher finishes in the League

19th C	Wolves	10-2 *(began at the start of the Football League in 1888, as both clubs are founder members)*
1900-WW1	WBA	9-6
1920s	WBA	10-0
1930s	WBA	6-4
40s+50s	Wolves	13-1
1960s	WBA	7-3
1970s	Wolves	7-3
1980s	WBA	9-1
1990s	Wolves	9-1
2000s	WBA	8-2
2010/12	WBA	2-0
TOTAL	WBA	58-55

Silverware (wins)

League	**Wolves**	3-1
FA Cup	**WBA**	5-4
League Cup	**Wolves**	2-1

Years in Top Tier	**WBA**	74-63

Biggest Wins	Home	WBA	7	Wolves	3 *(Dec 1929)*
		Wolves	7	WBA	0 *(Mar 1963)*
	Away	WBA	1	Wolves	4 *(Oct 1889)*
		Wolves	0	WBA	8 *(Dec 1893)*

History No. 3 – West Bromwich Albion v Wolverhampton Wanderers

There are a number of stories behind the biggest victories in Black Country derbies. West Brom's record 7-3 home win in December 1929 completed a huge League double, as they beat Wolves 4-2 at Molineux in the same season. In 1961/2, West Brom beat Wolves twice at Molineux, first in the cup and then by a massive 5-1 in the League later in the season. However, the next time they met, in March 1963, Wolves completed a remarkable turnaround by winning by their record margin of 7-0.

The most unusual story of all surrounds West Brom's 8-0 victory at Molineux at Christmas in 1893, which has to be one of the most amazing results of all time in English football. It rivals Sunderland's 9-1 win at Newcastle and remains Wolves' worst ever home defeat. In the previous season Wolves had also suffered their worst ever away defeat, losing 10-1 at Newton Heath. It would therefore seem safe to assume that Wolves were completely hopeless at this point in time and that Newton Heath were brilliant. Not so. Wolves were comfortably placed, whereas Newton Heath finished bottom of Division One, having won only six of their thirty games.

The circumstances surrounding the 0-8 hammering by West Brom were even stranger. Firstly, there was not much to choose between the sides that year. Both eventually finished in mid-table. However, coming into the seasonal derby match, Wolves were on a hot streak of form. In December they had won five and drawn one of six games, scoring seventeen goals and conceding just three. In that run they beat Everton, Blackburn and Villa, three teams who went on to finish in the top six, Villa as champions. West Brom on the other hand were in so-so form, having won two, lost two and drawn one of their games in December. If anyone was going to hand out a thrashing it surely should have been Wolves. To add to the mystery of this game, the teams again played League matches only three days later and normal service was resumed. Wolves won 3-0 at Stoke while West Brom, presumably still celebrating their 8-0 derby victory, lost 1-7 at Everton.

When the Football League began in 1888/9, West Brom were expected to be the top Midlands' club, challenged by Aston Villa. Albion had reached the previous three FA Cup finals, losing in 1886 and 1887, and then beating mighty Preston in the final of 1888. However, in the new League, it was not only Villa who made a bigger impression than West Brom. Wolves finished in the top four in each of the first three years and above Albion in ten of twelve seasons up to the turn of the century. The League's first few years proved to be a wonderful time for both clubs because, although neither could grasp the League title itself, both were very successful in the cup. In just eight seasons, Wolves reached four semi-finals, winning the cup in 1893 and reaching finals in 1889 and 1896. West Brom continued their excellent cup pedigree by also making it to semi-finals four times, winning the cup in 1892 and losing in the final of 1895. Altogether this meant Albion had been to seven semi-finals and on to five finals in ten years.

After a good start, Wolves did not fulfil their early promise. Relegated in 1906, they didn't return to the top tier until 1932. From 1911 to 1936, a period of twenty-one seasons, they finished below West Brom every time. However, as a run of the mill second tier side, they won the FA Cup in 1908, creating a huge shock by beating Newcastle in the final.

In the first season after World War One, West Brom emphasised their dominance over Wolves by becoming the second West Midlands' club to take the League championship (Villa already had six titles), while Wanderers were narrowly avoiding relegation to Division Three North. Albion's success in 1919/20 remains their only title in the League.

After years of playing second fiddle, Wolves began to emerge as a major force in the three seasons before league action was suspended for the duration of World War Two. In 1936/7, they were the top club in the West Midlands for the first time in thirty-two years. In the following two years, they were runners-up in the League and had a losing 'double' in 1939, as they were also beaten FA Cup finalists.

Meanwhile, in a complete reversal of fortunes, West Brom were relegated in 1937/8. This time Wolves did fulfil their promise. In nineteen seasons from 1936 to 1961, Wolves finished higher in the League than Albion eighteen times, but this was not because Albion were poor. On the contrary, in eight seasons from 1952/3, West Brom had five top-five finishes and yet, in all eight years, they were behind Wolves. Wolves, arguably even more so than Sir Matt Busby's Manchester United, were the team of the fifties. Wolves won the championship three times in six seasons (their only titles to date) and took the FA Cup in 1949 and 1960, at either end of their glory years.

Halcyon days for the Black Country reached their pinnacle in 1953/4 and it was a pinnacle that couldn't have been much higher. Wolves triumphed in the League, by four points from second placed West Brom. They beat Albion twice in their league clashes. In doing so they robbed the Baggies of an opportunity to become the first club in the 20th Century to complete a league and cup double, as Albion added to the success story by winning the 1954 FA Cup. So, in September 1954, 45,000 turned up at Molineux to celebrate the Black Country ruling the roost, as the two contested the Charity (Community) Shield. Ronnie Allen scored a hat-trick for Albion in a 4-4 draw.

Surely it couldn't get better – but it did, at least for Wolves. In December 1954, in front of another packed Molineux, Wolves recovered from a two goal deficit at half-time to beat Honved 3-2. This may not seem a big deal to younger readers, but Honved had provided the nucleus of the Hungarian side that thrashed England twice in the previous year. Victory for Stan Cullis's heroes in this game, and a series of others against top foreign sides, saw them proclaimed as unofficial 'champions of the world'. It was not a far-fetched claim and indirectly it led to the establishment of European club competitions soon afterwards. As an aside, Cullis is rarely included in the pantheon of truly great managers, but his record at Wolves deserves better recognition. He had one other claim to fame. In 1938, when England played Germany, Cullis was the only England player who refused to give a Nazi salute. His 'reward' for refusing to do so was to be dropped.

Times have never been as good in the Black Country since the heady days of the fifties. West Brom won their fifth FA Cup in 1968 to move one ahead of Wolves. There have been three triumphs in the League Cup between them, two to Wolves and one for Albion, but there have been at least as many bad times as good, especially for Wolves. In the 1980s they crashed, being declared bankrupt twice and experiencing relegation in three successive seasons from top tier to tier four. In those three seasons, Wolves won only twenty-five out of one hundred and thirty matches. They lost seventy-five.

More recently, both clubs have gained a reputation as being too good for the second tier, but unable to maintain a regular place in the top tier. In the 21st Century Wolves have been promoted to the Premiership twice and relegated twice. West Brom have been more extreme, recording four promotions and three relegations in nine years. The clubs exchanged places in the top tier three times in seven years. Finally, in 2010/11, they came together in the top tier for the first time since 1983/4 and, maybe surprisingly given their yo-yo existence in recent years, both survived. It lasted for only a season, as Wolves were relegated at the end of 2011/12.

In general, over the years Wolves have been the better supported club when the two sides have been in the same division. An exception was the glory year of 1953/4, when crowds at The Hawthorns outstripped those at Molineux. West Brom fans would also be quick to point out that their attendances never dipped anywhere near as low as the Wolves' crowds of 1985/6 when, in their darkest days at the foot of the third tier, they mustered an average of 4,020, fewer than neighbours Walsall in the same division.

There is one especially unusual aspect to the Black Country derby. Although the clubs have roughly equal records in head-to-head games in league matches, Wolves have an awful record in knock-out ties with the Baggies. In fact, they have the worst record of any club in the sixty derbies studied. In 1949, on their way to winning the FA Cup, Wolves beat West Brom, but that is the only time they have tasted victory, while over the years West Brom have dispatched Wolves from the FA Cup eight times. To give but one example. In 1930/1, Albion completed a league double over Wolves and pipped Wanderers to promotion. They also beat Wolves in the FA Cup and, as a Second Division side, went on to win the cup, having the added pleasure of beating First Division local rivals Birmingham in the final.

With that historical background in knock-out competitions, the events of 2006/7 will come as no surprise. The two shared home league victories and finished the season level on points in fourth and fifth places in the Championship. West Brom had already put Wolves out of the FA Cup, winning 3-0 at Molineux, before the two clashed again in end of season play-offs. Needless to say, West Brom won both games, thereby beating their rivals four times in one season and taking their knock-out tally against Wolves to nine-one.

The outcome of the 2001/2 season was arguably even more heartbreaking for Wolves' fans. Their team had led the second tier for most of the season and, at one stage, held an eleven-point lead at the top. West Brom had trailed, but a run of six wins in eight games saw them contesting automatic promotion. On the last day Wolves still had a chance of automatic promotion, but a draw for them, coupled with a win for the Baggies, saw West Brom finish second and Wolves third. West Brom were promoted. Worse was to come for Wolves, as they lost in the play-off semi-final and then saw local rivals Birmingham gain promotion, even though they had finished fifth, ten points behind Wolves, in the regular season.

For all their heartache at the hands of their Black Country foes, Wolves fans can still point to the simple fact that they have more silverware than Albion and they lie eleventh in the all-time success league table, three places ahead of the Baggies. Therefore, while the Baggies have had the better of the 21st Century so far and lead in most overall comparisons – derby wins, years at the top etc – Wolves have a better record of turning opportunities into silverware.

In 2012/13, the clubs are in different tiers again, but their derby looks in good health in comparison to the difficulties experienced by both clubs, especially Wolves, in the past few decades. Villa still pose a distraction, especially for older Baggies. Baggies v Villans takes on added significance in 2012/13, firstly because West Brom finished above Villa in 2011/12 for the first time since 1979 and secondly because they are the only two clubs from the West Midlands in the Premiership. However, there is little doubt any more that Villa's primary derby is with Birmingham and so the Black Country derby is getting even more focussed. If West Brom and Wolves could come together for a sustained period of time, their derby could yet challenge the North East for top spot.

Number 4 – Liverpool v Manchester United

Older club: **Manchester United**, as Newton Heath 1878 (Liverpool 1892)

Head-to-head record:

Number	180 games		
First one	Liverpool 2 United 0 *(April 1894 in an end of season*		
			test match)
Leader (wins)	**United 71-61**		

Higher finishes in the League

19th C	Liverpool	6-1	*(began in 1893/4 when Liverpool*
			joined the second tier of the League)
1900-WW1	Liverpool	8-7	
1920s	Liverpool	10-0	
1930s	Liverpool	10-0	
40s+50s	United	13-1	
1960s	Equal	5-5	
1970s	Liverpool	10-0	
1980s	Liverpool	10-0	
1990s	United	9-1	
2000s	United	9-1	
2010/12	United	2-0	
TOTAL	**Liverpool**	**62-46**	

Silverware (wins)	League	**United**	**19-18**
	FA Cup	**United**	**11- 7**
	League Cup	**Liverpool**	**8-4**

Years in Top Tier	**Liverpool**	**97-87**

Biggest Wins

Home	Liverpool	7	United	1 *(Oct 1895)*
	United	6	Liverpool	1 *(May 1928)*
Away	Liverpool	1	United	4 *(Dec 1969)*
	United	2	Liverpool	5 *(Nov 1936)**

*Modern Liverpool fans may treasure more their 4-1 victory at Old Trafford in March 2009. It was United's only home defeat in a season which saw them equal Liverpool's record of eighteen League championships. That having been said, Liverpool's win in 1936 ultimately ensured that United were relegated by two points.

History No. 4 – Liverpool v Manchester United

This is the derby between England's most successful clubs of all time. Those who argue it is not a true derby should note that it is the most often quoted number one English derby in international comparisons, no doubt reflecting worldwide interest in the clubs. If all competitions in domestic, European and world championships are taken into account, they have won an amazing 120 trophies (60 each). Famously, in 2010/11, United overhauled Liverpool's record of eighteen League championships and United lead 34-33 in major domestic trophies. Understandably, Liverpool fans will counter that statistic with the fact that they still lead United 5-3 in European Championship wins.

Their collective success is almost entirely a relatively recent phenomenon. In forty-seven seasons up to the Second World War, their combined trophy cabinet consisted of just six League titles (Liverpool 4 United 2) and a solitary FA Cup success for United in 1909. At the outbreak of war in 1939, Liverpool and United were 12th and 18th respectively in the all-time success list.

However, a measure of their post-war pre-eminence is that between them they have won nearly half the League championships since 1946/7 (thirty-one out of sixty-six).

From the start, the two Reds have been involved in crucial and sometimes controversial games against each other. Their very first meeting in 1894 was in a test match at the end of Liverpool's first season in the League. They had finished top of Division Two, whereas Newton Heath had finished bottom of Division One. Before the introduction of automatic promotion, test matches were held to determine promotion and relegation issues. The 'love' affair got off to a flying start, as Liverpool's victory ensured that they replaced United in the top tier.

Their first ever meeting in a regular League fixture in Oct 1895 ended with a 7-1 victory for Liverpool, a winning margin that has never been bettered in their derby encounters. Three weeks later, United beat Liverpool 5-2 in the return fixture.The biggest aggregate score in any of their meetings occurred in March 1908, when Liverpool won 7-4 at Anfield but, only weeks later, United were crowned League champions, having finished nine points clear at the top, with Liverpool nowhere in sight.

In February 1910, the clubs met to christen the spanking new Old Trafford ground and United were leading 3-1 with fifteen minutes to go. But Liverpool scored three times to ruin United's party. On the other hand, a year later, Liverpool started an end of season party for United. Aston Villa led on the final day by one point in a two horse race with United. United won and waited anxiously for Villa's result – they lost 3-1 at Liverpool and so United could thank their Scouse neighbours for making them champions.

In 1915, as football was being wound up for the duration of the First World War, a betting scandal rocked football. Bookmakers noticed unusual betting patterns on a crucial game and refused to pay out – nothing is ever new in football. Following an investigation, seven players were found guilty of fixing the match and betting on the outcome. They were all banned for life, although six were exonerated at the end of the war (one posthumously, as he had been killed at the Battle of the Somme). The purpose of the match fixing, apart from making money, was to save Manchester United from relegation. They won 2-0 and survived. Players from both teams conspired in the scandal. The other team involved? – it was Liverpool. It would be impossible to imagine this happening now, not because it is unlikely that United would be in a position to be relegated or that match-fixing/betting scandals are impossible, but surely no modern Liverpool player would be daft enough to risk being found guilty of saving Manchester United from relegation.

An odder result occurred on the last day of the 1927/8 season. It was a remarkable season. In a top tier with twenty-two teams, champions Everton finished only sixteen points clear of bottom club, Middlesbrough. Arsenal who finished *tenth* missed relegation by two points and seven sides ended the season level on thirty-nine points, one ahead of relegated Tottenham. Manchester United started the final day in bottom spot and were playing Liverpool at home. Liverpool had been a top side in the early twenties, whereas United had spent time in Division Two and had finished below Liverpool every season. In thirteen league and cup meetings since the war, Liverpool had won seven and the other six had been drawn. A draw was of no use to United this time and so the portents were not good – relegation loomed. Against all odds, United won 6-1 and survived. It was, and still is, their biggest win ever against Liverpool.

The inter-war period was mediocre to say the least, especially for United. Signs that things had changed significantly soon became evident when football resumed after the Second World War in 1946/7. United announced their arrival early in the season, by beating Liverpool 5-0 in September. By May 1947, Wolves were in the box seat for winning the League title, closely followed by United and Stoke City. Liverpool were still in contention, but were four points adrift, with an inferior goal average and only four games to play. However, early in May, Liverpool beat United 1-0 and at the same time the wheels began to come off for Wolves. The next crunch game was Liverpool against Wolves at Molineux. It was the final match of the season for both clubs. Liverpool won 2-1 to overtake both Wolves and Manchester United. The defeat for Wolves was enough to put United into second place on goal average. But, even then, the championship wasn't decided, because terrible weather that year had caused fixture delays. It meant that Stoke City's final game against Sheffield United was delayed for two weeks.

On into June Liverpool waited. Stoke went to Bramall Lane knowing that a win would give them their first title on goal average. But Blades beat Potters 2-1 and Liverpool were champions for a fifth time. Their victory over Manchester United in early May had been a catalyst for their excellent finish to the season. The only blot on their parade was a surprising defeat in an FA Cup semi-final to Second Division Burnley. It denied them the chance to become the 20th Century's first double winners. As for United, their second place heralded a run in which they finished in the top-two eight times in the next thirteen years.

The resumption of football had seen the previously 12th and 18th most successful clubs become champions and runners-up together for the first time. It was a foretaste of what was to come. Given their domination of post-war football in England, it is not surprising to find that their one-two finish in 1946/7 was not to be their last. Liverpool again beat United into second place in 1963/4, 1979/80 and 1987/8 and United reversed places in 2008/9.

Resumption of football after the Second World War also saw the arrival at United of a young Scottish manager called Alexander. No, Sir Alex isn't quite that old! This was Alexander Matthew 'Matt' Busby. As a player, he made over two hundred appearances for Manchester City and had been Liverpool's captain. He was groomed as a potential manager of Liverpool, but chose to join United for whom he had never played. The rest is history. Sir Matt created three great United teams and laid foundations for the club to become the biggest in England. His portrayal in a 2011 play about the Munich air disaster as a somewhat menacing, monosyllabic character was unfortunate, to say the least. He was one of the outstanding managers of all time and the fact that United erected a statue to this ex-Liverpool captain is no surprise. Incidentally, Liverpool did not lose out entirely. Sir Matt was a great friend and mentor to Bob Paisley, one of Liverpool's greats. Their friendship was not so odd at the time. The clubs are bitter rivals now, but the bitterness of this derby didn't really come to fruition until the late sixties and early seventies. By the nineties, it had reached a point where, when asked to name his greatest achievement, Alex Ferguson said *"knocking Liverpool off their fucking perch"*.

In addition to their many top of the league clashes, the clubs have met in four cup finals. United won both FA Cup finals, in 1977 and 1996, and Liverpool won both League Cup finals, in 1983 and 2003. The 1977 FA Cup final was especially pleasing for red Mancunians. As League champions and European Cup finalists (which they won), Liverpool were clear favourites. United's surprise 2-1 victory denied Liverpool a treble.

United completed that particular type of treble in 1999. In the FA Cup they trailed Liverpool 1-0 with a minute to go, but United scored twice in the dying moments. Ole Gunnar Solskjaer bagged the winner. After completing a domestic double, United went on to meet Bayern Munich in the Champions League final. With a minute to go they were again trailing 1-0 – United scored twice in injury time, with the winner being scored by.... Ole Gunnar Solskjaer.

Their overall records are very close, but the history of their rivalry is one of long periods of dominance by one club over the other, at least in league performance. Liverpool finished higher in the League every season from 1914/5 to 1946/7 (twenty two seasons in total) and completed another, even longer, top dog sequence (twenty three seasons) from 1968/9 to 1990/1. In fairness to United, Liverpool finished above virtually everyone during that period. On the other hand, since 1990/1 Manchester United have had the upper hand in every season except one (2001/2). Only in the years leading up to World War One, and in the 'swinging' sixties, have the clubs been on a par in the League.

In 2012/13, the derby is potentially at something of a crossroads. In one sense it is as strong as ever. Both clubs are global brands and have rival supporters' clubs across the world. Both are firmly top Premier League clubs and so the derby seemingly will be played regularly for a long time to come. On the other hand, Liverpool have consistently flattered to deceive in their attempts to catch Ferguson's United. They have yet to win the Premier League. Even more importantly, the emergence from past shadows of mega-bucks Manchester City and the thrilling all-Manchester chase for the 2011/12 title has significantly affected the primary derby map. The derby fully deserves its billing now, but it could slip.

Derby quote: " There's Man. Utd and Man. City at the bottom of Division 1, and by God, they'll take some shifting".
Bill Shankly

Number 5 – Sheffield United v Sheffield Wednesday

Older club	**Wednesday 1867** (United 1889)	

Head-to-head record

Number	126 games	
First one	United 1 Wednesday 1 *(Oct 1893 in Football League Div. 1)*	
Leader (wins)	**United 45-41**	

Higher finishes in the League

19th C	United	6-2	*(began when both were elected to the League in 1892/3 – Wednesday to Division One and United to Division Two)*
1900-WWI	Wednesday	10-5	
1920s	United	9-1	
1930s	Wednesday	8-2	
40s+50s	Wednesday	9-5	
1960s	Wednesday	7-3	
1970s	United	9-1	
1980s	Wednesday	10-0	
1990s	Wednesday	9-1	
2000s	United	10-0	
2010/12	Equal	1-1	
TOTAL	**Wednesday**	**58-51**	

Silverware (wins)	League	**Wednesday**	**4-1**
	FA Cup	**United**	**4-3**
	League Cup	**Wednesday**	**1-0**

Years in Top Tier	**Wednesday**	**66-60**

Biggest Wins	Home	United	7	Wednesday 3 *(Sept 1951)*
		Wednesday	5	United 2 *(Sept 1928)*.*

*Modern Wednesday fans may point to their 4-0 victory over United on Boxing Day 1979 as being greater than the 5-2 win recorded above, although it should be said that the points gained in the 1928 triumph ultimately ensured Wednesday won the League title

	Away	United	1	Wednesday 3 *(Nov 1907 and Jan 1954)*
		Wednesday	1	United 3 *(Dec 1904, Mar 1910, Jan 1931, Jan 1952 and Mar 1992).*

History No. 5 – Sheffield United v Sheffield Wednesday

Both Sheffield clubs owe their existence to links with cricket. 'Wednesday' was the name of a much older cricket club who played their cricket on (surprise, surprise) Wednesdays and who decided to form a football section in 1867. United were formed by the owners of Bramall Lane who included Yorkshire County Cricket Club and Sheffield United Cricket Club. Incidentally, the formation of SUCC was the first use of the name 'United' in sport, and the cricket clubs 'united' in their use of Bramall Lane included Wednesday CC.

The Wednesday, as they were known until 1929, were first to win the FA Cup (1896), but it was United who were first to win the League (1897/8 – their only League title to date). Both clubs were major forces in the early days of football, with United winning the FA Cup three times before the First World War and Wednesday claiming League titles twice and adding another FA Cup win in the same period.

United began the post-war period as the ascendant club. They retained their top tier League status continuously for thirty-seven seasons up to 1933/4, but the fact that they added only one more trophy to their collection, the FA Cup in 1925, indicated that their star was already beginning to fade. Wednesday spent much of the twenties in tier two, but when they finished above United in 1928/9, for the first time since 1912/3, they did so in style, as League champions. They repeated the feat the following season (now as Sheffield Wednesday) and won the cup in 1935. Wednesday's feats in this period established them as the bigger club, albeit only marginally. By the outbreak of the Second World War, Wednesday and United were still well up the all-time success table, lying fifth and eleventh respectively, ahead of the likes of Liverpool and Manchester United.

To say the least, both clubs have waned since the Second World War. In an overall post-war success league table, Wednesday would be in 21st place and United would not even make the top thirty. Wednesday's League Cup victory in 1991 is the only addition to either clubs' silverware collections since the war. They both had a brief twinkling of former glories in the early 1960s. Wednesday were runners-up to the magnificent Spurs double-winning side of 1960/1. In the following season, newly promoted Blades finished fifth, one point ahead of the Owls. It was the last time, and the only time since the war, that Sheffield had the country's top-rated derby. Wednesday's momentum in the sixties was checked when three of their best players were banned from football, after being found guilty of involvement in a major match-fixing scandal. United had a good side in the early seventies and Wednesday seemed to be emerging as a major force when finishing third in 1991/2, but their challenge quickly petered out.

Until the 1970s, their records had always been very close. Basically, they were good at the same time and they declined together. Both clubs, especially the Owls, bounced up and down between the top two divisions in the fifties. Neither club had been outside the top two tiers until Wednesday's relegation to the third in 1974/5. At that stage, the longest spell of dominance by either club had been United's eleven season period of superiority either side of World War One.

Things changed in the 1970s and both clubs have been through far more traumas than triumphs in the past thirty to forty years. First, United gained the upper hand throughout the seventies, but then plummeted down the League, eventually spending a season in the fourth tier in 1981/2. Wednesday had avoided a similar fate by only one point at the end of their first season in the third tier in 1975/6. The decline of the Blades heralded an unprecedented period of ascendency for the Owls, in which they finished above the Blades in twenty of twenty-one seasons from 1979/80 to 1999/2000.

The new century, however, saw a marked change in fortunes. United didn't do particularly well, but Wednesday ran into very difficult times. So, after a long period on top, the Owls found themselves behind the Blades for the first eleven seasons of the 21st Century, equalling United's best ever run of supremacy. At the end of 2010/11, United were relegated to join Wednesday in the third tier, together at that lowly level for only the second time. 2011/12 proved to be a dramatic season. The Blades had the edge for most of the year but faltered towards the end. The Owls finished stronger and took automatic promotion. Third placed Blades failed in the play-offs and so will spend 2012/13 a tier below their neighbours.

The derby won't be played in 2012/13 but it remains top-notch. It is by a long way the most competitive of England's single-city derbies. Its competitiveness is illustrated by historic races for promotion. 2011/12 was close and went to the last day of the season, but amazingly it is only their third-closest promotion battle.

Either side of the Second World War, the clubs were involved in even closer contests. In 1938/9, United beat Wednesday by one point to the second tier's second promotion spot. Had today's points system been in place at the time, the Owls would have taken second place by one goal, with the teams equal on points.

In 1949/50, Sheffield managed an even tighter finish. On the final day, Wednesday needed to beat Tottenham to pip United for promotion. A 0-0 draw would still have given the Owls promotion on goal average. However, a 2-2 draw would have handed promotion to the Blades. A 1-1 draw would have resulted in the teams being exactly equal and a unique play-off for promotion would have been required. Wednesday drew 0-0. Both finished with fifty-two points. Wednesday's for and against total was 67-48, compared with United's 68-49. United had nineteen wins to Wednesday's eighteen and so, under any points system except goal average, the Blades would have been promoted. But goal average was in force in 1949/50 and so the Owls achieved promotion by 0.008 of a goal, the closest ever finish between derby rivals.

A footnote to United's defeat in the 2011/12 play-off final, on penalties after a 0-0 draw, is that it marked the continuation of one of football's most miserable runs. United have not won a major 'neutral venue' match since their FA Cup semi-final victory in 1936. In the intervening years they have played in eleven such games in the FA Cup or promotion play-off finals. They haven't won any of them, which is remarkable in itself. Even more amazingly, including extra time, they have played for *eighteen* hours in these showpiece games and have scored just *one* goal.

The Steel City's derby has two distinguishing features. The first is that fear of losing appears to be all pervasive. Most local derbies are cagey, parsimonious affairs by their very nature, but Sheffield's derby takes the biscuit. In 126 meetings, one team or other have managed to score more than three goals on only six occasions (United four times, Wednesday twice) and neither has ever done so away from home. As a standard example for comparison, the Black Country derby has seen more than three goals scored by one of the sides twenty-seven times in 159 meetings and on ten occasions it has been the away team that scored at least four times.

The second characteristic is that on an unusually large number of occasions the underdog has prevailed in head-to-head meetings. In part this explains why the Blades, although slightly behind the Owls in terms of silverware, continue to lead the Owls in derby victories. A case in point is United's record 7-3 win in 1951. Given that more than six goals in aggregate have been scored only twice in Sheffield derbies, the city had obviously decided to hang it all and party on this particular day. The Blades followed it up by winning 3-1 at Hillsborough early in 1952 to complete their greatest ever derby 'double'. However, Wednesday lost only ten games that season and finished as champions of the second tier. United, on the other hand, ended the season in eleventh place in the second tier which, at the time, was their lowest position ever.

United's second biggest victory was 5-1 in 1933/4. The win completed another double, but that season saw them relegated to the second tier for the first time ever. Wednesday finished safely in mid-table. In 2008/9, the Owls completed a League double over United for the first time in ninety-five years, but finished the season nineteen points adrift of their neighbours. On the previous occasion, in 1913/14, Wednesday's double just secured their survival from relegation, whereas United finished the season safely in mid-table.

In 1979, the teams met on Boxing Day at Hillsborough. United had been relegated to the third tier for the first time in their history, having been in a higher division than Wednesday for most of the 1970s. United started the campaign well and led the table at Christmas. Understandably, they were confident of winning the derby. The history of Sheffield derbies should have warned them – Wednesday won 4-0. It proved to be a defining moment. The Owls went on to promotion, the Blades continued on a downward spiral and the long period of blue dominance, described earlier, had begun. Over thirty years later, the 'Boxing Day Massacre' is still the subject of terrace songs, especially amongst Blades, in a typical example of football fans' self-flagellation.

The clubs didn't meet again in the League until 1991/2, by which time Wednesday were one of England's top sides. Given their superiority, it will be obvious by now that they stood absolutely no chance when they met the Blades. Sure enough, the 'underdog' Blades completed a League double.

On one especially famous occasion, the 'underdog wins' principle didn't apply. In 1993, the clubs met in an FA Cup semi-final at Wembley, following a mass campaign in the city to have the game switched to the national venue. Wednesday were clear favourites and this time the favourites won but, even then, it was by 2-1 after extra time. In the midst of big-time famine for the city, Wednesday had a feast in 1993. They had already been to the League Cup final and their victory over United took them to the FA Cup final. The final had to be replayed, meaning that the Owls went to Wembley four times that year (as did opponents Arsenal, who won both finals).

Finally, just once in a while something or someone transcends usual derby enmities. Derek Dooley was one such person. Dooley was a prolific centre-forward for Wednesday. He scored at a goal a game and, in 1951/2, created the Owls' highest season total, bagging forty-six. Tragically, his career was terminated when an injury became infected with gangrene. It led to the amputation of Dooley's leg.

Later, Derek became manager of Wednesday. It was not an especially successful period. In what was not exactly one of football's finest hours, he was sacked – on *Christmas Eve*. Dooley vowed never to visit Hillsborough again.

Later still, he was employed by bitter enemies United, eventually rising to become Chairman of the Blades. Twenty years after his sacking, Derek finally relented on his vow and agreed to attend a Steel City derby at Hillsborough. In the midst of emotionally charged scenes, he was rapturously welcomed by both sets of fans. Amongst many lasting tributes to the great man, United erected a statue of him at Bramall Lane – to arguably the best striker *Wednesday* ever had.

Number 6 – Portsmouth v Southampton

Older club	Southampton 1885 (Portsmouth 1898)

Head-to-head record

	Number	70 games
	First one	Portsmouth 2 Southampton 0 (April 1900 in the Southern League)
	Leader (wins)	**Southampton 34-21**

Higher finishes in the League

19th C	Portsmouth	1-0 (began when Pompey joined the Southern League in 1899/1900)
1900-WW1	Southampton	10-5 (Southern League)
1920s	Portsmouth	6-4 (in 1920/1 both joined the new Football League Division Three)
1930s	Portsmouth	10-0
40s+50s	Portsmouth	14-0
1960s	Southampton	10-0
1970s	Southampton	10-0
1980s	Southampton	10-0
1990s	Southampton	10-0
2000s	Portsmouth	6-4
2010/12	Equal	1-1
TOTAL	**Southampton 59-43**	

Silverware (wins)	League	**Portsmouth 2-0**
	FA Cup	**Portsmouth 2-1**
	League Cup	**Neither club** has won the League Cup. Only **Southampton** have reached a final.

Years in Top Tier	**Southampton 35-33**

Biggest Wins

Home	Portsmouth	5	Southampton	1	*(Southern League 1919/20. Their biggest win in the Football League is 4-1 in Apr 2005)*
	Southampton	5	Portsmouth	1	*(Jan 1906 & Aug 1960)*
Away	Portsmouth	2	Southampton	5	*(Feb 1966)*
	Southampton	1	Portsmouth	4	*(Feb 2010)*

History No. 6 – Portsmouth v Southampton

Hampshire's south coast derby scores very highly on 'focus' and well in a number of other factors. However, it is one of the strangest derbies of all, in that it has been played so rarely in the Football League. The two enjoyed regular, closely fought battles for a relatively short time from when Portsmouth joined the Southern League in 1899/1900 until both clubs joined the Football League in 1920. By contrast, when they were drawn against each other in the FA Cup fifth round in 2010, it was only their thirty-sixth meeting in league or cup competitions since they joined the Football League. They have still spent as many seasons together in the same division of the Southern League as in the same division of the Football League (sixteen seasons together in each).

The all-time records of the clubs are close, but the history of the south coast derby is one of long periods of dominance by one club over the other, which largely explains why they have met each other so infrequently. To illustrate the point:- when Portsmouth finished higher than Southampton in the League in 2004/5, it was the first time they had done so since 1960/1, a continuous stretch of superiority for the Saints of forty-four seasons. This in turn followed a sequence of twenty-nine seasons of dominance for Pompey, dating back to 1924/5. That sequence would probably have been even longer had the Second World War not intervened to save the Saints from further punishment, in a football sense at least – much of the city was flattened during the war.

Their earliest meetings in the Southern League were dramatic. In April 1900, newcomers Portsmouth faced a Saints' side who, not only had been champions for the previous three seasons but, in that year, were also the first Southern League team to reach an FA Cup final. Needless to say, in the great tradition of unpredictable derbies, Portsmouth won 2-0. Just three days later the sides met again – and Pompey won again by the same score.

Southampton's 5-1 victory in their first FA Cup encounter with Portsmouth, in 1906, has still not been bettered in any match between the clubs. It was to be the start of a long run of cup triumphs in derbies for the Saints.

After spending many happy years together in the upper echelons of the Southern League, in which Saints were champions six times and Pompey twice, the clubs soon parted company after joining the Football League. It all began so well for Southampton. They completed a double over Portsmouth in one week in September 1920 in the first season in their new surroundings. Having narrowly missed out on promotion in that first season, Southampton gained promotion to Division Two the following year, leaving Pompey behind. However, two years later, Portsmouth joined them and, in 1926/7, Pompey completed a double over Saints on their way to achieving elevation to the top flight. Little would they have known at the time that those meetings would be the last derbies for thirty-four years. This long period of blue ascendancy reached its high point either side of World War Two. In 1939, Pompey won the FA Cup for the first time (and therefore held the cup for longer than any other club to date – as it wasn't competed for again until 1946). Then, in 1948/9 and 1949/50, Portsmouth won back-to-back League titles. During this period,

Southampton were pottering along in the second tier and, in the mid-fifties, they slipped into Division Three South.

Finally the tide began to turn from blue to red in 1959/60 and it did so dramatically. Southampton gained promotion from tier three to be on a par with Portsmouth for the first time since 1927. In their first clash at the start of the 1960/1 season they spelled out clearly a new dawn, by beating Portsmouth 5-1, equalling their biggest ever derby victory. Portsmouth were relegated at the end of that season and, although they bounced back, they didn't finish above Saints again until 2004/5. In 2004 they beat Southampton at Fratton Park for the first time in forty-one years, ending one of the longest and most frustrating droughts in football. The period of red heaven reached its crescendo in 1975/6 and it couldn't have been much better for Saints. They completed a league double over Pompey and a late goal in the second match consigned Portsmouth to relegation from Division Two, leading to running battles between fans. In the same season, as a second tier club, Southampton won their first and, to date, only national trophy, spectacularly beating Manchester United in the FA Cup final. Portsmouth-born Bobby Stokes scored the only goal.

Although both clubs had previously spent time in the top tier individually, they didn't meet each other at the highest level until as late as 1987/8 and even then it was for only one season, as Portsmouth went down. They added two more seasons together in the Premier League in 2003/4 and 2004/5, before Southampton went down. The clubs' ability to avoid each other has been so remarkable that, although they have spent a combined total of sixty-eight seasons in the top tier, in only three have they been together in the elite. 2004/5 was a momentous year for the derby and events helped further cement mutual animosity between the clubs and their supporters. First, Pompey's manager Harry Redknapp left in December 2004, only to become manager of Saints shortly afterwards. Next, a month later, Southampton beat Portsmouth 2-1 in the FA Cup, with former Pompey striker Peter Crouch scoring the decisive penalty for Saints in the last minute. But Portsmouth had the last laugh when Redknapp made his only return to Fratton Park as manager of Saints towards the end of the season. Pompey completed their record home win, 4-1, which effectively condemned Saints to relegation and ended their continuous run of twenty-seven seasons in the top tier. Finally, to add to the drama of an eventful year, Redknapp returned to Portsmouth in November 2005.

In 2008, Portsmouth won the FA Cup for the second time in their history. In doing so, they broke a monopoly of cup success for the Premiership's 'big four'. They also added to another odd aspect of the south coast derby. In most derbies, the club which leads in head-to-head victories; higher league finishes and most years in the top tier also, unsurprisingly, leads in the accumulation of silverware. But that is not the case on the south coast. Saints lead in all three comparisons of 'success', but their ability to turn good positions into silverware lags behind Pompey's, who boast two League titles and two FA Cups, against Southampton's solitary FA Cup triumph.

In 2010, Portsmouth knocked Southampton out of the FA Cup, winning 4-1 at St. Mary's. Not only was this Pompey's biggest ever away win against the

Saints in any senior game, it was the first time ever that Portsmouth had beaten Southampton in a cup derby, the Saints having won previously in one League Cup and four FA Cup encounters. Portsmouth therefore have had recent success in derbies. They completed record-breaking victories in their most recent encounters in the Premiership and FA Cup and managed two derby draws in an otherwise disastrous Championship season in 2011/12. Recent success doesn't alter the fact that Pompey have a terrible overall record in head-to-head meetings with the Saints. Their 21-34 record ranks as the twelfth worst of any club in the sixty derbies studied.

Throughout this account of the south coast derby, the clubs' official nicknames have been used. As in other derbies, fans themselves use derogatory terms for their opponents and Hampshire's insults are worth mentioning, because they are more interesting than most. Pompey fans call their Saints counterparts 'Scum' or more often 'Scummers'. Legend has it that the name stems from an incident in the 1930s when Southampton dockers supposedly broke a strike by dockers in Portsmouth, in an echo of the more famous Millwall/West Ham dispute during the General Strike of 1926. However, while the London equivalent is true, the south coast incident is almost certainly legend rather than fact. Portsmouth's commercial docks were always small and there is no clearly verifiable record of strike breaking by anyone from Southampton, in the 1930s or at any other time.

Saints' fans call Pompey fans 'Skates'. The use of the term for football fans is a recent phenomenon, but the insult itself is much older. It refers to the possibility that lonely sailors might resort to, shall we say, 'romantic liaisons' with the aforesaid fish. Saints' fans have made outrageous allegations that residents of a local Sea-life Centre are regularly subjected to 'interference' by men in blue shirts.

The south coast derby is undoubtedly one of the most fervent derbies in England. It is said to be fuelled by historic antipathy between the Royal Navy (Portsmouth) and the Merchant Navy (Southampton). That may be the case, but it is worth noting that the intensity of rivalry between the clubs has grown significantly in more recent times, rather than being constant throughout history. We should remember that, when Pompey won Hampshire's first ever trophy in 1939, they were invited to parade the FA Cup at The Dell (Southampton's old ground) and were received by delighted Saints' fans.

2011/12 saw Southampton join Portsmouth in the Championship, following Saints' promotion in 2010/11. They were together for only the third time in over twenty seasons and it soon became apparent that they would have very different seasons. As Saints pressed successfully for back-to-back promotions to take them into the Premier League, financially depressed Pompey crashed into tier three. The season showed what an excellent, fervent derby this is, but a two tier gap, if it lasts for any length of time, is not good for a derby.

Finally, Portsmouth have two additional historical claims to fame. Firstly, their 'Pompey chimes' song is probably the second oldest in England. Secondly, one of their earliest goalkeepers was an 'A.C. Smith', who is better known for his other pastime, as he was in fact Sir Arthur Conan Doyle.

Number 7 – Everton v Liverpool

Older club	Everton 1878	(Liverpool 1892)	

Head-to-head record

Number	213 games	
First one	Everton 3 Liverpool 0	*(Oct 1894 in Football League Div 1.)*
Leader (wins)	Liverpool 84-65	

Higher finishes in the League

19th C	Everton	4-3	*(began in 1893 when Liverpool joined the League).*
1900-WW1	Everton	10-5	
1920s	Liverpool	8-2	
1930s	Everton	6-4	
40s+50s	Liverpool	8-6	
1960s	Equal	5-5	
1970s	Liverpool	10-0	
1980s	Liverpool	8-2	
1990s	Liverpool	10-0	
2000s	Liverpool	9-1	
2010/12	Equal	1-1	
TOTAL	Liverpool	71-37	

Silverware (wins)	League	Liverpool	18-9
	FA Cup	Liverpool	7-5
	League Cup	Liverpool	8-0.

Years in Top Tier	Everton	109-97

Biggest Wins

Home	Everton	5	Liverpool	0 *(Apr 1909)*
	Liverpool	7	Everton	4 *(Feb 1933, although the Reds' 6-0 home victory in Sept 1935 might be considered more comprehensive)*
Away	Everton	0	Liverpool	5 *(Nov. 1982)*
	Liverpool	0	Everton	5 *(Oct. 1914)*

History No. 7 – Everton v Liverpool

The story of Liverpool's troubled birth, from the loins of their parent-cum-rival, Everton, was explained in the first half of the book. The city's derby has been played more often than any other. It is also the longest running continuous derby, having been played every year since Liverpool returned to the top flight in 1962/3. There has never been a league derby in Liverpool outside the top tier.

Everton were original members of the Football League. Their inclusion in the twelve pioneers was something of a surprise, as they hadn't achieved much; were not asked to attend early planning meetings and had not been mentioned in initial exchanges about who should be invited to form the new League. Clubs from longer established football heartlands appeared to have better claims, but the League was keen to get a foothold in Merseyside. Even then, Everton's biggest rivals on Merseyside, Bootle, were thought to have as good a claim to join the League. As it turned out, the choice of Everton was inspired. Not only were they the first club to unseat mighty Preston North End, by winning the title in the League's third season, but they were by some distance the best supported club in each of the League's first ten years. This was another surprise given that their city had been a traditional rugby stronghold.

Everton, therefore, had already been League champions, playing at Anfield, before the schism which led to the formation of Liverpool. Everton's Toffees, originally nicknamed the Black Watch because of the colour of their shirts, maintained the upper hand in the derby's early years. In forty-four derby meetings before the First World War, Everton won 23 times to Liverpool's 10 and the Toffees also had a better record in higher league placements.

Both clubs did reasonably well in the pre-war period, winning two League titles each. Everton also won the cup in 1906. On their way to the final at Crystal Palace, Everton beat Liverpool in the semi-final. As Liverpool were League champions in 1905/6 the city had its first taste of being at the top of English football. The clubs didn't have the pleasure of contesting the Charity Shield, because it didn't start until 1908 and, in any event, the tradition of the game being played between League and FA Cup winners was not introduced until later.

After World War One, Liverpool quickly established themselves as a top club, winning consecutive League titles in the early twenties, but from there their star began to fade. They spent the rest of the inter-war period as a fairly average top tier club who didn't win anything. Everton had a much more exciting time.

After playing second fiddle to Liverpool for most of the 1920s, Everton took the League title in 1927/8. William 'Dixie' Dean (by the way, Dean didn't like the name 'Dixie' and preferred 'Billy') scored a record sixty league goals that season, a record yet to be broken. Only two seasons later, Everton were relegated for the first time. They regained their top tier place at the first attempt, as Division Two champions, scoring 121 goals in the process and, in the following year, they became one of only five clubs to win a League title in their first season after promotion (the others being Liverpool in 1905/6; Tottenham in 1950/1; Ipswich in 1961/2 and Nottingham Forest in 1977/8).

Everton added the FA Cup to their trophy cabinet in 1933 and took the League title again in 1938/9, the final year before suspension of football for the duration of World War Two. Overall, Everton could claim to be the second best team in the country in the 1930s, albeit some way behind all-conquering Arsenal. By 1939, Everton led Liverpool five-four in League titles and two wins to nil in the FA Cup. Everton were second in the all-time success list, though well adrift of Aston Villa and only marginally ahead of Sunderland. Liverpool were twelfth. The Toffees had also usually been the better supported club, though not by much.

The post-war period started so well, with Liverpool retaining Everton's pre-war crown for the city in 1946/7. In 1950, the two met in an FA Cup semi-final. Liverpool's 2-0 victory sent them to only their second final. But from there, both clubs declined for a few years and the 1950s became the nadir for Merseyside's football. First, in 1950/1, Everton were relegated for the second time in their history. To put this into context, Everton have the best record of any club with regard to top tier appearances, having missed only four seasons at the top out of 113 (to 2011/12). Three of those four seasons in tier two began with their relegation in 1950/1. When Everton returned, they exchanged places with Liverpool, and the Reds' plight became even greater than Everton's, as Liverpool spent eight seasons in the second tier.

Both clubs emerged from the relative depths of the fifties as major and pretty equal forces in the 1960s. By 1970, each had seven championships, but Everton led 3-1 in FA Cup victories, Liverpool finally having tasted long-awaited cup success in 1965.

Equity between the clubs, which had broadly existed since their original split way back in 1892, then changed drastically, as Liverpool proceeded to win eight more League titles before Everton added to their own tally, in 1984/5. So dominant were Liverpool in the 1970s and 80s, many forget that in the eighties at least Everton were the second most successful side in England.

Merseyside football was at its zenith and it was amply demonstrated as the two clashed in three cup final derbies – in the League Cup (1984) and the FA Cup (1986 and 1989). Liverpool won all three, with Ian Rush bagging four of the seven Liverpool goals scored. The picture was even better in the League, as the city's finest monopolised the League championship for no less than seven seasons from 1981 to 1988. Everton had the pleasure of denying Liverpool the accolade of being the first club to win League titles four years in a row, when the Toffees ended the Reds' reign in 1984/5. The two finished in first and second places for three years running from 1984 to 1987. Everton, as League champions, narrowly missed out on the 'double' in 1985, losing the FA Cup final to Manchester United, who had beaten Liverpool in the semis. Liverpool went one better in 1985/6, achieving a League and FA Cup double, with Everton as runners-up in both competitions.

Despite their excellent record, the past forty years have been frustrating for Evertonians. When the Toffees finished above the Reds in the League in 2004/5, it was only the fourth time they had done so in forty seasons and, on all three previous occasions (1969/70, 1984/5 and 1986/7), Everton had had to win the League title to finish above their neighbours. Furthermore, Everton's achievement in 2004/5 went largely unnoticed, because Liverpool ended the season by taking the European club title in dramatic circumstances. Talk about setting the bar high! Equally frustrating is the fact that a number of Liverpool's best players in recent decades grew up as supporters of Everton. Examples include Michael Owen, Jamie Carragher, Steve McManaman, Robbie Fowler and Everton's tormentor-in-chief, Ian Rush. At least 'Billy/Dixie' Dean was a life-long Evertonian.

The city's record of success in the eighties could hardly have got better, and it didn't. Both clubs have maintained their positions as two of England's greatest, but the city hasn't seen a League title since Liverpool's success in 1989/90. By the end of the 1980s, Liverpool and Everton held the number one and two spots respectively in the all-time domestic success table, even though Everton had fallen a long way behind the Reds. The clubs are now second and fourth.

In addition to their high profile clashes in cup finals, there have been other significant derby results over the years. In October 1922, Liverpool beat Everton twice in a week on their way to winning the League title. In 1931/2, and again in 1938/9, Everton completed doubles over the Reds and the points gained were ultimately crucial in winning the League in both years. Liverpool's only consolation was to put the Toffees out of the FA Cup in 1931/2. The dark days around the fifties saw no league derbies for twelve seasons, but the only meeting in the period, an FA Cup clash in 1955, provided long term embarrassment for Everton. They were a top tier club, but lost 0-4 at home to second tier Liverpool. The clubs met five times in one season in 1990/1. Liverpool won twice in the League, but Everton eventually prevailed in the FA Cup after two replays.

Over the years, much has been made of the supposed lack of animosity between supporters of Merseyside's clubs. There is no real geographical split between them. There tend to be Everton and Liverpool pubs in the same areas across the city. Divided loyalties in families are not that unusual. Their rivalry has perhaps been diminished by Liverpool fans' greater hatred of Manchester United, as well as Merseyside's collective sense of solidarity in adversity. It is certainly the case that there is a good deal more mixing of blue and red at city derbies than would ever be found in Manchester, Sheffield or Bristol. However, camaraderie should not be exaggerated. This is a fierce derby by any definition and Everton fans harbour feelings of resentment and injustice about three things. First, as has been outlined above, the clubs traditionally were equally successful, and indeed the Toffees had a slight edge before the 1970s. Evertonians believe their own achievements have gone largely unnoticed because of their neighbours. Second, as with Manchester City fans in Manchester, Toffees think they are true Liverpudlians, whereas Liverpool are a global brand. Third, Evertonians feel that the behaviour of Liverpool fans at Heysel, which led to English clubs being banned from European competition, robbed the Toffees of a great opportunity to capitalise on their League titles and move on to a higher plane.

As with Manchester's city derby and the Liverpool v Manchester United clash, in 2011/12 Merseyside's derby is potentially at a crossroads. Everton fans have always seen this as their primary derby, but Liverpool fans have not done so for some time. Whether or not that situation continues will no doubt depend upon the performance of the four clubs in Manchester and Liverpool over the next few years. Everton's rare higher league placing over Liverpool in 2011/12, coupled with dramatic developments in Manchester, has given Merseyside's derby a significant shot in the arm. In any event, whether or not the derby reverts to its previously agreed primary status, it will certainly continue to be big – very big.

Derby quote: " I know this is a sad occasion, but I think that Dixie would be amazed to know that even in death he could draw a bigger crowd to Goodison than Everton do on a Saturday afternoon".
Bill Shankly at Dixie Dean's funeral

Number 8 – Ipswich Town v Norwich City

Older club   Ipswich 1878   (Norwich 1902)

Head-to-head record

Number	93 games	
First one	Ipswich 5 Norwich 0 *(Sept 1946 in Football League Division Three South).*	
Leader (wins)	**Ipswich 40-36**	

Higher finishes in the League

19th C	Nil	
1900-WWI	Nil	
1920s	Nil	
1930s	Norwich	1-0 *(began when Ipswich joined the League in 1938/9)*
40s+50s	Ipswich	10-4
1960s	Ipswich	9-1
1970s	Ipswich	9-1
1980s	Ipswich	6-4
1990s	Equal	5-5
2000s	Ipswich	7-3
2010/12	Norwich	2-0
TOTAL	**Ipswich**	**46-21**

Silverware (wins)

League	**Ipswich**	**1-0**
FA Cup	**Ipswich**	**1-0**
League Cup	**Norwich**	**2-0**

Years in Top Tier   **Ipswich   26-22**

Biggest Wins

Home	Ipswich	5	Norwich	0	*(Sept 1946, Feb 1977 and Feb 1998)*
	Norwich	4	Ipswich	1	*(Nov 2010)*
Away	Ipswich	1	Norwich	5	*(Apr 2011)*
	Norwich	1	Ipswich	5	*(Sept 1947)*

History No. 8 – Ipswich v Norwich

Ipswich are the older club, but remained amateur until 1936 and so played in minor leagues. For a short time, following Norwich's foundation in 1902, the two clashed in the Norfolk & Suffolk League. They both played second fiddle to the mighty Lowestoft Town, who thrashed Norwich 5-0 in City's first ever competitive outing. At the time, both Ipswich and Norwich played in blue and white.

In 1904 City, together with Lowestoft, were hauled before the FA, accused of professionalism. Lowestoft paid a fine in order to retain amateur status, but Norwich responded by turning openly professional and joining the Southern League. Had Lowestoft chosen a different course of action, City could have had a derby with the 'Trawler Boys' of Lowestoft, rather than the 'Tractor Boys' of Ipswich (incidentally, 'Tractor Boys' is an unofficial nickname, which didn't emerge until the 1990s). Instead, professional City and the amateur Towns of Lowestoft and Ipswich parted company.

In the following decades Ipswich developed a derby rivalry with Cambridge City, after outgrowing the likes of Lowestoft. The Citizens or Cits, as Norwich City were known, didn't have a local derby. Norwich may seem fairly isolated now, being almost fifty miles from their nearest current rivals, but when City opted for the Southern League it did not contain a single team within a hundred miles of Norwich. Along with other Southern League clubs, City joined the Football League in 1920/1, while their reserve side continued to play in the re-formulated Southern League.

Both East Anglian clubs have likeable, if slightly quirky images. To take Norwich as the example – they boast the oldest song in football ('*On the Ball City*'), which pre-dates the club itself and is decidedly odd to modern ears. In 1908, the club moved from a perfectly flat and sensible ground to a disused chalk pit called 'Ruymp's Hole'. One end had a concrete wall supporting a cliff (yes, a cliff in Norfolk!) on which supporters stood, and off which the ball would bounce back onto the pitch. Their centre-forward at the time was one Percy Varco, who became the hero of another odd song called, imaginatively, '*Give it to Percy Varco*'. The Canaries, as they had become, re-named Ruymp's Hole, 'The Nest', and it was their increasingly dangerous home until 1935.

More recently, an unusual ingredient has been added to the mix by celebrity chef, Delia Smith, who is not exactly a typical football club owner. Delia proved what all good football supporters know to be true – perfectly sensible at virtually all other times, supporters can do the daftest things at football matches. In 2005, an allegedly sober Delia invaded the pitch at half time, complete with microphone, to harangue fans for being too quiet. It is to her credit that her "*let's be 'avin' you!*" call to arms appeared to be met with a resigned '*fair enough*' response from assembled Canaries. Readers might ponder what would have happened had Ken Bates or Malcolm Glazer tried something similar.

In 1930/1, Norwich had to seek re-election. Having survived that scare they were promoted to the second tier for the first time in 1933/4. Meanwhile, in

1936/7, the newly professional Ipswich joined the Southern League and won it at the first attempt, beating Norwich City Reserves into second place. In the final year before the outbreak of World War Two, Ipswich were elected to the Football League, in place of Gillingham. Meanwhile, Norwich were relegated from the second tier. This set up the prospect of a new derby between established City professionals and the upstarts of Town, who had been only just better than City's *Reserves* two years earlier. However, the eagerly anticipated clash had to wait for another eight years.

Unfortunately for City they were at a low point when football resumed. They finished next to bottom of Division Three South in the first two seasons following the re-start and had to apply for re-election both times. Ipswich took full advantage, completing a derby double in 1946/7 and winning the very first home game 5-0, a record victory that has been equalled, but never bettered, since. They continued to rub in their advantage, by achieving their still record away victory, by 5-1 in 1947/8.

In 1953/4, Ipswich gained promotion for the first time to tier two. They came straight back down but, in 1956/7, an Ipswich double over Norwich helped them to another promotion, on goal average from Torquay United (Torquay have never subsequently been so close to achieving second tier status). To make things worse for Canaries, they finished bottom of the League and had to seek re-election for a fourth time.

By 1960/1, East Anglia's winds began blowing in the right direction. Norwich had recovered and both clubs were challenging for promotion to the top tier for the first time. They met twice in two days at Christmas 1960. The Blues won 3-0 at Carrow Road on Boxing Day and 4-1 the next day at Portman Road. They went on to win the Second Division championship by one point. City, although well behind, finished a respectable fourth. Therefore, in the same season, both clubs had achieved their highest ever places in the League.

If 1960/1 was a new high, 1961/2 was stratospheric, as East Anglia gained fifty per cent of its silverware to date in one season. City had a moderate year in the League, but took their first senior trophy by winning the League Cup, then in its second year of existence. Town, led by Alf Ramsey, achieved the unthinkable, by taking the League title at their first attempt in the top tier. In addition to their League Cup triumph, second tier Norwich managed to tarnish Ipswich's fantastic year just a little, by knocking them out of the FA Cup at Portman Road. The first glory period for Ipswich didn't last long. Ramsey left in April 1963, famously to become England's World Cup winning manager. In 1963/4, just two years after winning the title, Town finished bottom, having conceded 121 goals, and were relegated. Two years later, as Sir Alf gained immortality with England, Ipswich ended the season below Norwich, in fifteenth place in tier two.

In 1971/2, Norwich were promoted to make their debut in the top tier and, in 1972/3, East Anglia's derby took place at the top for the first time. City won the inaugural clash at Portman Road 2-1. This was, however, to be the start of Town's most prolonged golden era. Although they didn't repeat their stunning feat of 1961/2, the Blues were to finish in the top six of English football nine times in ten seasons, from 1972/3 onwards. In 1978, their centenary year, Ipswich won the FA Cup for the only time to date. They also won East Anglia's only European trophy, the UEFA Cup in 1981. This wonderful era in Ipswich's history may well become a museum piece. More recently, other relatively small clubs have attained short-lived, top-notch performances but, since Town's run, no other club of comparable size has achieved a sustained period of success to match them – and it seems unlikely that any will in future.

At the same time, Canaries had mixed fortunes, bouncing up and down between first and second tiers, and finishing below the Blues every year, except in 1977/8. However, they continued their good form in the League Cup, reaching semi-finals for three years in succession from 1973. They were beaten finalists in 1973 and 1975.

Norwich's League Cup odysseys continued in the 1980s. The clubs met in cup competitions four times in five years in the early eighties. Ipswich won a League Cup encounter in 1980/1 and Norwich an FA Cup clash two years later. Norwich then had the pleasure of putting Ipswich out of the League Cup twice in successive years, making it three cup knock-outs in three years.

1984/5 was one of the most spectacular years for the derby. Norwich came back from a first-leg deficit to beat Ipswich in a semi-final of the League Cup, on their way to beating Sunderland in the final. On the other hand, Ipswich completed a double in league derbies. At the end of the season they finished just one point ahead of Norwich. QPR and Coventry were also one point ahead, Coventry having pulled off the unlikely feat of winning their last three games to save themselves from relegation. So, having won their most important trophy to date, the Canaries went down. To add to their disappointment, Norwich were one of the victims of the European ban on English clubs following the Heysel disaster. The boot was on the other foot a year later, as Ipswich suffered relegation at the hands of Coventry's Houdinis and Norwich replaced them, having been second tier champions. This exchange of places heralded the Canaries' longest period of dominance, as they finished above the Blues for the next nine seasons.

It was also Norwich's most successful period. They were fifth in the top tier in 1986/7, fourth in 1988/9 and third, their best finish ever, in the Premier League's inaugural season in 1992/3. Even then, Town spoiled the year, by completing a league double in derby games. In 1994/5, both clubs were relegated together from the Premiership and, since then, both have had up and down experiences. The Tractor Boys returned to the top flight in 1999/2000, but survived for only two years. In 2003/4, the Canaries did the double over Ipswich on their way to winning the second tier championship, while Ipswich lost in the play-offs. But Norwich came straight back down in 2004/5 and Ipswich lost in the play-offs again.

In 2008/9, the Canaries were relegated to tier three, for the first time in fifty years. Their defeat at Portman Road towards the season's climax effectively sealed their fate, to the glee of baying Tractor Boys. The world looked decidedly blue for the Yellows when the lost their first game in the third tier 1-7, at home to Colchester United. However, hope springs eternal in football and fortunes can change dramatically. Norwich recovered from their day-one disaster to gain promotion in 2009/10 and to renew the derby days with Ipswich in 2010/11. The Canaries went on to achieve back-to-back promotions and, in doing so, they re-wrote the 'Old Farm' derby's record book. Their biggest ever home win over Ipswich came in November 2010. It was followed up by their biggest ever away win against the Blues in April 2011, as the Canaries marched on to the Premiership.

Overall, Ipswich still have the edge, especially in higher League finishes. Given that the clubs have been in the same division as each other for forty-one of sixty-seven seasons since Ipswich joined the League in 1938, it is surprising that the Blues have amassed such a big lead over the Canaries in league placements (46-21). The lead was established early. In thirty-three seasons, from 1953/4 to 1985/6, Norwich finished above Ipswich in the League on only two occasions. Norwich fans would point to two things. Firstly, the clubs' League records have been much closer in recent times and secondly, Norwich seem to have the 'eye' on Ipswich when it comes to derbies in cup competitions. Canaries lead 2-0 in FA Cup knock-outs and 4-2 in the League Cup. In the overall historical success list, Tractor Boys are 28th and Canaries 35th although both, especially Ipswich, gave many clubs a considerable head start, given their late entry into the League. If post-World War Two records alone are taken into account, Ipswich rise to 17th and Norwich to 28th.

Both clubs are generally seen by neutrals as well run, well supported and friendly clubs, providing models for how relatively small clubs can survive and prosper. The likeable image is usually well-deserved, but anyone who thinks of these two as 'cuddly' would be well advised to stay clear of Carrow or Portman Roads on derby days – make no mistake, this is one of the fiercest derbies in England. Their fans, comparatively welcoming of most other visitors, seem to think that a mixture of blue and yellow creates red – rage that is.

Norwich's elevation to the Premiership in 2011/12 and their survival for 2012/13 means that the derby will not be played in 2012/13, but it remains strong. It has been very competitive in the past thirty years and current ascendancy for the historical underdog will do it no harm.

Finally, East Anglia has had not two, but three England managers. Ipswich's two are, of course, the legends Sir Alf Ramsey and Sir Bobby Robson. Not in quite the same universe, the fictional England manager Mike Bassett gained his reputation by winning the 'Mr. Clutch Cup' with Norwich. Ipswich's contribution to movies was to provide many of the players in the 1981 film '*Escape to Victory*', alongside 'goalkeeper', Silvester Stallone.

Number 9 – Arsenal v Tottenham Hotspur

Older club   Tottenham 1882 (Arsenal 1886)

Head-to-head record

Number	167 games	
First one	Arsenal 1 Tottenham 0 (Dec 1909 in Football League Div. 1)	
Leader (wins)	**Arsenal 70-53**	

Higher finishes in the League

19th C	Nil	
1900-WWI	Tottenham	4-3 (began in 1908/9 when Spurs were elected to Division Two. Arsenal were already in Division One)
1920s	Arsenal	6-4
1930s	Arsenal	10-0
40s+50s	Arsenal	9-5
1960s	Tottenham	9-1
1970s	Arsenal	9-1
1980s	Equal	5-5
1990s	Arsenal	8-2
2000s	Arsenal	10-0
2010/12	Arsenal	2-0
TOTAL	**Arsenal**	**63-30**

Silverware (wins)

League	**Arsenal**	**13-2**
FA Cup	**Arsenal**	**10-8**
League Cup	**Tottenham**	**4-2**.

Years in Top Tier   **Arsenal 95-77**

Biggest Wins

Home	Arsenal	5	Tottenham	1	*(Oct 1934)*
	Tottenham	5	Arsenal	0	*(Dec 1911 and Apr 1983)*
Away	Arsenal	2	Tottenham	4	*(Dec 1926)*
	Tottenham	0	Arsenal	6	*(Mar 1935)*

History No. 9 – Arsenal v Tottenham Hotspur

The clubs grew from familiar sources. Tottenham emerged from an older cricket club and Arsenal were a work's team, originally called Dial Square, the name of a workshop in the Arsenal at Woolwich. Their first ever meeting in any game was in 1887 and it had to be abandoned because of 'darkness', which was presumably a reference to the light available, rather than the mood of these bitter enemies. Tottenham are older, but Arsenal were first to turn professional and the first southern club to join the Football League. In the 1890s, both clubs played in red shirts, Arsenal's having been given to them by Nottingham Forest.

The story of Arsenal's move north of the River Thames is covered in the first half. Suffice it to say here that they were not welcomed by Spurs or the local population, but were in financial difficulties and desperately needed bigger crowds, which they achieved almost immediately after their move. Also outlined earlier are the dubious circumstances that led to Arsenal being granted surprise promotion to the top tier after World War One, an elevation awarded to them at the expense of Tottenham. Arsenal didn't look back and have never been relegated since. Neither club was very successful in the early years. It was Tottenham who made the first impact, winning the FA Cup in 1901, while still in the Southern League, and winning it again in 1921, as a Football League outfit. By the end of the 1920s, Tottenham were at a lowly twentieth in the all-time success list, but Arsenal were not even in the top twenty.

That position was to change drastically in the next decade. In 1925, Arsenal had appointed as manager the legendary Herbert Chapman, who had inspired Huddersfield to their championship titles in the mid-1920s. In a mediocre, journeyman playing career, Yorkshireman Chapman had played for Spurs. As a manager he was certainly not mediocre. He re-invented the tactics of the game, introducing the WM formation and establishing Arsenal as a fast-moving, counter-attacking outfit, tactics that were frequently lambasted as 'boring' and 'lucky' – little is new in football.

Arsenal's first success was in the FA Cup final of 1930 when, ironically, they beat Chapman's old club, Huddersfield. Victory was the catalyst for the Gunners to become by far the most successful club of a decade in which they took the League title five times and the FA Cup again in 1936. They repeated Huddersfield's feat of three successive titles, though Chapman didn't live to see that achievement. By the end of the thirties, Arsenal lay sixth in the all-time success list. Spurs, having spent most of the decade in the second tier, were still in twentieth place and they have never been able to catch Arsenal since in the all-time table.

Tottenham's first League title came in 1950/1, but their greatest triumphs were achieved a decade later. In 1960/1, Spurs did the 'impossible', by completing a League and FA Cup 'double'. In recent years, achievement of the double has become fairly commonplace, but at the time it seemed an unattainable goal. Many teams had come close, but Spurs were the first club to 'do the double' since Aston Villa in 1896/7. People should have known that their manager, another Yorkshireman, Bill Nicholson would do something special in his managerial career – his first match in charge of Spurs ended in a 10-4 victory over Everton. Spurs have a strange habit of achieving success in years ending with '1'. Eight of their fourteen domestic titles have been gained in the first years of decades – in addition to both League titles, gained in 1951 and 1961, they won the FA Cup in 1901, 1921, 1961, 1981 and 1991 and the League Cup in 1971.

The 'double' eluded the great Arsenal side of the 1930s, but other Gunners have achieved it, not once but three times. Their first in 1970/1 included the added bonus of clinching the League title at White Hart Lane. It was a dramatic affair, as the Gunners scored the only goal four minutes from the end. Had they drawn, they would have been level on points with Leeds and conceded the title by one goal. The second double came in 1997/8 and they almost achieved a domestic treble, losing 4-3 on aggregate to Chelsea in a League Cup semi-final. Their third double in 2001/2 included a revenge mission, as they defeated Chelsea in the FA Cup final.

Amazingly, the Gunners have been involved in two even closer finishes for the League title than the one in 1970/1. They won on both occasions. Famously, they snatched the championship from Liverpool on the last day of the 1988/9 season, by beating Liverpool at Anfield. A late goal secured a 2-0 victory to put Arsenal on top by goals scored, as both clubs had the same points and goal difference. Less well known is that Arsenal shaded Preston North End to the title in 1952/3, on goal average by 0.099 of a goal.

Given that Arsenal and Tottenham are respectively the third and seventh most successful English clubs of all time, it is not surprising to find that a number of seasons contend for the honour of being North London's finest hour. For example, the clubs shared the Community Shield in 1991. Arsenal had won the League title and Tottenham the FA Cup. Spurs beat the Gunners in the semi-final, thereby denying them an opportunity to complete another double. However, the top year for the derby probably has to be 1970/1. Arsenal did the double, while Tottenham finished third in the League and won the League Cup, thereby completing a clean sweep of domestic honours for North London.

Over the years there have been many crucial derby games. Arsenal's record home and away victories over Tottenham were both achieved in the same season, 1934/5. The points and the 11-1 aggregate helped Arsenal to the title and Spurs to relegation. In Spurs' double year of 1960/1 they had the added satisfaction of another 'double', beating Arsenal 4-2 and 3-2 in derby games. In both 1968/9 and 1983/4, the Gunners completed league doubles over Spurs and knocked them out of the League Cup in the same years. In 1993, Arsenal beat Spurs in the semi-final of the FA Cup at Wembley, taking revenge for Tottenham's victory in the semi-final two years earlier. At least Spurs had the consolation of winning both derby games in the League that season.

The most memorable win for Arsenal over their old rivals possibly came in 2003/4. Arsenal were champions and became the first team since Preston, in the first year of the League, to complete a season in the top tier undefeated. On the way, the Gunners repeated their 'nose rubbing' of 1970/1, by clinching the title at a very frustrated White Hart Lane.

An unusual aspect of North London derby matches is that, on no less than *nine* occasions, one of the teams has scored four goals and yet not won the game. There have been four 4-4 draws and, in 2004, Arsenal won 5-4 at White Hart Lane. Whereas most derbies are cagey, it is rarely a turgid affair in North London, as was proven yet again in 2012 as Arsenal came from two down to win 5-2 at the Emirates.

The picture for the derby in 2012/3 is mixed. 2011/2 was an excellent season in which the clubs finished third and fourth in the Premiership, with Arsenal prevailing on the final day of the season – just. By any standards Tottenham are a very good club and their derby with Arsenal is fierce and strong. But sometimes being 'very good' is not good enough. The fact is that Spurs have not finished above Arsenal for seventeen seasons. Furthermore, in recent times, Chelsea have hunted down and overtaken Spurs as London's second most successful club of all time. The derby is therefore beginning to take on similar characteristics to those in Manchester and Liverpool, where the battle of the Reds has interfered with the pre-eminence of traditional city derbies. Tottenham fans still clearly see Arsenal as their primary derby and most Arsenal fans still agree, but an increasing number of Gooners are turning their attention to Chelsea.

Number 10 – Manchester City v Manchester United

Older club	United 1878	*(City 1880. City's founding date is often given as 1887, when Ardwick FC were born, or occasionally as late as 1894, when Ardwick re-formed to become Manchester City. However, arguably the club can be traced back further to the establishment of West Gorton in 1880 and this is the date accepted by the club.)*	

Head-to-head record

Number	160 games	
First one	City 2 United 5 *(Nov 1894 in Football League Div.2)*	
Leader (wins)	United 65-45	

Higher finishes in the League

19th C	Equal	4-4	*(began in 1892/3 when both were elected to the League, United to Div.1 and City to Div.2).*
1900-WWI	City	8-7	
1920s	City	7-3	
1930s	City	9-1	
40s+50s	United	13-1	
1960s	United	8-2	
1970s	City	6-4	
1980s	United	10-0	
1990s	United	9-1	
2000s	United	10-0	
2010/12	Equal	1-1	
TOTAL	United	70-39	

Silverware (wins)	League	United	19-3
	FA Cup	United	11-5
	League Cup	United	4-2.

Years in Top Tier	United	87-83

Biggest Wins	Home	City	5	United 1 *(Sept 1989)*	
		United	5	City 0 *(Nov 1994)*	
	Away	City	2	United 5 *(Nov 1894)*	
		United	1	City 6 *(Jan 1926 and Oct 2011)*	

History No. 10 – Manchester United v Manchester City

Manchester, like Liverpool, was originally a rugby city and this was reflected in the fact that the city's clubs had fairly quiet starts to their league and cup histories. United, as Newton Heath, were elected into the League's top tier in 1892/3, with City, as Ardwick, given a place in Division Two in the same year. United promptly finished bottom of Division One in their first two seasons and only survived after the first season via the test match play-off system. In two years, they won just twelve and lost forty of sixty games, a truly inauspicious start for the club later to become England's domestic number one. The clubs were evenly matched at the time, but it didn't seem that way when they first met in a competitive derby. In November 1894, recently relegated Newton Heath beat, recently re-named, Manchester City 5-2 away from home. It is still United's record away victory over their blue rivals. Later in the same season, United won again, 4-1 at home.

After promotion in 1902/3, City finished second in the top tier in 1903/4 and also won the FA Cup. They followed it up with a third place finish in 1904/5, while United lingered in the second tier. However, the season ended in uproar. Aston Villa captain, Alec Leake, claimed that City's Billy Meredith had offered him a £10 bribe to throw a crucial game. Meredith, one of the finest players ever to the grace the game, was found guilty and banned for a year. City refused him financial help and so Meredith decided to turn whistleblower. He gave evidence that City's recent successes had been built upon illegal breaches of the £4 per week maximum wage rule. Football authorities in those days had a good deal more bottle than their current counterparts have shown in response to recent scandalous breaches of league rules. City were forced to sell their players at an auction at Manchester's Queen's Hotel. United, of course, showed the expected 'solidarity' with their neighbours' plight – they bought four City players, including Meredith, at knock-down prices. If the derby wasn't hot before these events, it certainly was afterwards. That having been said, here was another example of how fans' attitudes were different in the past, because at the time most City fans welcomed the fact that United bought their players, rather than clubs from elsewhere, as it meant that Meredith and Co. could still be seen in Manchester. Modern City fans might not react in quite the same way!

Boosted by their City imports, United were promoted in 1905/6 and were League champions within two years, winning by a huge nine point margin. City had recovered sufficiently to finish third. It looked, therefore, as though Manchester would become a major player in English football. But it didn't happen. United won the FA Cup in 1909 and the League again in 1910/11, but then the clubs faded and both spent time in the second tier in the period between the world wars.

In the early 1930s, they faced a threat from a potential new derby rival, a third professional Mancunian club. Manchester Central were formed by the owner of Belle Vue, who had opposed Manchester City's move away from East Manchester in the twenties. When, in 1931, Wigan Borough resigned from the League in mid-season, Central applied to replace them. Initially, their application was looked upon favourably by the Football League, but it was vehemently opposed by the existing clubs, especially by United who were struggling financially and had attracted crowds of less than 12,000 in the previous season. The League ruled against Central, much to the disgust of many in East Manchester. What might have been?

City emerged the stronger club in those inter-war years, finishing above United in sixteen of twenty seasons, and they brought home Manchester's first silverware since 1910/11 by winning the cup in 1934. In the same season United avoided relegation to Division Three North by just one point. City pressed on and took the League title in 1936/7. United, who had been promoted in the previous season, were again relegated, completing what must have been a double celebration for City fans.

All looked rosy for the blue half of Manchester in 1936/7. Incredibly, however, the following season saw City's reigning champions relegated, despite scoring more goals than any team in the division and having a positive goal average. Across the city, United were promoted. Therefore, in an astonishing turnaround, the interruption of League football in 1939 began with United above City for the first time in eleven years. It was to be a truly historic turning point. Up to 1939, City and United were placed thirteenth and eighteenth respectively in the all-time success table. Both had three pieces of silverware, but City had a better overall record (for example, leading 28-15 in higher League placements). The Citizens had also been the better supported club in each of the previous fourteen seasons, including being the best supported club in the whole of England in 1927/8 (when in Division Two) and again in 1928/9. Since the Second World War, City have finished above United in the League on only eleven occasions in sixty-six years, most of which were in the seventies. Before their epic encounter in 2011/12, in thirty-three seasons from 1977/8 to 2010/11, City finished above United once (in 1990/1). Post World War Two, City's crowds have never exceeded those of United, even when the Reds dropped into the second tier.

If the 1920s were the low point for the Manchester derby as a whole, there are at least three contenders for the high point. Arguably, it was when the city's clubs met in the Charity Shield of 1956. The game itself, which United won 1-0, was not especially important, but Manchester was there in force, with its League champions (United) and FA Cup holders (City) from the 1955/6 season. The second contender would be 1967/8, when City took the League title from reigning champions United, who came second by two points and went on to become the first English winners of the European Cup. The third is, of course, 2011/12. The season began with a repeat of 1956, as League champions United beat FA Cup holders City in the Community Shield. It continued with a record equalling 6-1 victory for City in the season's first derby at Old Trafford and partial revenge for United, as they despatched City from the FA Cup. Things concluded with a nail-biting few moments in which City snatched the League title from United with virtually the last kick of the season. A derby double for City had proved crucial in the end.

Mention of the 6-1 derby drubbing in 2011 revives memories of very different times for City. It is also a reminder that fans can sometimes find succour in derbies, even when their overall position is dire. In 1925/6, City were relegated and conceded 100 goals in doing so, while United sat comfortably in mid-table. But, in this particular year, City's derby games with United provided consolation in abundance. In January 1926, they achieved their record away victory against United and the (now equal) biggest ever win by either side in a Manchester derby, beating the Reds 6-1. City followed it up less than two months later by beating United 3-0 in an FA Cup semi-final.

In 1954/5, both clubs finished reasonably well, United fifth and City seventh, but this was during a period when United were very dominant. They had finished above City in every year since the war and had been lower than fourth on only one occasion in the previous eight years. They also went on to win the League title in the following two seasons. In the midst of this era of misery for City fans, the derbies of 1954/5 again came to the rescue of those Sky Blues who may have been contemplating ending it all. City beat United 3-2 at Maine Road early in the season, knocked United out of the cup in January and capped it all by winning 5-0 at Old Trafford in the League two weeks later.

In 1969/70, the two met on no fewer than five occasions, as they were drawn against each other in both cup competitions. United finished above City in the League, but City not only completed a League double, they also beat United 4-3 on aggregate in the semi-final, on their way to winning the League Cup. United took revenge by knocking City out of the FA Cup, but lost in that semi-final too.

City's 5-1 win at Maine Road in September 1989, their biggest ever home victory over the enemy, was a meal that had to last a long, long time. City didn't beat United again until 2002. In the intervening period, they played sixteen derbies, losing ten and drawing six, including a run of eight defeats in a row from 1993 to 2000. In 1995/6, United completed a derby treble, when they not only won two league clashes, but also put City out of the FA Cup. United went on to complete a League and FA Cup double, beating Liverpool in the Cup final and, to ice an abundant cake, City were relegated. Even for Manchester United fans, it doesn't get much better than that.

Talk of relegation brings us to one of the most famous clashes of all between Manchester's clubs. In 1973/4, they met at Old Trafford towards the end of April. City won 1-0. The goal, a typically cheeky back-heel, was scored late on by Denis Law, one of United's all-time heroes (Law had in fact played for City before United as well as afterwards). It was Law's last contribution as a player, as he was substituted shortly after scoring and his glittering career ended there. Folklore says that Law's goal condemned United to relegation. In a sense it is true. Losing to City ensured that United were relegated on that very day and therefore gave City fans the satisfaction of wallowing in Red woe, while dancing around Old Trafford. However, it was not the last game of the season and United would have required a very fortunate series of results to save them, even if Law had not scored. United ended the season five points adrift of safety. Denis could retire in peace. He was not to blame.

The most vehement City fans take heart from their belief that their club is truly Mancunian. They deny that Manchester United are actually from Manchester (and hence the provocative 'welcome to Manchester' posters greeting the transfer of Carlos Tevez from United to City in 2009). In the technical sense of local authority boundaries, they are correct, as United's 'Theatre of Dreams' is just over the city border in Stretford, a part of Trafford local authority, rather than Manchester. However, few would wish to pursue this technical geographical point in Stretford's pubs and clubs. On the whole, City enjoy more support from the east of Manchester and United from the west. There is also something of a north/south divide.

In 2012/13, Manchester's derby is gathering steam at a breath-taking pace, after years of decline created by United's dominance. It is intertwined with Liverpool's city derby, because of United's battle of the Reds. It remains to be seen whether or not City's new found wealth will translate into long-term riches on the field but, in the light of their Premier League title, portents look good for lovers of sky blue. The comparative performance of the four Manchester and Liverpool clubs will in part determine which will be primary derbies in a few years time. Other things being equal, closeness of geography normally rules, but it is up to City to build upon their success in 2011/12 and change the course of history.

Derby quote: " I think the fact that Sir Alex Ferguson rested (referee) Howard Webb has a lot to do with the result".
Noel Gallagher celebrating City's 6-1 victory at Old Trafford

Number 11 – Luton Town v Watford

Older club	**Watford 1881** (Luton 1885)		

Head-to-head record

Number	120 games	
First one	Luton 2 Watford 2 (Oct 1898 in the FA Cup)	
Leader (wins)	**Luton 55-35**	

Higher finishes in the League

19th C	Nil		
1900-WWI	Luton	9-6	(began in the Southern League in 1900/01)
1920s	Luton	7-3	(Football League meetings began in 1920/1)
1930s	Luton	9-1	
40s+50s	Luton	14-0	
1960s	Watford	7-3	
1970s	Luton	10-0	
1980s	Luton	7-3	
1990s	Watford	7-3	
2000s	Watford	10-0	
2010/12	Watford	2-0	
TOTAL	**Luton**	**62-39**	

Silverware (wins)	**League**	**Equal.** *Neither club has won the League.* **Watford** *came closest, as runners-up in 1982/3*
	FA Cup	**Equal.** *Neither club has won the FA Cup. Both have been beaten finalists once*
	League Cup	**Luton 1-0.**

Years in Top Tier	**Luton 16-8**	

Biggest Wins	**Home**	Luton	5	Watford	0 *(Jan 1926)*
		Watford	5	Luton	2 *(Apr 1983)*
	Away	Luton	0	Watford	4 *(Oct 1997)*
		Watford	0	Luton	4 *(Sept 1929)*

History No. 11 – Luton Town v Watford

Watford are older, but Luton were the bigger and more ambitious club in the early years. Town were the first southern club to turn professional; they finished second to Millwall twice in the Southern League's first two seasons and were the second southern club, after Woolwich Arsenal, to join the Football League. The clubs first met in a major competition in the FA Cup of 1898/9. Luton won, after a replay, and soon became Watford's bogey team, meeting and beating the Hornets in the cup four times in six seasons either side of the turn of the century.

Luton's first adventure into the Football League nearly crippled them financially and so they returned to the Southern League in 1900/01. Waiting for them were Watford who, as West Herts, had joined the Southern League in 1896/7 and had achieved their first promotion to the top division in time for Luton's re-appearance (Town were big enough to be placed straight into Division One, rather than having to re-join in Division Two). Gradually, the gap between the clubs narrowed and it was Watford who won the derby's only Southern League title. They did so in 1914/5, the final season before war, after narrowly avoiding relegation in the previous season.

After the war, life in the Football League's new Division Three South was largely uneventful for both clubs, with Luton being marginally stronger in league positions, but Watford winning more derby encounters. In 1930/1, Watford succeeded in beating Luton in the FA Cup, at the fifth attempt. In the mid-thirties things changed dramatically. In April 1936, towards the season's finale and facing an injury crisis, Luton asked a rarely selected wing-half to switch positions to centre-forward. In his first appearance for seven months and on his *debut* up-front, Joe Payne scored ten goals in a 12-0 demolition of Bristol Rovers. Payne's feat is still the individual scoring record in any English League game. In the following season, Payne scored fifty-five goals, as the Hatters swept to the Division Three South title, completing a double over Watford on the way. He went on to play for England just once – he scored twice.

The clubs which, until that season, had been virtually inseparable in league status, were not to meet again until 1963/4. Luton finished above Watford for the next twenty-three seasons in a row. By 1958/9, lowly Watford had been placed in the new Division Four, whereas Luton, in addition to happily enjoying their fourth season in the top tier, were appearing at Wembley in the FA Cup final. Luton lost to ten-man Nottingham Forest. Ironically, the player to score Forest's first goal was Roy Dwight, cousin of Elton John (real name Reg Dwight), who was later to play a pivotal role in the emergence of a very different Watford.

By this time, the clubs were hardly rivals, as the gap between them was at its greatest. But, in 1959/60, Luton were relegated and, for the first time, perennial underperformers Watford achieved promotion, finishing fourth in the fourth tier. In 1962/3, Town went down again and so, in October 1963, the clubs met for the first time in twenty-six years – and Watford won. In their last home game of 1963/4 in tier three, Luton beat Watford 2-1 and, in doing so, ensured their own survival, while wrecking Hornet's hopes of promotion to tier

Love, Hope and Hatred

two. But tables had turned. In the following season, Hornets beat Hatters twice in three days over the Christmas period and ultimately those defeats condemned Luton to the basement of the Football League.

By 1968/9, the clubs were together again, chasing promotion from the third tier. Luton put Watford out of the League Cup and won a League fixture 2-1 in late April. It was a bad tempered affair. Three players were sent off. Trouble flared between supporters, in and outside Luton's Kenilworth Road, and also in neighbouring towns. Violence between this derby's rival fans has been fairly common in recent decades. Anyone who is shocked, perhaps because he or she thinks of Hertfordshire and Bedfordshire as being wholly leafy and genteel, clearly has not visited the two towns.

Defeat didn't stop Watford from winning the third tier title and rising to tier two for the first time. Luton came third and missed out, but gained promotion a year later. It proved to be another turning point in the derby. By 1974/5, the Hatters had risen again to the top tier, albeit only for one season, but Watford were on their way back to the bottom. The seventies belonged entirely to Luton.

Back-to-back promotions for Watford at the end of the seventies heralded the start of the derby's finest days. In 1981/2, the clubs were promoted together into the top flight, the Hatters as champions, eight points clear of the Hornets, who were to have their first taste of life at the top. Remarkably, in the following season Watford finished as runners-up to Liverpool, while Luton narrowly avoided relegation, by beating Manchester City at Maine Road on the last day of the season. Luton's late winner sent City down instead and prompted manager David Pleat's famous 'jig of joy' across the pitch. A wonderful year for Watford was made complete towards the season's end when they beat Luton by a record 5-2. In 1983/4, Watford's dream days continued as they defeated Luton on their way to their first appearance in an FA Cup final. They lost to Everton. A year later, Luton gained revenge, knocking Watford out of the FA Cup before eventually losing in the semi-final, also to Everton.

Altogether, the 'M1 derby' was played out at the top for six seasons in the eighties, the high point collectively being reached in 1986/7, when Luton finished seventh and Watford ninth, though the Hornets had the pleasure of doing the double in the season's derbies. In 1987/8, Luton won the League Cup, the partners' only silverware to date. By contrast, Watford were relegated and the two have not been together in the top tier since 1988. Luton soldiered on for a few more years, regularly escaping by the skin of their teeth but, in 1991/2, they lost out to the even greater escapologists of Coventry City, and a downward spiral followed.

In 1995/6, the clubs accompanied each other down into the third tier. Watford bounced back. In 1997/8, they not only won the third tier title, but achieved their biggest away win against Luton, 4-0, in a game where all four goals were scored in the first half-hour – the remaining hour for Kenilworth Road's faithful must have been one of the longest of their lives. Back-to-back promotions gave Watford a brief stay in the top flight while, in 2001/2, Luton spent another term at the bottom. By 2005/6, they were together again, comfortably placed in the second tier (Watford third, Luton tenth). Via play-offs, the Hornets achieved promotion for another brief stay at the top.

Their comfortable appearance was deceptive. Both had financial problems in the early part of the new century. However, while Watford's were nothing unusual, Luton's were truly catastrophic. Football fans are natural moaners. We almost all have a 'glass half empty' view of our clubs' fortunes, but few of us have experienced the real torment which befell a 21st Century Hatter. In three seasons, the Hatters plunged from Championship to Conference. On the way down, they picked up a ten point deduction in tier three and a record thirty point deduction in tier four. In effect, it condemned them to relegation before the season had started.

Of all the clubs to have faced demotion from the League, Luton are arguably the biggest. They share with Oxford United the distinction of being the only ones to have won a major trophy (the League Cup in both cases). Only Luton have appeared in a FA Cup final and the Hatters have spent sixteen seasons in the top tier, most of them in the past fifty years. This is comfortably ahead of their nearest 'demoteds" challengers, Grimsby, who spent twelve seasons at the top, all of them over fifty years ago. To add to their woes Luton, clearly the biggest club in the area historically, have been overtaken locally by the likes of Milton Keynes Dons and Stevenage. Meanwhile, Watford have basked in the glow of their relative success, as well as Hatters' misery. Having been cannon-fodder for the first forty-odd years of their Football League existence, Watford have spent the majority of the past forty-odd years in the top two tiers.

Luton's defeat in the Conference play-off final of 2011/12 meant that there remained a three division gap between Watford and their old Bedfordshire 'superiors'. The gap mirrors that which existed in reverse in the late 1950s. In one sense, the derby is suffering as a result, because it isn't being played. On the other hand, Watford are gradually making overall historical records closer and more competitive. The underdog truly is having its day.

Finally, a note about club nicknames. Watford's Hornets tag is a little confusing. It came into being when the club changed colours from blue to yellow and black in 1959, but more recently they have played predominantly in yellow and red – strange colours for a hornet. The hornet on their badge was also soon discarded in favour of Hertfordshire's hart (stag). Before becoming Hornets, Watford were the Brewers and then the Blues. Increasingly, they seem to be using the name 'the Golden Boys'. Hopefully, this will not emerge as a new nickname, as it sounds more like a troupe of male strippers than a football team. The Hatters of Luton used to be more often called the Strawplaiters, but at least Hatters is a simplified version of a name which continues to reflect a traditional industry in the town.

Number 12 – Blackburn Rovers v Burnley

Older club   **Blackburn 1875** *(Burnley 1882, as a football club, although most founders were also involved with Burnley Rovers, a club formed in 1881 mainly as a rugby club)*

Head-to-head record

Number	93 games	
First one	Burnley 1 Blackburn 7	*(Nov 1888 in the first season of the Football League)*
Leader (wins)	**Blackburn** **41-37**	

Higher finishes in the League

19th C	Blackburn	9-3.
1900-WWI	Blackburn	15-0
1920s	Blackburn	6-4
1930s	Blackburn	9-1
40s+50s	Burnley	13-1
1960s	Burnley	8-2
1970s	Burnley	8-2
1980s	Blackburn	10-0
1990s	Blackburn	10-0
2000s	Blackburn	10-0
2010/12	Blackburn	2-0
TOTAL	**Blackburn**	**76-37**

Silverware (wins)

League	**Blackburn**	**3-2**
FA Cup	**Blackburn**	**6-1**
League Cup	**Blackburn**	**1-0.**

Years in Top Tier   **Blackburn   72-52**

Biggest Wins

Home	Blackburn 8	Burnley	3	*(Nov 1929. Rovers have also won 7-1 (Oct 1889) and 6-0 (Nov 1914))*
	Burnley 6	Blackburn	0	*(Apr 1896)*
Away	Blackburn 1	Burnley	5	*(Oct 1926)*
	Burnley 1	Blackburn	7	*(Nov 1888)*

History No. 12 – Blackburn Rovers v Burnley

The East Lancs derby brings together two founder members of the Football League. Their history is one of long periods of dominance by one club over the other. In broad terms, Rovers held the upper hand up to World War Two and have done so again since 1980, while the Clarets held sway in the intervening thirty odd years. By the time the League started in 1888, Rovers had already established themselves as a power in the land, having won the FA Cup three years in a row from 1884 to 1886. They won the cup again in 1890 and 1891 and, overall, only Aston Villa achieved more than Blackburn in the 19th Century. Blackburn's ground, alas, was not in keeping with their exalted status. Named Oozehead, it had timber boards covering a watering hole in the centre circle.

Rovers had a number of earlier primary rivals, before focussing their loathing on Burnley. Originally it was Darwen – their fixture in 1880 was abandoned at half time due to fighting on and off the field. Then it was a cross-town derby with Blackburn Olympic and, when the League started, number one on Rovers' hit list were Preston North End.

Burnley started life as a rugby club. Their 'Clarets' nickname has taken over in recent years from older alternatives 'Moorites', 'Royalites' and, especially, 'Turfites'. The 'Royalites' tag allegedly arose because they were the first club to be visited by royalty, when Prince Albert attended a match in 1886. In early non-league or cup clashes Burnley did well, probably because Rovers didn't field their strongest sides. But, when things began in earnest, Blackburn made an overwhelmingly commanding start. Not only did they win the first Football League derby 7-1 at Burnley, they proceeded to win the first six derbies and scored an amazing thirty-one goals against Burnley's eight.

When Burnley finally won for the first time, in December 1891, they did so in controversial circumstances. The match was played in driving wind and snow and by half-time Burnley led 3-0. Following a sending off, the Blackburn players had had enough and all except their goalkeeper walked off. The referee ordered a re-start but, as the entire Burnley team bore down on his goal, the astute Rovers' goalie appealed for offside. Faced with a 'catch 22' rules dilemma, the ref abandoned the game and the 3-0 scoreline was allowed to stand.

Burnley's biggest win, 6-0, was achieved on the last day of the 1895/6 season. It was a wonderful way for the Clarets to start their summer holidays, even though they had finished slightly behind Rovers in the League. Controversy arose again in 1897/8, as the teams faced each other in end of season test matches to determine promotion and relegation. Division Two champions Burnley beat Blackburn twice in two days, 5-1 on aggregate, seemingly condemning their rivals to relegation for the first time. However, the play-off series ended with an infamous clash between Burnley and Stoke, both of whom went into the final game knowing that a draw would secure their First Division status. Not unexpectedly, the match ended in a 0-0 draw, with enraged supporters protesting about what became known as the 'game without a shot'. The scandal led to abandonment of the test match system and introduction of automatic promotion and relegation. A compromise was also found which involved extension of the First Division from sixteen to eighteen clubs; no relegation and, therefore, a reprieve for Rovers. Oddly, it was Burnley who proposed the change, probably to save face. Even stranger, or more principled, depending upon how you look at it, the Rovers' representative voted against the idea, on the grounds that more games and therefore more distractions for the masses would *"interfere with industrial life"*.

Rovers didn't face relegation from the top tier again until 1935/6 whereas Burnley, after a very good season in 1898/9, quickly slipped back. Only four seasons later, they finished bottom of the entire League and had to apply for re-election. They survived by five votes at the expense of Doncaster, even though Doncaster had finished five points ahead of them. In the same season, Blackburn avoided relegation by one place. The 20th Century hadn't started well for East Lancashire, with Rovers not pulling up any trees in the top tier and Burnley bumbling along in tier two. It was all to change soon afterwards, as their derby entered a golden era either side of the First World War.

It began in 1911/12, when Rovers won their first League title. It was considered an overdue accolade for a club who already had five FA Cup successes to their credit. They also lost narrowly in the cup semis. A year later, Burnley gained promotion (with Preston) and beat reigning League champions Blackburn in the cup, on their way to a narrow semi-final defeat. The pinnacle was reached in 1913/14, as the Cotton Towns ruled English football. Blackburn regained their League title, by seven clear points, and Burnley won their first major trophy, beating Liverpool in the FA Cup final. In the last year before war broke out, Blackburn beat Burnley 6-0 in their home league fixture, a win that ensured they finished third and Burnley fourth on goal average. However, the tide was turning claret.

Immediately after the war Blackburn struggled, but Burnley hit a purple, well claret, patch. After finishing second in 1919/20, Burnley won their first League title in 1920/1. They lost their first three games of the season, but then went on an unbeaten run of thirty league games, creating a single season record to last for over eighty years. They also beat Rovers in all four league clashes in those two seasons, scoring thirteen goals in the process. The halcyon days for Burnley didn't last and the inter-war years were largely unproductive for East Lancashire's clubs, apart from Blackburn's sixth FA Cup success in 1928. By the early thirties, Burnley were struggling near the foot of tier two and, in 1936/7, the clubs met outside the top tier for the first time.

Signs of better things to come again appeared either side of a war. Rovers achieved promotion in 1938/9 and Burnley did so in the next season, 1946/7, as well as reaching the FA Cup final. Blackburn's hopes were short-lived, as they quickly fell back into the second tier, but Burnley gradually emerged as a major force. Rovers' rare derby high point in the fifties was a 3-1 victory over Burnley, as a second tier team, on their way to an FA Cup semi-final in 1952.

By 1959/60, the clubs were back together at the top and Burnley were challenging for the League title. In March 1960, they met in an FA Cup quarter final. The first game ended in a 3-3 draw, after Burnley had led 3-0 with only twenty minutes to go. Blackburn won the replay 2-0 and went on to lose in the final, in which Dave Whelan (later to become famous as Wigan's owner) broke his leg, reducing Rovers to ten men. Burnley completed the season with their second League championship, becoming the only side to win the title having not led the table at any time until the very last day. In retrospect, therefore, Blackburn's comeback win in the cup robbed Burnley of the opportunity to become the first club to achieve the 'double' in the 20th Century (Tottenham achieved that feat the following season). Both clubs were strong in the early sixties, especially Burnley who, for example, were runners-up in both the League and the FA Cup in 1961/2. But the writing was on the wall for them, and many other medium sized clubs, once the maximum wage rule was abolished early in 1961.

The seventies started badly, with Burnley relegated from the top tier in 1970/1 and Blackburn relegated from the second tier in the same season. It was the first spell in tier three in the history of either club. And it didn't get better, despite the Clarets' return to the top tier in 1973/4. Burnley's derby double in 1978/9 effectively condemned Rovers to relegation to the third tier again but, in 1979/80, Burnley had their own first taste of relegation from tier two. To make things worse, they swapped places with Rovers. Burnley bounced back in 1981/2 but, in the following season, Blackburn's derby double returned the favour and sent Burnley back into the third tier.

This time the bouncing stopped and the clubs didn't meet again for nearly twenty years. Blackburn spent the eighties in the second tier, achieving little. Burnley endured a nightmare. Relegated from the third tier in 1984/5, and thereby falling from top to bottom divisions in ten years, they faced Orient on the last day of 1986/7. Burnley needed to win to avoid the unthinkable outcome of former champions falling out of the League. They won 2-1 and survived at the expense of Lincoln City. On their faltering way back from the abyss, Burnley became one of only three clubs to achieve the 'distinction', if that is what it is, of being champions of all four divisions (the others being Wolves and Preston).

As the Clarets struggled, the nineties brought sunshine to their neighbours. In 1991/2, Rovers returned to the top tier for the first time since 1966. They did so via play-offs, having finished only sixth in the regular season. Burnley were champions of the fourth tier in the same year. Backed by Jack Walker's millions, Rovers were an instant hit in the new Premier League, finishing fourth and second in its first two years. In 1994/5, Blackburn won their third League title, their first since before the First World War, and Kenny Dalglish became only the third manager to win the title with two different clubs (after Herbert Chapman and Brian Clough). It was a tense affair that went to the wire. Blackburn came into the last day leading Manchester United by two points, but Rovers lost to Liverpool and had to wait anxiously for the Red Devils' result. Manchester could only draw and Blackburn were champions. To complete the dream for die-hard Rovers' fans, Burnley ended the season relegated again to tier three.

From there on (to 2011/12) Rovers spent most of the time in the Premiership, although their only trophy was the League Cup in 2002, while Burnley spent most of their time in tiers two or three. Burnley caught up with their old foes just twice in the League after 1982/3 and still there was no happy ending for them. In 2000/01, they met in the Championship. Blackburn won both derby games by 2-0 and 5-0 and left Burnley behind, gaining promotion at the season's end. Then, in 2009/10, Burnley returned to the top flight, for the first time since 1976, but Blackburn beat them twice again and Burnley were relegated at the end of the season. In between they met in the FA Cup in 2005. Rovers won after a replay. Given recent history, any faint-hearted Burnley fans may have mixed feelings about the prospect of meeting Blackburn in 2012/13, following Rovers' relegation to the Championship. However, irrespective of recent events, most Clarets will relish the thought of locking horns again and dreaming of a sea change in fortunes.

Just how frustrating life has been for Clarets since the fateful season of 1979/80, when they swapped places with Rovers, can be demonstrated by a few statistics. Burnley have not finished above Blackburn in the intervening thirty-two seasons. Their higher league placements' comparison was very close, until 1980. It now stands at 76-37. In terms of years in the top tier, they now trail Blackburn 52-72 because, in twenty years of the Premiership (up to 2011/12), Blackburn were absent only twice, Burnley present only once. Arguably most hurtful of all, is their record in head-to-head meetings. As we saw earlier, Blackburn won the first six derbies but over the years Burnley hunted them down and, by the turning point 1979/80 season, the Clarets led 37-34. They have met eight times since then and Rovers have won seven, with one draw, changing the derby score to 41-37 in their favour. Burnley, not having won a derby since April 1979, have waited longer than any club in the sixty derbies studied for a sweet taste of victory. It is little wonder that the 'East Lancs'/'Cotton Mill'/'A666' derby is so venomous. In 1990/1, Burnley lost a fourth tier play-off game to Torquay, thereby condemning the Clarets to another year at the bottom. Shortly after the game ended, a plane flew over Turf Moor with a banner which read – *"staying down forever, luv Rovers, ha ha ha"*. A plane trying a similar stunt today would surely be shot down.

Number 13 – Reading v Swindon Town

Older club   **Reading 1871** (Swindon 1879).

Head-to-head record

Number	141 games	
First one	Reading 0 Swindon 3	*(1894 in the Southern League. The first game in the Football League took place on Christmas Day 1920 in the new Division Three. Swindon won 3-2 at Reading)*
Leader (wins)	**Equal 52-52**	

Higher finishes in the League

19th C	Reading	5-1	*(began in the first season of the Southern League in 1894/5)*
1900-WW1	Reading	8-7	
1920s	Equal	5-5	*(in the Football League from 1920/21)*
1930s	Reading	10-0	
40s+50s	Reading	12-2	
1960s	Swindon	7-3	
1970s	Swindon	9-1	
1980s	Reading	7-3	
1990s	Swindon	7-3	
2000s	Reading	10-0	
2010/12	Reading	2-0	
TOTAL	**Reading**	**66-41**	

Silverware (wins)

League	**Neither** club has won the League. **Reading** have the highest finish, eighth in 2006/7
FA Cup	**Neither** club has reached an FA Cup final. **Swindon** have appeared in the semi-finals twice, Reading once
League Cup	**Swindon** **1-0**.

Years in Top Tier   **Reading**   **2-1**

Biggest Wins

Home	Reading	7	Swindon	1	*(Jan 1933)*
	Swindon	9	Reading	1	*(Southern League 1909/10. 5-0 is their biggest win in the Football League – Nov 1965)*
Away	Reading	0	Swindon	4	*(Mar 1958)*
	Swindon	0	Reading	4	*(1901/2 and Oct 1959)*

History No. 13 – Reading v Swindon Town

Reading are the oldest Football League club in the south of England and sixth oldest of all. As with a number of clubs, there is debate about the year of formation of Swindon. It is often documented as 1881 or even 1883, but the club's website and badge says 1879. Swindon's relationship with Reading and other clubs in the area is discussed in the first half of the book. Suffice it to say here that what appears to be a natural primary derby is complicated and diffused by the hatred of Oxford, especially by Swindon fans. Their mutual loathing of anything Bristolian further muddies the water. It is a very competitive derby which, if it was more focussed, would be even higher in the Derby League Table. Oxford's re-entry into the League in 2010/11 and Reading's elevation to the Premier League for 2012/13 probably ensures that Reading v Swindon will not become clearly pre-eminent for the time-being.

The Royals of Reading and Robins of Swindon have discarded older and much more descriptive nicknames. Reading were the Biscuitmen and Swindon the Railwaymen. The making of biscuits may not have the macho cachet of, say, Mariners, Blades or Iron, but at least the name was distinctive of the town. As for 'Robins', it is the most common nickname of all and so is not special or distinctive in any sense. It is a very old derby, in fact the oldest league derby in southern England. It began in the inaugural season of the Southern League. Things did not start well for Swindon, as they lost their first ever league game 9-0 away to Millwall, the eventual champions. Swindon ended the season in bottom spot. There was improvement against Millwall in the following season. Swindon lost by 'only' 9-1. Reading had a brighter start to their league career. In the first thirteen seasons of the Southern League, up to 1906/7, Reading finished above Swindon in all but one.

Neither side won the title in those years, but Reading were runners-up twice. Swindon finished bottom of the table on three occasions and were saved from relegation only because there was no automatic demotion at the time.

At this point, the clubs' Southern League experiences reversed. Swindon finished above Reading in seven of the remaining nine seasons, before they both joined the Football League. The six seasons from 1908 to 1914 were Swindon's high point. They won the Southern League championship twice and were runners-up three times. They also appeared in their only FA Cup semi-finals to date, in 1910 and 1912, losing on both occasions to eventual cup winners. 1909/10 was an especially sweet season for Robins. Runners-up in the Southern League and FA Cup semi-finalists, Swindon beat Reading 9-1 and 4-1 in their derby encounters and had the pleasure of seeing their rivals relegated at the end of the season.

In the Football League, Town had the better start but, in 1925/6, Reading were first to progress to the second tier. They survived their first season and also enjoyed their only FA Cup semi-final to date in 1927. It began a period of dominance for Reading that saw them finish above Swindon in all but one of twenty-five seasons straddling the Second World War. It has to be said that neither club set the world alight. In thirty-one seasons from joining the

Football League to the creation of the new Divisions Three and Four in 1958, Swindon never made it out of Division Three South and Reading were with them in the bottom tier for all but five seasons. The Robins also had to seek re-election three times. However, both made the split in 1958 to become members of the new Division Three and that meant they were above the bottom rung together for the first time.

In 1962/3, Swindon achieved their first true promotion and, although they survived for only two seasons in tier two, a strong period in their history had begun. Its highest point came in 1968/9. The Robins not only won promotion again to the second tier, but also won the League Cup. They therefore became the only one of the two clubs to win a major national trophy. They were also only the second side from tier three to do so (Queen's Park Rangers had achieved the same feat two years earlier and a third tier success has yet to occur again). Swindon held sway over Reading for most of the sixties and seventies and it was during this period that derby rivalries began with newcomers to the Football League, Oxford United, who quickly supplanted Reading as the strongest competitors in the area for Swindon.

Reading overtook Swindon again in the eighties, but both had to play second fiddle to Oxford. The low points for this derby began in 1983/4, when Reading were relegated to join Swindon in the fourth tier for one year. The worst moment came a year later, as Oxford completed back-to-back championships to rise from third tier to the top. Of course, neither Reading nor Swindon had achieved such heady heights, despite years of toil. Reading were in tier three and Swindon in tier four, enviously peering upwards into the distance. It could have become even worse in the following season, as Oxford, still in the top flight, won the League Cup, but both Reading and Swindon gained consolation by winning their divisional championships. This was the beginning of better times for Swindon in particular. These culminated in their own first ever promotion to the top tier in 1992/3, albeit that they survived for only a season. In 1994/5, Reading were unlucky not to experience their first taste of life at the top. They finished as runners-up in the second tier, which would normally have ensured promotion. However, the Premier League was being reduced from twenty-two to twenty teams and this meant that Reading had to endure play-offs. They lost.

Reading fell backwards following the play-off reversal and both clubs entered the new century in tier three together. Oxford were there too. But, from thereon, paths have diverged significantly. The 21st Century so far has belonged solidly to Reading. They have finished above Swindon in the League every year and have been at least one division above the Robins since 2001/2. 2005/6 was a year in dreamland for Royals' fans. Swindon were relegated to tier four. Oxford's plight was even worse, as they dropped into the Conference and, after years of effort and the disappointment of 1994/5, Reading made it to the top. Furthermore, they did so as second tier champions. In their first season in the Premiership they finished eighth, higher than Swindon or Oxford have ever achieved, but next season they were relegated, on goal difference.

Overall, the clubs have been in the same division as each other for forty-six of their eighty-five seasons in the Football League and they have not been far apart for long. Even when Swindon reached the promised land of the top tier, for the one and only season in their history, Reading were third tier champions in the same year, and so again joined the Robins in 1994/5. As we have seen, the biggest gap between the clubs occurred in 2006/7 but again a big gap didn't last long. Swindon bounced back to the third tier straight away and Reading's reign in the Premiership lasted for only two years.

That having been said, the gap between the two is beginning to look potentially serious in 2012/13. Swindon narrowly missed out in the third tier play-off final of 2009/10, victory in which would have given them the chance to meet up again with Reading. The Robins then managed to finish bottom in 2010/11 and crash into tier four, where they were to renew hostilities with Oxford in the League for the first time since 2000/01. In 2011/12 Swindon secured a return to tier three by winning the fourth tier title, but the Royals won their own title in the Championship to make a welcome second visit to the Premiers League in 2012/13 and to retain a two division gap between them and their Wiltshire foes. In the great tradition of derby rivalry, Reading fans will not care a jot about the fact that the derby hasn't been played for over a decade as a result of their own club's superiority. Why should they? Neutral observers, however, will regret the recent demise of this, the oldest southern derby. It more than any other derby charts the development of football in the south. It is one of the best and most competitive derbies between those middle-range clubs who really form the heart of English football.

Historically, it is hard to say which club has the edge. Reading's record may be better, in that they have a big lead over Swindon in higher league placements. However, Swindon alone have won important silverware. The Robins not only took two Southern League championships but have the trump card of being the only ones to win a major national trophy. Their League Cup triumph over Arsenal in 1969, in front of over 98,000 at Wembley, and orchestrated by a fabulous performance from Don Rogers, is the stuff of dreams. Perhaps the head-to-head record between the clubs best illustrates the overall position – dead level on fifty-two each, in 141 meetings. Of all sixty derbies, this one is the closest in terms of results in head-to-head meetings. Neutrals will look forward to clash number 142.

Number 14 – Cardiff City v Swansea City

Older club	**Cardiff 1899** (Swansea 1912)

Head-to-head record

	Number	66 games
	First one	Swansea 1 Cardiff 1 *(Sept 1912 in the Southern League)*
	Leader (wins)	**Swansea 27-21**

Higher finishes in the League

	19th C	Nil	
	1900-WW1	Cardiff	3-0 *(began when Swansea joined Southern League in 1912/3)*
	1920s	Cardiff	10-0 *(in the Football League from 1920/1)*
	1930s	Swansea	9-1
	40s+50s	Cardiff	12-2
	1960s	Cardiff	10-0
	1970s	Cardiff	9-1
	1980s	Swansea	6-4
	1990s	Swansea	8-2
	2000s	Cardiff	9-1
	2010/12	Swansea	2-0
	TOTAL	**Cardiff**	**60-29**

Silverware (wins)	League	**Equal.** Neither club has won the League. **Cardiff** have the highest finish, 2nd in 1923/4.
	FA Cup	**Cardiff** **1-0**
	League Cup	**Equal.** Neither club has won the League Cup. **Cardiff** have reached one semi-final..

Years in Top Tier		**Cardiff** **15-3**

Biggest Wins	Home	Cardiff 5	Swansea 0	*(April 1965)*
		Swansea 5	Cardiff 1	*(Dec 1949)*
	Away	Cardiff 1	Swansea 3	*(Dec 1996)*
		Swansea 1	Cardiff 3	*(April 1959)*

History No. 14 – Cardiff City v Swansea City

Football in Wales first took root in the north and was late arriving in rugby strongholds of South Wales. Swansea and Cardiff adopted the colours of their cities' established rugby clubs, but not before the Bluebirds of Cardiff had tried out chocolate and amber quarters – evidently, football fashion was more daring in those days. Cardiff City grew out of an existing cricket club and, initially, they retained the cricket club's name, Riverside. Cardiff turned professional in 1910 and entered the Southern League. Two years later, they were joined in the Southern League's Second Division by newly formed Swansea. The two were immediately involved in a promotion battle. Cardiff won, although the Swans gained consolation by putting Cardiff out of the FA Cup. The Bluebirds did well in the Southern League's First Division and finished above the Swans in each of four seasons prior to the two clubs joining the Football League in 1920. The rest of the former Southern League teams created Division Three South, but Cardiff were given a place in Division Two, even though the Bluebirds had finished fourth in the previous season, behind Portsmouth, Watford and Crystal Palace.

Their stroke of luck heralded Cardiff's finest days. They won promotion to the top flight in their first season and very quickly became a significant power in the English League. Having been beaten finalists in 1925, 1927 saw Cardiff become the first (and so far only) non-English club to win the FA Cup. To rub English noses in it even further, the cup journeyed over the border to Wales on St. George's Day. In between Cardiff's final appearances, Swansea had their own bit of cup glory, reaching the semi-finals in 1926.

In 1923/4, the Bluebirds reached their highest point to date, when they came second in the League to Huddersfield, in what was the closest title finish ever. As the last day of the season dawned Cardiff had a one point lead. Huddersfield won 3-0, but Cardiff could only draw 0-0 against Birmingham, having missed the most important penalty in their history. This left both teams on 57 points. Huddersfield's goal tally was 60-33, Cardiff's 61-34 (i.e. both on plus 27). Had goal difference been in place at the time, Cardiff would have been champions, as they had scored more goals. However, in 1923/4, goal average was used to differentiate between sides where points were equal. So Huddersfield won what was to be the first of a hat-trick of titles, by 0.024 of a goal. (Incidentally, it is often said that Cardiff would have won the title that year had the *current* system been applied. That is not the case, because three points for a win has been introduced more recently. Huddersfield had won more games and so, had three points for a win been in place at the time, Huddersfield would have had 80 points to Cardiff's 79 and goal difference/average would have been irrelevant.)

Things changed dramatically in the late twenties and early thirties. Swansea plodded on, usually towards the bottom of the second tier, but Cardiff collapsed. In 1928/9, Cardiff were relegated from the top tier. They were seven points adrift of safety and yet bizarrely had the best defensive record in the division. In 1930/1, Swans finished above Bluebirds for the first time ever, as Cardiff were relegated again, this time from the second tier. By 1933/4, only ten years after their near miss for the League title and seven years after their glorious FA Cup victory, the Bluebirds were bottom of the bottom tier and had conceded 105 goals.

The pendulum swung violently again after the Second World War. In the first season after the resumption of football, the two clubs swopped places, Cardiff gaining promotion to the second tier and Swansea dropping into the third. With the exception of 1949/50, Cardiff then finished above Swansea for a period of thirty-two years.

Cardiff's most recent spell in the top tier ended in 1962 and, by the mid-seventies, football in South Wales was at low ebb. Cardiff were relegated to the third tier in 1974/5 and, even worse, Swansea had to seek re-election. In the following season, only 1,311 fans turned up at Vetch Field for a league game against Brentford. When the lengthy period of misery ended for the Swans, it ended with a bang. Emerging from tier four in 1978, they finally finished above Cardiff in 1979/80. Then in 1981/2, for the first time in Swansea's history, they made it to the top. Furthermore, they were to be no cannon fodder for the elite. They finished sixth, a mere seven years after seeking re-election. To complete their heaven-sent year, Cardiff were relegated from the second tier.

Surely the dream couldn't last for Swansea 'Jacks'. It didn't. By 1983/4, Cardiff were above them again. The Swans nosedived spectacularly through the divisions. Just over three years after being the sixth best team in country, the club was formally wound up. Things were no better for Bluebirds. In 1985/6, the cream of Welsh football clubs were relegated together to the bottom rung of the League and, in the following season, only 1,510 turned up for Cardiff's final home game. In 1985/6, for the first time ever, Newport County were the top club in Wales. Two years later they dropped out of the League and have not returned – it must have been the shock and responsibility of flying the nation's flag.

After bouncing along for a few years, things got even worse for Cardiff and Swansea. Off the pitch, in 1993, the derby created an unwelcome first when away fans were banned from attending games because of escalating violence. On the field, the nadir for South Wales came in 1997/8, when they finished fourth and fifth bottom of the entire League. Wrexham, safely ensconced in tier three, were now the best team in Wales. There is a slightly unusual footnote to the disastrous 1997/8 season. The record books show that Swansea finished above Cardiff. Both had fifty points. Swansea's goal difference was 49-62 (minus thirteen), whereas Cardiff's was 48-52 (only minus four). So how did Swansea finish higher? The answer is that, at the time, the League was experimenting with using goals scored as the determining factor in cases where teams finished level on points. This barmy idea didn't last long. Of course, it didn't make much difference for teams who were so low, but safe from relegation anyway, did it? – you bet it did in South Wales.

The 21st Century has seen a substantial revival in fortunes, with Cardiff recovering first. 2010/11 was arguably the highest point in history for the South Wales derby collectively, although memories for fans in the Welsh capital may not be so sweet. Both clubs qualified for second tier play-offs, having finished third (Swansea) and fourth (Cardiff) in the Championship and separated only on goal difference. The Bluebirds lost in the semi-finals to Reading, but the Swans beat the same opponents in the final to make it to the Premier League. 2011/12 saw them enjoying life at the top for only their third season and they survived in style to clock up another year in 2012/13.

There is one unique, and two unusual, features of the derby. The first unusual aspect is that, mainly because of long periods of dominance by one club over the other, the derby has not been played very often. To 2012/13, they have spent only twenty-seven seasons together in the same division of the Football League. Of the really big derbies, only Southampton v Portsmouth and Millwall v West Ham have seen fewer Football League clashes. The second unusual feature is that, in a majority of cases, the dominant partner overall in a derby also has the lead in head-to-head meetings between clubs. But in South Wales Cardiff's superiority overall is not reflected in their one to one meetings with Swansea. The Swans lead (marginally) in League; FA Cup and League Cup victories. It should be said that, if all derby clashes were taken into account, Cardiff have a massive lead, based largely upon victories in Welsh Cup and wartime games. In one of those, the 'Bluebirds' Blitzkrieg' of October 1940, Cardiff won 8-0. The unique aspect of the South Wales derby is that, in their twenty-seven seasons together, neither side has ever completed a League double over the other in a single season.

2012/13 will not see League derbies in Wales, but the derby is at a high point in terms of overall success. The history of the Swans and Bluebirds, in which both have experienced dramatic rises and falls, should ensure that fans will make the most of current good times

Finally, the Bluebirds' biggest ever win in a League derby against the Swans was 5-0 in April 1965. The scorers in blue that day were Ivor Allchurch, who helped himself to a hat-trick, and John Charles, who scored the other two. Both players would be included in any list of the finest ever to grace the English League. Both Cardiff scorers that day were sons of Swansea, although Charles never played for the Swans' first team. Allchurch was an all-time Swansea great who, in the following season, re-joined for his second spell with the club. Reportedly, although subjected to a hammering, Swans' fans enjoyed the spectacle of their local heroes performing so brilliantly against them. Modern fans might reflect upon what would happen if similar circumstances were re-created today.

Number 15 – Fulham v Queen's Park Rangers

Older club	**Fulham 1879.**	(QPR 1882, *though their date of formation has been disputed, with some authorities suggesting that it was 1885 or 1886. The club says 1882)*

Head-to-head record

Number	41 games	
First one	Fulham 2 QPR 2 *(1903 in the Southern League)*	
Leader (wins)	**Equal 16-16**	

Higher finishes in the League

19th C	Nil		
1900-WWI	QPR	5-3	*(began when QPR joined the Southern League in 1899, but Fulham subsequently left).*
1920s	Fulham	9-0	*(began again in the Football League when QPR joined the original Division Three South in 1920).*
1930s	Fulham	9-1	
40s+50s	Fulham	14-0	
1960s	Fulham	8-2	
1970s	QPR	10-0	
1980s	QPR	10-0	
1990s	QPR	9-1	
2000s	Fulham	10-0	
2010/12	Fulham	2-0	
TOTAL	**Fulham**	**56-37**	

Silverware (wins)	League	**Equal.** Neither club has ever won the League. **QPR** have the highest finish, second in 1975/6.
	FA Cup	**Equal.** Neither club has ever won the FA Cup, but both have been beaten finalists once – Fulham in 1975 and QPR in 1982. Both were second tier sides when reaching the finals
	League Cup	**QPR** 1-0.

Years in Top Tier		Fulham 23-21

Biggest Wins

	Home	Fulham	6	QPR	0 *(Oct 2011)*
		QPR	3	Fulham	0 *(Sept 1979)*
	Away	Fulham	0	QPR	3 *(Aug 1971)*
		QPR	0	Fulham	2 *(Oct 1930 and Jan 2001)*

History No. 15 – Fulham v Queen's Park Rangers

Fulham are London's oldest League club. They grew out of a church group and began life as Fulham St. Andrew's. Both QPR and Fulham would no doubt prefer to be the greatest derby rivals of Chelsea, rather than of each other. This is especially so in Fulham's case, as Chelsea's Stamford Bridge is actually in Fulham. However, Chelsea's record, even before the arrival of Abramovich's millions, is massively better than that of either Cottagers or R's. For instance, Chelsea lead Fulham 89-5 in higher League finishes and lead QPR 70-15 and so the Blues tend to look elsewhere for their primary derbies.

Fulham's rivalry with QPR is by far the most competitive derby in West London and is one of the most competitive derbies of all in terms of closeness of overall aggregate records. It would probably be a significantly fiercer derby were it not for their mutual hatred of Chelsea and the fact that they have so rarely been at the same level as each other. Although their *overall* records are similar and competitive, their relationship has been characterised by long periods of dominance by one club over the other. Up to 1967/8, QPR had finished above Fulham in the Football League on only one occasion in forty-one seasons. However, 1968 was a defining moment in their relationship. Fulham's first significant spell as a top tier club came to an end and their relegation coincided with QPR's first ever elevation to the top.

From there, QPR proceeded to finish above Fulham every year for thirty-one seasons. That run ended in 1999/2000, when Cottagers pipped R's by one point and Fulham have been ascendant since. The clubs were in the same division together only once (1948/9) in forty years between 1931/2 and 1971/2. Altogether they had been in the same Football League division as each other for only eleven seasons prior to 2011/12, leading to them having fewer derby meetings than almost any of the sixty derbies studied. Although they have a combined total of forty-four seasons in the top flight, remarkably 2011/12 saw them in the top tier *together* for the first time.

In recent years, both clubs have begun to adopt new nicknames. Traditionally, QPR have been the 'R's' or Rangers, Fulham the Cottagers. Increasingly, Rangers use Hoops or Super Hoops. Fulham have more reason than most to consider alternative names, given that 'cottagers' has taken on altogether different connotations than being from Craven Cottage. Whites, Lilywhites or even Badgers are gradually becoming preferred nicknames.

The derby began in the Southern League and the clubs were frequently involved in controversy in their first few years, starting with their entries into the league in the first place. Fulham joined in 1898/9 and were put into Division Two. QPR followed at the beginning of the next season, but were immediately given First Division status.

It took Fulham five years to gain promotion and, when they did so, it was in dubious circumstances. They finished top of the second tier in successive seasons, but lost out in the test match system, which still existed in the Southern League. In 1902/3, they lost their 'test' 7-2 against Brentford and, at a pre-meeting on the day before the League's AGM, it became clear that Watford would survive relegation and Fulham would probably be denied promotion. However, that evening, representatives attended a dinner thrown by Fulham and Plymouth. The next day, the party hosts were both placed in Division One and Watford went down – understandably complaining bitterly that something untoward had occurred on the previous evening.

Whites and Hoops therefore met for the first time in senior competition in 1903/4 and both games ended in draws. In 1906, Fulham beat QPR in the FA Cup and it started a trend. The clubs are level in overall head-to-head wins, but Rangers have never beaten Fulham in the FA Cup or League Cup. In 1905/6 and 1906/7, Fulham won consecutive Southern League championships. Their application to join the Football League was accepted and they departed to take up their derby with Chelsea, leaving QPR behind. In the following year, Rangers kept the Southern League title in West London and, as champions, they contested the first ever Charity Shield. They drew with Football League champions, Manchester United. But controversy arose again. Together with Spurs and Bradford Park Avenue (yes that 'southern' outpost of Bradford), QPR announced that they were leaving the Southern League. They thought they would be admitted into the Football League. The Southern League was less than happy and responded by expelling the two London clubs. At the last minute, possibly fearing that their Football League application was about to be denied, Rangers withdrew their bid and sought re-election to the Southern League. They were re-admitted, but only on a financially disastrous basis of having to play games in midweek. Tottenham's bid to join the Football League was rejected initially, but they entered via the backdoor when Stoke resigned. So, *Champions* QPR did not get their wish to join Chelsea, Fulham, Arsenal and Orient in the increasingly superior Football League. *Seventh-placed* Tottenham succeeded – the rest is history.

QPR didn't apply again, even when, in 1911/2, they won the Southern League championship for a second time. In 1920, they joined the new Division Three South of the Football League with most others from the Southern League's top tier. To say that Rangers didn't pull up any trees in their new surroundings would be an understatement. They didn't move out of the bottom tier before the Second World War and they finished bottom of Division Three South in 1923/4 and 1925/6. Fulham didn't fare that well either, though always ahead of QPR, except in 1929/30. After finishing fourth in the second tier in their first season, 1907/8, Fulham maintained a mid-table spot in virtually every year up to 1927/8, when they were relegated. For four seasons the derby was played at the bottom of the League, until Fulham returned to tier two. It should be said in passing that Brentford were the first West London club, other than Chelsea, to reach the top tier. Promoted in 1934/5, they ended the following season as the fifth best team in England and as London's top side. At this stage, Fulham and QPR were decidedly third and fourth in West London's pecking order.

Fortunes began to change after the war. First, in 1947/8, QPR rose from the depths for the first time. At the end of the next season, Fulham reached the top tier for the first time and, in 1950/1, they were the best team in West London. Although normal service was quickly resumed, as both clubs fell back, the signs of a better future were emerging. Finally, the sixties really swung for West London. Promoted in 1958/9, and led by 'maestro' Johnny Haynes, the Cottagers enjoyed a sustained period in the top tier. Then, in 1966/7, the R's won the only silverware to date for either club and, in doing so, became the first third tier side to win a major trophy, the League Cup. They also won the third tier championship by twelve points. Rodney Marsh epitomised the good times. He played for both clubs, transferring from Fulham to Rangers in 1966.

Back to back promotions for Rangers saw them into the top tier for the first time. They exchanged places with Fulham on the way and the long period of dominance for the R's had begun. Although Rangers moved up and down between top and second tiers, in the next three decades they frequently finished in the top ten of English football. The high point was achieved in 1975/6, when QPR were runners-up to League champions, Liverpool. Fulham struggled in the same period. Generally, they bounced to and fro from tier two to tier three but, in 1993/4, they crashed into the bottom tier. In the following season, both finished eighth in their respective divisions – Fulham in the bottom tier, QPR in the Premiership – the biggest gap ever between the two clubs. Things got even worse for Fulham. In January 1996, they played Torquay in a 'bottom two of the entire league' clash – and lost. Eventually they managed to survive the season on the field and a financial crisis off it.

In 1997, Fulham were taken over by Mohammed Al Fayed and his cash injection led to a dramatic reversal in fortunes. By 2001/2 they were back in the top tier, for the first time since 1968. On the way, Fulham won championships in tiers two and three. They would also have won the fourth tier championship in 1996/7, but were denied by the experimental rule change which gave preference to total number of goals scored, in cases where points were equal. In 2010/11, Fulham came eighth in the top tier, their highest ever finish.

Meanwhile, QPR had gone into reverse. Relegated from the Premier League in 1995/6, they avoided relegation to tier three on goal difference in 1998/9 and finally suffered the fall in 2000/1, for the first time since 1967. It was in the same season that Fulham returned to the top. Overall, in just seven seasons, the relative positions of the clubs had changed by *five* divisions. They met each other on their respective reverse journeys in two seasons and four derbies. Fulham won three, drew the other one and QPR didn't score. Rangers therefore went into their games against Fulham in 2011/12, having not scored against the Cottagers since May 1983. If Rangers' fans were relishing the prospect of rectifying history, they were to be sadly disappointed. History was written, but by Fulham, who won the first encounter of the season 6-0, the biggest victory ever in their derby. Fulham completed a derby double later in the season, winning 1-0 and so Rangers still haven't scored since 1983 and their fans have witnessed twelve goals at the other end. Strangely, prior to the most recent six games, Fulham had an awful Football League record against their neighbours. They had beaten QPR only three times in eighteen Football League matches and they still trail 8-12 overall in these fixtures.

The prospects for both clubs look very good in 2012/13. Both have substantial financial backing. Fulham have been reasonably comfortably placed in the top tier for some time. QPR, having gained promotion to the Premier League as champions of the Championship, survived a close relegation struggle in their first season back at the top and so West London can look forward to another round of derbies between Whites and Hoops in the top tier. The derby is at its zenith and, of course, there is the little matter of derbies against Chelsea too.

Historically, it is difficult to say which club is more successful. Only Rangers have won a major national trophy. Fulham have a healthy lead in finishing above QPR in league campaigns. However, their lead is dependent upon pre-war performances. Post-war, the two are almost equal. Fulham have spent two more years in the top tier, but Fulham's highest ever finish, eighth, has been bettered by Rangers four times and equalled on two other occasions. Neither has won the FA Cup. Both have made one losing appearance in an FA Cup final. Fulham, however, can boast six FA Cup semi-finals, against QPR's single appearance at that stage. QPR lead in head-to-head meetings in the League, but have never won a cup clash against Fulham. Altogether, this is a remarkably closely-fought derby in terms of historical achievement.

Finally, the clubs have a few things in common, apart from their loathing of Chelsea. They are the two most itinerant clubs in the entire League, having had more home grounds than anyone else (QPR the most, Fulham second). From 2002 to 2004, they shared Loftus Road during improvement work on Craven Cottage. This caused embarrassment for Fulham fans, as they had repeatedly mocked the awfulness of QPR's ground for years. There have also been at least two proposals to merge the clubs. Surprisingly, those attempts did not generate lasting, stronger animosity between the two sets of fans – perhaps a few more clashes in the top tier will do so.

Number 16 – Crystal Palace v Brighton and Hove Albion

Older club	**Brighton 1901** (Palace 1905)	

Head-to-head record

	Number	110 games
	First one	Brighton 2 Palace 1 *(1906 in the Southern League. Their first derby in the Football League took place on Christmas Day 1920 in Division Three's first year. Palace won 2-0 at Brighton. They played again two days later in London, with Palace winning again, 3-2).*
	Leader (wins)	**Brighton 41-39**

Higher finishes in the League

19th C	Nil		
1900-WWI	Brighton	6-4	*(began when Palace joined the Southern League in 1905/6)*
1920s	Palace	7-3	*(in the Football League from 1920)*
1930s	Palace	6-4	
40s+50s	Brighton	12-2	
1960s	Palace	8-2	
1970s	Palace	7-3	
1980s	Equal	5-5	
1990s	Palace	10-0	
2000s	Palace	10-0	
2010/12	Equal	1-1	
TOTAL	**Palace**	**60-36**	

Silverware (wins)

League	**Equal.** Neither club has won the League. **Palace** have the higher finish, third in 1990/1
FA Cup	**Equal.** Neither club has won the FA Cup. Both have been beaten finalists on one occasion each (Brighton in 1983 and Palace in 1990)
League Cup	**Equal.** Neither club has won the League Cup. **Palace** have come closest with three semi-final appearances.

Years in Top Tier	**Palace**	**13-4**

Biggest Wins

Home	Brighton	5	Palace	0	*(Jan 1956)*
	Palace	6	Brighton	0	*(Feb 1950)*
Away	Brighton	1	Palace	5	*(Dec 1928)*
	Palace	2	Brighton	4	*(Nov 1957)*

History No. 16 – Crystal Palace v Brighton and Hove Albion

Brighton v Palace is an unusual derby. Firstly, it is generally accepted as a true derby, even though the clubs are forty miles apart. Secondly, it didn't really emerge as a major derby until the 1970s. When it did, it did so in a blaze of publicity. For a couple of decades it was fashionable and fierce. In recent years, the clubs have rarely played each other and the derby has the feel of a fizzing rocket which may, but probably will not, soar to its former heights.

Both clubs had slightly unusual beginnings too. Albion's foundation in 1901 was the third attempt to establish a major club in Brighton, and they took over the ground and Southern League place of a previous club that had folded. The original plans for the founding of Palace faced objections from the F.A., who didn't want the venue of the Cup Final to have a resident club. Objections having been overcome, Palace joined the Southern League in 1905. They lost their first game, but then went through the rest of the season unbeaten, gaining promotion to meet Albion for the first time in 1906/7.

Palace and Brighton therefore have a long history together. They met each other twenty times in the Southern League and had similar records of success. Brighton were champions in 1909/10 and beat Aston Villa, Football League champions, in the Charity Shield. Palace narrowly missed out on the championship in 1913/4, trailing Swindon only on goal average. However, although they were general rivals, their clash was not a derby. At the time, Palace had an alternative true local derby with Croydon Common, whose ground, the Nest, was taken over by Palace when Common folded in 1918.

Brighton and Palace joined the new Division Three together in 1920 and their regular rivalry continued, but it was largely due to mutual under-achievement. The Glaziers of Palace were the first champions of the new division and, briefly, it looked as though they would rise above the also-rans, but it didn't last. By 1925/6, they were back with Brighton and the two stayed together in Division Three South continuously until 1957/8, when Brighton finally made it into the second tier for the first time.

In truth, not a great deal happened in those intervening years. Palace finished second in the division three times, missing promotion on goal average in 1928/9 to South London rivals, Charlton (remembering that, at the time, only one club was promoted from Division Three South and one from Division Three North). Brighton came second twice in the 1950s, before their success in 1957/8. Brighton had finished bottom of the whole League pile in 1947/8 and Palace did so in both 1948/9 and 1950/1. Neither had any difficulty in achieving re-election, but clearly they were not strong clubs. Oddly, the biggest ever win in this derby was Palace's home victory by 6-0 in 1950, in the middle of a period when they were one of the worst teams in the country. One individual feat of note occurred in 1930/1. Palace came second to Notts County. They scored 107 goals and Peter Simpson hit an amazing nine hat-tricks in the season. Palace had the edge in the inter-war period, in both head-to-head victories and higher league placings. Brighton took over leadership after the war, but there was never much in it between the two.

Albion may have been first to show signs of breaking the leash of the bottom tier, but it was the Glaziers who first made the rest take notice. In 1960/1, they rose from the fourth tier and this time they didn't fall back. By the end of the sixties, the eternal under-achievers of Palace were enjoying their first spell in the top tier. It did not last long and it wasn't especially successful, but it was light years ahead of anything in the past and it laid foundations for the glorious seventies. In fact, the seventies did not start well. In 1973, the Glaziers of Crystal Palace became the Eagles. Apparently, the new emblem was supposed to be a phoenix, but fans mistook it for an eagle and so an eagle it was. The Gods of sensible and descriptive nicknames promptly dished out appropriate punishment, as 'the Eagles' were relegated in successive seasons to the third tier. There they re-joined a struggling Albion, who had adopted the nickname 'Seagulls', allegedly in response to the cries of Palace fans.

Past mutual failures were not to be repeated. In 1976/7, they were promoted together from tier three. Famously, they met five times during the season, twice in the League and three times in the FA Cup before Palace prevailed. Brighton didn't win any of the five derbies (Palace won two), but had the comfort of finishing above Palace in the League, though both were behind champions Mansfield. The derby between the two had become firmly established and was often in the headlines, thanks to the antics of their fans and, in particular, their managers. It got even better. In 1978/9, the two were promoted to the top tier, with Palace snatching the championship from second placed Brighton on the last day of the season and thereby fuelling the ever more ferocious derby. They were together at the top for only two seasons, before Palace were relegated. Brighton won three and drew the other of the four, rare top tier derby clashes.

In 1981/2, the Seagulls had their highest finish ever, thirteenth, and in the following season they reached their only FA Cup final. They should have won the first game against Manchester United. In the last minute, with the score 2-2, Gordon Smith was through on goal, leading the TV commentator to scream *"and Smith must score"*. He didn't and Albion were battered 4-0 in the replay. Unfortunately, cup glory coincided with relegation from the elite.

Ironically, having by now firmly established their derby as one to be respected by the best, the clubs began to part-company for the first time in their history. At that point in time their overall histories were almost exactly equal. For example, by 1984/5, Brighton led 35-34 in higher league placements. However, from 1984/5, the Eagles finished above the Seagulls for twenty-six years in a row. As Brighton began their bumpy spiral into serious difficulties, Palace were about to embark upon their most successful period to date. Promoted into the top tier in 1988/9, Palace reached the FA Cup final in their first season back in the top flight. They beat Liverpool 4-3 in the semi-final, having been given no chance, as Liverpool had beaten them 9-0 in a League fixture earlier in the season. Palace lost the final, in a replay, also against Manchester United. Next season, the Eagles soared to their highest ever League finish, third behind Arsenal and Liverpool, by which time they were being seriously touted as potentially the 'team of the nineties'.

It didn't happen. The rest of the nineties were spent bouncing up and down between the top two tiers and, in 1998, Palace fell into administration. However, any trials experienced by the Eagles paled into insignificance compared with the nightmare faced by the Seagulls. As Palace were gaining promotion back into the top tier, via the play-offs, in 1996/7, Albion were fighting for their lives. They were kicked out of their Goldstone Ground and had to share Gillingham's home, fifty miles away. Even worse, they came into the last day of the season facing a gladiatorial contest with Hereford United – the loser would get the ultimate thumbs-down, relegation to the Conference. Brighton had also already been deducted two points. In the end, however, they had a stroke of luck. Going into the game, their goal difference was minus seventeen, compared with Hereford's minus fifteen. Under usual rules, a draw would have saved Hereford. But the experimental 'goals scored' rule was in place and Albion had scored three more goals than United. A draw would therefore favour Brighton – and they duly drew.

Albion finished next to bottom again at the end of the following season, but this time they were well ahead of bottom placed Doncaster. On the field, things improved for the Seagulls from there onwards – they could hardly have got much worse. But, off the field the long saga of their home ground was just beginning. They returned to Brighton, but the Withdean Stadium was always unsatisfactory, given that it is primarily an athletics stadium (Hammers' fans take note). Brighton's new Falmer/Amex Stadium was at last ready for 2011/2, fifteen years after they had to leave the Goldstone. In the early 21st Century, Brighton were promoted twice to the second tier, but didn't survive for long. In 2002, they must have been delighted to finally catch up with Palace again, after thirteen seasons without a derby. After the game, Albion fans must have wished they hadn't bothered. They lost 5-0. The Eagles have spent most of the new century in tier two, but had one season at the top, after gaining promotion via the play-offs in 2003/4. In 2009/10, they diced with relegation from the second tier and avoided the drop by drawing with Sheffield Wednesday on the last day of the season, thereby sending the Owls down.

Their earlier history together in the Southern League means that this derby is one of the elite twenty-one to have been played more than a hundred times, but since 1988/9 they have been together in the same division only three times. Palace's dominance in recent years has given them the lead overall, but Brighton still have more derby victories to their credit. In 2011/2, following Brighton's promotion as champions to the second tier, the derby was revived. Seagulls in their new stadium were full of confidence, while the Eagles had endured difficult times – needless to say, in the great tradition of football derbies, Palace pooped on Brighton's party with a 3-1 away victory in the season's first derby. However, the Seagulls ended the season flying above the Eagles for the first time since 1984/5. It could be that Palace's long run of superiority has come to an end. The derby is interesting again, but the glorious days of media attention, fedoras and public spats seem a long, long time ago.

Number 17 – Bristol City v Bristol Rovers

Older club	**Rovers 1883**	(City 1894)

Head-to-head record

	Number	107 games
	First one	City 1 Rovers 0 *(1899 in the Southern League. Rovers won the first Football League clash 1-0, at City, in Sept 1922 in Division Three South)*
	Leader (wins)	**City 43-30**

Higher finishes in the League

	19th C	City	1-0 (began in 1899 when Rovers joined the Southern League).
	1900-WWI	City	1-0 (there was only one season together in this period, because City joined the Football League in 1901)
	1920s	City	9-0 (began again in 1920 when Rovers joined the original Division Three)
	1930s	City	6-4
	40s+50s	Rovers	12-2
	1960s	City	8-2
	1970s	City	10-0
	1980s	Equal	5-5
	1990s	City	7-3
	2000s	City	10-0
	2010/12	City	2-0
	TOTAL	**City**	**61-26**

Silverware (wins) League		**Equal.** Neither club has won the League. **City** were runners-up in 1906/7
	FA Cup	**Equal.** Neither club has won the FA Cup. **City** were beaten finalists in 1909
	League Cup	**Equal.** Neither club has won the League Cup. **City** have appeared in the semi-finals twice.

Years in Top Tier		**City 9-0**

Biggest Wins

	Home	City	5	Rovers 2 (Feb 1948)
		Rovers	5	City 1 (Dec 1933)
	Away	City	2	Rovers 4 (Oct 1991)
		Rovers	0	City 5 (Sept 1926)

History No. 17 – Bristol City v Bristol Rovers

While former rugby strongholds such as Manchester and Liverpool crumbled to the onslaught of football, Bristol and the South West generally stayed loyal to the oval ball. It is sometimes said that, as Bristol is at the heart of Rugby Union country, the city's football derby is insignificant. Not so. Football derby passions run high in Bristol and mutual antipathy between City and Rovers is a good deal stronger than in many derbies higher in the Derby League Table. However, this is not a top derby because in competitiveness City clearly hold the upper hand in every factor.

Rovers are older, by over a decade, and both turned professional in the same year (1897). It must therefore have been annoying, to say the least, for Rovers' fans to have seen City quickly establish themselves as a moderately powerful force in the country. City were already in the Southern League and competing against other local rivals, Bedminster, before they were joined by Rovers in 1899. Bedminster, whose ground Ashton Gate became City's home, finished above both 'Bristols' that year but before the next season they merged with the Robins of City. City pipped Rovers only on goal average in their first season together. Although they didn't win the title, the Robins were strong in their four seasons in the Southern League. Having been runners-up three times, they made a successful application to move to the Football League in 1901. Rovers, having initially had two neighbours in their league, were left on their own.

City were the first southern club to make a real impact in the Football League. After promotion as tier two champions in 1905/6, they were runners-up to Newcastle in their first season at the top. Two seasons later, in 1909, they made it to their only FA Cup final, losing 1-0 to Manchester United at Crystal Palace. A contemporary report said that *"more than a thousand spectators brought their own stands with them and animated scenes took place while the amateur carpenters hammered together their apparatus"* – their own stands! City spent five seasons in the top tier in the first spell, but never reached the heights of a top three finish again. Their second period of four seasons at the top didn't occur until the late 1970s and their highest finishing position during those years was thirteenth in 1978/9. The Pirates of Rovers were in the shadow of rampant Robins in the early days, but they did at least have the satisfaction of beating the new Football Leaguers 3-2 away from home in their FA Cup clash in 1901/2. Rovers also achieved something to have eluded City, by winning the Southern League title in 1904/5.

The inter-war years were pretty uneventful. On the whole, City continued to dominate, but they yo-yo'd between second and third tiers. Rovers ambled along in Division Three South. In the final season before World War Two, the Pirates finished bottom of the Football League and had to seek re-election.

After the war, portents were still not good for men in blue and white quarters. On the resumption of the FA Cup in 1945/6 and League football in 1946/7, City proceeded to win the first six derby encounters in a row, scoring twenty goals and conceding only four. However, a 3-1 victory for Rovers near the start of 1948/9 heralded their most successful years to date, and their only prolonged period as top club in Bristol. For the next fourteen seasons, until their relegation from tier two in 1961/2, Rovers finished above City and, having won promotion to the second tier in 1952/3, Rovers finished in the top half of the table for seven years in a row. Their highest ever position in the League (sixth in tier two) was achieved in 1955/6, when they missed out on promotion to the top by just four points. In 1958/9, they finished sixth again, but were further off the pace. Arguably, the crowning glory was when Rovers dispatched the Busby Babes from the FA Cup in 1956, by the seemingly improbable scoreline of 4-0, in front of nearly 36,000 ecstatic Pirates. Yes, in the 1950s Bristol Rovers were nearly as fashionable as Teddy Boys. Unfortunately, however, they still are as fashionable as Teddy Boys. Having re-established the natural order of things in 1962/3, City went on to finish higher in the table than Rovers for the following nineteen seasons, their longest ever period of ascendancy.

Having said that City's dominant position is the natural order, it is also fair to point out that their dominance has never been as great as is the case in many other derbies. The clubs have been in the same division as each other in forty-four of the eighty-five seasons since Rovers joined the Football League and Bristol's derby is one of the elite twenty-one to have been played over a hundred times. Alas for Rovers, things have been getting worse recently. The clubs play their 2012/13 campaigns in different divisions and this is their longest-ever spell apart from each other.

The lowest point for the Bristol derby collectively arguably came in 1980/1, when they crashed out of the second tier together, winning only twelve of their combined eighty-four games and scoring only sixty-three goals between them. Predictably, both derby games ended as 0-0 draws. Individually, the clubs have been through some very difficult times. The Robins' second spell in the top tier in the late seventies ended with the League's most spectacular fall from grace. They went down in successive seasons from top tier to fourth, the first club to do so. Bankruptcy followed, though they were the first modern example of a club escaping debts and sanctions by going into liquidation. During these dark days, heroes emerged. The 'Ashton Gate Eight' were players who carried on regardless, completing the club's fixtures, even though there was no certainty of receiving pay.

Times became even bleaker for Gasheads across the city. A fire caused considerable damage to their old home at Eastville. They were then forced out of the ground and had to take refuge at Twerton Park – in Bath. For ten years, from 1986, they didn't play in their home city and, during this period, seven City fans were convicted of setting fire to Rovers' new home.

On the field, however, there was a glimmer of hope. In 1989/90, the clubs were promoted together from tier three, with Rovers beating City to the championship by two points, thanks to a 3-0 win over City late in the season. The Robins then bounced up and down between tiers two and three for a number of years, but the Pirates ran into troubled waters again. In 1999/2000, Rovers narrowly missed the play-offs in tier three, after losing their final game to the dreaded Cardiff. At least they finished above the Robins. However, rather than build upon that relative success, in 2000/1 Rovers struggled and were relegated. They were unlucky, as they went down by only one point, with a goal difference of just minus four, which was far superior to the nearest survivor, minor rivals Swindon Town. It was Rovers' first excursion into the fourth tier – they had previously been able to gloat that City were the only Bristolians to stoop so low. 2001/2 was a disaster for Rovers, as they finished next to bottom of the Football League. This time they were lucky because, in the following season, the automatic two-down rule was introduced. In 2001/2, it was still only one down and so Rovers escaped. In the same season, Cheltenham Town were promoted to the third tier to play a brand new local derby, with City. From Rovers' standpoint, one shudders to think what may have happened to them had the two-down rule been introduced a year earlier.

The 21st Century has been consistently red. In 2002/3, City had their own heartache at the hands of Cardiff, losing to them in tier three play-off semi-finals, after finishing three places above the Bluebirds in the regular season. But, after more narrow failures, City returned to tier two in 2006/7. In their first season back, they finished fourth, made it to the play-off final, but lost 1-0 to Hull City and so didn't quite make it to the promised land of the Premier League. As for Rovers, they clambered out of the fourth tier, via the play-offs in the same 2006/7 season. The clubs approach season 2012/13 with City in the second tier with no huge pretensions or fears. Rovers, however, face another season at the bottom, having suffered relegation in 2010/11. They will meet Cheltenham. They haven't faced City in a major competition since 2000/1 and so the Bristol derby is falling behind the pace.

Derby times generally have been tough for Rovers over the years and it is difficult to find a minor crumb of comfort for their fans. One perhaps is that, if there was in existence a 'best names in the league' League, Bristol Rovers would be up there as potential champions. Their original (in both senses of the word) real name was the Black Arabs and at the time they were known by the nickname 'Purdown Poachers'. Their official nickname now is the Pirates and their unofficial one is Gasheads. Gasheads was originally an insult thrown at them by City fans but, as in notable examples covered earlier, such as Boca Juniors, an insult has become a badge of honour. If any club has a better array of magnificent names than Bristol Rovers, let them step forward. City, on the other hand, are the Robins which, as we saw in the case of Swindon, is the most common and least original nickname imaginable. They have toyed with the unofficial name of Ciderheads. But City had the chance to be far more distinctive. Their shirt colours were originally dedicated to Italian revolutionaries and, way back in the days when Bedminster were their main derby enemies, City were known as the 'Garibaldis'. Gasheads versus Garibaldis! – bring it back City, bring it back.

Number 18 – Hull City v Grimsby Town

Older club   Grimsby 1878 (Hull 1904)

Head-to-head record

Number	51 games	
First one	Hull 0 Grimsby 1 *(Dec 1905 in Football League Div. 2)*	
Leader (wins)	**Hull 20-18**	

Higher finishes in the League

19th C	Nil	
1900-WWI	Hull	9-1 *(began when Hull were elected to the League in 1905)*
1920s	Hull	8-2
1930s	Grimsby	10-0
40s+50s	Hull	8-6
1960s	Hull	6-4
1970s	Hull	9-1
1980s	Equal	5-5
1990s	Grimsby	9-1
2000s	Equal	5-5
2010/12	Hull	2-0
TOTAL	**Hull**	**53-43**

Silverware (wins)

League	**Equal.** Neither club has won the League. **Grimsby** have the highest finish, 5th in 1934/5.
FA Cup	**Equal.** Neither club has won the FA Cup. **Grimsby** lead 2-1 in semi final appearances
League Cup	**Equal.** Neither club has won the League Cup or reached the semi finals.

Years in Top Tier   Grimsby 12-2

Biggest Wins

Home	Hull	5	Grimsby	0	*(Mar 1913)*
	Grimsby	4	Hull	1	*(Nov 1933)*
Away	Hull	2	Grimsby	3	*(Mar 1927, Feb 1929, Aug 1960)*
	Grimsby	1	Hull	3	*(Dec 1906, Jan 1914)*

History No. 18 – Hull City v Grimsby Town

Hull and Grimsby have a strange derby history and one that possibly explains why derby feelings on Humberside are not as fervent as they should be. Although both clubs have spent the vast majority of their time in tiers two and three, they have spent only twenty-three out of ninety-six seasons in the same division as each other. In the past forty-seven years, they have been together for only three seasons and they last played a League derby in 1987. In recent years, their fortunes have fluctuated wildly.

Like many other clubs, Grimsby's foundation had connections with cricket. They were also another club who had more daring dress sense in their early years, playing in chocolate and blue quarters, before adopting their familiar black and white stripes. Grimsby were elected as members of the original Division Two in 1892/3 and, after winning promotion in 1900/01, they had two seasons in the top tier before Hull had even been formed. Hull were relatively late arrivals on the scene, largely because the city was, and still is, a hotbed of Rugby League. They are Hull City AFC, to distinguish them from Hull FC, the earlier rugby team with who City share a ground.

Once they had entered the fray, the Tigers of Hull became dominant, finishing above Grimsby's Mariners in seventeen out of eighteen seasons either side of the First World War. This period included a year out of the League for Grimsby, as they failed to gain re-election in 1910. In the same season, Hull narrowly missed out on promotion to the top tier. In the final game, Hull met Oldham and needed only a draw to secure promotion, but they lost 3-0 and Oldham took the promotion berth on goal average. It was not to be the last unfortunate close shave for the Tigers and they had to wait almost a century to reach the top.

Grimsby re-emerged as a considerable force, not only on Humberside, but in the country as a whole, towards the end of the twenties. After gaining promotion to the top tier in 1928/9, the Mariners spent ten of the next twelve seasons at the top. They finished fifth in 1934/5, with clubs such as Liverpool, Spurs and Villa trailing in their wake and Manchester United not even in the same division. The 1930s were the high point for both clubs in the FA Cup. Hull had a largely uneventful and unsuccessful time in the League in the period, bouncing between second and third tiers and starting with relegation to tier three in 1929/30. However, in the same season, they reached their first and, to date, only FA Cup semi-final. They lost 1-0 to Arsenal in a replay, after a 2-2 draw.

Grimsby did even better. They made it to two semi-finals, again their only appearances to date. In 1936, they lost 1-0 to eventual winners Arsenal. In 1939, they took a beating, losing 5-0 to Wolves. In fairness, Grimsby had to play their second team goalkeeper, who was then injured early in the game. With no substitutes allowed, the Mariners had ten men and an outfield goalkeeper, against a Wolves' side who had finished runners-up in the League. A strange footnote to the 1939 game is that the crowd, 76,962, is still the biggest ever at Old Trafford and the Mariners therefore sit proudly in Manchester

United's record books. Incidentally, Manchester United's biggest crowd (and a record for any League match) is 83,260, but it gathered at the home of Manchester City, Maine Road, to see United play Arsenal in 1948. United were sharing their neighbours' ground because of bomb damage to Old Trafford.

At the outbreak of war, Grimsby were a mid-table top tier club in good condition. Hull, though safely in the third tier playing wise, were in desperate straights financially and facing an uncertain future. Things changed after the war. In 1948, Hull signed thirty-four year old Horatio Stratton Carter. Better known as Raich, Carter was in the twilight of a brilliant career, in which he had starred for Derby and, especially, Sunderland. He proceeded to score goals which propelled Hull to the Division Three North title in 1948/9. City's average crowd in the season immediately prior to the war was just over six thousand. In stark contrast, nearly fifty thousand fans turned up to see them play a crucial third tier game against Rotherham United on Christmas Day 1948.

Meanwhile Grimsby began to slide from their pre-war height. Relegated from the top tier in 1947/8 (and never to return to date) they were relegated again in 1950/1 to Division Three North, dropping past Hull on the way. The Mariners then had a particularly bad stroke of luck in their first season back in the third tier. They were beaten to the championship, and the single available promotion spot, by local rivals Lincoln City despite gaining the modern equivalent of ninety-five points (twenty-nine wins and eight draws in forty-six games). No other team in the Football League has gained the equivalent of so many points and yet failed to be promoted.

For most of the period after World War Two, up to the end of the 1980s, the clubs settled largely in tiers two and three. Hull had the upper hand overall. Grimsby's star had waned sufficiently for them to have to seek re-election in 1955 and 1969. When the re-election system was in place, Grimsby had to apply five times in total, once unsuccessfully in 1910. Hull never had to seek re-election

In 1970/1, Hull were in the race for promotion to the top tier until late in the season, but they didn't make it. Grimsby were struggling in tier four. But tables turned at the end of the seventies. In 1979/80, the Mariners completed back-to-back promotions, to rise from fourth to second tiers. On the way, they passed Hull, ending a period of dominance for the Tigers. By 1981/2, Grimsby were safely in tier two. Hull were in the bottom tier and in receivership. It was not their first brush with financial disaster and it would not be their last.

The Tigers began a recovery and, in 1983/4, had another of their 'miss out on goal difference' moments. Their final game of the season, away to Burnley, was delayed and so, by the time it was played, Hull knew that they needed to win by at least a three goal margin to shade Sheffield United for promotion from tier three. Not surprisingly, Burnley's 'home' crowd was significantly enhanced by travelling Blades. Hull won, but only 2-0. They missed promotion on goals scored.

The derby was last played in a major competition in 1989/90, when Grimsby beat Hull in the League Cup, thereby avenging a defeat in the same competition in 1986/7. Since then, the fortunes of the clubs have fluctuated more wildly than probably any derby. By 1989/90, Hull were in tier two, while Grimsby were paying a short visit to tier four. Successive promotions for the Mariners and relegation for the Tigers saw Grimsby in tier two by 1991/2, overtaking Hull on the way. Hull then continued on a journey almost into the abyss. In 1997/8 and 1998/9, Hull finished third and fourth bottom of the entire League, whereas Grimsby ended the 1998/9 season comfortably placed in mid-table in tier two.

Off the field, the new century brought immediate financial problems for both clubs. At one point in 2000, Hull were even locked out of their ground in a dispute about money and ownership. On the field, the new century brought ever more dramatic ups and downs. By 2004/5, the clubs had changed places yet again, with Grimsby falling into the fourth tier and Hull rising to the third, following what was to be the first of three promotions in five years. In 2007/8, Hull's amazing resurgence saw them at last reach the top tier for the first time, winning promotion in the play-off final. As Hull were ending their first ever season at the top in 2008/9, having just survived for another year in the sun, Grimsby avoided relegation from the League by four points. Unlike for Hull in the nineties, there was to be no bounce-back or reprieve for Town. In 2009/10, they dropped out of the League. Hull fell back into the second tier too.

2012/13 sees the clubs three tiers apart and not having played each other in the League for twenty-six years. Clearly, their derby is on a downward spiral. Historically, however, this is a very competitive example, despite their amazing ability to pass each other in reverse directions without meeting. Hull have a slightly better record in terms of head-to-head encounters and higher placements in the League. Grimsby have not beaten Hull in the League since 1966, although there have been only six League derbies in the period, and the Mariners have won more recently in the League Cup. As with England, for Grimsby the years of hurt since 1966 continue to mount. But Grimsby can still point to past glories and the facts that they have enjoyed more years in the top tier; a higher best League placing and more FA Cup semi final appearances than the Tigers. To bring back memories of the good times, 1930s fashions are no doubt in evidence in Grimsby or, more appropriately, in Cleethorpes, where the Mariners have made their home.

Number 19 – Blackpool v Preston North End

Older club **Preston 1881** (Blackpool 1887). *Dates of foundation are not clear cut. The Lilywhites of Preston arose from an older cricket club, who dabbled with other sports including rugby, lacrosse and even rounders. They first played an association football game in 1878. They voted to adopt football as their main sport in 1880. The usual date given for their foundation, 1881, is when they first played a major game as a football club. Blackpool's 1887 date is when the Blackpool Football Club was founded following a dispute, but some would argue that their roots can be traced back to an earlier incarnation dating from 1877*

Head-to-head record

Number	93 games	
First one	Blackpool 1 Preston 4	*(Nov. 1901 in Football League Div. Two)*
Leader (wins)	**Preston 44-30**	

Higher finishes in the League

19th C	Preston	4-0	*(began when Blackpool were elected to Division Two in 1896).*
1900-WW1	Preston	15-0	
1920s	Preston	8-2	
1930s	Preston	6-4	
40s+50s	Equal	7-7	
1960s	Blackpool	10-0	
1970s	Blackpool	8-2	
1980s	Preston	7-3	
1990s	Blackpool	6-4	
2000s	Preston	9-1	
2010/12	Blackpool	2-0	
TOTAL	**Preston**	**62-43**	

Silverware (wins)	League	**Preston**	2-0
	FA Cup	**Preston**	2-1
	League Cup	**Equal.** Neither side have won the League Cup. Only **Blackpool** have reached a semi-final (1962).	

Years in Top Tier **Preston** **46-28**

Biggest Wins

Home	Blackpool	5	Preston	1	*(Feb 1930)*
	Preston	6	Blackpool	4	*(Mar 1926 – although their 4-1 victories in March 1927 and April 1960 might be considered more comprehensive)*
Away	Blackpool	2	Preston	6	(Oct 1955)
	Preston	0	Blackpool	7	(May 1948)

History No. 19 – Blackpool v Preston North End

Blackpool's 7-0 away win at Deepdale on 1st May 1948 is one of those remarkable oddities that occur in football from time to time. Preston won the corresponding fixture at Blackpool in the same season, although by only 1-0. They also finished two places above Blackpool at the end of 1947/8. As this is Preston's worst league defeat, home or away, Preston share with very few clubs the ignominy of having their deadliest rivals etched onto their records. It is also Blackpool's equal best league victory and so is proudly in their record book too. If anything, Preston might have been expected to thrash Blackpool, as not only were the Seasiders recovering from the disappointment of losing the FA Cup final the previous Saturday, but also their biggest star, Stanley Matthews, was not playing. McIntosh scored five. Originally a Blackpool player, McIntosh had been transferred in controversial circumstances to Preston, only to return to the Seasiders to play a starring role in this famous victory on the final day of the season.

Lilywhites of Preston may have to live with this aspect of their record book, but they can claim a clear edge in the West Lancashire derby in all factors. That having been said, their lead was established in the very early days of League football and the clubs' records have been almost equal since then. For example, Preston lead in terms of silverware won, but they already had two League titles and one FA Cup success to their name before Blackpool had entered the League. During the years when both have been in the League, each has won only one FA Cup (Preston in 1938 and Blackpool in 1953) and neither have gained League titles. Preston comfortably lead Blackpool 62-43 in higher League placements. However, Blackpool didn't finish above Preston in any season until 1925/6, which was their twenty-sixth attempt to do so. Excluding those first twenty-five years, Blackpool are slightly ahead.

Preston were the first great power in the Football League. In the season before the Football League came into existence, Preston won forty-two consecutive matches. It made them red-hot favourites for the 1888 FA Cup final, but they lost 2-1 to West Brom. Next year, in 1888/9, they won the very first League title and didn't lose a game in doing so. Only two other teams, in any division in the history of the League, have repeated Preston's feat of remaining unbeaten in a whole season. Liverpool did so in 1893/4, but in the second tier. Arsenal equalled the Lilywhites' record in the 2003/4 Premier League. Arsenal's achievement was greater, in that they played thirty-eight games, whereas Preston played only twenty-two. However, Arsenal were beaten in the semi-final of the FA Cup in 2003/4. In 1888/9, Preston went on to complete a League and FA Cup double and, in that sense, they remain as the only undefeated side in any season. At the time, Preston's great rivals were Blackburn Rovers and, to a lesser extent, Burnley, who they beat 5-2 in their first ever League game. The derby rivalry with Blackpool arose much later and didn't really take off until after World War Two.

Having achieved the 'double' and been unbeaten in their first League season, things could only go one way for Preston's 'Invincibles' – downwards. They won the League title again in season two and finished as runners-up in the following three seasons but, after that, they didn't seriously challenge for the title again in the 19th century. In the first season of the 20th century, Preston were relegated for the first time and so, also for the first time, they made acquaintance with Blackpool in Division Two. Blackpool were returning to the League after a year's break, having failed re-election in 1899, despite finishing third from bottom. Ironically, later they finished bottom of the League twice, only to be re-elected on both occasions. The remaining years up to 1930 were fairly uneventful. Preston bounced up and down between the top and second tiers, challenging for the title only once, when they were runners-up in 1905/6. They also reached the Cup final of 1922, but lost to Huddersfield. Reportedly, the game was awful and was won by a penalty awarded for a foul that was clearly committed outside the area. Blackpool sat in the second tier, when it was the lowest tier, and continued to sit there after a third tier had been introduced. The only other thing of note in these years was that, unusually for derbies, there were lots of goals scored. For example, Preston beat Blackpool 6-4 at Deepdale in 1925/6. Blackpool won 6-4 at Deepdale in 1929/30 and also won the home tie 5-1.

Having finished above Preston for the first time in 1925/6, the Tangerines achieved their first promotion in 1929/30. Life in the top flight proved tough and Blackpool soon fell back. But, they had hinted at better times to come and they had finally established themselves as worthy opponents for Preston. In 1937/8, Blackpool joined Preston in the First Division and, for the first time, the derby was played at the top. Preston had become a force again. Beaten FA Cup finalists in 1937, in 1938 they finished third in the League and also won the FA Cup. The 1938 final produced a series of amazing co-incidences. Preston played Huddersfield, as they had in 1922. The score was again 1-0, this time to Preston. Most remarkably, the winner was scored with the last kick in extra time – and it was another controversial penalty, awarded for what appeared to be a foul committed outside the area.

As far as it was possible to do so, Tangerines had a good war. Blackpool was the base for a major RAF training centre and it allowed the club access to many guest players. Wartime games are not considered official matches and so are generally ignored in this book. In passing, however, it is worth mentioning Blackpool's victory over Arsenal in 1943 for the unofficial 'championship of England'. Half the side playing that day were not actually Blackpool's own players and one of them, a guest from Stoke, was to play a huge role in the Seasiders' post-war success.

The golden years for West Lancashire's derby commenced immediately after the resumption of football. Blackpool have reached three FA Cup finals in their history and all three came in a six year period not long after the war. Beaten finalists in 1948 and 1951, the Tangerines came back from 3-1 down to beat Bolton 4-3 in 1953.The man from Stoke, Stanley Matthews, took the plaudits, in what was one of the best finals ever. Another Stan, Mortensen, scored the only hat-trick in a Wembley final and in the whole of the 20th Century.

(Incidentally, it is often recorded that Mortensen's is the only hat-trick in *any* FA Cup final. This is incorrect. Townley for Blackburn Rovers in 1890 and Logan for Notts County in 1894 both scored hat-tricks in finals).

In fourteen seasons up to 1960, Blackpool finished in the top half of the top tier in all but two seasons. Preston achieved similar end of season finishes eight times in the same period, despite spending two of those years in the second tier. Blackpool's highest placing was second in 1955/6. Preston were runners-up twice, in 1952/3 and 1957/8, and it was they who came closest to taking the title. In 1952/3, as the Seasiders were winning the FA Cup, the Lilywhites almost completed a double for West Lancashire, losing out on goal average to Arsenal, in one of the tightest ever finishes for the League title.

The derby came to prominence in this period. Burnley were also in the top half of the top tier for most of the fourteen seasons, but Preston's traditionally biggest and geographically closest rivals, Blackburn, spent most of the late forties and fifties in the second tier. The brilliance of Preston and Blackpool at the time is perhaps best illustrated by a fact about their individual superstars. Only four British footballers have been knighted solely for their on-field talents. Two of the four graced the West Lancashire derby in the years following the war – Sir Stanley Matthews for Blackpool and the home-grown 'Preston plumber', Sir Tom Finney (the other two are Sir Bobby Charlton and Sir Geoff Hurst. Incidentally readers may be surprised to learn that Bobby Moore, England's World Cup captain in 1966 was *not* knighted).

In 1960/1, Preston were relegated and Blackpool escaped by just one point. The writing was therefore already on the wall for the clubs before the scrapping of the maximum wage took its full effect. When it did so, West Lancashire went into severe decline. Blackpool were relegated in 1966/7 to join Preston in the second tier. To date, the Lilywhites have not returned to the top tier. Desperate times lay ahead.

In the derby itself, the sixties and seventies belonged to Blackpool. From 1960, Blackpool finished above Preston for eighteen seasons in succession. In 1969/70, Blackpool bounced back to the top tier. Towards the season's end, a Fred Pickering hat-trick at Deepdale, in a 3-0 victory, sealed promotion for Blackpool and ensured that Preston were relegated to the third tier for the first time. The derby, which until then had been a relatively good-natured affair, became anything but from that night onwards.The Tangerines survived for only one season and they were not to return to the top again until 2010/11.

Tables turned in 1977/8, as Blackpool crashed into tier three for the first time. In the same year, Lilywhites gained promotion into tier two. There was further decline in 1980/1, when Preston dropped into tier three again and Blackpool dropped down for their first spell in the fourth tier. Two years later, the Seasiders finished twenty-first, three places from bottom of the League pile. Two years after that, Blackpool were promoted, as Preston fell into the bottom tier for the first time. If Preston fans thought things couldn't get worse, they were wrong. In 1985/6, Preston ended the season next to bottom of the bottom tier. Had current rules been applicable at the time, 'Proud' Preston would have dropped out of the League altogether. From there, the clubs exchanged places from time to time, as both moved up and down between tiers three and four. In 1999/2000, Preston returned to the second tier, for the first time in almost twenty years, as Blackpool paid yet another visit to the bottom.

Preston had a good start to the 21st century, frequently challenging, but ultimately failing, to make it into the Premier League. In 2006/7, after an absence of almost thirty years, Blackpool returned to tier two to join them. Preston had been dominant for over a decade and might have expected to be first to return to the top tier. But they were not. In 2009/10, Blackpool gained an unlikely promotion to the Premier League, via the play-offs, having only squeezed into a play-off berth on the last day of the regular season. Their spell in the sun lasted for just one year but, on their return to the second tier in 2011/12, they didn't find Preston waiting for them. The Lilywhites had been relegated again and so derbies in the League will have to wait. Preston's demotion was the cause of an unwelcome celebration in Bamber Bridge. Whenever the Lilywhites are relegated, residents of the village bury a special relegation coffin. It is a tradition that has been played out far too often in recent times.

Finally, mention should be made of the dramatically different experiences of these derby rivals in end of season play-offs. Preston have qualified for play-offs eight times. They have made it to three finals, but have yet to achieve promotion via this method. On the other hand, Blackpool have qualified for seven play-off stages and have gained promotion no less than four times. They are unique in having gained promotion from all three tiers of the League by means of play-off finals. However, sympathy for Preston will be in short supply amongst those who believe that highest placed teams deserve to prevail in play-offs, or that the entire system should be abandoned in favour of automatic promotion for the next in line teams. On none of the eight occasions when Preston have qualified for play-offs have they been the highest placed team in the regular season. By contrast Blackpool have been the highest placed team three times and so their four play-off successes are not quite as lucky as they might at first seem.

Number 20 – Aston Villa v Birmingham City

Older club   Villa 1874 (City 1875)

Head-to-head record
Number	120 games	
First one	Villa 4 City 0 (Nov 1887 in the FA Cup)	
Leader (wins)	Villa 51-38	

Higher finishes in the League
19th C	Villa	8-0.
1900-WWI	Villa	14-1
1920s	Villa	9-1
1930s	Villa	7-3
40s+50s	Villa	10-4
1960s	Villa	7-3
1970s	Equal	5-5
1980s	Villa	10-0
1990s	Villa	10-0
2000s	Villa	9-1
2010/12	Villa	2-0
TOTAL	**Villa**	**91-18**

Silverware (wins)	League	**Villa**	**7-0**
	FA Cup	**Villa**	**7-0**
	League Cup	**Villa**	**5-2.**

Years in Top Tier	**Villa**	**101-57**

Biggest Wins

Home	Villa	7	City	3	*(Sept 1895, although 5-0 in the Oct 1988 League Cup clash might be seen as more comprehensive)*
	City	4	Villa	0	*(Sept 1968)*
Away	Villa	2	City	4	*(Oct 1967)*
	City	0	Villa	4	*(Feb 1931)*

History No. 20 – Aston Villa v Birmingham City

Birmingham's clubs are two of the ten oldest current League clubs. Many football clubs were founded by churches. Many others arose as a result of cricketers seeking a winter sport. The Second City's finest were both formed by church-going cricketers, from Wesleyan Chapel (Villa) and Holy Trinity Church (City). Villa's stronghold is generally in the north of the city and Birmingham's in the south but, as elsewhere, a geographical split is by no means absolute and mixed families are not uncommon. Birmingham's derby is intense and even fierce at times but, frankly, competitive it is not. Villa have nineteen major domestic trophies in their cabinet and are one of only five English clubs to have won the top European trophy. Birmingham have just two League Cups to their name. Villa have appeared in ten FA Cup finals, winning the cup seven times. City have reached two FA Cup finals and lost in both. Villa have finished in the top three of the League on nineteen occasions. The Blues haven't. Their best effort was to finish sixth in 1955/6. In domestic competitions, Villa are the fifth most successful English club of all time. Birmingham do not feature in the top twenty of the same list and historically they have never done so.

It is not all bad news for City. Villa have a massive lead over them, but most claret and light-blue success was achieved generations ago. Villa were not only the top club in England in the early years, they were also the best supported club in the country at the turn of the 20th Century, having overtaken previous holders of the top-support crown, Everton, in 1898. Given Villa's feast, in comparison with Blues' famine, perhaps three examples in history should be highlighted when Birmingham held sway. In 1955/6, Birmingham had their best ever year in the League and also reached the FA Cup final, losing 3-1 to Manchester City. To cap a wonderful year for the blue half of the city, Villa avoided relegation to the second tier only on goal average. Then, in May 1956, City became the first English club to play in European competition. They drew 0-0 away to Inter Milan. The dream couldn't last and it didn't. In 1956/7, normal order was restored, as Villa finished above City in the League. To make matters worse for the Blues, both clubs made it to semi-finals of the FA Cup but, as Birmingham were losing to Manchester United, Villa beat their old local foes West Brom. Villa went on to win against the 'Busby Babes' in the final, thereby bringing home the cup to the city for what to date, over half a century later, has proven to be the last time.

A second good time for Blues occurred in the mid-sixties. In 1966/7, Aston Villa were relegated to the second tier and, for the following eight years, they were not only outside the top tier, but were also behind Birmingham. To put this period into perspective, Villa have missed only twelve years in the top tier in total, in one hundred and thirteen seasons since the League was formed, a record bettered only by Everton. The Blues were not particularly successful at the time, but it is their only prolonged period of ascendancy over the Villans. For the derby itself, this period was its nadir. The clubs played together for three seasons in the second tier, before Villa dropped even lower into tier three.

It may have been a low point for the derby, but the sheer joy of witnessing the fall from grace of Villa must have been worth as much as any trophy to a long-suffering Blue. Furthermore, City could point out that, at the time, they had never stooped so low themselves (City have been in the third tier since, but slipped down only in 1989).

Again, City's good times were not to last. The Villans were promoted back to the top tier in 1974/5 and, in thirty-seven seasons since, they have finished below Birmingham only once (in 2002/3). In 1980/1, Villa were League champions and in 1982, just ten years after clawing their way out of the third tier of English football, the Villans were champions of Europe. Even for hard-nosed Blue pessimists, Villa's turnaround must have been hard to take. They did at least gain a morsel of comfort, by beating Villa 3 - 0 in their first derby after Villa's European triumph.

For the third example, we come to what was arguably the greatest moment for Blues' fans. In 1963, City won their first major trophy. Birmingham triumphed over two legs in the final of the League Cup. At the time, the League Cup was probably even less of a big thing than it is now, but the victory in the final was against none other than the Villa. Moreover, Villa fans could hardly dismiss the League Cup as a Mickey Mouse competition, as they had been its first winners two years earlier. Leek, with two, and Bloomfield scored priceless goals in a 3-1 win at St.Andrews and the second leg at Villa Park ended in a scoreless draw – happy days indeed for Blues.

Having outlined three of the rare better times for City, it would be remiss not to return to earlier days, to pay tribute to the magnificent Villa of old. When the Football League began in 1888, Villa were in much the same position as they are today. They had a very good side; they had, after all, won the FA Cup in 1887. However, they were not thought of as the best club around. Lancastrian giants, Preston and Blackburn, were expected to be better, and local rivals West Brom were considered to have the edge over Villa. Furthermore, no-one was quite sure how good Everton would be and big non-Football League clubs, such as Sunderland, were developing in the wings. In fact, Villa excelled in the first season and were runners-up, albeit a full eleven points behind champions, Preston. For the next four seasons, Villa performed to expectations – good, but not great. However, from 1893/4, Villa became to the turn of the 20th century what Manchester United were to be at the turn of the 21st. In seven seasons to 1899/1900, Villa were champions five times and FA Cup winners twice. In 1896/7, they did the double, a feat which no-one else achieved for over sixty years.

In the first years of the 20th century up to World War One, Villa added another League title in 1909/10, were runners-up in the League five times and FA Cup winners twice more, in 1905 and 1913. In twenty-three attempts in these years, Birmingham finished above Villa once. That was in 1905/6 and the Blues were only one point ahead. By 1914, Villa were far away leaders in the all-time success table. Indeed, they notched up such a huge lead before World War One that it took Liverpool until 1982 to overhaul Villa as the domestic number one club in history. Ironically, Villa lost top spot domestically in the year they became European champions.

In the past three decades, Villa have been constants in the top tier, except for one year in 1987/8. They have been runners-up in the League twice since their title winning season in 1980/1 but, on both occasions (1989/90 and 1992/3), were well behind the champions and so have never come close to repeating their success. It has been a frustrating period for a club of Villa's ambitions. Trailing in Villa's wake for virtually the whole period, City have spent time in first, second and third tiers.

In 2010/11, Birmingham won only the second trophy in their history and again it was the League Cup which brought joy to the blue streets of England's Second City. Their victory added spice to a derby that looked to be in good health in 2010/11. Unfortunately, as Jasper Carrott's demeanour will demonstrate, joy is rarely long-lasting for a City fan. At the end of the season Birmingham were relegated. Villa, always keen to rub a bluenose in it, added to the wake by taking City's manager in controversial circumstances. City fans could at least take heart from the fact that the manager survived for only one turbulent season in which Villa came perilously close to relegation. But the Villans were not relegated and the Blues were not promoted and so the derby will not be played in the League in 2012/13. Villa will extend their better League finishes count to at least 92-18 over the Blues and the lack of competitiveness in this otherwise excellent derby will continue to hamper any chance of progress up the Derby League Table.

Number 21 – Chesterfield v Mansfield Town

Older club   **Chesterfield 1866**. (Mansfield 1897). *Chesterfield are the fourth oldest club in the League. Mansfield's date of foundation is disputed, with some authorities suggesting that it was as late as 1905, but the club officially states that they were formed in 1897, as Mansfield Wesleyans.*

Head-to-head record

Number	70 games	
First one	Mansfield 0 Chesterfield 3	*(Oct 1933 in Division Three North)*
Leader	**Chesterfield 28-26** *(Mansfield lead 25-24 in League games)*	

Higher finishes in the League

19th C	Nil	
1900-WWI	Nil	
1920s	Nil	
1930s	Chesterfield	7-1 *(began in 1931/2 when Mansfield were elected to the League).*
40s/50s	Chesterfield	12-2
1960s	Mansfield	9-1
1970s	Chesterfield	6-4
1980s	Chesterfield	7-3
1990s	Chesterfield	7-3
2000s	Chesterfield	10-0
2010/12	Chesterfield	2-0
TOTAL	**Chesterfield 52-22**	

Silverware	**League**	**Equal.** Neither club has won the League.
	FA Cup	**Equal.** Neither club has won the FA Cup. Only Chesterfield have appeared in an FA Cup semi-final
	League Cup	**Equal.** Neither club has appeared in a League Cup final or semi-final

Years in Top Tier   **Equal.** Neither club has ever reached the top tier. **Chesterfield** have spent more years in the second tier by **10-1**.

Biggest Wins

Home	Chesterfield	5	Mansfield	2	*(May 1995)*
	Mansfield	6	Chesterfield	2	*(1970)*
Away	Chesterfield	0	Mansfield	4	*(Sept 1961)*
	Mansfield	0	Chesterfield	5	*(1971)*

History No. 21 – Chesterfield v Mansfield Town

There is an oddity about Mansfield's biggest home win and biggest home defeat against Chesterfield. Both occurred in the League Cup and were in successive years. Having beaten the Spireites 6-2 in 1970, the Stags must have been very confident of winning a home tie in 1971, after drawing 0-0 at Chesterfield's Saltergate. Instead, they lost 0-5. It heralded a tough year for Mansfield, at the end of which they were relegated from the third tier by one goal, having finished in a four-way tie on points.

When people think about particularly toxic derbies, Chesterfield versus Mansfield probably doesn't spring to mind, but this one can be thoroughly unpleasant. The reason for the venom? – the answer is coal and specifically the Miners' Strike of 1984/5. The social and economic scars of the strike run deeper than the mines upon which communities are or (more accurately) were based. It is common for all Nottinghamshire clubs to be greeted with chants of 'scabs, scabs, scabs' when visiting their South Yorkshire or North Derbyshire neighbours. Nottingham itself, however, is not at the heart of the Nottinghamshire coalfield. Mansfield is, and Chesterfield is the opposite number for North Derbyshire's mining community. The battle lines are set, as they were in 1984/5.

It was not always thus. There has always been inter-county rivalry to boost antagonisms between the clubs but, when Mansfield were elected to the League in 1931, Chesterfield would not have viewed the Stags as emerging bitter rivals. Firstly, Chesterfield were about to enter the most successful period in their history. After gaining promotion as Division Three North champions in 1935/6, the Spireites were to spend the next eight seasons, either side of World War Two, in the second tier. Secondly, Mansfield took Newport's place in Division Three *South* and they were moved to and fro between south and north three times, before settling as a 'northern' club in 1947/8. The combined effect was that Mansfield spent only three seasons together with Chesterfield before 1951/2. Thirdly, during their first twenty-three years in the League Mansfield finished above Chesterfield only three times.

Chesterfield's best finishing position was fourth in the second tier in 1946/7 and, after relegation in 1950/1, they have never returned to those heights. In one respect, Mansfield have the upper hand, in that they tasted second level football more recently. Their single season in the second tier was 1977/8 and they finished next to bottom. They had been promoted as champions, ahead of the infinitely more fashionable Brighton and Hove Albion and Crystal Palace, who rose with the Stags. Three seasons later, Brighton and Palace were lording it in the top tier. Mansfield were relegated to the fourth.

Mansfield's only significant period of dominance over Chesterfield occurred in the 1960s, but this was due to the inadequacies of Chesterfield, who spent most of the time in the doldrums of tier four, rather than to any great achievements by the Stags.

Overall, Chesterfield have the edge in all factors and for Mansfield things are getting worse and worse. They haven't finished higher than Chesterfield for nineteen seasons and that run will continue for the time being, because the Stags lost their League place in 2007/8 and have yet to return (as at 2012/13). Recently, Chesterfield have bounced between tiers three and four. As champions of tier four in 2010/11, they enjoyed derby clashes in the higher tier against both Sheffield clubs in 2011/12, but the season ended in relegation for the Spireites.

The clubs have managed only one major cup run between them, but what a magnificent run it was. In 1997, Chesterfield became one of the few third tier sides to make it to an FA Cup semi final. Most observers would concur that they were robbed of the opportunity to be the first third tier side to reach the final. In an excellent game, and leading 2-1, Chesterfield were denied a goal which clearly crossed the line. Premier League Middlesbrough recovered to draw 3-3 and won the replay 3-0.

Arguably, the biggest games in the history of Chesterfield v Mansfield fixtures happened in fourth tier play-off semi-finals of 1994/5. Chesterfield had finished in third place, sixteen points clear of Mansfield in sixth, but Mansfield had won both derby encounters in the normal season. The first leg was drawn at Manfield's Field Mill 1-1 but, in the second leg, Chesterfield achieved their biggest ever home win over their rivals (5-2) and went on to gain promotion, by winning the final at Wembley.

Many neutrals have a soft spot for Chesterfield. Not necessarily because of the injustice of their 1997 FA Cup semi-final defeat, or even the fact that they became one of the first 'peoples" clubs, after driving out their chairman in the early 2000s (he was subsequently sentenced to four years for fraud). But, Chesterfield are unique in having given us the blessed Mr Banks. Gordon Banks, surely England's and, arguably, the world's greatest ever goalkeeper, came from over the county border in Sheffield, but it was Chesterfield who discovered him. He played for their youth team, who amazed everyone by reaching the FA Youth final in 1956. They lost 4-3 on aggregate to the latest wave of Manchester United Busby Babes, who included Bobby Charlton. In 1959, Chesterfield sold Banks for a measly £6000 to Leicester and they spent most of the following decade regretting having done so, as they languished in the fourth tier. As the glorious Gordon helped win the World Cup in 1966, his mentors finished twentieth in the bottom rung of the League.

Finally, back to the Miners' Strike of 1984/5. At the time, Chesterfield and Mansfield were together in the fourth tier. They met on Boxing Day, the Christmas period being particularly poignant for families who had been on strike for many months. They met again in April 1985, shortly after the strike had ended in defeat for the miners. For the only season ever in meetings between the clubs, both derbies ended in 0-0 draws. Given the circumstances, it is probably good that there were no goals for either set of fans to celebrate. Chesterfield won promotion, as champions, at the end of the season but for striking Spireites it no doubt came as scant compensation for the bigger defeat suffered earlier in the year – 'football is more important than...?' – no, it is not.

Number 22 – Exeter City v Torquay United

Older club	**Torquay 1899**	(Exeter 1904)

Head-to-head record

Number 112 games *(NB an exception has been made to include the four derbies played in the Conference in 2007/8, because those games were so important – see below – although, as both sides won two games each, it doesn't make much difference to overall records)*

First one Torquay 1 Exeter 1 (Aug 1927 in Division Three South)

Leader (wins) **Exeter 41-36**

Higher finishes in the League

19th C	Nil	
1900-WWI	Nil	
1920s	Equal	1-1
1930s	Exeter	6-4
40s/50s	Torquay	10-4
1960s	Torquay	7-3
1970s	Exeter	8-2
1980s	Exeter	9-1
1990s	Exeter	6-4
2000s	Torquay	6-4
2010/12	Exeter	2-0
TOTAL	**Exeter**	**43-35**

Silverware **Equal.** Neither club has won the League, FA Cup or League Cup and neither has appeared in a final or semi-final.

Years in Top Tier **Equal.** Neither club has been in the top tier or the second tier of English football. **Exeter** lead **16-10** in the number of years spent above the lowest tier of the league (ie in the third tier, when there has been a fourth tier below it).

Biggest Wins

Home Exeter 5 Torquay 0 *(Dec 1927 and Jan 1933. The victory in Dec 1927 was in the first derby played at Exeter's ground).*

Torquay 5 Exeter 1 *(Dec 1951)*

Away Exeter 0 Torquay 3 *(Aug 1962 and 1967)*

Torquay 0 Exeter 4 *(Apr 1989)*

History No. 22 – Exeter City v Torquay United

The appearance of this particular Devonian derby in the top thirty may surprise readers, even those in Devon. Many would consider Exeter's meetings with Plymouth to be the bigger derby. However, historically, Plymouth's Pilgrims v Exeter's Grecians is far too one-sided to be considered competitive, whereas Grecians v Torquay's Gulls has been very competitive indeed. There has been only one prolonged period of dominance, when Exeter finished above Torquay in the league for fifteen seasons in a row from 1972/3 to 1986/7. It is the seventeenth most played derby of all and, given their relatively late start in 1927, it would be even higher in a more recently played list. Unfortunately, the fact that the clubs have met so often is testament to their mutual failure over the years to break out of the League's bottom tier.

Torquay is closer to Exeter than is Plymouth. The explanation for Exeter's fascination with Plymouth, rather than their nearer and more comparable neighbour, is largely historical. They have been playing Plymouth for much longer. There is also more rivalry between the cities in general, and their senior clubs clash in rugby union, the South West's passion. Overall, Torquay v Exeter probably ranks as the friendliest derby of all those studied although, as with all derbies, it has had its moments. In their early existence, United played in black and white stripes and were called the Magpies. At the time, City played (and still play) at St.James's Park. Had satnavs existed, there could have been some very confused people wandering the streets of Devon, seeking Newcastle United's home ground.

Although the Gulls are older, the Grecians turned professional earlier and joined the Southern League in 1908. There they met Plymouth Argyle, who had finished as runners-up in the previous season. The early professional derbies saw Plymouth lead Exeter 9-3 (with four draws) in head-to-head clashes and finish above Exeter six times in eight seasons up to 1919/20. Plymouth's domination increased even further when the two clubs joined the Football League in the new Division Three South. In fact, the Pilgrims have finished below a fellow Devonian club on only ten occasions in eighty-five league seasons and until 2011/12 they had *never finished below* both Exeter and Torquay in the same season.

Meanwhile, Torquay Town were playing in the Plymouth League against the reserve sides of their Devonian rivals. In 1921, they amalgamated with Babbacombe and turned professional. Six years later, they won the western section championship of the Southern League, finishing above Argyle Reserves for the first time, and made an audacious bid for election to the Football League. They were elected, after a tied vote, in place of Aberdare Athletic, and promptly finished bottom of the League in their first season. Their first ever league fixture was at home against Exeter. They drew.

Gulls and Grecians began a journey of underachievement together which lasted for many years. There were occasional exceptions. The first was in 1932/3, when Exeter finished second in Division Three South, at a time when only one club gained promotion. It was the closest Exeter have ever come to promotion to the second tier. In 1956/7, Torquay came even closer. On the last day of the season United were in the box seat, but they drew at Crystal Palace, while Ipswich won at Southampton and so took the divisional championship and promotion on goal average. Five years on, their paths had diverged dramatically. Ipswich were English Champions. Torquay were facing relegation to Division Four. Torquay's 1956/7 season was momentous in another sense, as it was the first time in their Football League careers that either Torquay or Exeter had finished above Plymouth.

Both Torquay and Exeter were allocated to the newly created Division Four in 1958, thereby retaining their unenviable record of having always been in the lowest tier available. United were first to achieve promotion from the bottom tier, in 1959/60. City finally rose from the depths in 1963/4. Since then, Torquay have come closest to reaching tier two, finishing fourth in 1967/8 in tier three. Exeter's best in tier three has been eighth, which they achieved in 1979/80 and repeated in 2010/11. For only one glorious season, in 1991/2, the clubs played their derbies above the bottom rung of the League. Exeter avoided relegation by two points, but Torquay went down and they have never since reached such dizzy heights together.

Overall, Torquay vie with Rochdale for the dubious distinction of being the most consistently unsuccessful club in the whole League and Exeter are not that far ahead. The Gulls do, however, have a record in escapology of which Houdini would be proud. In both 1984/5 and 1985/6, they finished bottom of the League. These happened to be the last two seasons before the introduction of automatic relegation to the Conference. United went into the final day of the following season next to bottom with 47 points, one ahead of bottom placed Burnley and one behind Lincoln City. In this first year of automatic relegation, only one club was to be doomed. Burnley won on the day and, as the Gulls were trailing 0-2 at half time, their time in the League seemed to be up. In the second half they pulled a goal back. Then, a police dog called Bryn became an unlikely hero. With time running out, Bryn decided to take a chunk out of a Torquay player who Bryn thought was about to attack his handler. At the time, Gulls' fans, facing relegation, would probably have liked to join in with the dog. During the long delay, news came through that Lincoln had lost, meaning that an equaliser for the Gulls would see them survive on goal difference – the equaliser came in the third minute of a very unusual injury time.

In 1994/5 and 1995/6, both Devonian clubs benefitted from the League rule which insisted that the grounds of Conference champions had to be suitable for promotion to be confirmed. First, Exeter finished bottom of the League on goal difference, but escaped because Macclesfield's ground was deemed inadequate. Next year, Torquay finished bottom by eleven points, but survived again because Stevenage's ground was ruled out. In 2000/1, the Gulls escaped yet again by beating Barnet on the last day of the season to send the Bees down instead. After all Torquay's close shaves, it was Exeter who faced the trap door first, losing their League place in 2002/3. As Torquay gained promotion at the end of the following season, 2004/5 saw Gulls two tiers above Grecians for the first time ever. It didn't last. In 2006/7, there was no escape and eighty years of League football finally ended for Torquay, as they joined Exeter in the Conference.

Devon's year in the Conference, in 2007/8, set up what were arguably the most important games ever played between the clubs. They had finished in third and fourth spots in the regular season, with Torquay three points ahead of Exeter. So, when Torquay won the first leg of the play-off 2-1, away at St. James' Park, they became odds on favourites to reach the final. Four days later, the Gulls scored first at Plainmoor, to lead 3-1 on aggregate, but Exeter stormed back, scoring four goals in eighteen minutes to win 5-3. They went on to success in the final, thereby leaving Torquay stranded in the Conference. However, in 2008/9, Torquay were promoted from the Conference and, as Exeter went straight through the fourth tier, gaining promotion in second place, relatively good times were back. It was a deserved return, especially for Exeter, who had endured horrendous and dubious financial problems in the early 21st century, which almost wrecked the club and culminated in a police raid. Out of the mayhem, Grecians were taken over by the Exeter City Supporters' Trust. The Trust has become a model for others to follow in how to successfully hand over power to fans.

2012/13 will be especially exciting in Devon. Exeter were relegated from the third tier at the end of 2011/12. Torquay missed out in the fourth tier play-offs and Plymouth, who have been in freefall, survived despite dicing with a possible plunge into the Conference. Therefore, all three meet in the fourth tier, with the historical top dogs playing the role of underdogs. Competition between Devon's clubs in 2012/13 is potentially in a uniquely interesting phase.

Finally, a note about goalkeepers – goalies are frequently said to be mad and, undoubtedly, many of them are, but they also have more than their fair share of famous characters from other fields. Pavarotti, Albert Camus, Pope John Paul II and Sir Arthur Conan Doyle all plied their trade between the sticks. Exeter can add to the list, as Sir Stanley Rous, later President of FIFA, began his football journey as Exeter's reserve keeper.

Number 23 – Millwall v West Ham United

Older club	Millwall 1885	(West Ham, as Thames Ironworks, 1895)

Head-to-head record

	Number	60 games
	First one	Millwall 2 West Ham 1 *(Dec. 1899 in the FA Cup)*
	Leader (wins)	**Millwall 22-19**

Higher finishes in the League

	19th C	Millwall	2-0 *(began when Thames Ironworks joined the Southern League in 1898/9).*
	1900-WW1	West Ham	9-6
	1920s	West Ham	9-0
	1930s	West Ham	9-1
	40s+50s	West Ham	14-0
	1960s	West Ham	10-0
	1970s	West Ham	10-0
	1980s	West Ham	8-2
	1990s	West Ham	10-0
	2000s	West Ham	10-0
	2010/12	West Ham	2-0
	TOTAL	**West Ham**	**91-11**

Silverware (wins)	League	**Equal.** Neither club has won the League. **West Ham** have the highest finish, third in 1985/6
	FA Cup	**West Ham 3-0**
	League Cup	**Equal.** Neither club has won the League Cup. **West Ham** have been beaten finalists twice.

Years in Top Tier		**West Ham 54-2**

Biggest Wins	Home	Millwall 5 West Ham 1 *(Southern League 1911/2)*
		West Ham 4 Millwall 1 *(FA Cup Feb 1930)*
	Away	Millwall 1 West Ham 3 *(Southern League 1912/3)*
		West Ham 0 Millwall 3 *(Southern League 1902/3)*

History No. 23 – Millwall v West Ham United

The clash between Hammers and Lions is undoubtedly high in the list of fervent derbies. It loses so much ground in the Derby League Table because it is very one-sided. In fact, since the First World War this has been the least competitive derby of all sixty studied. Given its lack of competition and the fact that Millwall are from South London, whereas West Ham are from East London, *north* of the Thames, people may wonder why on earth this derby is so important in the first place. To find the answer, we have to delve into history and it is a story that could alternatively have appeared in the 'bitter early derbies' section of the book.

It is often said that the fans' hatred of each other stems from a dispute that developed in the General Strike of 1926, when the docks in which most West Ham fans worked were on strike, while those of Millwall fans were not. This may well be so, but their rivalry has significantly deeper roots. Anyone trying to locate 'Millwall' may be a bit confused to find that the place itself is on the Isle of Dogs, *north* of the River Thames, within the loop in the river made famous by the opening credits of 'Eastenders'. Millwall Football Club began life here, as Millwall Rovers in 1885, in the East End of London, not in South London where they now reside. West Ham and Millwall were both formed by workers from firms who, though not dock companies themselves, were associated with different docks in direct competition with each other for contracts. To add to the mix, many Millwall supporters were Scots and, indeed, their original colours stem from 'Dundee' blue.

In the early days of professional football in London, Millwall were top dogs north of the river. The Lions' most serious rivals at the time, for the crown of best side in London, were Woolwich Arsenal, from south of the river. However, firstly, Arsenal soon went off to join the Football League and, secondly, Arsenal were not suitable candidates for an exclusive derby, because everyone in London hated Arsenal – nothing new there then. Millwall were major players in creating the new Southern League and their devotion to it was to shape Lions' history. On the first day of the Southern League's inaugural season, in 1894, the Lions beat Swindon 9-0. It was a sign of things to come. They emulated Preston's achievement in the Football League, by completing the first season undefeated. They romped home to the championship six points clear of nearest challengers, Luton Town. At the end of season one, Millwall were invited to join the Football League. They declined the offer, partly because of concerns about the travelling involved and partly because there was genuine optimism that the Southern League could rival the Football League. In the quest to become London's biggest club in the longer term, it was the first missed opportunity – 'strike one', in baseball parlance.

Millwall retained their Southern League championship in the second season, although they were not undefeated this time. They lost once, meaning that in thirty-four games, over two seasons, the Lions won twenty-eight and lost just once, away to Southampton in their final away fixture of season two. Millwall finished second to the Saints in the third season, and never won the championship title again.

West Ham's forerunner, Thames Ironworks, made a much less auspicious entry into the Southern League. They won the London section of the Second Division at the first attempt, in 1898/9, but struggled at the higher level. Then in 1900, after a disastrous share issue, the club folded. A new club was re-launched, as West Ham United, shortly afterwards. In 1899/1900, Iron met Lion for the first time. Millwall won the FA Cup tie 2-1 and the only surprise was that the score was so close. Millwall went on to their first FA Cup semi-final, where they lost to their nemesis Southampton. The Lions returned to the semi-finals again in 1903, but lost to Derby.

Iron had joined Tottenham Hotspur, as well as Millwall, in the Southern League. For ten seasons, the clubs had a healthy three-way tussle, which Tottenham won on six occasions; Millwall three times and West Ham once. However, in 1908/9, Spurs joined Woolwich Arsenal in the Football League. Millwall and West Ham were left behind in the Southern League. At this point, they were still deadly East End derby rivals. It was also at this time that Millwall missed another opportunity to establish themselves as one of London's top clubs. They continued to stay loyal to the Southern League, even though the wind was blowing firmly in favour of the Football League. Spurs caught up with other ex-Southern League clubs, Fulham, Clapton Orient and Bristol City, and also met Arsenal and Chelsea, who had never been in the Southern League – 'strike two' for Millwall's long term future.

In 1904/5, West Ham moved to their new Boleyn Ground (the correct name for Upton Park). It was christened by a clash with Millwall. The Hammers won 3-0, which is still their equal best league victory over the Lions. So incensed was Millwall's huge goalie, 'Tiny' Joyce, that he punched a hole in the new dressing room door.

Millwall moved south of the river in 1910 and, in 1911/2, over 28,000 turned up to the new Cold Blow Lane to witness the Lions beat the Hammers 5-1, the biggest ever victory in the derby. But, gradually, Millwall's star began to fade and West Ham's became brighter, although they never won the Southern League title. United were higher in the league than Millwall in all three seasons preceding the outbreak of war. Those seasons were to be their last together in league competition until 1932.

When football resumed after World War One, the Southern League was rocked by further defections. In particular, West Ham applied and were accepted to join the Football League. By now, every big club north of the River Thames was in the Football League, but South London, arguably the original home of club football in the capital, did not have a single representative. Millwall were in the south and, although challenged by Crystal Palace, the Lions were by far the best established professional club in South London. They had the opportunity to stake a claim as the Football League's big beast in the territory. The Lions were not denied – they simply didn't apply. The enormity of Millwall's decision to stay faithful to their baby began to unfold one year later. The Southern League bowed to the inevitable and its members, including Millwall, became members of the new Football League Division Three. The Lions were faced with a fight against formidable southern clubs for just one place in tier two, a fight which, ironically, was won by South London's Crystal Palace.

Meanwhile West Ham, having had the foresight to jump ship a year early, were already safe in tier two and doing quite nicely. Only two years later, in 1922/3, the Hammers gained promotion to the top tier and, to cap a wonderful season, they made it to the first FA Cup final to be held at Wembley. Watched by the biggest crowd ever to witness a game in England (just over 126,000 officially, but unofficial estimates ranged up to 200,000), United lost the historic 'white horse' final to Bolton Wanderers. Lions must have wept – 'strike three' and, as far as being one of London's biggest clubs was concerned, Millwall were out.

The Lions/Hammers scene was, therefore, very well established long before 1926 and their mutual animosity was simply further cemented by events in the General Strike. Alas, violence in the derby was also established early. For example, trouble between players at a game in 1906 quickly led to fighting between rival supporters on the terraces. Their history since they joined the Football League has been largely one of separate development. The two clubs rarely meet. In 2011/12, they came together in the same division for only the twelfth time in eighty-five seasons and West Ham's promotion meant that year thirteen will have to wait. In only one season (1989/90) have Millwall been in a higher division than West Ham and in only three seasons have Lions finished above Hammers in the Football League.

In truth, from the 1920s to the 1960s very little of note happened. West Ham spent most of the twenties in the top tier, without ever challenging for silverware in the League. They were relegated in 1931/2 and didn't return to the top until 1958/9. Millwall were third tier champions in 1927/8 and spent a few years at the higher level. A year after falling from the top tier, West Ham avoided relegation to tier three by one point. It is the closest they have come to being outside the top two tiers. For that one season in the period, 1932/3, Millwall finished above the Hammers. The Lions faced relegation a year later and they would have to wait for over fifty years to finish above West Ham again. Apart from West Ham's 1923 final appearance, the highlight of the period came in 1937 when Millwall became the first third tier side to reach an FA Cup semi-final. They lost 2-1 to eventual cup winners Sunderland. The lack of impact of Hammers and Lions is perhaps best demonstrated by the fact that neither were in the top thirty in the all-time success league table before World War Two.

Life for Millwall was hopeful in 1938/9. Their cup run was fresh in the memory and they ended the last season before war in the second tier, alongside West Ham, and only two points behind their claret and blue foes. Post-war, it all went wrong. Relegated to tier three in 1947/8, things got worse for the Lions in the fifties. They finished bottom of the League in 1950 and next to bottom in 1958, having to seek re-election on both occasions. Things for West Ham were very different. As Millwall sought re-election in 1958, United celebrated winning the second tier title. An era began in which the Hammers would emerge as a significant power in English football. They won the FA Cup in 1964, 1975 and 1980. They never really challenged for the League title, their best effort being to finish third in 1985/6, but the Hammers were fairly constant members of the top tier for decades. Overall, it added up to West Ham becoming the thirteenth most successful English League club in the post-war period.

Given that the Hammers were rarely out of the top tier and Millwall didn't rise to that level, it is not surprising to find that, between 1947/8 and 1988/9 the derby was played out in only one season, 1978/9. Millwall achieved back-to-back promotions from fourth to second tiers between 1964 and 1966, but they couldn't catch the Hammers, who were basking in the glow of providing essential components for England's World Cup triumph. The Lions came closest to reaching the top tier in 1971/2, missing promotion by one point. Finally, in 1987/8, Millwall made it to the promised land, winning the second tier title on the way. For one glorious season, the derby was played at the top and, as West Ham were relegated that year, Millwall held sway for the first time in well over fifty years. Even then, Lions' fans had to put up with the Hammers completing a League double in the derbies that year. Millwall's place in the sun didn't last for long. They were relegated at the end of the following season and have not been above the Hammers again. The only joy for Millwall in recent years came in March 2004, when they beat West Ham 4-1, in the derby's biggest Football League victory. It was eventful, involving three penalties (two missed), a red card and a spectacular own-goal. Most Lions would consider the 'Mothers' Day massacre' as their best ever win.

Looking at overall results, readers may think that a 22-19 head-to-head lead for Millwall in the records' section is a mistake. It isn't. Admittedly, Millwall ran up a fairly substantial lead long ago, during their time together in the Southern League. However, in twenty-four Football League meetings to the end of 2011/12, West Ham lead by only 8 wins to 5. In fact, Millwall have an unusual hold on their derby rivals generally. Both Crystal Palace and Charlton Athletic also have better overall records of success than Millwall. For example, Charlton have spent twenty-six seasons in the top tier and Palace thirteen. Millwall have had just two years at that level. But, in head-to-head contests, Lions lead Eagles 43-40 and, astonishingly, they lead the Addicks of Charlton 33-11. To put this into perspective – of all sixty derbies studied, only two clubs have a worse statistical record against their partners than Charlton's against Millwall. Those two are Fulham, whose head-to-head record against Chelsea accurately reflects their overall relative performance, and Morecambe, who have yet to beat Accrington (but they have only played eleven times).

Finally both clubs, especially Millwall, have a hard reputation. The Lions' Den was closed four times before 1950, as a result of crowd trouble. A testimonial match between the clubs in 1972, on behalf of Lions' stalwart Harry Cripps, ended with police horses on the pitch trying to separate fans. Lions' fans mock their reputation by singing the traditional song 'let 'em come' and the more recent 'no-one likes us, everybody hates us, we don't care'. They may not be lovable, but anyone reading an account of Millwall's history would be hard indeed not to have sympathy for them. Had they not been so loyal, for so long, they could have been the biggest club in London – no wonder they get a bit grumpy at times.

Number 24 – Shrewsbury Town v Wrexham

Older club	**Wrexham 1873** (Shrewsbury 1886)	

Head-to-head record

Number	52 games	
First one	Shrewsbury 0 Wrexham 1 *(1945 in the FA Cup)*	
Leader (wins)	**Shrewsbury 21-20**	

Higher finishes in the League

19th C	Nil	
1900-WW1	Nil	
1920s	Nil	
1930s	Nil	
40s+50s	Wrexham 2-1	*(began in 1950/1 when Shrewsbury joined the League, but they played in different Division Threes for most of the fifties)*
1960s	Shrewsbury 9-1	
1970s	Wrexham 8-2	
1980s	Shrewsbury 10-0	
1990s	Wrexham 8-2	
2000s	Equal 5-5	
2010/12	Shrewsbury 2-0	
TOTAL	**Shrewsbury 31-24**	

Silverware (wins)

League	**Equal.** Neither club has won the League. **Shrewsbury** have the highest finish, 8th in the second tier in both 1983/4 and 1984/5	
FA Cup	**Equal.** Neither club has appeared in the final or a semi-final	
League Cup	**Equal.** Neither club has appeared in the final but **Shrewsbury** reached the semi-finals of the first ever League Cup in 1961.	

Years in Top Tier — **Equal.** Neither club has played in the top tier. **Shrewsbury** lead **10-4** in seasons in the second tier.

Biggest Wins

Home	Shrewsbury 6 Wrexham 1 *(League Cup 1966/7)*	
	Wrexham 3 Shrewsbury 1 *(Jan 1974)*	
Away	Shrewsbury 1 Wrexham 2 *(achieved four times).*	
	Wrexham 1 Shrewsbury 3 *(Feb 2007)*	

History No. 24 – Shrewsbury Town v Wrexham

There are a couple of oddities about the record scores between the clubs. First, the two biggest scores in the derby were both registered by Shrewsbury in the same season, 1966/7, and both were in cup competitions. In addition to their 6-1 win in the League Cup, Town dumped Wrexham out of the FA Cup by 5-1. Second, although the two sides have an almost equal number of victories in games against each other, Wrexham have an amazingly poor record of scoring against Town. In fifty-two clashes, Wrexham have scored more than two goals on only two occasions, and one of those was in a 3-3 home draw. On the other hand, Shrewsbury have scored more than twice against Wrexham eleven times.

As with a few 'smaller' derbies, the appearance of Shrewsbury v Wrexham in the top thirty may surprise people, especially as Wrexham's number one enemy traditionally has been Chester. Chester is considerably closer to Wrexham and Chester's Deva Stadium actually straddles the English/Welsh border. The Wrexham v Chester derby started earlier than Shrewsbury v Wrexham, as Shrewsbury didn't enter the League until 1950. Furthermore, having initially joined Division Three North, Shrewsbury were switched to Division Three South after their first season and so didn't take part in League derbies with Wrexham or Chester until later. All of that having been said, the fact remains that, in terms of its competitiveness, if not its focus and fervour, Shrewsbury v Wrexham is right up there with the best whereas, even before Chester City's demise, Wrexham were clearly the more successful club in that derby. Shrewsbury have an even bigger lead over Hereford. In contrast, although Shrewsbury lead Wrexham in all factors, their advantage is marginal and so it is by far the closest run derby in the area.

Both clubs are older than might be expected. Football in Wales began in the north and Wrexham, formed by cricketers in 1873, are older than all but six current English League clubs. Shrewsbury Town may not have joined the League until 1950, but football in the town was established very early and Shrewsbury School provided a number of the first internationals for England and Wales. Foundation in 1886 makes Shrewsbury as old as Arsenal. Both clubs had early brushes with violence. Town had connections with a club called Castle Blues, who developed a reputation for 'robust' play, a reputation the new club was determined to cast off. Wrexham's first FA Cup tie was marred by crowd trouble, so much so that it led the club briefly to change its name to Wrexham Olympic, presumably in the belief that Olympian sprit would prevent future disturbances.

Wrexham are another 'Robins', although increasingly they use the more distinctively Welsh 'Dragons' as their nickname. They were original members of Division Three North. Thus, they had a thirty year head start on the 'Blues/Shrews/Town' in the League, but the Robins didn't achieve a great deal in those years. Only once did they come close to gaining promotion, finishing as runners-up by two points in 1932/3. On a more positive note, they were rarely in trouble, never having to seek re-election in the years before Shrewsbury joined the League. Their closest shave came in 1949/50, when the Dragons finished third from bottom. Indeed, it was Shrewsbury who were first to have to seek re-election. Having made a shaky start to their League career, Shrews came next to bottom in 1952/3, but had no difficulty in retaining their League place.

When the third and fourth tiers were created in 1958, Shrewsbury missed the cut, whereas Wrexham got their first 'promotion', edging out York City on goal average for the final third tier spot. But Town were promoted in the fourth tier's inaugural season and the Robins were relegated a year later. From there, the sixties belonged to Shrewsbury. They established themselves as a solid third level side and narrowly missed out on promotion to a higher tier in 1967/8. Meanwhile, Wrexham's fortunes fluctuated and in, 1965/6, they finished bottom of the League and had to apply for re-election, for the first and only time.

Things changed in the seventies and the Robins were first to rise to the second tier, as they took the tier three championship in 1977/8. It began the most successful period for the derby, because Shrewsbury were third tier champions in the following season. Swansea were promoted with the Shrews and so Wrexham had the added pleasure and distraction of Welsh derbies with Swansea and Cardiff. For three seasons, the Shrews/Robins derby was played at the higher level, with Shrewsbury finishing just above Wrexham on all three occasions. The one that really mattered was in 1981/2, when the Robins were relegated, as Town survived by two points. Incidentally, Cardiff joined Wrexham in the fall to tier three, while Swansea enjoyed their best season ever, sixth in the top tier. Shrewsbury's good times rolled on for ten years, their best seasons in the second tier being 1983/4 and 1984/5, when they finished eighth. Neither club has made a return to this level.

The seventies and early eighties were also the best times for the clubs in the FA Cup. Town reached round six in 1979 and 1982 and Wrexham made it to the same round in 1974 and 1978. Robins' fans would point to another glorious period for their club. Although at a lower level than in 1978 to 1982, in 1993/4 Wrexham became the top club in Wales for the first time and they led the Principality's challenge for seven of the next eight seasons. The nineties was also a time for excellent cup runs. The longest came in 1997, as Wrexham reached the quarter-finals again, but the greatest story was written in January 1992. Fourth tier Wrexham faced reigning League champions Arsenal and famously the Dragons won.

The derby's low point occurred more recently. The early years of the 21st Century have largely been a nightmare for the Shrewsbury/Wrexham/Chester axis. It started badly in 1999/2000, as Shrewsbury and Chester fought to avoid the drop into the Conference. Shrews escaped on the last day of the season to send Chester down. The reprieve didn't last very long. Shrewsbury were relegated in 2002/3, their demise being confirmed by a defeat to Wrexham, which left only the Robins with League status. In the following season, Shrewsbury won the Conference play-off final and returned to the League, along with champions Chester.

In the meantime, Wrexham had severe problems. Difficulties started off the pitch, but quickly translated into results on it. First, they had a long running saga with their chairman who tried to sell the Robins' ground. Second, the club fell into administration. In 2004/5, Wrexham became the first club to suffer, the now familiar, ten point penalty for entering administration. The penalty directly resulted in them being relegated to the fourth tier and it prompted a decline.

In 2006/7, Wrexham narrowly avoided falling into the Conference. The highlight of their season was being the last team ever to win at Shrewsbury's old Gay Meadow ground. Ironically, the Shrew's have won five of the last six derbies, but the one they lost was when they should have been celebrating the end of an era. The boot was on the other foot a year later. Defeat to Shrewsbury just about ended Wrexham's League career. Their relegation to the Conference was confirmed shortly afterwards following defeat against Hereford. Chester were relegated from the League again in 2008/9 and subsequently went into liquidation, all of which meant that only Shrewsbury retained Football League status. All was not joy for Town either. They made it to tier four play-offs in 2008/9, by winning on the final day of the regular season. In the play-off final they met Gillingham, who the Shrews had beaten 7-0 earlier in the year. Gillingham won 1-0, courtesy of a last minute goal.

In 2010/11 and 2011/12, Wrexham lost out in the Conference play-offs. Their experience in 2011/12 was especially harrowing as they gained ninety-eight points in the regular season, fifteen points more than promoted York City. So Shrewsbury are still alone in having League status. In the summer of 2011, Wrexham were taken over by a partnership between their Supporters' Trust and Glyndwr University. After their travails of the past decade, neutrals will wish them well.

The Robins need to return to the League quickly for the sake of the derby. In their absence, there are signs that Town are looking elsewhere, not only to Hereford, but also to Walsall or Port Vale, though they are never likely to prize the latter away from their city neighbours. Waiting in the wings too are Shropshire rivals Telford United, should their paths ever cross. For their part, Wrexham would still prefer the shorter trip to Chester and they too have interests other than Shrewsbury, for example Tranmere and anyone from South Wales. The derby, never a clear cut primary example of the species, is therefore not secure in the top thirty.

Finally, a couple of goal scoring feats deserve mention. The most prolific striker in the history of English League football is not Dixie Dean or Jimmy Greaves or Bobby Charlton or Gary Lineker. It is Arthur Rowley. The magnificent Arthur scored more than half his 434 goals for Leicester, but he finished his career with Shrewsbury and scored 152 for the Shrews. For most forwards that would be a complete career's worth. For Rowley it was a mere dessert. Secondly, when Wrexham overwhelmed Hartlepools United 10-1, in 1962, they registered a record first, because three different players scored hat-tricks (Ron Barnes – a Ken Barnes played too, Davies and a man named Ambler – clearly he was not justly named!).

Number 25 – Northampton Town v Peterborough United

Older club	**Northampton 1897** (Peterborough 1934)		

Head-to-head record

Number	62 games	
First one	United 1 Town 1 *(Dec 1946 in the FA Cup)*	
Leader	**United 26-19**	

Higher finishes in League

19th C	Nil		
1900-WW1	Nil		
1920s	Nil		
1930s	Nil		
40s/50s	Nil		
1960s	Town	7-3	*(started in 1960 when United were elected to the League)*
1970s	United	9-1	
1980s	Equal	5-5	
1990s	United	7-3	
2000s	United	7-3	
2010/12	United	2-0	
TOTAL	**United**	**33-19**	

Silverware	League	**Equal.** Neither club has won the League.
	F.A.Cup	**Equal.** Neither club has won the Cup or appeared in a semi-final.
	League Cup	**Equal.** Neither club has won the Cup. **Peterborough** came closest, appearing in a semi-final in 1966.

Years in Top Tier	Town	1-0

Biggest wins

Home	Town	3	United	0	*(FA Cup Nov 1986)*
	United	6	Town	0	*(Apr 1984)*
Away	Town	1	United	4	*(FA Cup 1980/1)*
	United	0	Town	5	*(Oct 1985)*

History No. 25 – Northampton Town v Peterborough United

This part of the country has a number of potential derbies and it is fair to say that United v Town is not a secure primary derby. Peterborough fans have tended to view their all-Cambridgeshire clash with Cambridge United as their chief derby, partly because of closer geographical proximity and, partly, because they are both relatively new kids on the block, Cambridge United having joined the League in 1970, ten years after Peterborough. In fact, Peterborough v Cambridge is not far adrift of Peterborough v Northampton in the Derby League Table and the former has fallen behind largely because Cambridge United dropped into the Conference in 2004/5. Cambridge's demise gave the animosity between Posh and Cobblers a strong shot in the arm. Northampton have probably paid more attention to Peterborough than the other way round. But the Cobblers too have had their distractions, especially when brash, Dr. Marten's backed, Rushden and Diamonds entered the League to threaten Town's dominance in Northamptonshire. However, R+D followed Cambridge back into the Conference the following year and, so, Posh/Cobblers will do for the time being at least.

Northampton are by far the older club. Formed by teachers in 1897, they joined the Southern League in 1901. For a short while, they were part of a Northamptonshire trio with Kettering and Wellingborough, before those local derby rivals dropped out. Life was hard for the Cobblers and, in 1905/6 and 1906/7, they finished rock bottom of the Southern League's First Division.

In the following season, they were touched by the genius that was Herbert Chapman. Chapman is best remembered for his Football League title triumphs with Huddersfield and Arsenal, but he performed his first miracle with Northampton. Taking over a useless team, he transformed the club into Southern League champions in less than two years. In 1909, Northampton lost to Football League champions Newcastle in the second ever Charity Shield showpiece. The Cobblers continued to be a force in the Southern League, until Chapman returned to his native Yorkshire with Leeds City in 1912.

In 1920/1, Town accompanied the rest of the Southern League in transferring to the new Football League Division Three. And there they remained, year after year, rarely challenging for promotion, but never finishing so low as to have to seek re-election. In 1958, the Cobblers were allocated to the new Division Four, having just missed the cut to be part of Division Three. Therefore, by 1960, Northampton were a well-established League club, with a thoroughly unremarkable history, none of which had included clashes with Peterborough. For many years, Northampton shared a dubious distinction with Sheffield United of being the only clubs playing on three-sided grounds, their homes also being used for cricket. The Cobblers were the last club to get four sides, moving to Sixfields in 1994.

Peterborough were born in 1934, making them one of the youngest League clubs.There had been an earlier club in Peterborough, but it was suspended by the FA in 1932 for owing precisely 248 pounds, 1 shilling and 11 pence. The new professional club was formed, in part out of the ashes of the old Peterborough and Fletton. There are two unusual things to note. Firstly, Peterborough United's nickname, the Posh, pre-dates the club itself. The earlier club's official nickname was the Brickies, another great example of how nicknames often used to describe – and sometimes still do - the features, or main industries, of places represented by clubs. Northampton, of course, are still the Cobblers. 'Posh' developed as an unofficial nickname in the early twenties, because a player-manager of the old club advertised for *'posh players for a posh team'*. The name stuck and was adopted by the new United over a decade later. The second point to note is that many clubs have debatable links to earlier outfits, in circumstances similar to those described for Peterborough but, wherever possible, clubs almost always claim as long a history as is possible. The foundation dates given in this book generally concur with clubs' official claims. Peterborough are unusual, because they accept the later start date of 1934 and that there was a clean break with the former club.

Northampton and Peterborough first met in an FA Cup 2nd Round tie in 1946, long before Peterborough joined the League. Things did not go well for Posh. After two creditable draws against the Cobblers, United lost the second replay 8-1. It remains their heaviest defeat ever against anyone (incidentally, this 8-1 drubbing doesn't appear in the biggest wins stats above, because the game, being a second replay, was not played at home or away. It was held at a neutral venue, Coventry).

Peterborough burst onto the League scene, following their election in 1960. In their first season, they won the fourth tier championship and scored what is still a League record number of goals in doing so (134, of which Terry Bly bagged 52). United's success highlighted the nonsense of the 'old pals act', which protected weak League clubs and denied access to better non-league outfits. Posh, for example, had been applying for entry every year since the Second World War and had been rejected every time. When given the opportunity, Posh were rampant.

Peterborough's triumphal arrival into the League overshadowed another notable event in 1960/1. After decades of failure, Northampton finished third behind United and so joined them in promotion to the third tier. For the first time, Town had stepped up. From then on in the sixties, it was the Cobblers who made all the headlines. Like a dragonfly emerging from a murky pond, Northampton rose and majestically flew. Two years after their first promotion, they were third tier champions and, two years after that, they joined Newcastle United as newly promoted clubs from the second tier. And so remarkably, in 1965/6, the mighty Northampton Town hit the big time. Though relegated in their first season, they were far from disgraced, picking up what, under the modern points system, would have been 43 points from 42 games. They ended the season only three points from safety and thirteen points clear of bottom club, Blackburn Rovers.

1966 was a special year for all English football fans but, in this part of the midlands, it was especially special. Not only did the Cobblers reach the heights of the first tier, the only time that either club has done so, but Posh reached the only cup semi-final that either club has experienced. They lost 6-3 on aggregate to the eventual winners of the League Cup, West Bromwich Albion. Joe Mercer was prompted to remark that *"the miracle of 1966 was not England's World Cup victory, but Northampton reaching Division One"*.

If Northampton's ascent to the top was spectacularly speedy, their descent was even more dramatic. They suffered three relegations in four seasons and so, having started the 1960s in the fourth tier, they ended the decade back where they had started. No other club has risen and collapsed as quickly as Northampton. Faithful Cobblers must have felt like daredevil balloonists, rising to the summit of Everest, only to crash land shortly afterwards. The descent must have been terrible, but it is odds-on that those who experienced it never have regretted the journey.

As if exhausted by their exploits in the sixties, the low point for this derby came shortly afterwards in 1972/3. Northampton came next to bottom of the League and had to seek re-election. Had current rules been in place at the time, they would have lost their League status, only seven years after appearing in the top division. Peterborough fared only marginally better, ending the season fifth from bottom of the League. As an individual club, Peterborough fans would probably point to even darker days five years earlier, when they were demoted from the third tier for offering illegal bonuses

After their record breaking first season, Posh's history over the past fifty years has been relatively sedate. They made their first visit to the second tier, via the play-offs in 1991/2, after they had finished sixth in the regular season. They survived for only two seasons, with their highest position to date being tenth in 1992/3. Posh returned to the second tier in 2009/10, but had a difficult time and were relegated again. In 2011/12, they made their third attempt to establish themselves at second tier level and survived to tell the tale.

Sedate they may have been, but Peterborough have spent much of the past half century comfortably placed in the third tier. On the whole, they have a better record than Northampton, who have spent more time in tier four. The Cobblers had another near disaster in 1993/4, when they were fortunate to retain League status. For the first time in their Football League history, Town finished bottom of the entire League pile. They had narrowly avoided bottom place one year earlier and the bottom club, Halifax, had been relegated to the Conference. However, in 1994, Conference champions Kidderminster Harriers were controversially denied promotion, because their ground was deemed not to be up to League standard.

Peterborough's dominance over Northampton must be galling for Cobblers' fans, given Posh's relatively late arrival on the League scene. It could have been worse, had more recent newcomers Rushden and Diamonds' flame not dimmed as quickly as it glowed into life. Also, Cobblers can always look back dewy-eyed to the fab sixties, when they were the ones who made it to the top. The derby is reasonably competitive, but it will not be played in 2012/13 and its future as a top thirty derby is uncertain, given the gaggle of clubs potentially vying for the 'affections' of Posh and Cobblers.

Number 26 – Colchester United v Southend United

Older club	Southend 1906 (Colchester 1937)	

Head-to-head record

Number	68 games	
First one	Southend 4 Colchester 2 *(Oct 1950 in Division Three South)*.	

Leader (wins) Southend **28-25**

Higher finishes in League

19th C	Nil	
1900-WW1	Nil	
1920s	Nil	
1930s	Nil	
40s/50s	Southend	7-3 *(began in 1950 when Colchester were elected to the League, joining Southend in Division Three South)*
1960s	Southend	6-4
1970s	Colchester	7-3
1980s	Southend	7-3
1990s	Southend	8-2
2000s	Colchester	8-2
2010/12	Colchester	2-0
TOTAL	Southend	**33-29**

Silverware	League	**Equal.** Neither club has won the League. **Colchester** have the highest finish, 10th in the second tier in 2006/7.
	FA Cup	**Equal.** Neither club has won the Cup or reached a semi-final.
	League Cup	**Equal.** Neither club has won the Cup or reached a semi-final.

Years in Top Tier	**Equal.** Neither club has appeared in the top tier. **Southend** lead **7-2** in years spent in the second tier.

Biggest wins	Home	Colchester 4 Southend 0 *(Nov 1968)*
		Southend 6 Colchester 3 *(Nov 1964 – they have also beaten the U's 4-0 on two occasions)*
	Away	Colchester 3 Southend 6 *(Aug 1955)*
		Southend 2 Colchester 5 *(Jan 1985)*

History No. 26 – Colchester United v Southend United

Essex's blue and white striped derby has not been an especially fervent affair. It is very close run and therefore it may seem strange that the derby does not generate more heat. There are two possible explanations. Firstly, there are geographical reasons. Although both towns are in Essex, they are about forty miles apart. Colchester is closer to Ipswich in Suffolk. Southend is as near to and, in many senses, has closer ties with, East London, than it has with North Essex. Secondly, there are historical reasons. The clubs had significantly different histories before they belatedly came together in the Football League in 1950.

Both clubs had links with earlier amateur outfits. Southend are older and their foundation as a professional club in 1906 was at the expense of another club, Southend Athletic. The Shrimpers immediately joined the Southern League and won its Second Division title at the first attempt. Unfortunately, they were denied promotion, because the League chose to tempt Bradford Park Avenue with a top tier berth, as part of a tit-for-tat battle with the Football League. Southend promptly repeated the feat in their second season and this time were promoted but, after a promising start, the Shrimpers were not especially successful. At the time, Southend had minor rivalries with West Ham, Millwall and Leyton (not to be confused with Leyton Orient who, as Clapton Orient, had joined the Football League in 1905).

Colchester grew out of a decision, in 1937, by members of amateur club Colchester Town to form a professional outfit. Town could trace their history back to 1873. As an aside, it is a pity that United chose 'U's' as their nickname, rather than taking Town's 'the Oysters' moniker. Shrimpers versus Oysters would have created a far tastier derby. Colchester joined the Southern League but by that time Southend were long gone. They had become members of the Football League's new Division Three in 1920. On their entry to the Southern League, Colchester had a potential derby with closer neighbours Ipswich, but Ipswich were elected to the Football League shortly afterwards in 1938.

The U's were successful at the lower level. They won the Southern League title in 1938/9 and were contenders in most years. In 1947/8, Colchester sprang to the attention of the nation, as they embarked upon a sparkling cup run. Along the way, they became the first non-league club to defeat a top tier Football League side, since the League had been extended. It was a thoroughly ungrateful thing for them to do, as their opponents were Huddersfield Town. Huddersfield had been the inspiration for the U's blue and white colours.

Colchester's entry into the League in 1950 was of little concern to Southend. The U's struggled and had to apply for re-election in 1954 and 1955. The Shrimpers were top dogs every year. However, in 1956/7, from nowhere, Colchester not only finished above Southend for the first time, but came very close to being first to achieve promotion to tier two. They just missed out, failing by one point to prevent rivals Ipswich from becoming third tier champions.

Both clubs gained their first 'promotion' of sorts in 1958. Both made the cut to join the new Third Division, when Third and Fourth Divisions replaced

Divisions Three North and South. From there until the end of the eighties, the Essex clubs bounced between third and fourth tiers, without threatening to rise any higher and rarely running into severe difficulties. The wonderful exception to the humdrum years came in 1971, when Colchester hit the headlines again as a result of their FA Cup exploits. At a time when top tier clubs still fielded first elevens in cup ties, the U's, eighth in tier four, were drawn against top of the League Leeds United. Colchester led 3-0 and, despite a fight back by Leeds, the U's hung on to win 3-2 and complete one of the greatest cup upsets of all time. Just two years later, Colchester finished third from bottom of the entire League and had to seek re-election.

Having spent years entwined together like low flying blue and white kites, things changed dramatically in 1989/90. Southend soared. They gained promotion to the third tier, as Colchester crashed and faced the ignominy of relegation to the Conference. The Shrimpers' upwardly mobile surge continued and, after successive promotions, they reached the pinnacle of their League achievements to date, by finishing twelfth in the second tier in 1991/2. The U's were still languishing outside the League, although 1991/2 was quite enjoyable for Colchester fans, as they were Conference champions.

Although back in the League, Colchester remained in tier four, while Southend enjoyed six seasons in tier two, the longest period of clear blue water between the clubs. Perhaps in part because of Southend's superiority at this time, Colchester developed an unusually hostile rivalry with Wycombe Wanderers, a rivalry which many U's fans still consider more important than their derby with Southend. It started in 1985, when non-league Wanderers bit the famous cup biters, putting Colchester out of the FA Cup. It continued with battles in the Conference.

By 1997/8, Shrimpers and U's were switching places with each other, between third and fourth tiers. It was Colchester's turn to be top dogs. In total, the clubs spent sixteen years apart, from 1989/90 onwards. Their coming together again in 2005/6 sparked the high point for the Essex derby. For the first time, the two were promoted together to the rarefied heights of the second tier. Southend pipped their rivals to the third tier championship, but it was Colchester who settled better at the higher level. U's beat Shrimpers 3-0 in both derby encounters in 2006/7 and enjoyed their most successful year ever, ending the season in tenth place. Southend, alas, were relegated. Colchester joined them at the end of the following season and normal service was resumed, with both clubs in the lower reaches of the League.

The clubs are not together in 2012/13. Colchester are in tier three and Southend a tier below, having narrowly missed out on promotion in 2011/12. The Essex derby is never likely to be a world beater, but it is gradually growing in stature. To an extent, it reflects a cultural gap between South and North Essex. In relative terms, it is still fairly new and its focus is blurred, but the clubs have been in the same division together for thirty-one seasons over the past sixty-one years. They have rarely been far apart and it is a pretty equal contest. If the trend continues, the derby should rise up the Derby League Table.

Number 27 – Port Vale v Stoke City

Older club	Stoke 1863	(Vale 1876). *Stoke's foundation date is often contested. The club's official history accepts that "uncertainty clouds the actual date of formation". That having been said, the date of 1863 is officially accepted by the authorities. It makes City the second oldest current League club.*	

Head-to-head record

Number	50 games	
First one	Stoke 1 Vale 0 (Oct 1887 in the FA Cup)	
Leader (wins)	**Stoke 19-14**	

Higher finishes in League

19th C	Stoke	6-0	*(began when Vale joined the original Football League Division Two, but Vale were out of the League for two seasons in the decade, having failed re-election in 1896)*
1900-WWI	Stoke	7-0	*(Vale resigned and left the League again in 1907)*
1920s	Stoke	6 4	*(began again in 1919/20 when both were re-elected to Division Two)*
1930s	Stoke	9-1	
40s/50s	Stoke	13-1	
1960s	Stoke	10-0	
1970s	Stoke	10-0	
1980s	Stoke	9-1	
1990s	Vale	6-4	
2000s	Stoke	10-0	
2010/12	Stoke	2-0	
TOTAL	**Stoke**	**86-13**	

Silverware	League	**Equal.** Neither club has won the League. **Stoke** have finished 4th twice (1935/6 and 1946/7).	
	FA Cup	**Equal.** Neither club has won the FA Cup. Only **Stoke** have reached the final (2011).	
	League Cup	Stoke	1-0

Years in Top Tier		**Stoke**	**56-0**

Biggest wins

Home	Stoke	4	Vale	0	*(Sept 1931)*
	Vale	3	Stoke	0	*(Feb 1932 and Aug 1925)*
Away	Stoke	0	Vale	3	*(Sept 1925)*
	Vale	2	Stoke	4	*(Jan 1922 and Oct 1923)*

History No. 27 – Port Vale v Stoke City

The geographical split in support for the clubs is accentuated by the fact that the City of Stoke is an amalgam of six towns. Port Vale are from Burslem in the north of the city. Stoke are from Stoke, the town that is, that forms part of Stoke, the city that is! The Potters are associated more with the centre and south of the city and their move to the Britannia Stadium involved a further shift southwards. As in all geographically based derbies, however, the division of fans by location is far from absolute.

The City of Stoke derby is very one-sided historically. It has similarities with Nottingham's derby, but it also differs in two respects. Firstly, they may not have been top dogs in Nottingham for many years, but Notts County have been the dominant club for significant periods of time in the past. Vale have never had a prolonged period as top side in Stoke. Nevertheless, the second difference explains why Stoke's derby ranks higher than its counterpart in Nottingham. Nottingham Forest's dominance over Notts County has led them to seek a more competitive derby elsewhere and they have found a willing accomplice in Derby County. When Stoke City have been particularly dominant, as they are currently, there has been a tendency for their fans similarly to seek out another derby. Wolves, West Brom and, for altogether different reasons, a rivalry with Cardiff, have been promoted as alternatives to Vale. To no avail – no-one has taken up the offer of accepting the Potters as their primary dance partners, but Vale are always willing and available. Make no mistake, in times when their teams are close in ability, derbies between Stoke's clubs are as vehement as any, as witnesses to the riot which took place at Vale Park in 2001 will testify. That having been said, switches of allegiance by players and managers are considerably more common than is the case with most vehement derbies. Even Stoke legend Sir Stanley Matthews spent time as manager of Vale.

The clubs are old and they first met in the FA Cup in 1887. That meeting was, however, a one-off and it was not to be repeated at a senior level for many years. Neither club had happy early years. Stoke were elected as founder members of the Football League, but the euphoria did not last long. They promptly finished bottom of the League in both its first two seasons and failed to be re-elected for season three. The Potters returned a year later when the League was extended and, although it was not exactly a triumphal return, they became an established mid-table side for a few seasons. In 1899, they also reached the FA Cup semi-finals, but lost to Derby.

Stoke were relegated in 1906/7 and, after one mid-table season in the lower tier, the club went bankrupt and resigned from the League. In fact, having resigned, Stoke changed their minds, but it was too late. They then spent the next few years applying to get back the place they had voluntarily given up, only to be rejected each time. Finally, in 1915, they were successful in their application to return, only to find that football was suspended, because of the outbreak of war. Somehow, Potters' fans should have realised there and then that Stoke and luck were never going to be regular bedfellows.

If Stoke fans think they had it tough in the early days, they should take the very unlikely step of sparing a thought for Vale. Burslem Port Vale entered a bright new future in 1892, as one of the original members of the new Division Two. They made a so-so start, but won two and lost three of their first six homes games. In December 1892, they met Sheffield United, also newcomers to the League. The Blades had made a storming entrance in their home games, but had failed to win any of their first four away fixtures. A close-fought match was guaranteed surely? United won 10-0. It is the only time in any division in the history of the English League that an away side has scored double-figures. As luck would have it, the fixture list threw up a return, just one week later, at Bramall Lane. The Blades won again, but by only 4-0. Rarely can a 0-4 defeat have been celebrated as a resounding result by the vanquished.

Vale finished in the bottom three of the League in all but one of their first four seasons. They were promptly booted out. They returned after a two-year absence and generally did better, without ever threatening to gain promotion. But in 1907, just as they were looking forward to their first League derby with newly relegated Stoke, Vale went bankrupt and resigned from the League. So, in 1906/7, the city had two League clubs. By 1908, it didn't have any.

Stoke, as Stoke City, made their return to the League in 1919 on the resumption of football. Eight games into the same season the Valiants made a dramatic re-entry. They had failed by one vote in the election process but, following Leeds City's expulsion for financial irregularities, Vale took over their fixtures. They were also awarded Leeds' points (Leeds had started quite well) and are the only club to date to have taken on points gained by another club. Finally, thirty-three years after their first senior meeting in the FA Cup, the city's clubs met in a League derby. City won 3-0 at Vale's ground. In spite of that poor start, the 1920s were to prove relatively good for the Valiants. They completed the first League double in the derby in 1920/1 and it helped them finish above the Potters for the first time.

Stoke spent one year in the top tier in the decade but, in 1925/6, they were first to fall into the third tier. They bounced straight back as champions. In 1928/9 and 1929/30, Port Vale repeated the trick, being relegated, but returning immediately with the Division Three North crown. On their return, Vale finished fifth in the second tier, six places above City. To date, it is their best ever end-of-season position. From there, the fortunes of the clubs diverged for many decades. After their excellent season in 1930/1, Vale would finish above City only once (by one point in 1955/6) in the next fifty-one seasons. After promotion back to the top in 1932/3, Stoke went from strength to strength. In 1935/6, they achieved their best ever position, fourth, in the same year that Port Vale plunged back into Division Three North. By the outbreak of war, City had become a serious force, while Vale were fifth from bottom of the League, now in Division Three South.

Potters' fans were very optimistic about the club's title ambitions in the first season after the war. They had a fine side which included the 'wizard of dribble' Stanley Matthews. Their optimism was well founded, as Stoke were contenders throughout a season hugely disrupted by appalling winter weather. Games dragged on into June. City's title push was dealt a severe blow in May, with only three games to go, when their talisman Matthews left to join Blackpool (in the days before transfer windows and deadlines). By the final day of the season, all other games had been completed. Stoke faced an all or nothing trip to Sheffield United. A win would crown the Potters as champions. Defeat, or even a draw, would leave them in fourth place. United won 2-1 and Stoke have yet to achieve a top three place, let alone a League title. It was downhill from there for Stoke and they were relegated in 1952/3.

Port Vale, meanwhile, were making something of a recovery. In 1950, they moved back to Burslem to a new home at Vale Park (they had been in Hanley, a predominantly City 'town'). The original plans for the ground were overly ambitious, leading to talk of creating the 'Wembley of the North', which was a little odd for a club still plying their trade in Division Three *South*. It was, nevertheless, a good ground and demonstrated new found ambition. Stoke promptly spoiled the party mood, by beating Vale at their new ground in an FA Cup replay.

In 1953/4, Port Vale had arguably their most successful season to date. They stormed through their third tier campaign, losing only three games and winning the title by eleven points. In the FA Cup, Vale made it to their first, and to date only, major semi-final, joining a select band of third tier teams to have done so. In an incident which presaged the furore in the later Chesterfield v Middlesbrough semi-final, Vale had a goal dubiously ruled out for offside. They lost 2-1 to eventual winners West Bromwich Albion.

Port Vale's elevation to the second tier brought them face-to-face with City in the League, for the first time in twenty-two years. Parity and optimism for Valiants didn't last long. Vale were relegated again in 1956/7 and, by 1958, they were in the newly created fourth tier – they were its first champions. Stoke returned to the top in the early sixties and, by 1965/6, the gap between the clubs was at its greatest, with Stoke in mid-table in the top tier and Vale only four points from the bottom of the entire League. The gap continued and Vale faced a different crisis in 1968. They were expelled from the League for financial irregularities. Sir Stanley Matthews was their manager at the time. Fortunately for them, the old pals' act in the League was at its most potent. Vale were re-elected and performances improved for the next few years.

Those years in the early seventies were to be City's finest. Tony Waddington's side were very good and were widely admired for the quality of their football. In 1971 and 1972, they reached semi-finals of the FA Cup, although they lost on both occasions to Arsenal, after replays. In 1972, the Potters went one better in the League Cup. They beat Chelsea, to grasp their only major piece of silverware to date. In successive seasons, 1973/4 and 1974/5, they finished fifth in the League. Unfortunately, the side aged and broke up. By 1977, Stoke were back in the second tier and Vale were on their way back to the bottom. Stoke recovered, though not to the heights of the early seventies, but the Valiants hit their lowest point, when they ended the season fourth from bottom in 1979/80. The three tier gap between the clubs was firmly in place again.

By 1989/90, the world looked very different. Having been promoted to tier two, Valiants met Potters in the League for the first time in over thirty years. Moreover, while Vale survived easily, City fell into tier three, after sixty-three years in the top two tiers. Two seasons later, Vale joined City in the third and it led to a titanic struggle for promotion in 1992/3. Vale had the pleasure of putting Stoke out of the FA Cup, but the Potters completed a League double and it proved to be crucial. Stoke went up as champions, four points ahead of Vale. The Valiants lost out on automatic promotion on the last day of the season and were beaten in the play-off final.

The Football League Trophy is not mentioned elsewhere in the book, as it is not a senior competition, but it does have a special place in the hearts of Vale fans. Valiants visited Wembley in successive weekends in 1993. Before losing in the play-off final, they had won the Football League Trophy. Furthermore, they beat holders Stoke on their way to the final. Co-incidentally, they followed Stoke as winners of the Trophy again in 2001.

The 1990s was the most competitive period ever for the derby. In 1997/8, the clubs were involved in another epic struggle, this time at the bottom of tier two. On the final day of the season, Port Vale saved themselves whilst, in the midst of mayhem, Stoke joined Manchester City tumbling into tier three. At the end of the nineties, Vale finished above City for four seasons in a row, their longest span of superiority ever. Wonderful days for Vale didn't last for long. Vale were demoted to the third tier in 1999/2000 and the new century has belonged firmly to the Potters. They last played together in the same division in 2001/2. Stoke were promoted, via play-offs, to leave Vale behind. Like many smaller clubs, in 2002/3 Vale faced administration. In 2007/8, Stoke rose to the Premiership, while Port Vale slipped into the bottom tier, thereby re-establishing a three tier gap. Tony Pulis's side may not be as lovable as Tony Waddington's in the seventies, but Stoke are having a great time at the top. In 2011, their improvement culminated in the Potters reaching their first ever FA Cup final. They lost, but after 148 years of precious little, few in red and white cared about the result.

The paucity of silverware on the city's shelves suggests that the clubs are poor historically, but that would not be an entirely fair assessment. In 2012/13, Stoke are completing their fifty-seventh season at the top. Only nineteen clubs have spent more time at that level. Alas, only Birmingham (also fifty-seven seasons) have been in the top tier as often without ever achieving a top three finish. At a level lower, Port Vale have a similar unfortunate record. Of all the clubs not yet to have experienced the sweet taste of life at the top, Vale have spent the most years (forty-one) knocking on the door in tier two (although Plymouth might argue that their forty years at the same level is unluckier, as they have been accumulated in a much shorter period).

The past few decades have seen the clubs, concertina-like, coming together and then moving apart quite dramatically. Vale fans, and lovers of single-city derbies, will hope that someone pushes hard on Vale's half of the concertina as soon as possible.

Number 28 – Barnsley v Rotherham United

Older club	**Rotherham 1870 or 1884** *(Barnsley 1887. Rotherham's date of birth is disputed and there is more dissent about United's origin than in most other doubtful cases. United were born from a merger of clubs, one of which could trace its roots back as far as 1870 and this is the founding date in Rotherham's official records. However, most football historians do not credit Rotherham with being the sixth oldest League club, which would be their status if 1870 is correct. 1884 is the date usually accepted, still older than Barnsley).*	

Head-to-head record

Number	60 games	
First one	Rotherham 1 Barnsley 0 *(Sept 1919 in Football League Division Two)*	
Leader (wins)	Equal 21-21	

Higher finishes in League

19th C	Nil	
1900-WWI	Nil	
1920s	Barnsley	10-0
1930s	Barnsley	10-0
40/50s	Equal	7-7
1960s	Rotherham	8-2
1970s	Rotherham	8-2
1980s	Barnsley	9-1
1990s	Barnsley	10-0
2000s	Barnsley	6-4
2010/12	Barnsley	2-0
TOTAL	**Barnsley**	**58-28**

Silverware	**League**	**Equal.** Neither club has ever won the League. **Barnsley** have the highest finish, as only they have been in the top tier.
	FA Cup	**Barnsley 1-0**
	League Cup	**Equal.** Neither club has won the League Cup, but **Rotherham** were beaten in the very first final in 1961.

Years in Top Tier		**Barnsley 1-0** *(The Tykes' one year in the sun was in 1997/8. They also lead Rotherham **53-26** in number of years spent in the second tier).*

Biggest Wins	**Home**	Barnsley 5	Rotherham 1 *(Jan 1934)*	
		Rotherham 4	Barnsley 0 *(Oct 1951)*	
	Away	Barnsley 2	Rotherham 3 *(Feb 1953)*	
		Rotherham 2	Barnsley 4 *(Nov 1981)*	

History No. 28 – Barnsley v Rotherham United

This South Yorkshire clash is not one of the most fervent derbies in England, but it is fairly competitive in its overall history. Their relative lack of passion for each other is due in part to both clubs being more interested in their big neighbours from Sheffield. It probably also stems from the fact that their relationship has been characterised by long periods of dominance by one club over the other. Barnsley have a big lead in relative League success, but the basis of their lead was established very early. Their League derbies started in 1919 when Rotherham, as County, not United, were elected to the expanded League after the resumption of football. It then took twenty-six attempts for Rotherham to finish above Barnsley, a feat they finally achieved in 1951/2. The Merry Millers became dominant throughout the sixties and seventies and Barnsley's Tykes have again held sway for most of the time since.

What was arguably Barnsley's high point came as a major surprise, and at a time when Rotherham were not even in the League. In most years before World War One, the Tykes were a run of the mill second tier side. Yet, in 1910, they made it to an FA Cup final, where they lost to Newcastle. In the following season, Barnsley had a terrible time. They finished next to bottom of the League and had to seek re-election. Performance in the League improved in 1911/2, but sixth in tier two hardly hinted at what was to come. Remarkably Barnsley, fresh from re-election, returned to the FA Cup final again and this time they won, after extra time, in a replay against West Brom. It is the only major trophy gained by either of these derby rivals.

Given Barnsley's early pre-eminence and their cup exploits before the First World War, it might be assumed that they were first to join the League, but they were not. Rotherham (as Town, not as County or United) were elected to the League in 1893, along with four other clubs, including future giants Liverpool, Newcastle and Arsenal. Town didn't survive for long and had left the League before Barnsley joined in 1898. At least Rotherham can claim to have done better than the fifth new entrant of 1893, which was Middlesbrough Ironopolis.

Both clubs have suffered major misfortunes in their quests to reach the top tier. Barnsley's is more famous and has been documented elsewhere in the book. Basically, they finished third in the second tier in the season before World War One, but Arsenal were elected to the top tier after the war, even though they had finished two places and four points behind Barnsley in the preceding season. Rotherham's unlucky year was 1954/5. They finished the season in third place in tier two on the same points as the two promoted teams, Birmingham and Luton. Had the three points for a win system been in place at the time, Rotherham would have been champions and would have tasted the high-life forty years before Barnsley were able to do so. The Millers have never come so close again.

In the same 1954/5 season, the Tykes were champions of the third tier. The fifties represented the high point for the derby, firstly, because it was at its most competitive and, secondly, because both clubs spent most of the fifties in the second tier. The relatively good times ended in 1958/9, when Barnsley were relegated to the third and Rotherham escaped a similar fate by one point.

In 1961, Rotherham, still in the second tier, met mighty Aston Villa in the final of the first ever League Cup. Their place in history as its first winners seemed reasonably secure when they won the first leg 2-0, but Villa bounced back in the second leg to win 3-2 on aggregate, after extra time.

The derby was at its lowest ebb collectively from 1973 to 1975, as both were in tier four, alongside fellow South Yorkshire rivals Doncaster Rovers. Rotherham emerged first and the eighties showed early promise for both clubs. In 1980/1, both were promoted to the second tier, the Merry Millers as champions, two points ahead of second placed Tykes. The following season ended with the clubs in sixth and seventh places in tier two, Barnsley edging out Rotherham on goal difference. Had good times returned? Alas not, at least not for Millers, who were soon back alternating between tiers three and four. The Tykes had a prolonged spell in tier two and it culminated in promotion to the top tier in 1996/7. At long last, Barnsley took up the place they should have had in 1919. Rotherham were relegated to tier four in the same year and so a three tier gap developed for the first time. It lasted for one season, as Barnsley dropped back into tier two, despite famously (in Barnsley at least) "*playing like Brazil*". In 1999/2000, Barnsley nearly returned to the top flight, losing out in the play-off final, after ending the season in fourth place.

At the turn of the century, successive promotions for Rotherham saw the derby played in the League for the first time in nearly twenty years of dominance by the Tykes. In 2001/2, it was Rotherham's turn. Barnsley were relegated to the third tier, while Rotherham, just one point better off, survived. Fortunes reversed again later in the decade. Not for the first time, Rotherham faced huge financial difficulties. But their 21st century experience has been much worse than anything which went before. For three seasons running, the Merry Millers faced points' deductions, culminating in a massive seventeen point deduction before the start of the 2008/9 campaign. They also lost their home at Millmoor and moved to play their games in Sheffield.

2012/13 sees Barnsley in the second tier and Rotherham in tier four. The Merry Millers may not be so merry any more, but the resilience of their fans and team over the past few years demonstrates that no-one should bet against their ability to survive. Things are also looking considerably brighter, as United returned home from their sojourn in Sheffield to their new, impressive (and even more impressively named) New York Stadium. Whether or not they can improve on their 5-27 higher League place record against Barnsley since 1980 is another matter.

Number 29 – Coventry City v Leicester City

Older club   **Coventry 1883** (Leicester 1884)

Head-to-head record

Number	86 games	
First one	Leicester 1 Coventry 0 *(Sept 1919 in Football League Division Two)*	
Leader (wins)	**Leicester 37-25**	

Higher finishes in the League

19th C	Nil	
1900-WWI	Nil	
1920s	Leicester	10-0
1930s	Leicester	10-0
40s/50s	Leicester	10-4
1960s	Leicester	8-2
1970s	Equal	5-5
1980s	Coventry	8-2
1990s	Coventry	6-4
2000s	Leicester	6-4
2010/12	Leicester	2-0
TOTAL	**Leicester**	**57-29**

Silverware (wins)   **League**   **Equal.** Neither club has won the League. **Leicester** came closest, when second in 1928/9. Coventry's best effort was sixth in 1969/70.

FA Cup   **Coventry 1-0.** Coventry won in 1987 in their only final appearance. Leicester have been beaten finalists four times, but have never won it.

League Cup   **Leicester 3-0.**

Years in Top Tier   **Leicester 46-34**

Biggest wins   **Home**   Coventry 4 Leicester 1 *(Mar 1981 and Jan 1952)*
Leicester 5 Coventry 1 *(Dec 1984 and Jan 1925)*

Away   Coventry 1 Leicester 8 *(Dec 1964 in the League Cup)*
Leicester 0 Coventry 3 *(Jan 1999 and Sept 1975)*

History No. 29 – Coventry City v Leicester City

Both clubs originate from familiar sources, Coventry from factory workers at Singers cycle works and Leicester from old school chums. Both have had different nicknames over the years. Coventry, now the Sky Blues, were the Bantams until the early 1960s. Leicester, now definitely the Foxes, were often also called the Filberts in earlier times.

The derby between these two midland cities is a relatively low key affair, for three principal reasons. First, both clubs have a surfeit of general derbies available to them in the West and East Midlands and it seems that both clubs would prefer to have primary derbies against clubs other than each other. For example, in the Football Fans Census, Leicester fans name Forest and Derby as their chief rivals, ahead of Coventry. Coventry fans name Villa ahead of Leicester. However, of course, Derby and Forest target each other, rather than Leicester. Meanwhile, neither Villa fans, nor any other fans in the West Midlands, place Coventry in their lists of top three rivals. All of which leaves the Sky Blues and Foxes stuck with each other, almost reluctantly.

Second, they have two geographical differences. Their first choices of primary derbies are dictated by the fact that Coventry are from the West Midlands while Leicester are from the East. Also, the traditional north/south dividing line in football is variable, but it tended to run between the two clubs. Coventry's first taste of major league football began in 1908 in the Southern League, where they were not especially successful. Once in the Football League, with the exception of one year spent in Division Three North, Coventry were always allocated to the southern division when in the third tier. Leicester, on the other hand, joined the Football League as early as 1894 when, with the exception of Woolwich Arsenal, it was an entirely northern and midlands institution. They too, as Leicester Fosse, were not successful in their early years, venturing into the top division for only one season before the First World War (1903/4) and having to seek re-election in 1904 and 1915.

Third, until after the Second World War, Coventry rarely appeared on the radar of Leicester. They spent only seven seasons in the same division as each other in the twenties and thirties and the Foxes finished higher in the League than Coventry in all twenty seasons. Leicester achieved their only top three finishes in this period. It was a short lived spurt of brilliance. In 1927/8, Leicester came third behind Everton and Huddersfield. In the following year, they were beaten to the title by The Wednesday, ending the season just one point behind the Owls and with a better goal average.

Just before football stopped for the duration of World War Two, Coventry finally flickered into life. They were Division Three South champions in 1935/6 and, in the following seasons, challenged for promotion to the top tier, though falling short each year. In the final year before war, Leicester were relegated and so, when football resumed in 1946/7, the two clubs met in the second tier. For the first time ever, Coventry finished above Leicester.

1948/9 was an exciting year for both. The Foxes reached their first ever FA Cup final, despite being involved in a desperate relegation battle at the bottom of tier two. They lost to Wolves in the final, but survived relegation one week later on the last day of the season. The contest to avoid the second relegation spot was intense. Thirteen clubs, including Coventry and Forest, as well as Leicester, finished within five points of each other. Sky Blues and Foxes shared the joy of seeing Forest ending up as the unlucky thirteenth. Normal order in the derby was restored shortly afterwards, as Coventry fell backwards. In 1951/2, the Bantams won an FA Cup tie between the clubs, but a League double for the Foxes effectively relegated Coventry to tier three. Subsequently, Coventry were allocated to the new Division Four in 1958. Leicester, meanwhile, bounced between the top two tiers.

The 1960s began very well for Leicester. They were safely placed in the top tier and had fabulous cup runs. They reached FA Cup finals in 1961 and 1963, but lost both times. The first defeat to double winners Tottenham came as no surprise. However, they were favourites to beat Manchester United in 1963, as Leicester had ended the season in fourth position, whereas United were fourth from bottom. In the League Cup, Leicester won in 1964 and were beaten finalists in 1965.

Coventry meanwhile were steadily charting their way through the League, from their fourth tier starting point. After two promotions, they had a near miss in 1965/6, failing to gain their first ever elevation to the top tier by one point. In 1966/7, the Sky Blues set off on a run of twenty-five games unbeaten. On the last day of the season, over fifty thousand fans turned up at their Highfield Road home to see them clinch the title, by beating second placed Wolves.

The derby was therefore played in the top tier for the first time in 1967/8. Coventry survived in their first year by one point. This was to set the scene for the next thirty-four years, as Coventry regularly performed amazing Houdini-like escapes. One of their more amazing feats occurred in the following season and it involved Leicester. The Foxes reached another FA Cup final and lost again, which means that they hold the record as the club with most final appearances without taking the FA Cup home. Partly as a result of their cup run, Leicester still had five League games left after Coventry had completed their fixtures. Leicester had to pick up seven points to survive. They got six and were relegated. Coventry survived again.

Incidentally, Coventry's record of remarkable escapology is even older. When they joined the Football League's Division Two in 1919/20, they failed to win a game until Christmas Day. They saved themselves from relegation to the new Division Three on the final day of the season. Quite why Coventry had been elected to Division Two after the First World War is a story in itself. They had achieved very little in the Southern League and had finished fifth in its poor division two in the season immediately before the war. Yet, when the voting took place for the Football League's second tier in 1919/20, Coventry received more votes than anyone else. Someone mentioned bribery!

Surprisingly, following their hair-raising escapes in their first two seasons at the top, in 1969/70 Coventry achieved sixth place, their highest ever League placing to date. Leicester re-joined Coventry in the top tier in 1971/2. In many senses, the seventies and eighties were very successful years for the derby, although very little of note happened until 1987. Coventry spent the entire period at the top and Leicester accompanied them for most of the time, but neither club finished higher than seventh in the League. The Foxes made it to two FA Cup semi-finals and the Sky Blues to one in the League Cup, but neither reached a final. Then something of considerable note happened in1987. For once Coventry were not involved in a relegation battle, which perhaps left them with energy to concentrate on the FA Cup. In one of the most exciting finals of the 20th century, the Sky Blues beat Tottenham 3-2 to win their first ever major trophy. To add to the sky blue glow, not only Leicester, but Aston Villa too, were relegated to the second tier.

In the late 1990s, Leicester embarked on another period of success in the League Cup. They triumphed in 1997 and 2000 and were beaten finalists in 1999, but difficult times lay around the corner for both clubs in the 21st century. In 2000/1, after thirty-four years at the top, Coventry couldn't escape relegation. Leicester followed them into the second tier a year later. Both clubs ran into financial difficulties. In 2007/8, they struggled with each other to avoid the drop into the third tier. It may surprise people to learn that Leicester were part of an elite group of clubs that had never been out of the top two tiers until that year. Against anyone else they would have been favourites to survive. Against the sky blue Houdinis they had no chance. Leicester dropped into the third tier by one point and with a better goal difference than Coventry. Leicester bounced back as champions after one year. At the end of 2011/12 Coventry slipped into tier three for the first time in almost fifty years and so parted company with Leicester again.

The 'M69' derby may not have been one of the classic derbies in its early days, but since the 1960s the clash has become one of the more competitive and consistent encounters. In their first forty years in the League, they played together in the same division only thirteen times and the Foxes led 36-4 in higher League placements. In their more recent forty-six seasons, they have been together twenty-nine times and the Sky Blues lead 25-21. It is a close contest which is rising up the Derby League Table despite the seeming ambivalence of its participants.

Finally, Leicester fans will get a bitter/sweet feeling if they look at their club's record books. Their record defeat was suffered in their first year at the top, back in 1909. Towards the end of the season they met arch enemies Nottingham Forest. Forest won 12-0 to equal the biggest victory ever in a top tier match in the English League. Leicester (Fosse as they were) conceded over one hundred goals in thirty-eight games that season and were relegated by nine points. On a sweeter note, for Foxes that is, their record cup victory was achieved on their way to the League Cup final in 1965. They beat the Sky Blues 8-1 – at Coventry.

Number 30 – Bradford City v Huddersfield Town

Older club   **Bradford 1903** (Huddersfield 1908)

Head-to head record

	Number	47 games
	First one	Huddersfield 1 Bradford 0 (Sept 1920 in Football League Div 1)
	Leader (wins)	**Huddersfield 19-13**

Higher finishes in League

19th C	Nil		
1900-WWI	City	5-0	*(began when Town joined the League in 1910)*
1920s	Town	8-2	
1930s	Town	10-0	
40s/50s	Town	14-0	
1960s	Town	10-0	
1970s	Town	8-2	
1980s	Equal	5-5	
1990s	City	6-4	
2000s	Town	6-4	
2010/12	Town	2-0	
TOTAL	**Huddersfield 67-24**		

Silverware (wins)

League	**Huddersfield**	**3-0**
FA Cup	**Equal**	**1-1**
League Cup	**Equal.** Neither club has appeared in a final. **Huddersfield** reached the semi-finals in 1968.	

Years in Top Tier   **Huddersfield 30-12**

Biggest wins

Home	Bradford 4	Huddersfield 0	*(Apr 1922)*
	Huddersfield 6	Bradford 3	*(Jan 1983)*
Away	Bradford 3	Huddersfield 4	*(Sept 1994)*
	Huddersfield 1	Bradford 2	*(on five occasions. Bradford have scored three goals away to Huddersfield only twice, once in the record 6-3 defeat of 1983 and once in a 3-3 draw).*

History No. 30 – Bradford City v Huddersfield Town

Bradford City versus Huddersfield Town is not a stable primary derby. West Yorkshire's derbies tend to shift in focus according to the relative strength of clubs at points in time. In 2012/13 Huddersfield v Leeds United will take centre stage, as Town's Terriers gained promotion in 2011/12 to join Leeds in the Championship, whereas Bradford remained in tier four. Arguably both Bradford and Huddersfield hate Leeds more than they do each other. The fact remains, however, that in the past fifty years Leeds have rarely been in the same division as either Terriers or Bradford's Bantams. United have finished above Huddersfield in every one of those fifty seasons and above Bradford in all but two. By contrast, in the past thirty-seven seasons, Terriers and Bantams have been in the same division as each other nineteen times and their records in those years are close, with Huddersfield leading 20-17 in higher League placements. It is therefore the City v Town clash which scrapes into the top thirty, but it is not possible to tell their story without reference to Leeds United and also to non-League Bradford Park Avenue.

Having both been formed in the early 20th century, City and Town are among the youngest in the League. The late arrival on the scene of West Yorkshire's clubs is not a coincidence, as development of association football in the area was stunted by the primacy of rugby. West Yorkshire was at the epicentre of battles between amateur rugby union and professional rugby league and also between rugby and football. These battles are reflected in the early histories of Town and City. Huddersfield was the birthplace of Rugby League in 1895. Bradford's clubs had even closer ties with rugby as both emerged from decisions by existing rugby clubs to switch codes. Manningham, the forerunners of Bradford City, were Rugby League's first ever league champions in 1895/6 and Bradford FC, Park Avenue's parents, were its league champions in 1903/4 and Challenge Cup winners in 1905/6, shortly before the 'great betrayal' of 1907 saw the majority of the club switch to football. Needless to say, at this point in time and for decades to come Bradford had its own single-city derby.

Football's determination to break into rugby strongholds is demonstrated by its treatment of Bradford's clubs. City were immediately elected to the Football League in 1903 even though they had never played a game of association football. Newly switched Park Avenue were denied a similar favour in 1907 by the Football League, but were offered a place in the Southern League as part of a tit-for-tat argument between the two football leagues. Park Avenue joined the Football League a year later, in the same year that City made their debut in the top tier and two years before Huddersfield's maiden season.

Given West Yorkshire's late start and the strength of competition offered by rugby league, it might be expected that the area's football clubs would have struggled in the early decades of their Football League careers. Far from it. For three of the four clubs this was the greatest period in their histories. Only Leeds City had a hard time.

First to make the nation take note were Bradford City. In 1910/11 they finished fifth in the top tier, their highest-ever League standing. Even better, they won the FA Cup for the only time to date. The cup had been replaced that year and the new cup (the one still in existence today) was made by Fattorinis of Bradford. Even more remarkably co-incidental, the Fattorinis had been heavily associated with Manningham FC. In 1914/15 City were joined in the top flight by Avenue, while Huddersfield and Leeds fought out their own secondary duel in tier two. For three seasons, either side of the First World War, Bradford had two clubs comfortably placed at the highest level of the English game. Park Avenue were relegated in 1920/21 and in the following season both Bradford clubs were relegated. Avenue were never to return to the top. It took City seventy-seven years to do so.

The demise of Bradford's clubs heralded the incredible rise of Huddersfield Town. Their rags-to-riches story remains the greatest in English League history. Their first few years in the League prior to World War One had been unremarkable on the field, as they finished roughly mid-table in the second tier each year. Off the field they quickly ran into trouble and faced liquidation in 1912. Immediately after the war, football in Huddersfield seemed doomed. Leeds City had been disbanded and plans were put in place to replace them, by re-locating Town from their Leeds Road ground all the way to Leeds itself. The local community rallied, saved the club and, in the opening season of post-war football, the Terriers gained promotion to the top tier for the first time and made it to the FA Cup final, also for the first time.

Huddersfield then appointed the genius Herbert Chapman as manager and he built a team around his captain, Clem Stephenson, a player whose place in the pantheon of football's greats has not been fully acknowledged. What happened next was simply astounding. In 1922, Town returned to the FA Cup final and this time they won. They also finished above Bradford City for the first time and it was to be fifty-five years before the Bantams ended a season above the Terriers again. In 1922/23 the Terriers came third in the League. It was to be their *poorest* finishing position until 1928/29. In 1923/24, merely five years after facing oblivion, Town won their first League title, in the closest ever finish. They defended their title more easily in 1924/25 and completed the first ever League treble in 1925/26, by which time Chapman had left to join Arsenal. Huddersfield were runners-up in the following two seasons and in 1928 they were also runners-up in the FA Cup. By the end of the twenties, Huddersfield was the centre of the sporting universe. Far from fading in the shadow of their football counterparts, in the twenties Huddersfield's Rugby League side added two League titles and one Challenge Cup victory to the town's overflowing trophy cabinet. In 1930 Huddersfield lost in the FA Cup final to Chapman's new loves. It was the Gunners first national title and it was a portent of things to come in the thirties. Huddersfield were still a top side, achieving five top-six finishes in the decade and another losing trip to Wembley in 1938, but they were never again to rise to the magnificent heights of the roaring twenties.

Throughout the period of Town's greatness, Bradford City sat in the second or third tiers, engaged in a ding-dong battle with Park Avenue. City edged things in the twenties but Avenue were the better side throughout most of the thirties. The only primary derby in the area was Bradford's single-city affair. Huddersfield and Leeds had a general derby but by then Town had eight top-three finishes in the League and five FA Cup finals to their credit. They lay ninth in the all-time success table in 1939. Leeds had achieved nothing, other than establishing themselves as a run of the mill first tier side and overtaking both Bradford clubs in terms of years spent at the top.

The post-war era did not start well for West Yorkshire. Huddersfield were constantly involved in battles to avoid relegation in the late forties and finally, in 1951/52, they dropped through the trap door for the first time in their history. For City it was worse. They continued in Division Three North, a tier below their Bradford rivals and, in 1948/49, faced the humiliation of seeking re-election after ending the season bottom of the whole pile. Leeds meanwhile had been relegated in the opening season after the war and in the following season they finished below Avenue. By 1952/53, West Yorkshire had no clubs in the top tier for the first time since 1907/08.

In 1953/54, Huddersfield had one last flicker of potential greatness. Promoted back to the top they chased Wolves and West Brom for the League title, ending the season in third spot. They quickly returned to tier two and have never finished in the top half of the top tier since 1954. The rest of the fifties were fairly uneventful. Park Avenue had to seek re-election for the first time in 1956 and their poor run continued so that, when the new Divisions Three and Four were created in 1958, Avenue were allocated to Division Four, a tier below City.

In the 1960s West Yorkshire's football world was turned upside down. The decade started poorly. Leeds were relegated to the second tier in 1959/60. Huddersfield narrowly avoided a first taste of third tier football in 1960/61, while City fell into tier four switching places with Avenue. In 1961/62, only a final day victory saved Leeds from relegation to the third tier and, in the next season, Avenue were relegated and City had to seek re-election for a second time. The emergence of Leeds United from this mire was almost as amazing as Huddersfield's in the early twenties. Don Revie's side was often criticised at the time and has frequently been vilified with benefit of hindsight. But even their harshest critics have to acknowledge Revie's outfit as one of the most effective and successful teams in the history of the English game. Town and City could only watch Leeds disappearing into the distance and stand helpless as United sought new 'friends' across the Pennines in Liverpool and especially Manchester.

In 1966 Bradford City had more pressing matters on their minds as they had to reach for their begging bowls again to seek re-election for a third time. But it was not they who should have been most worried. From a position of relative comfort Bradford Park Avenue suddenly nose-dived. Next to bottom in 1966/67 they ended the next three seasons at the bottom of the entire League. Even their most ardent fans could not justify a continued League existence for a club which had won fifteen and lost eighty-seven of their games in those three years. Avenue duly departed in the opposite direction to Leeds, leaving Town and City behind. Bradford's clubs had always been close in standard. Avenue left the League still leading City 26-25 in higher league placements, though City had spent more time in the top tier and had won the FA Cup. They had also both been well and roughly equally supported clubs. Incidentally, Huddersfield were never particularly well supported, even in their championship winning years.

In 1971/72 Huddersfield went down from the top flight and to date they have not returned. City were relegated to tier four in the same year. For Town it was the start of a nightmare journey which saw them relegated three times in four seasons. And so in 1975 Town met City in a League derby for the first time in over fifty years. Their previous meeting in 1922 had been in the top flight, towards the end of the Bantams' glory days and at the start of the Terriers' golden era. Fifty odd years on they met in very different circumstances, in tier four. In the seasons that followed, the clubs had yo-yo existences between tiers three and four before Town returned to the second tier in 1983/84. At the end of 1984/85 City won the tier three championship, but their joy in qualifying to meet Town (and Leeds) again in 1985/6 paled into insignificance as, in the midst of the celebrations, fire swept through their Valley Parade home killing fifty-six people in one of the three great football tragedies of the 1980s.

The three clubs stayed together for three seasons and Bradford were top dogs twice but, by 1991/92, as Leeds were winning their third League title, City and Town were back in tier three. As the new century approached, both had returned to the second tier. Then, in 1998/99, Bradford scrambled into the Premier League, at the top again after an absence of a mere seventy-seven years. Life in the sun lasted for only two seasons and the new century brought financial problems rather than continuing glory for City and they gradually made their way down to their 2012/13 position in tier four. Huddersfield dipped back into tier four in the new century too, but are back in the second tier for 2012/13.

Finally, a word about nicknames. Bantams and Terriers are both fairly recently adopted names. For most of their existence, Town were simply 'Town'. They probably felt entitled to purloin the 'Town' tag as, until Ipswich won the League title in 1961/62, Huddersfield were the only 'Town' to win anything. Terriers was adopted after a vote by fans. Originally, City were the Wasps. For most of their existence they were known as the Paraders, named after their Valley Parade ground, before becoming the Bantams. There is another nickname in Bradford which bears testament to the longevity of derby hostilities. City fans call fans of Avenue 'Stans'. It is a reference to a cartoon character 'boring Stan the Avenue man' who, according to City's fanzine, can't come to terms with his loss. Over forty years after their demise, no doubt some Avenue fans can't forget – and City fans won't let them.

In Memoriam of Darlington v Hartlepool United

As a reminder, the rules adopted for choosing sixty derbies to study discount any club lower in the league pyramid than what is currently the Conference National, the fifth tier of the pyramid. Unfortunately, at the end of 2011/12, the long-standing travails of Darlington FC finally resulted in them being demoted from the Conference and placed way down the structure into the Northern League. Their derby with Hartlepool therefore cannot be considered. There are of course other derbies to have fallen by the wayside over time, the single-city derby in Bradford and more recently Wrexham v Chester are prime examples. But the 'minor' north east derby was special. Had it still qualified for inclusion, Darlington v Hartlepool was so good that it would have been challenging for a top ten spot in the Derby League Table. In the hope that a new Darlington eventually recover sufficiently to re-enact this previously close fought and superb derby, its history is remembered here.

History: Darlington v Hartlepool United

When the 'minor' north east derby began in the 1920s, it was not the geographically isolated affair it became. South Shields, later to relocate and become Gateshead, were already in the League when Darlington and Hartlepool, together with Ashington and Durham City, joined as original members of Division Three North. None of the teams were successful, and Ashington and Durham didn't survive for long. However, South Shields/Gateshead led the way, finishing as 'minor' north east 'champions' thirteen times in eighteen years between the wars (Hartlepool three times and Darlington twice). Despite playing second fiddle to South Shields, it was in this period that Darlington reached their own highest point, when they were Division Three North champions in 1924/5 and spent two seasons in the second tier. Such dizzy heights have never again been attained by either the Quakers or Pool. To this day, South Shields/Gateshead remain more successful, having spent nine seasons in tier two. Even when Gateshead failed re-election in 1959/60 they were unlucky, as they ended their final season six points ahead of bottom placed Hartlepool.

Inevitably, debates about 'success' are relative, but everything in the Darlo/Pool derby is close. United just lead in head-to-head meetings, but the clubs are equal in higher league finishes. Darlington alone have reached the second tier and only they have won a divisional championship (Division Four in 1990/1, as well as the Division Three North title in 1924/5). However, Hartlepool have spent more seasons above the lowest tier of the Football League, by twelve seasons to six and they will continue to add to their tally as they are in the third tier for 2012/13. When re-election to the Football League existed for the weakest teams in the League, Hartlepool had to seek re-election fourteen times, an awful record equalled only by Lincoln City. The Quakers of Darlington had to seek re-election 'only' eight times. On the other hand, for all their brinkmanship, Hartlepool have not faced the nightmare of relegation to the Conference, whereas Darlington are in their second spell out of the League.

Darlington v Hartlepool United

Older club	Darlington 1883 *(Hartlepool 1908)*	

Head-to-head record

Number	148 games	
First one	Hartlepool 0 Darlington 0 *(Mar 1922 in Division Three North)*	
Leader (wins)	**Hartlepool 60-58**	

Higher finishes in the League

19th C	Nil	
1900-WWI	Nil	
1920s	Darlington	8-0 *(began when both were founder members of Division Three North in 1921/2)*
1930s	Darlington	6-4
40s/50s	Hartlepool	9-5
1960s	Darlington	7-3
1970s	Hartlepool	7-3
1980s	Darlington	8-2
1990s	Equal	5-5
2000s	Hartlepool	10-0
2010/12	Hartlepool	2-0
TOTAL	**Equal**	**42-42**

Silverware	**Equal.** Neither club has ever won the League, FA Cup or League Cup or appeared in a final or semi-final.
Years in Top tier	**Equal.** Neither club has ever appeared in the top tier. Only **Darlington** have appeared in tier two.

Biggest wins

	Home	Darlington 6 Hartlepool 3 *(Jan 1932). They have also won 5-0 on two occasions (Sept 1923 and Sept 1927)*
		Hartlepool 6 Darlington 1 *(Mar 1951)*
	Away	Darlington 0 Hartlepool 3 *(Mar 2007). Hartlepool did once score more than three goals at Darlington, but it was in a 5-5 draw (Nov 1936)*
		Hartlepool 2 Darlington 5 *(Aug 1929 and Aug 1987)*

One of the best years ever for Hartlepool was 1954/5. In an otherwise nondescript season, bearing in mind that 'uneventful' is usually a success story for clubs at the bottom of the pile, Pool completed a league double over Darlington, finished above them in the League and put them out of the FA Cup. In 1967/8, Pool completed a double over the Quakers and the points helped United achieve a rare promotion from the fourth tier. Incidentally, in October 1965, Hartlepool had appointed the youngest manager in the League, Brian Clough, but they sacked him and his assistant Peter Taylor in May 1967. Clough and Taylor, of course, went on to work wonders at Derby and Forest. Had they done so at Pool, they really would have deserved the status of deities.

The most exciting period for the derby was in the early nineties. Given that Darlington have spent virtually their whole time in the bottom tier of the Football League, the eight years from 1984 to 1992 were positively thrilling. Promoted from tier four in 1984/5, the Quakers fell back again two seasons later and, two seasons after that, they finished 92nd of ninety-two and dropped out of the League. But, in 1989/90, the Quakers took the Conference championship and followed it up by winning back-to-back titles, taking the fourth tier by storm in 1990/1. Alas, it didn't last and Darlo finished bottom of tier three in 1991/2 and dropped again into the League's basement.

In general, United chugged along, as their neighbours bounced up and down but, in 1990/1, the two gained promotion together. Darlington were champions and Pool third, but there was only one point between them. For the first time, the two rose *together* from the bottom. In 1991/2, Hartlepool finished eleventh, but Darlington were relegated and, to date, it is still the only season in which both clubs were above the League's lowest level. For the record, Darlington won 4-0 in the first derby that season, but United won 2-0 in the return and, in between, United put Darlington out of the FA Cup with a 2-1 away victory.

In 1999/2000, Darlington beat Hartlepool twice in fourth tier end-of-season play-offs. They had finished above United in the regular season, but had lost one and drawn one of the derby meetings. Unfortunately, the Quakers lost the play-off final.

In 2007/8, the collective joy of derbies played in tier three was almost repeated. Hartlepool had already reached the third tier, having gained promotion in 2006/7, but Darlington missed the opportunity to join them, by losing out in fourth tier play-offs. Only two years later, the Quakers were saying goodbye to the League, again.

In recent times, the clubs have been at least as famous for their odd characters as they have been for their football. From 1999 to 2004, Darlington were owned by George Reynolds, who gained notoriety earlier in life as a safe-cracker. His behaviour and methods were unusual, even by the 'impeccable' standards set by his fellow club owners. Mr.Reynold's grand plans ultimately produced little and the Quakers sank into administration for the first and, unfortunately, not the last time.

Hartlepool's character is arguably even odder. Their mascot, named H'Angus the Monkey, had a chequered and occasionally controversial career. It was therefore something of a shock when he decided to stand for Mayor of the town. The mascot's name, by the way, was derived from an unfortunate incident during the Napoleonic Wars, in which people from the town were persuaded to hang a ship's monkey as an alleged French spy. In a move that seemed to show that the good people of Hartlepool had learned very little in the intervening two hundred years, H'Angus (aka Stuart Drummond) won the election. However, contrary to expectations, Mr. Drummond took to mayoring like a monkey to bananas and so, perhaps, the judgement of the people of Hartlepool shouldn't be questioned. Maybe the swopping of politicians for mascots and vice versa should become more widespread. Tony Blair and David Cameron could stun their doubters by turning out as mascots for their 'beloved' Magpies and Villans respectively. Furthermore, maybe the monkey was a spy after all.

In 2012/13, the derby is at such a low point that it effectively no longer exists. Hartlepool fans may not agree that this is a problem as they bask in the sun of tier three. Pool finished above the Quakers throughout the new century and thereby closed the gap in historical league performance. It is welcome happy days for Hartlepool, but a town without a derby is fish without a sauce. A potential new partner is Gateshead, but they are still two divisions below Pool. One of the great virtues of the Hartlepool v Darlington derby was its purity of focus and it is highly unlikely that United can find a replacement of such quality. Lovers of football in general and of great derbies in particular will lament this one's passing.

General derbies

As stated on page 119, there are six general derbies which would also have been included in the top thirty had they been primary derbies.

The six examples are very competitive derbies and are often more closely fought than the primary derbies of the clubs concerned. For example, Crystal Palace v Millwall and Aston Villa v West Brom are much more competitive in terms of historical records than Millwall v West Ham or Aston Villa v Birmingham. However, in all six cases, it is clear that they are not primary derbies. Statistical records of the six are listed in the following tables.

Blackburn Rovers v Bolton Wanderers

Older club	**Bolton 1874** (Blackburn 1875)		

Head-to-head record

	Number	160 games	
	First one	Blackburn 6 Bolton 2 (Nov 1881 in the FA Cup)	
	Leader (wins)	**Bolton 64-59**	

Higher finishes in League

	19th C	Level	6-6 *(began in 1888 as both were founder members of the Football League)*
	1900-WW1	Blackburn	13-2
	1920s	Bolton	9-1
	1930s	Blackburn	6-4
	40s/50s	Bolton	13-1
	1960s	Blackburn	8-2
	1970s	Bolton	9-1
	1980s	Blackburn	10-0
	1990s	Blackburn	9-1
	2000s	Blackburn	6-4
	2010/12	Bolton	2-0
	Total	**Blackburn**	**61-52**

Silverware (wins)	League	**Blackburn**	**3-0**
	FA Cup	**Blackburn**	**6-4**
	League Cup	**Blackburn**	**1-0**

Years in Top Tier		**Bolton**	**73-72**

Biggest wins

	Home	Blackburn 7 Bolton 1 *(Dec 1889)*	
		Bolton 6 Blackburn 0 *(Apr 1925)*	
	Away	Blackburn 1 Bolton 6 *(Jan 1928)*	
		Bolton 0 Blackburn 5 *(Feb 1964)*	

Arsenal v Chelsea

Older club   Arsenal 1886 (Chelsea 1905)

Head-to-head record
	Number	174 games
	First one	Chelsea 2 Arsenal 1 *(Nov 1907 in Football League Div 1)*
	Leader (wins)	**Arsenal 71-52**

Higher finishes in League

	19th C	Nil	
	1900 –WW1	Arsenal	6-4 *(began when Chelsea joined the League in 1905)*
	1920s	Arsenal	8-2
	1930s	Arsenal	10-0
	40s/50s	Arsenal	11-3
	1960s	Equal	5-5
	1970s	Arsenal	10-0
	1980s	Arsenal	8-2
	1990s	Arsenal	9-1
	2000s	Chelsea	6-4
	2010/12	Equal	1-1
	Total	**Arsenal**	**72-24**

Silverware	League	**Arsenal**	**13-4**
	FA Cup	**Arsenal**	**10-7**
	League Cup	**Chelsea**	**4-2**

Years in Top Tier   **Arsenal   95-77**

Biggest wins	Home	Arsenal 5	Chelsea 2 (Apr 1979)
		Chelsea 4	Arsenal 2 (Sept 1969)
	Away	Arsenal 0	Chelsea 5 (Nov 1998)
		Chelsea 1	Arsenal 5 (Nov 1930)

Crystal Palace v Millwall

Older club	Millwall 1885 (Palace 1905)		

Head-to-head record

Number	114 games	
First one	Millwall 2 Palace 0 *(1906 in the Southern League)*	
Leader (wins)	**Millwall 43-40**	

Higher finishes in League

19th C			
1900-WWI	Equal	5-5	*(began when Palace joined the Southern League in 1905)*
1920s	Palace	6-4	
1930s	Millwall	8-2	
40s/50s	Millwall	11-3	
1960s	Palace	9-1	
1970s	Palace	6-4	
1980s	Palace	8-2	
1990s	Palace	10-0	
2000s	Palace	8-2	
2010/12	Millwall	2-0	
Total	**Palace**	**57-39**	

Silverware	League	**Equal.** Neither club has won the League. **Palace** have the highest finish (3rd in 1990/1).
	FA Cup	**Equal.** Neither club has won the FA Cup. Both have been losing finalists once.
	League Cup	**Equal.** Neither club has reached the final of the League Cup. **Palace** have been to four semi-finals.

Years in Top Tier	**Palace**	**13-2**

Biggest wins	Home	Millwall 5	Palace	1	*(Apr 1968)*
		Palace 5	Millwall	0	*(Nov 1935)*
	Away	Millwall 1	Palace	4	*(Mar 1996)*
		Palace 1	Millwall	6	*(May 1927)*

Charlton Athletic v Crystal Palace

Older club		Both clubs were formed in 1905.	

Head-to-head record

	Number	63 games	
	First one	Charlton 1 Palace 1 *(Nov 1925 in Football League Div3 South)*	
	Leader (wins)	Palace 30-18	

Higher finishes in League

	19th C	Nil	
	1900-WW1	Nil	
	1920s	Palace	7-1 *(began when Charlton joined the Football League in 1921)*
	1930s	Charlton	10-0
	40s/50s	Charlton	14-0
	1960s	Palace	6-4
	1970s	Palace	7-3
	1980s	Charlton	6-4
	1990s	Palace	8-2
	2000s	Charlton	7-3
	2010/12	Palace	2-0
	Total	**Charlton**	**47-37**

Silverware	League	**Equal.** Neither club has won the League. **Charlton** have the highest finish (Runners-up in 1936/7)
	FA Cup	**Charlton 1-0**
	League Cup	**Equal.** Neither club has won the League Cup. **Palace** have the better record with four semi-final appearances to nil.

Years in Top Tier		**Charlton**	**26-13**

Biggest wins	Home	Charlton 4	Palace	2 *(Sept 1933)*
		Palace 5	Charlton	0 *(Nov 1927)*
	Away	Charlton 0	Palace	4 *(Mar 1928)*
		Palace 0	Charlton	2 *(Jan 1969 and Oct 1928)*

Bristol City v Cardiff City

Older club	**Bristol City 1894** (Cardiff 1899)		

Head-to-head record

Number	84 games	
First one	Bristol City 2 Cardiff 0 *(1915 in the FA Cup).*	
Leader (wins)	**Bristol 35-29**	

Higher finishes in the League

19th C	Nil		
1900-WW1	Nil		
1920s	Cardiff	9-0	*(began when Cardiff joined the Football League in 1920).*
1930s	Bristol	9-1	
40s/50s	Cardiff	14-0	
1960s	Cardiff	8-2	
1970s	Bristol	9-1	
1980s	Equal	5-5	
1990s	Bristol	10-0	
2000s	Cardiff	7-3	
2010/12	Cardiff	2-0	
Total	**Cardiff**	**47-38**	

Silverware	League	**Equal.** Neither club has won the League. Both have been runners-up once (Bristol in 1906/7 and Cardiff in 1923/4).
	FA Cup	**Cardiff** **1-0**
	League Cup	**Equal.** Neither club has won the League Cup, but **Cardiff** were beaten finalists in 2012.

Years in Top Tier	**Cardiff** **15-9**

Biggest wins	Home	Bristol City 5	Cardiff	1	*(Aug 1992)*
		Cardiff 5	Bristol City	1	*(Dec 1966)*
	Away	Bristol City 0	Cardiff	6	*(Jan 2010)*
		Cardiff 1	Bristol City	5	*(Nov 1933)*

Aston Villa v West Brom

Older club   Aston Villa 1874 (West Brom 1878)

Head-to-head record
            Number   158 games
            First one   Villa 0 WBA 0 *(Jan 1885 in the FA Cup)*
            Leader (wins)   Villa 74-52

Higher finishes in League
            19th C   Villa   11-1 *(began in 1888 as both were founder members of the Football League)*
            1900-WW1   Villa   14-1
            1920s   Villa   8-2
            1930s   Equal   5-5
            40s/50s   Villa   8-6
            1960s   WBA   8-2
            1970s   WBA   6-4
            1980s   Villa   10-0
            1990s   Villa   10-0
            2000s   Villa   10-0
            2010/12   Equal   1-1

            Total   Villa   83-30

Silverware (wins)   League   Villa   7-1
                    FA Cup   Villa   7-5
                    League Cup Villa   5-1

Years in Top Tier   Villa   101-74

Biggest wins   Home   Villa   7   WBA   1 *(Apr 1899)*
                            WBA   6   Villa   1 *(Jan 1967)*

                Away   Villa   0   WBA   7 *(Oct 1935)*
                            WBA   3   Villa   6 *(Oct 1893)*

Answers to the Derby Daze Quiz

A 1   Nottingham's city derby – 1 point.

A 2   Ipswich and Norwich. It is, however, a close-run thing with Accrington and Morecambe depending upon the route chosen between the two Lancastrian towns. Therefore either answer gains 1 point.

A 3   Liverpool's city derby – 1 point.

A 4   Cardiff v Swansea – 1 point.

A 5   Newcastle 1-9 v Sunderland - 1 point. Newcastle had the last laugh because they were champions that season – another 1 point.

A 6   Torquay (formerly the Magpies) v Exeter (who play at St. James's) – 1 point.

A 7   Fulham v Chelsea. 9 wins and 43 defeats, so a record of minus 34 – 1 point.

A 8   West Brom v Wolves. 8 wins and 1 defeat – 1 point.

A 9   Burnley v Blackburn – 1 point

A 10   Fulham v QPR – 1 point.

A 11   The best answer is probably Reading v Swindon, because they have 52 wins each. However, Bury v Bolton (28 wins each) and Barnsley v Rotherham (21 wins each) are also acceptable answers – 1 point.

A 12   Manchester United buying Manchester City players – 1 point.

A 13   The more famous example is Manchester United's statue of Sir Matt Busby - 1 point. Busby didn't play for United but was a star for both Manchester City and Liverpool.

The second example is Sheffield United's statue of Derek Dooley, who didn't play for United but was a record breaking striker for Wednesday – another 1 point. (Arsenal also erected a statue to their great manager Herbert Chapman, who never played for the Gunners but did turn out for Spurs. However, Chapman could hardly have been described as a 'star' player).

A 14   There are a surprising number of instances (14 out of 60) where the 'inferior' club overall in a derby has a better record in derby clashes against their 'superior' opponents. The best overall record belongs to Millwall – 1 point. Millwall lead not only West Ham (when Southern League records are included), but also Palace and Charlton in derby encounters, even though Millwall trail all three in terms of their overall record. Their head-to-head record against Charlton is outstanding – Millwall lead 33-11.

A 15   Sheffield Wednesday v Sheffield United -1 point. In 1949/50 Wednesday pipped United by 0.008 of a goal on goal average. It was important because it determined promotion to the top tier that year – another 1 point.

A 16   In terms of *time*, Burnley fans have had the longest wait, as they have not enjoyed a victory over Blackburn since April 1979. They have met eight times in the intervening period. Blackburn won seven with one draw. In terms of *number of games,* Fulham have not beaten Chelsea in their last thirteen meetings, but Fulham did win as recently as 2006. That win was Fulham's only success in the last thirty-two derby clashes. Technically another acceptable answer is Morecambe against Accrington. Accrington beat Morecambe in the FA Cup in 1956 and, in the only ten Football League games played to date, Morecambe have yet to win. Therefore, arguably, Morecambe fans have been waiting longest. However, their Football League clashes didn't begin until 2007 and Morecambe did win twice when the clubs met in the Conference. (It should be said that all three of these derbies will be played in the League in 2012/3 so Burnley, Fulham and Morecambe will have at least two opportunities each to end their droughts). Burnley, Fulham and Morecambe are all acceptable answers – 1 point.

A 17   Blackpool (Sir Stanley Matthews) v Preston (Sir Tom Finney).

A 18   Reading v Swindon

A 19   Bristol's city derby. Purdown Poachers was an early unofficial nickname of Rovers. Garibaldies was City's original official nickname.

A 20   The clubs involved were Cardiff and Swansea – 1 point. The reason was that the League was experimenting with the idea of giving preference to total goals scored, rather than goal difference or goal average, in situations where clubs finished equal on points – another 1 point. In 1997/8, both clubs were near the bottom of the fourth tier. Swansea had a goal difference of minus 13. Cardiff had a goal difference of only minus 4 but, as Swansea had scored one more goal than Cardiff, they were placed higher in the League table.

How did you do out of a maximum score of 24?

If you scored less than 5, you haven't been concentrating – the answers to at least four questions are in the first half of the book.

If you scored between 5 and 10, that's fine. There's no point in getting a book like this if you already know the answers.

If you scored between 10 and 19, you know your stuff. Well done.

If you scored 20 or more, you *really* know your stuff. My advice is that you should buy another copy of the book. However, please make sure you get it from a bookshop – you need to get out more!

Extra time – the future of derbies

Having looked at the best *current* derbies, the final part of the book explores the question; will current derbies stay much the same in years to come, or will new derbies emerge?

The derby landscape can be compared to the earth's tectonic plates (pretentious, but bear with the analogy!). Many primary derbies have been around for well over a century and 'plates' are highly unlikely to shift in the future. For example, it would take something pretty catastrophic to change the primacy of Newcastle v Sunderland, Southampton v Portsmouth or the Sheffield derby. A few primary derbies, although around for considerably less time, are nevertheless firmly set in stone and are unlikely to be disrupted by anyone else. The best example is probably Norwich v Ipswich, which started in earnest only after the Second World War.

There are mid-range primary derbies elsewhere that are fairly stable, but have been prone to shifts over time. They could change again, even where the clubs involved *remain the same*. Examples include derbies in the West and East Midlands; Lincolnshire and Humberside; West Yorkshire and the area north of Manchester. It is worth remembering that, had this book been written in the early part of the 20th century, passionate derbies in the top thirty would have included Blackburn v Preston, Villa v West Brom, Nottingham Forest v Notts County and Bolton v Bury.

The most interesting areas of all are those where there could be seismic shifts in derby plates and where *different* clubs could become involved. Most of these areas are in the south of England or in the south midlands. As a broad general rule, over the past fifty years, the make-up of the Football League has been adjusting to the reality of the nation's population structure. The Football League was a northern and midlands invention. The League was in its sixth season before the first southern club joined. At the outbreak of the First World War, by which time the League had been in existence for twenty-seven years, only six of its forty clubs were from the south. The Football League therefore did not properly reflect the population at the time. Furthermore, in recent years, the country's population has been drifting southwards.

The re-election arrangement that previously existed in the League was used to make relatively minor adjustments, but it was a slow and distorted mechanism for change. In the period from 1960 to 1987, when automatic promotion and relegation finally arrived, the League lost just six clubs. They were all from the north (Gateshead, Accrington, Bradford Park Avenue, Barrow, Workington and Southport). With the exception of Wigan Athletic, all replacements were from the south or midlands (Peterborough, Oxford United, Cambridge United, Hereford and Wimbledon).

The advent of automatic promotion from the Conference hastened the process of demographic adjustment. Only two northern clubs in the League in 2012/13 have entered the League since 1987, Morecambe and Fleetwood. By contrast, of current League clubs, new southern and midlands' entrants are Barnet, Wycombe, Cheltenham, Yeovil, Dagenham and Redbridge, Burton, Stevenage, Crawley and AFC Wimbledon. The reverse is true of 'leavers' since 1987. The north has lost Darlington, Halifax, Chester, Mansfield, Wrexham, Grimsby, Stockport and Lincoln. Only Luton, Newport and Hereford have gone from areas further south.

The geographical basis of the League has therefore changed very significantly and this has implications for the development of future derbies. Automatic promotion and relegation between Football League and Conference effectively makes the Conference a fifth division, thereby opening up even more possibilities for new derbies, or for re-alignment of existing derbies. It is a sweeping generalisation but, on the whole, derbies in the north are longer established and more stable. Further south there is greater potential for new derbies to emerge, or for existing derbies to be de-stabilised.

It would be foolish to suggest that ancient conflicts will be forgotten or easily exchanged for new sparring partners, but it is possible at least to highlight where challenges are most obvious. Watford v Luton is an example. It is a passionate and historic derby and fully deserves its current billing in the Derby League Table. However, it has long been a straightforward derby between neighbouring Hertfordshire and Bedfordshire. The fairly recent arrival of Barnet and Wycombe Wanderers was not really a threat, even though both are not far from Watford. However, the arrival of Milton Keynes Dons and Stevenage, especially at a time when Luton are not in the League themselves, is an altogether different threat.

Another case in point is Brighton v Crystal Palace. Despite the distance between them, this has always been an understandable geographical derby for Brighton, because they have been the only club in Sussex. But now Crawley Town, also from Sussex and equidistant from the two existing foes, have entered the fray. Those who believe that new kids on the block cannot disturb historical derbies should be mindful that it has happened before. Reading v Swindon is the oldest southern derby and a very strong one too. That didn't stop Oxford United quickly poking their noses into Berkshire and Wiltshire's business, once United showed signs of success. Relative success over a reasonable period of time is probably the key to how derby arrangements will develop in these areas.

Relative success is likely also to determine the development of derbies in areas where existing derby relationships are not as clear cut as in the examples above. The part of England which potentially is most fluid and most open to new derbies is probably the one around Birmingham, largely to the west of the city and heading south west towards Bristol. There are existing derbies in the area, but they are not entirely stable. For example, Cheltenham Town traditionally have a derby with Gloucester City, but their difference in status now has a long term feel to it. Shrewsbury have a derby with Hereford, but currently usually look further north to Wrexham. Shrewsbury are one of the longer established League clubs in the area, but even they didn't join the League until 1950, so the area does not have a long tradition of League status. Now, in addition to relatively new League clubs in Shrewsbury and Cheltenham, together with longer established Walsall, the area boasts a number of Conference Premier teams. There is recently relegated Hereford; Telford (close to Shrewsbury), Tamworth and Nuneaton (close to Walsall), Kidderminster (roughly in between all three current League clubs), and Forest Green (close to Cheltenham).

Predicting precisely which local rivalries may develop into full blown primary derbies of the future would be a bit like betting on greyhounds. Educated guesses may be made, but ultimately there are too many unseen factors. Outcomes will be affected by the performance of clubs as well as geography. In football the greatest unknown is whether or not an old style sugar daddy, or a new style spotty speculator, will take a shine to a club and give it power beyond the club's apparent means and current status.

There are two other issues in football generally which affect derbies or could affect them in the future. First is the competitiveness of the League. Premier League bosses and media pundits constantly try to tell us how exciting English League football is. They have a vested interest in doing so. The fact is that, despite the excitement of the finale to 2011/12, the League has become increasingly stale due to the domination of a tiny elite. Two examples will demonstrate the problem. In the past fourteen years, the Premiership title has been won by only four clubs and Manchester United have won it eight times. By contrast, in fourteen seasons from 1958 to 1972, no fewer than eleven clubs took the title and no club did so more than twice. Even worse is the fact that, in the twelve seasons of the 21st century, on only eight occasions has a club other than Manchester United, Arsenal, Chelsea or Liverpool finished in the top four (Newcastle, Tottenham and Manchester City twice and Leeds and Everton once each). Never in the history of the League has there been such a closed-shop. Similarly, the FA Cup has been dominated by bigger clubs to an extent never seen previously.

What has this to do with derbies? The answer is that lack of competitiveness has tended to enhance still further the importance of derbies. In the absence of any chance of winning anything at a national level, the battle to finish above local rivals has become the litmus test of success or failure for many clubs. Animosity between neighbouring supporters has grown steadily over the decades and seemingly these gulfs continue to widen.

The second issue revolves around the future of European football. Europe's biggest clubs have mooted the idea of a European League on numerous occasions and many would argue that they have already created a de facto European League, via the Champions League format. However, the Champions League still leaves big clubs competing in their domestic competitions and stifling opportunities for smaller clubs. If big European clubs were to compete in their own league and either quit their domestic championships or play only second elevens domestically, new opportunities for competition would arise, distasteful as the concept may appear. Should this situation arise in the future, it would significantly alter the concept of a derby. In the first half of the book it was explained that Manchester United v Arsenal or Chelsea v Liverpool are great rivalries, but could not be derbies because of geography. However, within a European League, these would become 'local' derbies and most English people presumably would adopt a favourite club in the European League, in addition to the club they support in the domestic league.

The Final Whistle

The book is a celebration of the greatest, heart-stopping occasions in the greatest sport on earth. As in any human activity that really matters, derby feelings can sometimes overflow into unacceptable behaviour. We should all remember that football is *not* more important than life and death, and that the differently coloured 'monsters' in the stand opposite are actually our neighbours and even our friends – most of the time.

But let us also remember that few other human activities create the collective buzz of joy or the shared gut-wrenching despair of football's great derbies. We are social animals. We *thrive* on collective experiences. People will rightly say that collective joy and sadness are also felt by opera buffs, film-goers or crowds at rock concerts. The big difference is that almost everyone at these events experiences *either* joy *or* sadness *at the same time*. There isn't an alternative group on the other side of the auditorium expressing precisely the opposite feelings, while booing your favourite performers. Those who dismiss football as merely a game, and derbies as unnecessarily hostile occasions, are missing a point about humanity. And those who haven't witnessed the joy and despair of a derby crowd are missing one of life's truly great and colourful experiences where love, hope and hatred are emotions shared collectively by thousands of souls.

Appendices

Top twenty derbies – the most focussed + ferocious (ie taking into account only Factors 8 and 10 of those listed on pages 116 and 117)

1. Cardiff v Swansea
2. Portsmouth v Southampton
3. Newcastle v Sunderland
4. Blackburn v Burnley
5. Ipswich v Norwich
6. Millwall v West Ham
7. Sheffield Utd v Sheffield Wed
8. Derby v Nott'm. Forest
9. West Brom v Wolves
10. Aston Villa v Birmingham
11. Arsenal v Tottenham
12. Liverpool v Man Utd
13. Man City v Man Utd
14. Port Vale v Stoke
15. Chesterfield v Mansfield
16. Bristol City v Bristol Rovers
17. Luton v Watford
18. Brighton v Crystal Palace
19. Everton v Liverpool
20. Blackpool v Preston

Top Twenty Derbies – the most competitive (ie taking into account only Factors 2, 3, 4, 5 and 6 of those listed on page 116).

1. Derby v Nott'm. Forest
2. West Brom v Wolves
3. Newcastle v Sunderland
4. Liverpool v Man Utd
5. Blackburn v Bolton*
6. Sheffield Utd v Sheffield Wed
7. Fulham v QPR
8. Crystal Palace v Millwall*
9. Exeter v Torquay
10. Shrewsbury v Wrexham
11. Luton v Watford
12. Arsenal v Chelsea*
13. Everton v Liverpool
14. Grimsby v Hull
15. Ipswich v Norwich
16. Colchester v Southend
17. Reading v Swindon
18. Bristol City v Cardiff*
19. Portsmouth v Southampton
20. Arsenal v Tottenham
21. Charlton v Crystal Palace*
22. Northampton v Peterborough
23. Blackburn v Burnley
24. Brighton v Crystal Palace
25. Man City v Man Utd
26. Aston Villa v West Brom*

Twenty-six rather than twenty derbies are listed here because the six marked with an asterisk are not primary derbies. They are excluded from the main lists earlier in the book and can be taken out here if readers wish to do so.

Incidentally, the appearance of one of the six, Arsenal v Chelsea, at 12th in the competitiveness list may seem high, given that historically Arsenal's record is much better than Chelsea's. However, this derby scores very highly in Factor 6, the 'recent competitiveness' factor. In fact, since the founding of the Premier League, Arsenal v Chelsea has been the most competitive derby of all sixty studied.

The all-time success league table up to World War Two (ie taking into account success in the League and FA Cup and years spent in the top tier up to the suspension of football in 1939)

1. Aston Villa
2. Everton
3. Sunderland
4. Blackburn
5. Sheffield Wed.
6. Arsenal
7. Newcastle
8. Preston
9. Huddersfield
10. West Brom
11. Sheffield Utd.
12. Liverpool
13. Manchester City
14. Bolton
15. Wolves
16. Derby
17. Burnley
18. Manchester Utd
19. Notts.County
20. Tottenham

Note that only current professional clubs are included in the list. If all clubs were included, the Wanderers (at 17th) and Old Etonians (at 20th) would still have been in the all-time top twenty by 1939 as a result of their exploits in early FA Cup competitions.

The all-time success league table post World War Two (ie taking into account success in the League, FA Cup, League Cup and years spent in the top tier since football resumed in 1946).

1. Manchester Utd
2. Liverpool
3. Arsenal
4. Chelsea
5. Tottenham
6. Everton
7. Leeds
8. Wolves
9. Manchester City
10. Aston Villa
11. Nottingham Forest
12. Newcastle
13. West Ham
14. West Brom
15. Leicester
16. Derby
17. Ipswich
18. Portsmouth
19. Burnley
20. Blackburn

Note the change in geographical balance pre and post-war. Thirteen clubs appear in both lists. All seven clubs which are present in the pre-war list, but missing from the post-war list are northern. Of the replacements, five are from further south.

The appearance of thirteen clubs in both lists may give an impression of continuity. However, a look at the top ten in each list gives a very different picture. Only three clubs, Arsenal, Aston Villa and Everton, are in the top ten of both lists and even then they are in reverse order, with Villa, by far the most successful pre-war club, only just scraping into tenth place in the post-war league. Furthermore, four of the top ten pre-war clubs disappear altogether from the top twenty post-war.

Burnley leading Blackburn *post-war* may come as a surprise. It is close-run, but Burnley amassed sufficient points in the early part of the post-war period to still have a slight lead despite having played second-fiddle more recently.

The all-time success league table, taking into account overall success throughout history – to the end of the 2011/12 season.

1. Manchester Utd.
2. Liverpool
3. Arsenal
4. Everton
5. Aston Villa
6. Chelsea
7. Tottenham
8. Newcastle
9. Sunderland
10. Manchester City
11. Wolves
12. Blackburn
13. Sheffield Wed.
14. West Brom
15. Leeds
16. Preston
17. Nottingham Forest
18. Derby
19. Bolton
20. Sheffield Utd.

Supporters – the most popular derby by year (taking into account combined home attendances)

Years	No. of seasons	Top Derby
1888/90	2	Preston v Blackburn
1890/91	1	Blackburn v Burnley
1891/92	1	Aston Villa v West Brom
1892/93	1	Nottingham's derby (*1)
1893/98	5	Liverpool's derby
1898/1900	2	Newcastle v Sunderland
1900/01	1	Liverpool's derby
1901/02	1	Birmingham's derby (City were still Small Heath)
1902/03	1	Newcastle v Sunderland
1903/04	1	Manchester's derby
1904/05	1	Newcastle v Sunderland
1905/06	1	Liverpool's derby
1906/09	3	Newcastle v Sunderland (*2)
1909/10	1	Liverpool's derby (*2)
1910/13	3	Manchester's derby (*2)
1913/14	1	Arsenal v Chelsea (*2)
1914/15	1	Liverpool's derby
1919/21	2	Arsenal v Chelsea (*2)
1921/23	2	Liverpool's derby (*2)
1923/24	1	Arsenal v Chelsea
1924/25	1	Liverpool v Manchester Utd
1925/26	1	Arsenal v Chelsea
1926/29	3	Liverpool's derby
1929/32	3	Arsenal v Chelsea
1932/35	3	Arsenal v Tottenham
1935/39	4	Arsenal v Chelsea
1946/48	2	Arsenal v Chelsea
1948/53	5	Arsenal v Tottenham
1953/55	2	Arsenal v Chelsea
1955/57	2	Arsenal v Tottenham
1957/59	2	Liverpool v Manchester Utd
1959/61	2	Arsenal v Tottenham (*2)
1961/64	3	Liverpool's derby
1964/2003	39	Liverpool v Manchester Utd
2003/05	2	Manchester's derby
2005/09	4	Liverpool v Manchester Utd
2009/12	3	Manchester's derby

Notes to previous page:

*1 Strictly speaking, the alternative Merseyside derby between Everton and Bootle had higher combined crowds than Nottingham's clubs had in 1892/3. However, this was entirely due to Everton having much bigger crowds than anyone else. Bootle had the 4th poorest attendances of twenty-eight clubs in the League.

*2 Chelsea v Tottenham is not one of the sixty derbies studied. If included, Blues v Spurs had the top crowds in nine seasons (six seasons from 1908 to 1914, two from 1920 to 1922 and again in 1959/60).

Summary – the top derbies overall by combined attendance.

Liverpool v Manchester Utd	46 seasons
Liverpool's derby	17
Arsenal v Chelsea	16
Arsenal v Tottenham	12
Manchester's derby	9
Newcastle v Sunderland	7
Preston v Blackburn	2
Blackburn v Burnley	1
Birmingham's derby	1
Nottingham's derby	1
Aston Villa v West Brom	1

Individual club attendances.

By some distance, Everton were the best supported club in each of the first ten Football League seasons. They were then overtaken by Aston Villa who reigned for the next six seasons. Things became much tighter in the years immediately preceding the First World War, with Manchester City, Newcastle, Tottenham and Chelsea vying for top spot. Chelsea probably edged that period. They were the best supported club of all in 1911/12 despite being in Division 2 (Tottenham had the best crowds in Division 1 in the same season, demonstrating that southern clubs in the Football League were very popular).

Post-war, the Twenties saw Tottenham slip back a little. Newcastle continued to draw big crowds and Everton, Liverpool and Arsenal joined the fray. But Chelsea and Manchester City could probably argue that they were the best supported clubs in the period, as they maintained excellent attendances despite being pretty poor teams. Both managed to draw the biggest crowds of all despite being second tier sides – Manchester City in their promotion year of 1927/8 and Chelsea in 1925/6, when they didn't even win promotion. Huddersfield, *the* side of the Twenties, were never well supported. In fact, incredibly, in 1926/7, the year after Huddersfield had achieved a hat-trick of League titles, the lowest crowd in the top division all season (just over 6000) saw their home game against Liverpool – Town were *only* runners-up that year. Something strange happened in 1924/5. Liverpool had the best crowds and Manchester United second best. Not only was this the only time pre-war that they finished one and two in the attendance league, it was the only time in the inter-war period that United were in the top three and yet they were in Division Two at the time.

The 1930s belonged to Arsenal in every sense. They were by far the best side and they had the biggest crowds in every season of the decade except in 1938/9 when they were pipped by Aston Villa.

Newcastle were the best supported club immediately after World War Two, twice having the biggest crowds in the country whilst in the second tier. They were overtaken by Tottenham in the early 1950s. Arsenal retained excellent support, but Manchester City, Everton and Liverpool all went through relatively lean periods in terms of attendances.

In 1956/7, for the first time ever, Manchester United had the biggest crowds in the League. Spurs briefly took over again in the early sixties and Everton regained the crown in 1962/3 and 1963/4. But, in forty-eight seasons since 1963/4, Manchester United have been the best supported club in England forty-two times. The only club to displace them is Liverpool and they last did so in 1992/3 when Old Trafford was being re-developed. For most of the period Liverpool have also been runners-up to United in the attendance league but, more recently, Newcastle and then Arsenal have taken over second spot.

In short, the attendance league has become even more predictable than the League itself. Gone are the days when a number of clubs could challenge for top spot. For the foreseeable future Manchester United will be the best supported club, and the best supported derby will depend upon whether Manchester City or Liverpool have the biggest crowds – that will almost certainly be City until Liverpool are able to develop their ground.

Summary – best supported club.

Manchester United	45 seasons (last time 2011/2)
Everton	13 (last time 1963/4)
Arsenal	11 (last time 1953/4)
Chelsea	9 (last time 1954/5)
Aston Villa	8 (last time 1938/9)
Newcastle	8 (last time 1948/9)
Liverpool	8 (last time 1992/3)
Tottenham	7 (last time 1961/2)
Manchester City	4 (last time 1928/9)

Only these nine clubs have ever led the top support list.

Selected Bibliography

Alcock Charles W. – The Association Game (Bell, London 1890)

Alegi, Peter – African Soccerscapes (Hurst & Co, London 2010)

Association of Football Statisticians – The Early Years 1863–1888 (Basildon)

Bennett, Dirk – Chariot Racing in the Ancient World (History Today 1997)

Booth, Keith – The Father of Modern Sport, the Life & Times of Charles W Alcock (Parrs Wood, Manchester 2002)

Brailsford, Dennis – British Sport, A Social History (Lutterworth, Cambridge 1998)

Brimson, Dougie & Eddy – Derby Days (Headline, London 1998)

Butler, Bryon – 100 Seasons of League Football (Lennard, Queen Anne, London 1998)

Cavallini Rob – The Wanderers FC (Dog N Duck, Worcester Park 2005)

Chandos, John – Boys Together: English Public Schools 1800-1864 (Yale University Press 1984)

Clarebrough, Denis & Kirkham, Andrew – Sheffield the Home of Football (Hallamshire Press, Sheffield 2009)

Dunning, Eric & Sheard, Kenneth – Barbarians, Gentlemen and Players (Routledge, Abingdon 2005 – first published 1979)

Edworthy, Niall – The Official F.A. History (Virgin, London 1997)

Foer, Franklin – How Soccer Explains the World (Harper Collins, London 2004)

Gardner, Paul – The Simplest Game: The Intelligent Fan's Guide to the World of Soccer (MacMillan, London 1994)

Foster, Stephen – She Stood There Laughing (Scribner, London 2004)

Goldblatt, David – The Ball is Round (Viking, London 2006)

Golden, Mark – Sport in the Ancient World from A to Z (Routledge, Abingdon 2003)

Goodhead, Giles – Us v Them: Journeys to the World's Greatest Football Derbies (Penguin, London 2003)

Granville, Brian – Football Memories (Robson, London 2004 – first published 1999)

Harvey, Geoff & Strowger, Vanessa – Rivals (Aesculus, Swadlincote 2004)

Heatley, Michael – Football Club Origins and Nicknames (Allan, Hersham 2008)

Inglis, Simon – The Football Grounds of England and Wales (Harper Collins, London 1996 - first published in 1983)

Jackman, Mike – Blackburn Rovers: a Complete Record (Breedon, Derby 2009 – first published 1990)

Joannou, Paul – Pioneers of the North (Breedon, Derby 2009)

King, Martin – Rivals (Head-Hunter, London 2004)

Kuper, Simon – Football Against the Enemy (Orion, London 1994)

Lovejoy, Joe – Glory, Goals and Greed – Twenty Years of the Premier League (Mainstream, Edinburgh 2011)

McComb, David – Sports in World History (Routledge, Abingdon 2004)

Midwinter, Eric – Parish to Planet (Know the Score Books, Studley 2007)

Mitten, Andy – Mad for It (Harper Sport, London 2008)

Morris, Peter – Aston Villa (Sportsmans Book Club, London 1962)

Murray, Colin – A Random History of Football (Orion, London 2009)

Needham, Ernest – Association Football (Soccer Books, Cleethorpes 2003 – first published in 1901)

Oliver, Guy – Almanak of World Football (Headline, London 2008)

Radnedge, Kier – Complete Encyclopaedia of Football (Carlton, London 2007 – first published 1998)

Rollin, Jack – Soccer at War (Collins, London 1985)

Sharpe, Graham – The Book of Bizarre Football (Robson, London 2000)

Soar, Phil – Hamlyn A-Z of British Football Records (Hamlyn, London 1981)

Steele, John A – The Countrymen (Sheffield 1986)

Tabner, Brian – Football through the Turnstiles.... Again (Yore, Harefield 2002)

Twydell, Dave – Denied F.C. (Yore, Harefield 2001)

Tyler, Martin – The Story of Football (Marshall Cavendish, London 1976)

Tyler, Martin – Cup Final Extra (Hamlyn, London 1981)

Walvin, James – People's Game: A Social History of British Football (Allen Lane, London 1975)

Ward, Andrew – Football's Strangest Matches (Robson, London)

Williams, Graham – The Code War (Yore, Harefield 1994)

Young, Percy M – A History of British Football (Stanley Paul, London 1968)

Young, Percy M – Football in Sheffield (Dark Peak, Sheffield 1981 – first published in 1962)

Also referenced: various magazines, newspaper articles and official and unofficial websites. The following deserve particular mention:-

World Soccer magazine
Footballderbies.com
Thefa.com (archives)
Soccerbase.com
Statto.com
Footballpools.com
Footballfanscensus.com